"This does what no book on production has done before — you actually can go out and make a movie after you read it. Maureen Ryan is one of the best independent producers working today and this book will show you why. Like her, it's thorough, thoughtful, and highly enjoyable. Whether you are a novice or a professional, there is much to learn here."
  — Ben Odell, Producer, *Padre Nuestro*; Partner, Panamax Films

"You never will ask 'what does a producer do?' once you read Maureen's brilliant book. She has fully described, in detail, all aspects of production, along with her own personal experiences. If you want to be the producer everyone raves about, this book is for you. I consider it 'The Production Bible' for all producers — it has everything you need to produce your feature, short, or documentary film."
  — Carole Dean, Author, *The Art of Film Funding*
    www.FromTheHeartProductions.com

"Where was this book when I needed it? The table of contents alone would have saved me days and dollars. For the first time ever, no filmmaker can make the excuse 'I didn't know!'"
  — Jeff Pucillo; Actor/producer, *Roots in Water*

"An awesomely clear, detailed, and readable, step-by-step guide to everything you ever needed to know about indie film production. And it comes from someone who knows what she's talking about — Maureen Ryan is one of the most effective and accomplished producers on the independent film scene today. This is the book we've all been waiting for! A must-read for everyone making, or even contemplating, an independent film."
  — Susanna Styron; Writer/director: *Shadrach; 100 Centre Street*

"Finally, a book that lays out, practically, how to get through a shoot. No one ever tells you this stuff — you're expected to learn it the hard way… until now. Written by one of the best producers I've ever worked with."
  — Paul Cotter, Writer/director: *BOMBER; Estes Avenue*

"This book, like Maureen Ryan herself, is an absolute gift for any filmmaker to know and work with. The material is both accessible and comprehensive, distilling Maureen's clear-eyed wisdom into doable directives. Her thorough approach, peppered with tangible experiences, is a great read for filmmakers hungry for knowledge and the ability to manifest their visions. I wish this book had been required reading in my Sight and Sound class! The lists and tools provided create a map for navigating the journey of production and troubleshooting its many unexpected variables. Maureen's attention to every detail and her veteran outlook provide the assurance, guidance, and clarity for filmmakers to successfully deliver their creative babies. She not only outlines the physical jumps that need to be navigated in production, but deftly handles the psychological preparation necessary to make crucial decisions. Her straight-shooting tone sets this book apart from 'how to' and theory books — truly marrying experience with the nuts and bolts that bring the process of filmmaking to life."

— Domenica Cameron Scorcese, Writer/director: *Roots in Water; Spanish Boots*

"This is THE book for producers. Nowhere else will you find the wisdom, insight, and tried-and-true, nuts-and-bolts know-how found here."

— Sheila Curran Dennin, Writer/director: *RED FLAG; Becoming Medusa*

"Maureen Ryan shares her extensive, first-hand experience as an independent producer and shepherds aspiring producers, step-by-step, through the entire process, creating a unique road map that will inevitably make both the creative and business journeys easier."

— Sharon Badal, New York University, Tisch School of the Arts; Author, *Swimming Upstream – A Lifesaving Guide to Short-Film Distribution*

PRODUCER TO PRODUCER

A Step-By-Step Guide to
LOW-BUDGET INDEPENDENT FILM PRODUCING

MAUREEN A. RYAN

MICHAEL WIESE PRODUCTIONS

Published by Michael Wiese Productions
12400 Ventura Blvd. #1111
Studio City, CA 91604
(818) 379-8799, (818) 986-3408 (FAX)
mw@mwp.com
www.mwp.com

Cover design by MWP
Interior design by William Morosi
Copyedited by Arthur G. Insana
Printed by Sheridan Books

Manufactured in the United States of America
Copyright 2010

Library of Congress Cataloging-in-Publication Data

Ryan, Maureen A.
  Producer to producer : a step-by-step guide to low-budget independent
film producing / by Maureen A. Ryan.
       p. cm.
  ISBN 978-1-932907-75-9
  1. Motion pictures--Production and direction. 2. Low-budget films. I. Title.
  PN1995.9.P7R93 2010
  791.4302'32--dc22

                              2010001871

Printed on Recycled Stock

For Rick

CONTENTS

FOREWORD

Maureen Ryan has been producing my films from the time of our very first meeting in the spring of 1997. Our first project together was a daunting, ambitious period film with no obvious commercial prospects and a tiny budget provided by the BBC.

You'd have to be crazy to want to produce this film — it involved elaborate historical recreations that needed to be filmed across all four seasons, on location in Wisconsin. There were stunts with horses and steam trains, hangings, shootings, and burnings. The script called for a 19th century mansion to be burned down. All of this was achieved — and more — across a production that sprawled over two years on a budget that was little more than a well-funded music video of the time. It turned out that Maureen wasn't crazy at all — she was just methodical, resourceful, and bold. Looking back now, I still don't know how we did it. Or, rather, how she did it — though some of the answers can now be found in this book.

The resulting film, *Wisconsin Death Trip*, premiered at the Telluride and Venice Film Festivals and was theatrically released in the U.S. and the UK. It even turned a small profit. Our collaborations have grown in budget and scope, since then. We've worked together on documentaries and features and have grown together in our experience of production. Like all filmmakers we've never quite had the resources we wanted. The genius of a great producer is to never let you feel that is a problem.

So, Maureen knows what she is talking about. In this book anyone who's involved — or wants to be involved — in film production, at any level, will find answers to every question and pitfall a production generates. Like her productions, the book is clear, detailed, generous, and inspiring.

— James Marsh, February 2010

ACKNOWLEDGEMENTS

A sincere thanks to all the talented students I've been blessed to work with over the last decade. You constantly remind me of why I love what I do. Especially my students at Columbia University's School of the Arts Graduate Film Program — I've learned more from you than you can imagine.

Thanks to Carole Dean for your constant support and encouragement throughout the writing of this book. Your insights, weekly notes, and intuition have been a steady beacon while I wrote draft after draft.

Thanks to all the contributors for their interviews and expert experience. You took the book to a whole other level with your contributions — Ira Deutchman, Ben Odell, Christine Sadofsky, George Rush, Zach Seivers, Paul Cotter, Dave Anaxagoras, Rick Siegel, and especially Sheila Curran Dennin for the materials used in the case study.

My thanks to the directors I have had the pleasure of working with and learning from over the last two decades — John Nathan, Michael McNamara, James Marsh, Albert Maysles, Sheila Curran Dennin and Paul Cotter. You all live the mantra "it's all about the project" and I am grateful to have been able to produce your work.

Thanks to my mentors. This is a tough industry and your example and guidance made all the difference during the forks in the road — Marc Sarazin, Jon Fontana, Lewis Cole, Annette Insdorf, Dan Kleinman and Ira Deutchman.

Thanks to my dear friend Sheila Curran Dennin — your writing tutorials made all the difference. A big thank you to my old friend Adam Sexton, this book would not be what it is without your invaluable expertise and guidance. My gratitude to my literary agent Jennifer Unter for all of your help. Thanks to copy editor Arthur G. Insana — your invisible work made this a better book indeed. Thanks to Michael Wiese and Ken Lee at MWP — your support and hard work is much appreciated. Thank you to research assistant Geoff Quan, designer Bill Morosi and cover artist John Brennner. I also want to thank the staff at Le Grainne Café and Café 202 in NYC for keeping me hydrated and fed as I worked on the many drafts.

I want to thank all the crews I have had the honor to work with. Your dedication and commitment to the work is a moving thing to watch and be a part of. Thanks for making my heart skip a beat every time I walk onto a film set.

Finally, thanks to my partner Rick. Your kind heart, great eye, and constant love is a deep source of encouragement and inspiration.

INTRODUCTION

I T'S A HOT AUGUST afternoon somewhere in Appleton, Wisconsin.
The corset I'm wearing under
this Victorian-era peasant dress
is digging into my ribs. I and it are
filthy because I'm lying in a pit of
mud in a chicken coop on some god-
forsaken farm. Did I mention I'm in
rural Wisconsin? As I try to distract
myself from the pain and filth, I hear
the shout of "Action!" from the film
director who sits comfortably behind
the video monitor as the key grip and
production assistants begin pelting me
with potatoes. They actually are trying
to hit the wooden slat above my head
but they often miss and hit me instead.

Trying not to think about the
bruises that are beginning to form
on my limbs and back, I concentrate
on the very obvious question that I
should have asked about an hour ago,
"how the hell did I get myself into
this?" It's too late now. There's only
one answer — I'm producing a low-
budget film and we can't afford any
more extras.

And the truth is, I wouldn't want
to be anywhere else. Why? Because I
love what I do — I'm an independent
film producer.

> *Be passionate. Be serious.*
>
> *Wake up.*
>
> *— Susan Sontag*

This book in your hands is about film producing. Every page is filled with all the knowledge I think is essential to produce well. Because that's the goal here — to produce *well*.

Anyone can learn to make a budget, hire a crew, and take all the steps necessary to produce a film and this book will teach you all of those steps. The ultimate goal of this book is to teach you how to produce in a way that gets the project completed on time and under budget, to teach you how to stretch the precious dollar in the right places, but also how to produce with integrity, decency, respect, and wit. I hope that's what makes this book different.

To me, that's the prize. That's what makes all the hard work worthwhile and that's how it should always be. Nothing else will do. If that appeals to you, then please read on.

By the way, my scene never made it to the final cut. But that's ok, that film was the first of five films I would make with that director — the last one won an Academy Award. It's the journey, not the glory, that makes film producing so satisfying. It's about jumping in and doing what it takes. Even if it involves a Victorian dress and a chicken coop on some farm in northern Wisconsin.

— Maureen Ryan, April 2010

HOW THIS BOOK WORKS AND WHOM IT IS FOR

I'M ALWAYS ASKED "What does a Producer do?" My simple answer is "They make the project HAPPEN." Without a producer, there isn't a project. When I teach university producing classes which focus on no/low-budget filmmaking there is always a directing student or two who say "I can't afford a producer" and I always say "You can't afford *not* to have one."

Producer to Producer teaches you how to produce independent low-budget productions — narrative features, documentaries, and shorts. The principles and steps involved are the same whether it is for a six-day shoot or a 28-day schedule. If you are gathering all the materials, cast, and crew for a short film, you still need to follow all the same rules and regulations as you would for a feature-length film.

This book is put together in general chronological order for the steps to make a film. All aspects of film producing are here and reflect, directly, my specific background as a producer. I came up through the production ranks as a line producer so this book will be grounded in that particular perspective. I'm the type of person who likes to make films and not just

> *What man needs is not a tensionless state but rather the striving and struggling for some goal worthy of him. What he needs is not the discharge of tension at any cost, but the call of a potential meaning waiting to be fulfilled by him.*
>
> *— Victor Frankl*

talk about making films. I find that often, if you can produce it for less money, you can make it happen faster and easier. I'd rather do it and get it done on less than waste time gathering up more resources or collecting more money with strings attached. This book will take you through all the steps to produce your film well — with creativity and finesse.

I think it's helpful to define what a producer does and there are many different kinds of producers with several different titles. Let's go through them here. The Producers Guild of America is a good resource for information. Their website is *www.producersguild.org*. I've included a summary based on their definitions for each title:

Executive Producer — the person who brings in financing for the project or makes a significant contribution to the development of the literary property.

Producer — the person who puts together various elements for the project, such as purchasing the rights to underlying material, coming up with the idea for the project, hiring a screenwriter, optioning and/or purchasing a script, attaching actors (talent) to a film, hiring key department heads, overseeing production and postproduction, and bringing in financing.

Co-Producer — the person who is responsible for the logistics of the production of the film or a particular aspect of the film.

Line Producer — the person who is responsible for the logistics of the production, from preproduction through completion of production.

Associate Producer — the person responsible for one or more producing functions delegated by the producer or co-producer.

Depending on your budget, your film may only have a few of these positions, but the producing principles are the same.

Please note that in this book I will refer to any production (no matter what format or genre) as a "film." So many projects are shot on video, but to simplify the grammar I'll use the word "film" in a generic sense, whether it was shot on, or completed in, film or video. I will refer to the reader of this book as a producer. You may be a director, production manager, screenwriter, filmmaker, or producer (or a combination of several of these), but this book is for the producer or the producer *in* you.

In addition, this book is directed toward low-budget, independent productions. There are other books out there that concentrate on Hollywood and big-budget features. There also are lots of books dedicated to the topics of development, finance, and distribution. This is *not* that. I will discuss those topics only insofar as they impact the low-budget side of the spectrum of filmmaking. This book is for the **low-budget, independent filmmaker** and I will assume, throughout the book, that you have limited funds for your film and that the project's ambitions go beyond what those dollars can normally afford. I say "normally" because this book will help you to stretch your dollars as far as humanly possible to give you the highest production values at the lowest cost.

On the philosophical side, as a producer, I truly believe that all people want to be a part of something that is bigger than themselves. People like being a part of something special that inspires them — and that's what a good film does. And good film producing can provide that experience for all those associated with it. Often that experience is worth more to someone than a paycheck. A good producer can do that and that's what I intend to do with this book.

Throughout each chapter there will be words in **bold** that I'll define along the way. At the end of each chapter there will be points that I wish to highlight and you will find them under the **Recap** heading. And finally, there is the *www.ProducerToProducer.com* website that will contain tons of information that you can use, like downloadable documents, essential production information and important links for you to refer to when making your film.

So let's get started.

> For free downloadable production templates go to
> *www.mwp.com*
> Click *Virtual Film School*
> Click *Resources*
>
> and also
> *www.ProducerToProducer.com*

CHAPTER 1

DEVELOPMENT

DEVELOPMENT REFERS TO THE time period and resources it takes to bring an idea to full maturation as a final script. Financing for the film also happens during this phase. Ideas can be completely original or be derived from underlying material — such as a novel, magazine article, comic book, theater play, television show, Web series, or graphic novel. This process involves the creative aspects of writing and revising a screenplay, as well as the legal aspects of optioning or owning underlying material and procuring the proper releases and contracts. Simultaneously, you are looking for and finalizing the financing, as well. Once you have completed these steps, you will enter the next one — preproduction. The process from first idea/concept to final distribution is usually anywhere from **two–five years** for a feature. Some projects have an even longer gestation period. The length of your development period will impact your overall schedule for producing your film. Keep that in mind as you begin the journey.

There is a vitality, a life-force, an energy, a quickening that is translated through you into action. And because there is only one of you in all of time, this expression is unique. And if you block it, it will never exist through any other medium and be lost. The world will not have it. It is not your business to determine how good it is nor how valuable it is nor how it compares with others' expressions. It is your business to keep it yours clearly and directly, to keep the channel open… Above all else, keep the channel open.

— Martha Graham

Finding the Idea or Material

So, with the knowledge of how long it will take you to create a project from start to finish, the first thing you need to keep in mind is that you need to LOVE the project. As the producer, it's going to be in your life for the rest of your life, so choose wisely. Make sure it's a project you are passionate about because there will be so many twists and turns on the road to completion. It's just too damn hard otherwise.

I really recommend taking some time to think about what excites you, energizes you, holds your attention. Figure out what makes you laugh, what's your particular take on things. For documentaries, think about what topic inspires you; what do you want to explore? It needs to sustain you intellectually and emotionally for a long, hard time.

When deciding what film or films you want to produce, also consider where this project fits in with your vision for your career. Is it in keeping with where you want to be in five years? Is it a step forward in the right direction or is it a path down another road that doesn't lead to where you ultimately want to go? Is it the perfect vehicle for you to get from where you are now to where you want to be? When I decided to produce my first feature documentary, *Wisconsin Death Trip,* I was line producing country music videos and commercials in Nashville, Tennessee. I loved the treatment for the film and believed in the project with all my heart. It was also a way for me to move toward my dream of producing documentaries, full time. So I worked part time on WDT for 2 1/2 years while I made a living producing videos for country artists like Dolly Parton and Junior Brown. It was really hard to do but when the film premiered it was well received, won many awards and played in theaters and on television... and I had taken a big step toward my goal.

Study Scripts

Spend time learning what makes a great script. Read lots of scripts and educate yourself by determining what makes an excellent one. Go to a library or online to find classic brilliant scripts like *Citizen Kane, Chinatown,* and *Star Wars* and study them. Watching them on screen is *not* the same thing. You need to read it line by line, analyze the structure, figure out the beats, and decide what makes a compelling protagonist, to really understand what makes a stellar screenplay. Producer Shelby Stone (*Lackawanna Blues*) calls it "mapping." She takes a great, already-produced script and breaks it down, beat by beat and maps the beginning and end of each act on paper so she can analyze what makes that particular film work so well. Then she uses that info and compares it to the scripts she is developing to make sure she is on track. You don't need to reinvent the wheel, just use great past work as a template for your great future work.

Better yet, buy books that contain great screenplays in which the author analyzes them and shows how they are crafted. Or take a screenwriting class to learn the principles of the screenplay form. Even if you don't want to be a writer, you will learn the basics of screenwriting and it will be invaluable as you develop a script with a writer.

Lastly, read lots of scripts — good and bad — in the genre you wish to produce. Webster's New Collegiate Dictionary defines genre as "a category of artistic, musical, or literary composition characterized by a particular style, form, or content." It is the type of film you plan to make, such as horror, comedy, drama, sci-fi, fantasy, or animation. There are sub-genres too, like coming-of-age films, road movies and buddy films. These genres have a specific set of rules that drive the narrative and character development. The audience gets its enjoyment from the creativity of the film itself, but also how the film follows the "rules" of that genre. Learn them so you can combine them in a different way or subvert them. Decide what you want to produce and really go to school on it.

Development Process

The development process is focused on five areas — 1) Ownership of original or underlying materials; 2) Creation of log line, screenplay, and revision; 3) Creation of proposal and pitch for the film; 4) Acquisition of financing; 5) Creation of tentative distribution plan. We'll go through them:

Obtaining Rights to Underlying Material

Your film will be produced from a finished screenplay, but how it gets to that format can happen in many different ways. It may originate as a screenplay or it could come from some other material that needs to be adapted to the screenplay format. Such possible material includes magazine or newspaper articles, short stories, novels, comic books, graphic novels, blogs, theater plays, TV shows, Web series, screenplays, or another film. If the idea comes from such a format, you'll need to obtain the rights to the material so that you can be on solid legal ground for your project. Don't write a screenplay without obtaining the proper rights first. It could be a big waste of time. Inquire first to make sure someone else doesn't own the film rights already. Hollywood studios and film production companies have departments dedicated to discovering new material for potential film projects. They often get a book in galley format so they can see it before everyone else and have a chance to purchase the rights ahead of the pack.

Documentaries are often based on already-published material about the subject matter. *Man on Wire*, a film I co-produced, is about Philippe Petit, the wirewalker who walked between the World Trade Center towers in 1974. In 2002, Philippe wrote a book titled *To Reach the Clouds* about the miraculous event. The film's producer, Simon Chinn, purchased the rights to that book and negotiated a deal for Philippe's involvement in the film before he went to financiers to discuss the funding of the film. This important step assured the investors that the producer held the proper rights to the underlying material to make the film, without fear of any rights problems further down the line.

But before we get into the particulars, let's discuss the meaning of the word "rights." **Rights** is short for copyright — or the right to copy. According to Michael Donaldson, in his comprehensive book *Clearance and Copyright*, "copyright law does not protect ideas. Copyright law only protects 'the expression of an idea that is fixed in a tangible form.'" For our discussion in this chapter, we will concentrate on literary-type rights listed above. Music rights will be covered in the *Music* chapter, later in this book.

Here's what you need to consider regarding obtaining the rights for a film:

1. Do you need **exclusive** or **non-exclusive** rights? Is it ok for someone else to also own the rights to material that you use for the basis of your screenplay? Or do you need to own it exclusively? The price will be higher if you require exclusivity.

2. For how long do you need the rights? In perpetuity or less time? Generally, you want to own rights **in perpetuity** (forever) but sometimes you may want to purchase rights for a shorter period of time, especially to start with. You could also get an **option** for the rights for a year or two with the option to acquire the rights for a longer period of time, automatically. With an option, you can develop the project more cost effectively and then pay a higher fee once you know your film project is funded and is going to be produced.

3. Who is the proper and legal rights holder? Make sure you are in contact with the person who owns the rights to the underlying work. They must own the copyright and be able to prove it, legally. Otherwise you could be purchasing rights from the wrong person and it would not be legally binding and would be a waste of money.

4. What rights do you need? Worldwide or just a particular kind of rights? There are all different kinds of rights: theatrical (domestic and foreign); domestic TV; domestic cable TV; international TV; VOD; DVD; Internet/online; film festival; cell phone; and probably a few more, since this book was published. Usually, it's best to purchase all of them, which is commonly referred to as **worldwide** rights. But sometimes you don't need all those rights, or you can't afford them, or they are not available. You have to weigh all of these possibilities with what you know and what you anticipate your needs will be, now and in the future. Technology is changing so quickly that you need to be looking ahead and staying on top of the current and future state of the industry.

5. Life rights are the rights to the details of a private person's life that are not in the public domain. If you have these rights, the individual can't sue you for using his or her life story.

6. Film festival rights are usually affordable. Some of my students option the rights to a short story when producing their short films. Often the author will give them non-exclusive film festival rights to the story for free or almost free. This is helpful and allows you to screen at film festivals for almost no money. But if your film does well and someone wants to buy the rights to your film for a television broadcast or some other distribution, you are going to have to go back to the rights holder and re-negotiate for additional rights. The rights holder could ask for more money than you can afford and then you won't be able to make the deal. You always want to plan for your film's success. A good way to future-proof your film is to make a deal for the festival rights but also negotiate fees for the additional rights you would need if your film was successful — Internet, DVD, television, etc. And get it in writing — so you'll know the costs before you begin to produce your film and be able to refer to it when you go back to the rights holder later on.

7. Make sure to add **future technology rights** to any agreement that you sign. You want to future-proof your ability to exploit your film. Having rights for "media known and unknown" is necessary to make sure the rights will follow any new technology that has yet to be invented.

8. All of this should be done with the assistance of an entertainment attorney. Make sure you have your lawyer look over the final contract *before* you sign it.

Screenplay Creation and Revision

I've discussed how important it is to know what makes a great screenplay. Your entire film rests on its foundation. Work hard to get it right and learn to give good, clear, and helpful notes to the screenwriter. "Writing" is actually a misnomer. It's actually *rewriting*. It's the revision process that will make all the difference. Make sure the script is rewritten and rewritten until it is the best you and the writer can possibly create. It is up to you as the producer to make that happen. I am not a screenwriter and don't pretend to be. Benjamin Odell (*Padre Nuestro*, *Ladrón que roba a ladrón*), the talented producer and president of Panamax Films (*www.panamaxfilms.com*) has a lot of experience regarding script revision and the development process. Below is the transcript from our interview.

Maureen: What are the most important steps a producer needs to take to develop a project successfully?

Ben: First and foremost is ownership of material, what will eventually be called "chain of title." One of the first things [a distributor or a studio] asks for is chain of title, which follows who owns the rights to the underlying material and how those rights were transferred from the original source material, whether it be a novel or a documentary or an idea, to the screenwriter, to the producer, and then to the distributer who's going to control those rights for some period of time.

So when you're developing material, the question you have to ask yourself is: Where are the ideas coming from? Where is the material coming from? And are those rights controlled? If they're not controlled by you, the first thing you have to figure out is how to control them long enough to develop the material into something that you can use to raise the money and make the film.

So many first-time producers get really far into projects — they find a script they like, they develop it with the writer, and they put a lot of energy into sort of shaping the material so it'll work. Then, at some point, when they're ready to do the deal, they haven't discussed and signed and sort of buttoned down the terms of the deal, and the writer walks away or extorts them or feels like he or she deserves more. So buttoning down rights is, by far, the first thing to think about before you think from a creative point of view.

Secondly, as a producer, I think you always have to think about and ask yourself: Who's my audience? Who am I developing this material for? Who is the end user? I think that's the huge difference between a producer and a screenwriter/director. Producers have to really think about the end game where the filmmakers are thinking about their vision and, to some degree, I think producers have the obligation when they're looking for material to say, "*Is this a movie I can sell?*" And if it's going to be a hard sell or if you want to take an artistic approach to material, as a producer, you have to go in knowing that.

In other words, if you're going to make a movie like *Padre Nuestro* — Spanish language, no-name actors, dark ending, dark opening, [you need to be] conscious of the fact that the budget has to reflect the reality of the marketplace. In other words, it would be ridiculous to try to make a $20 million hyper art house film, very small intellectual movie. It's going to go nowhere, even if you pack it full of stars.

When you're searching for material ask yourself: "*Who's going to want to see this?*" I think it's important, too, before you get into development, to sort of see where the business is. I mean, just in the last year, watching all of these art house divisions of studios close shop you have to ask yourself: Where are the opportunities for small movies?

If you already have a project you like, I think you have to ask those tough questions before you buy any material or spend any time really developing. People don't really consider this part of development but the truth is, as a producer, I think your obligation first is to understand the reality of the business.

Then sometimes it's like — throw all caution to the wind and do it because there is no logic to it and you don't know if there is an audience there, but you love it and that's fine, too. But I think you have to go into it clear about the reality. I see so many producers so delusional about the ability of their films to perform — they're developing material that leaves them so shocked when they can't find anywhere to take their movies and they don't know what to do with them.

Maureen: You are a writer yourself and you've written screenplays. I feel that you, as a producer, come to that revision process — note giving — with a lot more than a lot of producers, and I'd love to hear your philosophy and what you think are the most important things for a producer to know.

Ben: First off, when you're in this position of making low-budget films, the one thing you obviously don't have is money to buy scripts. So, more often than not, what you're going to do is option a script for a period of time, while you develop it and then you're going to try to get it made or raise the money.

Draw up an option, negotiate it and sign it with the writer. Obviously there is going to be very little money involved and I think that inherently changes the nature of the relationship between the producer and the writer, because you have to be much more diplomatic in your approach to development.

Development money is the riskiest money — I don't like to spend money early on. I like to develop at least to a certain point before I spend any money.

One of the first things I'll do if I read a screenplay that I think is 50% there is I'll sit down with the writer and try to understand his or her vision of the screenplay. In other words, not what's on the page but what they tried to get on the page. Because oftentimes I think where the problems come between a producer and a screenwriter is that the producer doesn't try to understand where the screenwriter is going. So when the producer is giving notes to the writer, the writer is fighting those notes because, in her head, the movie is something completely different.

So I think there is a process early on and I think it's pre-option, where you're really trying to figure out what the writer's vision is and then you try to also sort of say, *Okay. Is that my vision? Is that what I liked about the screenplay?* And if it isn't, then you need to have that conversation and you have to be very transparent about how you envision the movie, because it has to be all clear beforehand, it's like entering into a marriage. If you don't understand where the writer envisions the movie going and where you envision it and those things aren't cleared up, most likely you'll find yourself, a year later, incredibly frustrated and won't have gotten anywhere. So that's the first process. Try to bring the writer's complete vision to the foreground, even if it's not in the screenplay, and then compare it to your own.

Then, even pre-option, I would recommend that you sort of say, *Okay, this is what I feel like the movie needs.* Oftentimes what I'll do is say, *Watch this movie because I feel like that's the tone. The tone that you have isn't right.* Try to find movies or novels or whatever it is that you can give to the other people to express where you think the screenplay needs to go. Then sit down again—and this could take a month or two—and see if you can get on the same page.

The clearer your notes, the better the record of your directory. At the end of the day, what I do is I keep a log, like a development log. Every time I give notes to a writer I keep those notes in a log so that I know where the script went at the end of the process and I know how I impacted that script — and that's for a lot of reasons. It's also for legal reasons, and I guess, on some level, for my own gratification to understand my impact on the script, and it's also because sometimes you find yourself with a screenplay that's developed and it's gone in a direction that you hadn't imagined.

It's always good to be able to go back and see where it all went wrong and say, *Remember, the original idea that we talked about is that this movie is about a man who will go to all ends to stay…. It's the strength of paternal love. And, look, we've gone off. Let's go back and look at these original notes and look at what you said.* You can always go back to that original idea that got things going.

Maureen: Do you ever put your notes in writing and send to the writer? Or is that done in your conversations and they take notes from that meeting?

Ben: I usually go in, take notes, write them down, email them to the writer, get on the phone with the writer, and go through the notes. What I try to do—and I'm not sure that I always succeed—is let them air their complaints because it's such a personal thing. It's people's egos and their lives and their emotions are wrapped up in their characters. So often the main character is some reflection of the writer.

So when you're giving notes it can get very touchy and emotional; so you sort of let them react to your notes. First, let them read them, digest them, you give them a couple days to react to the notes, and then you sit down, chew on them, and then take it from there.

I think every development process with every writer is completely different and part of your job as a producer is to be a psychologist and figure out how to best get where you need to go and the way they need to deliver notes. So, often, if you have an idea that you think would work, the best way to get it to work for the writer is to somehow make her think it's her own ideas.

It just not to make them think it is. It's to somehow get them engaged with the idea in such a way— I can't tell you how many times I'll give a writer an idea and a week later he or she will call me up and say, *I got this idea.* They'll tell you the idea exactly as you proposed it to them and it's hard on the ego but you've got to say, *That's a brilliant idea* and then everything is good.

It's one of the hardest things about being a producer. Sometimes I've even demanded credit when I felt like I needed it. It's hard as a producer but you have to be prepared on some level that you are going to support this movie, creatively, on so many levels that you will never get credit. The only way a producer ever is seen as a creative force is over time with a body of work… but never on a single film will somebody say, *It's obvious that you, the producer, had a great creative impact on the script.*

What I always say is if you can't handle it then become a screenwriter, which is frankly what I've done. I'm writing two or three scripts a year now because I got tired of it. But that's definitely part of the process. I think the hardest part is when a producer has a vision of a movie and thinks it's the same vision as the writer, and then, only through the act of rewriting, you find that it's not.

Maureen: As the producer, you need to know more than anybody, what you want.

Ben: Definitely. I also think you don't have to be a writer but you should, as a producer, have tried to write and you should read the books. You should read *Save the Cat* by Blake Snyder, and you should read Syd Field and you should read Robert McKee (screenplay teaching gurus)— you don't have to know how to write but you should be able to at least speak the language. I frankly think any producer should go through the painful act of trying to write a screenplay to understand how bloody hard it is and therefore why you shouldn't beat your writers up when they don't do exactly what you think they should. Because the movie you have in your head is never the movie that ends up on the page. It never translates that fluidly unless you're a genius screenwriter, but there are very few. I think the more you can empathize with the writing process, the easier it is to deal with the writers.

The other thing that I think is really important to mention is the pacing of [the rewriting process]. No good screenplay comes in less than 15 or 20 drafts, but you can't get all your notes in one draft. When you read a screenplay and you love it but it needs a lot of work and it needs structural work and it needs work on character and it needs work on dialogue… you have to start with the macro first and fix the structure and make sure there is a through line and a premise and that there are themes and all those sort of larger concepts first and then you go in.

If you send them a 30-page document—and I know this because I've done it and it's a disaster—with every note from like *"the second act, it doesn't work"* to *"on page 33 the line of dialogue—blah-blah-blah— doesn't feel funny enough,"* writers will feel so overwhelmed that they'll burn out. You shouldn't try to get everything in one draft and I think that anyone who tries to do that finds it takes much longer to get to a good screenplay. Pace yourself in terms of how you're trying to deconstruct and reconstruct the screenplay.

Also, after a draft let the writer rest and don't come at him three days later with aggressive notes because you can really burn out a writer fast if you don't watch how you're pacing. That's why I [think it's good to] write a screenplay and then you'll understand just how hard it is.

Richard Price, a novelist and screenwriter, said that "writing a screenplay is like carrying a piano up five flights of stairs." He had written a screenplay called *Clockers* for Scorsese and so he got it up the five flights of stairs and then Spike Lee decided to direct the movie. He said it was like all of a sudden you had to take the piano down the five flights and carry it back it back up again. That's sort of the way it feels, as a writer, to go through a draft. So the more you can put yourself in their heads and realize how difficult it is— I think producers always underestimate how hard it is to be creative and execute those creative ideas. Because of that they sometimes beat the writers up, unnecessarily.

Maureen: Any other advice regarding the rest of the screenwriting process — getting to the point where you finally have a script that's ready to go into production?

Ben: One is if you're dealing with a screenwriter who's not the director, [you need] to know when to bring a director in and you shouldn't bring a director in at the end. If you bring in a director at the end you're losing the advantage. It is a director's medium and the director needs to come in early enough to shape the material.

At the same time, you have to be very clear about who controls the ultimate vision of the screenplay because you may bring in a director who takes control and takes it in a direction you don't want. So you almost have to do the same thing with a director. You have to interview your directors, make sure they have the vision that you want and that they're only going to bring out more of what you had in mind. If it's a writer/director you don't have that problem, necessarily, but you can have other problems because they're so tied to it in so many different ways.

I think the other big piece of advice is patience. Too often producers take their material out too early. They have one connection to one executive at one studio or they have one potential financier and they take the screenplay to them when it's not ready. It's always harder to get that person to read a screenplay a second time. They don't read as carefully. They remember the things they didn't like. Even if they aren't in the screenplay any longer, they still sort of linger in the mind of the reader and so it's very hard to get somebody to become excited about a screenplay the second time. There is only one time for the first impression.

I think producers so often make the mistake, especially when they're doing it cheaply and they raise the [money] independently where nobody has invested that deeply in it. It's $10,000 here or there and you make it for $200,000. No one contemplates that by not spending those six extra months to get the screenplay right you will have to live with that flawed movie for the rest of your life. Forget about the fact that you have two to three years between preproduction, production, editing, and distribution of just dealing with the movie. Why would you not spend those additional six months to get the script further along—first, to raise money and then to go into production? People are really impatient and often young producers will go into production before they should.

Maureen: How do you know when it's time to go into production?

Ben: I think one thing is that you should surround yourself with people you trust. I'll send my screenplays undeveloped out to three or four readers and I ask the screenwriter to do the same. Look for people who are neutral, don't know the story and some who do. Some who've read a previous draft and some who haven't. Every time we feel like the script is taking a giant leap forward, we try to find that little group of people— some of them are the same, some are new, [to read it and give notes]. I never take their advice 100%. I listen and what you'll find, if you take it to enough readers, is the film's patterns. Things that you were feeling and then you hear three people say the same thing and you'll go, *Okay, I have to change that.*

Then you'll get a note from somebody whom you really respect but it's the only time you've ever heard that note and, frankly, often—it's not that the person is wrong but it's not the right note for the movie you're making and so you have to ignore it. It's a process. [But] don't depend on just your [opinion] and constantly refresh yourself by finding new people to read it. But always keep an arm's length from those notes because they don't always work. They may not like the genre. They may not have been paying attention when they were reading. That's why you need enough readers to really rely on.

Don't rely only on yourself and certainly you have to be very in touch with your ego and the need to make a movie. Never discount how much your ego plays into making films because we all want to be recognized as filmmakers and there is always that glamorous side of it. Sometimes we're so hungry for that part that we rush through the rest because we're imagining receiving the Oscar. Frankly, because you rushed through things you won't get close to getting even a theatrical release. It's about getting your ego in check and not being too eager to be a producer and tell everybody that you're making a movie because they'll see it a year later and say, *That sucked* and then you'll really regret that you didn't take more time.

Maureen: As you're getting ready to go into production, anything else to keep in mind?

Ben: Screenplays are fluid and what's amazing about the process of making films is that when your art director gets involved, when your actors get involved, when your DP gets involved, they all see your movie from their own particular angles and they all bring really interesting energy and ideas. At that point the director really needs to be in control and all of those ideas need to be filtered through the vision of the screenplay. But as long as the parameters of the idea of the movie you want are firmly place, all of that new energy and those new ideas are good. As a producer and then with the director, of course, you create an atmosphere of collaboration where those ideas can be absorbed, because in the process of making the movie you're still writing. I think as a producer you have to stay very alert, especially in the low-budget world, to how the budget is impacting the storytellers.

So it's a process of seeing what's in front of you and being able to weave it into your screenplay, taking advantage of the resources you do have rather than trying to force a screenplay using the resources you don't have. In other words, trying to make a big-budget movie with a low budget. Keep the writing process open as you go into production because you'll find that so many opportunities continue to expand and make the script better.

So often you'll find that the things that are right in front of you, that you have access to, that can work as well or better than what you had imagined in the screenplay and will cost you less money. That process is using your resources and continuing to develop your screenplay as you go and keeping your eyes open to opportunities within the reach of your budget that are functional to low-budget screenwriting. I think all the good, interesting low-budget movies have that story in which there is a lot of exploration that came out of the limitations.

Maureen: If you are open and if you're looking, if you're seeing and hearing and then you just throw out an idea, it could really take the scene to a whole other level and it didn't cost anything. That's probably a major part of my philosophy about producing.

Ben: I think we, the producers, have to establish that atmosphere of collaboration and willingness to change early on. When you talk about development, I think it does leak into preproduction and production and you need a director who's going to have that kind of spirit. Too often you'll find directors who are so set in their ways that, because they're not willing to make changes based on the reality of the budget, they undermine the film and end up with something that doesn't work. So it's interesting. It's hard in low-budget filmmaking especially, to separate the development of the screenplay from the development of the film itself.

Maureen: How important is a good log line to the development process?

Ben: Screenplays need a focus and usually that focus can be summed up some way in a log line. It may not be in the traditional Hollywood sense of the log line but there is this kind of concept that will carry you through, all the way to the marketing of the movie. It's like that very same thing that hooked you into wanting to make the film is the same thing that, captured properly in a trailer, will hook an audience into going into a movie. That can be very effective.

Producers, from the day they decide to make a movie until it's marketed at the end, need to be able to sum up a movie quickly for a hundred different people. First for investors and for actors, then for your director, then for a great DP, and then when you've got to get into a festival and they ask you to chop up your film and send in a log line. If you get in, that log line ends up in the catalog and that catalog ends up being sent to every major distributer. Or it ends up showing up at the festival with people reading the log lines to decide whether or not they're going to see the movie.

So, in a way, if you don't have a quick way of summing [up] your film, it will make it harder every step of the process. I believe that with most great films, you tend, somehow, to catch their essence in a very simple way, even if it's not some sort of Hollywood hook.

It's a tough question because I do feel like there are filmmakers who make movies that you can't sum up and it's just like they're such an original vision. Even a movie like *Napoleon Dynamite* is not a movie that's easily summed up. It's more in the sort of execution and the weird humor. The point is as a producer, you should find a way to capture them, even for films that are not easily summed up. To say, imagine if this were David Lynch making *The Matrix*. I don't know what that means, but somehow I'll go see that movie and that's probably an art-house film.

I think that as a producer you're constantly forced to reduce your movie to a concept that's salable and so it is effective to figure out how to sell it from the beginning.

The other point is that it also depends who you're talking to as to how you want to sell your movie. So you may want to have sort of different pitches depending on who you're talking to. Certainly if you're trying to pitch name actors, that log line should be about the characters they would be playing. It depends who you're talking to.

Maureen: I think that if I can't come up with a log line that makes sense, I find it to be a red flag. You've got to go back and make sure you get it right. Do you agree with that?

Ben: I completely agree. I fully believe that and frankly I won't make a movie unless I feel like there is a really interesting concept in it. Partly it's because I've come to a point where I tend to like movies frankly that are a little more concept driven, even if it ends up *Being John Malkovich*. *Being John Malkovich* is a pretty weird concept, but there was a log line. A guy finds a portal into the brain of John Malkovich.

Now, that's not going to get the masses running to go see it but, certainly for its audience, that log line was brilliant. I definitely feel that's the way to develop screenplays and that, truthfully, once you have that concept you sort of have to ask yourself as you're developing it: *Are you being true to it?* If you find that in the middle of Act II you're off on some tangent that has nothing to do with that original concept, you're probably lost.

But the only reason I don't say that out loud is because you get that, *How would you discover the next Fellini then? How would you pitch Amarcord?* It's true. It's like the exception, in a sense, proves the rule that once in a while there is a movie that's so brilliant and so impossible to sum up in a phrase.

I think as a responsible producer you want to have more than a log line. It's a concept that conveys your movie in some way that's interesting and unique and more often than not — emotional. If there is some sense of emotion in the concept and you're true to that emotion in your movie, it tends to make more sense.

Maureen: I know you've worked with a lot of writer/directors. Is there anything in the development process that would be different if it were a writer/director?

Ben: One thing that I do see happen often is that writer/directors tend to think—young ones, new ones, and some who maybe aren't fully developed—they don't need everything on the page. They say, *No, but I had this in my head and I've envisioned—*

The problem is that a screenplay is a tool that many people who collaborate on a movie have to use and so it does two things. One is that you need to communicate to other people and also it's always better to force your writer/director to articulate his vision on the page first. Because often when they don't, you realize they really didn't have it that clear and when they try to execute, it didn't work.

So it's always better to try to get them to get as much of their vision in screenplay form as possible and that's one of the areas that you can run into problems.

I think there is one other area of development that's hugely important, which is finding your director. How do you find your director based on your material? Obviously you have them read the script. You have them sit down and articulate their vision and then one of the things that I often do is have them list several movies that they feel in some way capture what it is they want to do. Like how many different ways can we have them visualize their vision before you take them on as a director? I think you have to get a sense of what they're going to bring to the table before you get them involved. It's not just about seeing their previous films and thinking that they have the right sensibility. It's also about articulating their vision on that movie before you sign them on. Because once you sign a director you now have three people opining about every little nook and cranny and it gets more complicated.

Screenwriting Software

There are many scriptwriting software programs out there. Final Draft is one of the most common and is compatible with EP Scheduling and EP Budgeting software. There are many others and you can check the *www. ProducertoProducer.com* website for more listings.

Getting Feedback on the Script

Once you have a great draft of the screenplay it's a good idea to send it to people who have different tastes in film from yours to give you some notes. It can be very enlightening to have a different perspective on the screenplay from someone who may not be a ready cheerleader and yet can give constructive criticism for your film. I don't suggest that you ask for script notes from family and friends unless they are talented and experienced filmmakers themselves. Otherwise the chances are slim that anything they say to you will be very useful. No offense, but I wouldn't ask my mom to read my x-rays and give me her opinion about possible surgery options for my foot unless she were a trained radiologist. It's fine for family and friends to read your screenplay but I would take whatever they say with many grains of salt.

Doing a **table read** or a **staged reading** will also be invaluable in the final stages of the script-revision process. Gather up the best actors you can find for each role and send the script at least a week ahead of time to the actors. Plan for a few hours of rehearsal time with the director (if attached at that time) or whoever will do the best job. Then invite trusted filmmakers and insightful colleagues and have the actors read the script, start to finish, without stopping. A quiet space that allows the actors to sit proscenium-style in front of the audience works best. The thing that matters most is that the actors understand each of their roles and have the time to rehearse with the director so they can convey the essence of the screenplay and the characters. Afterward, you can poll the audience on key questions that you want feedback on or you can talk/correspond directly to individuals and get their notes about the reading.

It's one thing to read the script and hear the voices in your head. It's a revelation to watch great actors read the dialogue and act out the words. Jokes that just laid there on the page can come alive and things that you thought would be incredibly moving or funny might not deliver the dramatic punch or laughs when exposed to the light of a staged reading. Caution — don't get too caught up in the individual performances and gloss over any needed changes in structure and tone. There have been times that producers become so enamored with a brilliant actor's performance that it blinds them to the weak third act or the lack of a clear want or need in one of the other characters. We've all heard the adage — If it's not on the page, it's never going to get onto the screen. You still need to attend to those issues before you begin official preproduction. Now is the time to do it.

Veteran producer/executive producer and managing partner of Emerging Pictures, Ira Deutchman (*www.EmergingPictures.com*), weighs in on the development process:

Maureen: When you're putting a project together, do you do staged readings?

Ira: There are a couple different parts to that. It really depends on the project. Some projects read well and some projects don't. I think it's very difficult for people, in general, to sit through readings, unless, first of all, the acting is really very good. I always recommend that the script be cut dramatically.

If you're doing it for investors and for outsiders, for any sort of audience, I think [the length of] most screenplays will definitely try their patience. So in those kinds of circumstances, if that's what you're going after, it would be an edited version of it. Sometimes you can just have a narrator read the stage directions, sometimes there are better ways of doing that.

I've seen people do very clever things at readings including use of music. I would just caution that if you're going to do something like that, make sure people are rehearsed so that they really know what they're doing.

Maureen: If you're doing a reading for investors, do you have any suggestions of where to do it — a stage? A conference room? Is there anything that you think is very important that you need to try to make happen?

Ira: I think it's partially whatever is available but it's also partially what's going to get people interested in coming. So a venue like a bar — and I'm not saying a loud bar, but like the back room of a bar — so there is, sort of, a promise that there is going to be refreshments or just some place interesting. Like if it is at one of these trendier kind of homey clubs, those would be things that might make it feel like more of an event. Whereas doing it in a conference room definitely doesn't feel like an event.

Maureen: What about actor rehearsals before production?

Ira: Readings, as rehearsal, are a little different when there isn't anybody around and I would highly recommend that, particularly for comedies. Comic timing is so important and I feel like the films that I've been involved with — the low-budget films that had any real comic repartee — one of the problems with working with a low-budget film is you don't have enough rehearsal time, you don't have enough takes, usually, to get it on the ninth take or something. So those are the places where I would say that doing a couple of readings where the cast can actually bounce the lines off of each other [is invaluable]. It's a way of finding laugh lines and making up for the lack of time to do it on the set.

Script Doctors

Sometimes it makes sense to bring in a **script doctor** to work on the screenplay. A script doctor is an experienced screenwriter who is brought in to rewrite parts of a screenplay such as dialogue, pacing, or other aspects. It is common for script doctors to not receive screen credit for their work. If you decide to hire a script doctor you should consult a lawyer and research any guild rules, if applicable.

Writer's Guild of America

The Writer's Guild of America is the union for screenwriters in the U.S. The West Coast chapter is located online at *www.wga.org* and the East Coast chapter can be found online at *www.wgaeast.org*. If you hire a union screenwriter you'll need to follow the guild rules for fees and work regulations.

Log Line — Don't Leave Home Without It

It's never too early to start working on the log line for your film. The log line is a sentence (or two) that describes the protagonist(s) and the plot line of the film in a very specific way. Some people insist it must be one sentence only. I believe it can be two if the alternative is a jammed sentence that is so grammatically mangled that it's hard to understand the meaning. The log line describes what the film is about, using verbs as much as possible. Verbs are action words and that's what makes a good film.

You want it to capture the essence of your film and elicit the reaction "I want to see that!" from most of the people you tell it to. If it's a comedy, the log line should come across as funny. If it's a documentary then you want it to communicate the topic effectively so that listeners can engage immediately with the subject.

If people aren't interested after hearing the log line, you need to revise it until it works. If you change it and you still get lukewarm responses, then you might not have a great film yet and you'll need to change the script or the treatment until you do. Log lines can be a great reality check to find out if you are onto a good thing. One of my favorite log lines was from a film I produced a few years ago titled *The Team*. The documentary was directed by James Marsh and Basia Winograd in 2004-5. James wrote the log line — "Shot over a period of five months in the spring and summer of 2003, *The Team* chronicles the efforts of a homeless agency in New York to recruit and train a soccer team of homeless people to compete in the first annual homeless world soccer championships in Graz, Austria." Most people were generally intrigued by the log line and we were able to get funding for the film off of the short treatment written by the co-directors. Don't underestimate the power of a good log line.

Log Line Creation

Writing a log line requires skill and there are certain principles for creating a great log line. Dave Anaxagoras (*www.davidanaxagoras.com*) has come up with the best rules for log line creation. He's been kind enough to let me reprint some of his info in this book.

Here is Dave's advice for the essential elements of effective log lines:

TONE AND GENRE

What is the tone and genre of your screenplay? If your log line describes the humorous adventures of a robot butler, it is a safe assumption you have a sci-fi comedy. But if there is any chance of confusion, explicitly state the genre and tone.

A MOTIVATED PROTAGONIST

Whose story is this? What flaw must your hero overcome? What motivates your protagonist to undertake his or her goal? The subject of your log line (and your screenplay) is the protagonist. We must also understand what motivates this protagonist. Why this protagonist for this story?

Protagonists' motivations could be an emotional problem, a character flaw, or an incident in their past that still haunts them.

Sometimes, a single adjective is enough to give us a sense of the protagonist's motivations — not just a pet store clerk, but a lonely pet store clerk. Not just a fourth-grader, but a timid fourth-grader. Remember, these aren't extraneous adjectives; they are relevant to the story and describe motivation. A bald man doesn't suggest motivation . . . unless he's stalking the president of the hair-club for men.

INCITING INCIDENT

What sets the story in motion? This is the spark that ignites the fire, the event that sets the whole story in motion. It gives your protagonist (and your script) focus and direction. The Inciting Incident is the meat of our log line.

MAIN OBSTACLE

Without some serious conflict, without an obstacle, you could just write *and they lived happily ever after* and the story would be over. The inciting incident sets the story in motion. The conflict *is* the story. In order to sustain a script for 110 script pages, we need big conflict. This would be a good place to mention the antagonist.

ULTIMATE GOAL

This is the end-game, the desired outcome of the protagonist's efforts. This is what the protagonist is after, what they truly desire more than anything else in the movie. You have to have it in your script, or the story could meander and end up anywhere.

STAKES

A very legitimate question that many people ask is "Who Cares?" or, put another way, "So what?" What they are really asking, for our purposes, is "What's at stake?" The outcome has to matter in a way that we care about. So what hangs in the balance? What happens if the protagonist doesn't reach his or her goal? In other words, we are talking worst case scenario. What catastrophe we are trying to avoid?

RECAP

The six essential elements of the log line are:

1. Tone and genre

2. The protagonist's identity and motivation

3. The inciting incident

4. The main obstacle or central conflict

5. The protagonist's ultimate goal or desired outcome

6. The stakes, or what happens if the goal is not accomplished

A prototype log line might look like this: TITLE OF MY SCREENPLAY is a GENRE with overtones of TONE about a PROTAGONIST who HAS A FLAW/MOTIVATION when THE INCITING INCIDENT HAPPENS and s/he must then overcome THE MAIN OBSTACLE in order to accomplish THE ULTIMATE GOAL or else there will be CATASTROPHIC CONSEQUENCES.

Don't be a slave to the formula. Not all elements must be explicitly stated, and not always in this order. But the idea is to cover this essential information, one way or another, as economically as possible. I find it easiest to write everything into one long, unwieldy and awkward sentence first and then edit down to something elegant and economical.

For BOMBER, a feature film I produced with writer/director/producer Paul Cotter, our log line is: "A bittersweet comedy about love, family and dropping bombs on Germany. An 83-year-old man goes back to find and apologize to a village he accidently bombed during the Second World War."

Notice that the essential elements in any effective log line are also the essential elements of any viable movie. Working out a thorough log line can be an important first step in developing a solid movie concept.

Creating a Proposal

For any project that requires funding you will usually need to put together a proposal. There is a general format for such a proposal although you can customize it to fit your particular film. There are differences in what you include when creating one for a narrative film versus a documentary film. I have included an example of each at the end of this section. A proposal should be only a few pages long. Less than five pages is best. People don't have a lot of time and you need to make sure to include only the information that is essential for them to make a decision. If they are interested and want more info, they will ask for it and you can supply it. Narrative proposals can be different from proposals for documentaries. When applicable, there are separate requirements for narrative and documentary below.

OVERVIEW OR PROJECT INFORMATION —

Narrative format: Describe the project briefly. Include the title, running time, type of project, and the log line. If you have any important attachments such as cast or executive producer, mention them here, as well. You also could choose to include a pitch line, as well. The pitch line is when you take two fairly recent successful films or television shows that have elements of your film and put the word "meets" between them and it creates a filmic child that represents your particular film. When you put them together you should get an instant image in your mind of what the film will be, i.e., "*Cinderella* meets *My Big Fat Greek Wedding*." Make sure to include the format, production schedule length, and estimated budget.

Documentary format: Similar to the narrative format. Include more discussion of the film's topic, giving the reader some background — historical or otherwise. Then you'll go into some detail about how your film will focus on the topic. It needs to be clear about your "take" on the topic and what the trajectory of the film will be.

COMPARISON FILMS —

Narrative format: Just as you studied great scripts from past films, once you decide what project you want to make you should do some research on similar projects to compare to yours. Comparison films take into consideration a film's theme, demographic (gender and age of your intended audience), storyline, subject matter, similar characters, casting, scenarios, and genre. You want to look at these films and research several things — what were the production budgets? Where did the money come from? How much money did it make at the box office (domestic and international)? DVD sales and Internet sales? Create a grid for yourself and analyze four to six films for comparison. The films should be fairly recent, within the last seven years is best — so the economics are relevant. There are many websites that provide box office information about past films to fill in your grid. You will begin to see which films were financially successful and which were not, and where they were able to make their money.

For those films that were not successful (i.e., did not make back all the money spent on budget, prints & advertising (P&A), and distribution), figure out why not. Was the budget too high for what could be made at the box office? Did they spend too much on P&A so they couldn't make back their investment? Was it a great script but poor execution (bad acting or directing)? Was it bad timing — two similar films released around the same time in the same market? Or was the film just not very good? Did it tank at the box office but then do really well in DVD sales? Is it destined to be a cult classic and do really well in DVD sales, long term?

All those factors are important to know because they will be the predictors of your possible success, they will give you ideas as to where to go for funding and how to distribute and market the film when completed. You'll have your own ideas and contacts but you don't have to reinvent the wheel here. If a strategy worked successfully before on a comparison film, it has a good chance of working for your film, too — as long as the same conditions apply. Remember everything is constantly evolving in the film industry, faster and faster than ever, so keep up on the trends. Discover what factors may impact your film in the marketplace two years down the line and plan for it now. For the proposal, only include the comparison films that were financially successful. You don't want to give the potential investor the impression that your film won't be a hit.

Documentary format: Comparison films are important for documentaries, as well. Recently there have been many feature documentaries that have strong theatrical releases that you can use as examples. Your topic and scope of your film will be different, so concentrate on the same target audience, not necessarily the content, when picking comparison films.

INVESTMENT PARTICULARS —

Narrative/Documentary format: Discuss the budget and how the money will be raised — pre-sales, equity investment, other monies. Put in the distribution plan. Lastly, include how the investor will be paid back for what level of investment. Remember to consult your attorney before finishing the investment sections. There are Security and Exchange Commission (SEC) rules that need to be followed, for legal reasons.

SYNOPSIS —

The synopsis is probably the most critical part of your proposal. Write it and rewrite it until it represents the essence of your narrative arc and it is an easy-to-read document. Keep it visual. You want the readers to be able to "see" your film by the time they finish reading the last paragraph.

Narrative format: Describe the main characters and the key plot points of the film. Keep it to no more than three or four key character descriptions. More than that number and it becomes difficult to keep them all straight in your head. You should list the character's name, then age and then a quick description like "petulant teenager" or "biker chick" — instant identification through an adjective and a noun. Remember that conflict = drama. Keep it to three to five paragraphs and no more than one page. Work hard to make it concise and easy to read.

Documentary format: Use the same principles for a narrative when writing the documentary synopsis. Bring the film to life for your reader. Introduce characters and plot points (if applicable) so the synopsis has the dynamism of a clear narrative arc. You'll want to give some context to the film's subject matter for the reader.

BIOS —

Narrative/Documentary format: Include one paragraph bios of any key personnel — executive producer, director, and producer. If cast is attached put their bios here. If a key department head (i.e., cinematographer, production designer, editor, composer) has an impressive resume include them, as well.

BACKGROUND/HISTORY OF THE PROJECT –

Narrative format: If there is additional useful information put it here. Add details like if the screenplay has won any awards or if it participated in a Sundance workshop or if the underlying material has an interesting story behind it.

   Documentary format: In addition to the above, you can list any of the grants your project has previously been awarded.

BUDGET AND/OR SCHEDULE —

Narrative format: Add the budget's summary page or top sheet only and a schedule, if you have one. If there is any important tax information that is relevant, put it here. Many states have tax incentives and the rules should be outlined here if you plan to take advantage of them.
The proposal should outline the key elements of the film so a potential investor gets all the pertinent details to make a decision about her investment. The proposal is usually accompanied by the script. Don't send out the proposal until you have a FINAL draft of the script. You only have one chance to make a first impression.

Documentary format: Include the budget info as described above. Instead of a script, you can include a trailer if you have one.

LEGAL DISCLAIMER

As I have stated at the beginning of this book, I am not an attorney and am not dispensing any legal advice in this book. You should always consult with your entertainment lawyer before proceeding. In the case of putting together a proposal you need to be aware that the Security Exchange Commission (SEC) has very strict rules about raising money for a business or a film. You need to discuss these issues with your attorney before you send out a proposal to make sure that you do not run afoul of any federal statutes.

Proposal Examples
Narrative Film Proposal example

NOTE ABOUT FILM:

Padre Nuestro was completed in the fall of 2006. It was accepted into the Sundance Film Festival 2007, where it won the grand jury prize. It was an official selection in more than a dozen major international films festivals including the San Sebastian Film Festival, Miami International Film Festival, Havana Film Festival, and Pusan International Film Festival and was the closing night film at the Morelia Film Festival in Mexico. It was released by IFC Films in May 2008. *Sangre* received two Independent Spirit Awards nominations, for best first feature and best screenplay. *Padre* was distributed in over 20 foreign territories and sold to IFC Films in the U.S. where it was distributed under the title *Sangre de Mi Sangre.*

THIS BUSINESS PLAN WAS PREPARED BY PRODUCER BENJAMIN ODELL IN 2005.

Thanks to the talented writer/producer Benjamin Odell (*Sin Memoria, Ladrón que roba a Ladrón*) and writer/director Chris Zalla (*Padre Nuestro, Law and Order*) for allowing me to include their proposal for *Padre Nuestro* as a narrative film proposal sample.

PADRE NUESTRO
an independent feature film

FILM COMPANY
ADDRESS
PHONE
EMAIL

2

TABLE OF CONTENTS

PROJECT INFORMATION

Two teenage Mexican boys meet on their way to New York City. Juan goes in search of the father he never met; Pedro flees from a criminal past. When Juan arrives to the city, he finds that Pedro has not only stolen his bag, but also the letter that contains Juan's father's address. Without it Juan not only can't find his father, but has to learn to survive on New York's mean streets. Meanwhile, Pedro shows up at Juan's father's house claiming to be his long lost son...

PADRE NUESTRO is Spanish-language drama about the struggle of Mexican immigrants in the U.S. Following in the footsteps of recent Spanish language hits such as AMORRES PERROS, Y TU MAMA TAMBIEN and MARIA FULL OF GRACE, PADRE NUESTRO caters not only to the biggest minority group in the U.S. - the Latino population - but has the ability to crossover into a theatrical distribution domestically and throughout the world. Spanish-language cinema is in demand, and OUR FATHER has the emotional power to reach a large audience.

PADRE NUESTRO is the first feature for writer-director Chris Zalla. The project was selected as one of twenty finalists out of 5,000 applicants for the 2004 Sundance Institute's Feature Screenwriting Lab. Based on the strength of PADRE NUESTRO, Mr. Zalla was hired to write the feature film, MARCHING POWDER, based on the international eponymous best seller, for Brad Pitt's Plan B Entertainment.

PADRE NUESTRO is budgeted at $**XXXXXXXXX**. The producers seek to finance the film either entirely through equity investment or through a combination of equity and other sources.

Upon completion of the film, the producers will target the top film festivals such as Sundance, Berlin, Venice, Cannes and Toronto in order to create maximum publicity and to garner the most competitive distribution deals. After recouping their equity investment, the investors will become profit participants, sharing in all profits generated by the film. By keeping the budget low, assembling a top-notch creative team, and casting name actors, the producers aim to maximize the film's marketability and profitability.

PADRE NUESTRO will be shot on film on location in Mexico and New York City.

4

YOUR INVESTMENT IN <u>PADRE NUESTRO</u>

The budget of PADRE NUESTRO is $**XXXXXXXXXX**, being raised primarily through equity investment. It is possible that the film will be funded through 100% equity. Otherwise, there will be a portion financed through a distribution deal, foreign presales, or other funding. Any changes in the structure will be pre-approved by all investors.

After the film is completed, the producers will seek both a domestic and foreign distributor. The distributors will sell the film worldwide -- theatrical, pay cable, home video/DVD, basic cable, video on demand, broadcast television, and miscellaneous smaller markets. Often, sales contracts allow for a film's rights to revert back to the producers after a finite period of time (such as seven years), at which point the film can resell to other buyers in these markets. The film will be produced through an LLC dedicated to this project. All of the revenues that flow back to the producers (minus minor operating and delivery expenses) will be distributed to the investors on a quarterly basis as follows:

PHASE ONE: The first profits returned to the LLC go entirely to the investors, pari passu to their original investment. When the investors have received a cumulative **XXX**% of their original investment ($**XXXXXXXXX**), then the profit distribution reaches the second phase. Most of the revenues from a film tend to be received in the first year or two after selling of the film.

PHASE TWO: All "deferments" will be paid. This "deferred compensation" is given to actors, key crew, postproduction facilities, etc., to entice top caliber people to work below their normal rate, keeping up-front costs low. The deferments will be capped at $**XXXXXXXX**.

PHASE THREE: From here on out, all profit participants will receive "points" in the film. There will be 100 points total, and investors will receive 50 of these points on a pari passu basis. For example, an investor of $**XXXXXX** (a quarter of the budget) would receive 12.5 points in the film. The other 50 points will be allocated by the producers to actors, writer, director, producers, and other key contributors. As with deferments, the point system enables the producers to keep the costs low while maintaining high production value.

For example, the investor puts in the $**XXXXXXXX** for PADRE NUESTRO. From the "Phase One" revenues, they would receive 100% of the money coming in until reaching **XXX**% of the original investment ($**XXXXXXX**). Then, after deferments are paid, they would own 50% of all profits thereafter. As these points have no cutoff time, investors will continue to receive income over the entire profit-earning life of the film.

SYNOPSIS

JUAN, 17 and PEDRO, 15, meet in the back of a tractor-trailer filled with illegal Mexican immigrants headed for New York City. Pedro shows Juan a sealed letter that his mother, now dead, has given him - an introduction to the father he never knew. He brags to his new friend that his father, DIEGO-- who left Mexico many years before - has become a wealthy restaurant owner and will surely rejoice at the arrival of the son he always wanted. Juan doubts Pedro's confidence and challenges his expectations. Juan's father left him when he was four with two things -- a switchblade... and the scar it made on his chest.

When the truck lands in New York City, Pedro finds that Juan has not only stolen his bag, but also the letter with Diego's address. With that letter, Pedro shows up at Diego's house knocking on the door, introducing himself as his long lost son, Pedro. Diego doesn't believe he has a son and Juan spends his first night sleeping in the hall outside Diego's door.

But Juan's dogged persistence to win over his "father" and Diego's mounting guilt ultimately compels the old man to offer the boy shelter. Juan plays along and contrives to maintain the image of the hardworking, devoted son. But rather than working during the day for money, as he claims he is doing, Juan picks pockets, steals from beggars, and solicits prostitutes. Even as Diego sleeps, he prowls about his room, looking for the old man's money stash. But something else happens, too: despite himself, Juan seems to be growing fond of 'his father.'

In the meantime, Pedro has been forced to survive on the mean streets of Brooklyn. He meets MAGDA, a prostitute who dupes him and steals his last possession: a locket containing a picture of his mother and Diego. When he finds her again, he demands that she help him find his father, but she'll only listen to money. In order to earn her payment, though, Pedro must partake in her way of life.

When Juan finally discovers a shoebox beneath a loose floorboard, he is disappointed to find it only contains a few old love letters and some random tools. After prying up the entire floor, Juan realizes there is no stash, and makes the difficult decision to leave. He runs into Diego returning from work and agrees to go out for a last drink with his coworkers. Juan wins them all over with his bravado. For the first time, Diego experiences fatherly pride. He insists that "his son" come back home. Juan relishes the human contact as they stumble home, arm-in-arm.

Though Diego and Juan discover a father-son relationship they have both secretly longed for, Fate conspires against them. Pedro, with the help of Magda, finds the restaurant where his father works, learning through co-workers that Juan has stolen his identity. Before long, Pedro and Juan find themselves facing off against each other with knives. While Pedro has learned quickly how to survive in the streets, Juan is fiercer and faster...

6

Diego returns home to find Juan, covered in blood, hiding in his hallway. As sirens approach, Juan, terrified, tells him that he killed someone and must go away. Diego acts quickly. He grabs the hammer and chisel and knocks several bricks from the wall, revealing dozens of large rolls of cash behind. He tells Juan that he must take the money and meet him in Mexico, for the police will confiscate it and deport him anyway. Juan caves under the weight of the gesture and the moment. He finally confesses that Diego isn't his father, but Diego won't hear any of it... not from his own son.

Money in hand, Juan runs frantically across the Williamsburg Bridge, away from the only father he ever had and to an unknown fate.

The Mexican and Latino Greater Latino Markets in the U.S.

Two films with similar styles to PADRE NUESTRO are the Mexican features AMORES PERROS and Y TU MAMA TAMBIEN. Both of these films were Spanish language, edgy in content, and used actors with little or no international star power. And yet, they were both successful in both box office and ancillary revenue streams. Much of their success came from the U.S. Latino marketplace including theatrical, TV, cable and home video. (See Exhibit A).

According to the U.S. Census taken in 2000, the combined Latino and Hispanic population was 35,305,818, or 12.5 percent of the total U.S. population. With a constant new influx of immigrants and continued growth rates in the current population, the number is currently estimated to be 40 million.

The Selig Center for Economic Growth at the University of Georgia did a study on minority spending power in the U.S. and found the following:

> ➤ Latino spending power is projected to reach $927.1 billion in 2007, up from $580.5 billion in 2002 and $686 billion projected in 2004
> ➤ Latino spending power should outpace African-American spending power in 2005
> ➤ Latino market share should reach 9.4 percent in 2007, up from 5.2 percent in 1990.

This tremendous spending power has undoubtedly boosted box office, TV and video sales of Spanish language films in the U.S. Recent Spanish language films that have succeeded in the U.S. market place include:

Film	US Box Office
El Crimen del Padre Amarro	$5.7 million
Tortilla Soup	$4.5 million
Amores Perros	$5.38 million
Y Tu Mama Tambien	$13.6 million
Maria Full of Grace	$6.2 million
A Day without a Mexican	$4.17 million
Like Water for Chocolate	$21.7 million
The Motorcycle Diaries	$14 million*
	*still in US theaters

U.S. Box Office is only one component of a film's net profits, which includes domestic and international television, cable and DVD/Home Video rights. In fact, the U.S. box office makes up significantly less than half of the total revenues on a film.

Of the eight films mentioned above, six of them are Mexican or Mexican-American stories. This is important, as the Latino market is diverse and sometimes difficult to navigate. Tastes between immigrants of different Latin American countries can vary greatly even if they share a common language. The largest sector of the Latino population is Mexican, making up over 60% of the

8

U.S. Latino population. The producers of PADRE NUESTRO believe that the appeal of this story to the Mexican-American market could generate significant revenues in the U.S. alone, even without counting the non-Mexican Latino audience in the U.S., the Latino audience in Central & South America, and the Spanish-speaking audience in other foreign territories. If, like the above films, PADRE NUESTRO appeals to the international non-Latino audience as well, then revenues could increase dramatically.

THE CREATIVE TEAM

BIOS OF ALL CREATIVE PLAYERS GO HERE.
DIRECTOR
WRITER
PRODUCERS
EXECUTIVE PRODUCERS
ACTORS (IF ANY ATTACHED)
DIRECTOR OF PHOTOGRAPHY (IF ANY ATTACHED)
COMPOSER (IF ANY ATTACHED)
ETC

10

BUDGET

BUDGET TOP SHEET GOES HERE.

STATEMENT OF RISK

This memorandum outlines the formation and operation of a limited liability company to engage in the business of the production and exploitation of a motion picture.

The contents of this memorandum are confidential and are disclosed pursuant to a confidential relationship and may not be reproduced or otherwise used except for the purpose intended herein.

The partnership interests described in this memorandum will not be registered under the Securities and Exchange Act of 1993 or any local securities law, and are described for investment only and not with a view to resale or distribution.

The purchase of membership interests described herein entails a high degree of risk and is suitable for purchase only by those who can afford a total loss of their investment. Further, factors as contained in this memorandum (which does not include all possible factors) should be carefully evaluated by each prospective purchaser of a limited membership interest.

The contents of this memorandum are not to be construed by any prospective purchaser of a limited membership interest as business, legal, or tax advice, and each such prospective purchaser will be required to demonstrate that he or she has the ability to evaluate the purchase of the limited membership interest described herein or has retained the services of a representative who has such knowledge and expertise as may be necessary to evaluate said purchase.

This memorandum is neither an offer to sell nor a prospectus, but is informational in nature. A full investment prospectus will be provided upon request and at the sole discretion of the Managing Member.

EXHIBIT A: Film Profit ROI reports*

	Title	Comparison Film #1	Comparison Film #2
Domestic Release	*Distributor*		
	Release Date		
	Maximum Screens		
	Opening Gross		
Costs	*Budget*		
	Prints & Ads		
	Total Costs		
Domestic Income	*Box Office Gross*		
	Rentals		
	Video Units		
	Video Revenue		
	Domestic Ancillaries		
	DOMESTIC ROI		
Foreign	Foreign Box Office		
	Foreign Rentals		
	Foreign Home Video		
	Foreign Ancillaries		
	Int'l Revenues		
	Total Global Revenues		
	Distribution Fees		
	Income After Distribution Fees		
	Library Value		
	GLOBAL ROI		

Documentary Film Proposal Example

The award-winning team of writer/director/producer Susanna Styron (*Shadrach, In Our Own Backyards*) and producer Jacki Ochs (*The Secret Agent, Letters Not About Love*) created a wonderful proposal for their documementary *9/12: From Chaos to Community* (www.912film .com). They have been kind enough to allow me to include it here as an excellent documentary proposal sample:

CITY OF FRIENDS

A documentary film

Produced by Jacki Ochs & Susanna Styron
Directed by Susanna Styron
Co-producer: Stephanie Zessos

Contact: The Human Arts Association, 212-343-0078.

CITY OF FRIENDS

"I dream'd in a dream, I saw a city invincible to the attacks of the whole of the rest of the earth;
*I dream'd that was the new **City of Friends**;*
Nothing was greater there than the quality of robust love – it led the rest:
It was seen every hour in the actions of the men of that city,
And in all their looks and words."

-- Walt Whitman, Leaves of Grass

On the evening of September 11, 2001, John Casalinuovo, a retired sheetmetal worker living in Chinatown, climbed into the ruins of the World Trade Center and began digging for survivors. Within days, he and his wife, Denise Lutrey, had set up tables, and eventually a makeshift tent at the edge of "the pile" to serve rescue workers water, food, coffee, clean clothes, boots, first aid – anything they could get their hands on, anything anyone needed. The tent grew, was absorbed by the Salvation Army's relief effort which began to stock it with supplies twenty-four hours a day seven days a week, and was eventually dubbed the Hard Hat Café.

The Hard Hat Café was an island of relief and replenishment in a sea of pain and exertion for countless firemen, police officers, ironworkers, asbestos workers, construction workers, sanitation workers and others who worked round-the-clock shifts for nine months in their effort to recover the remains of those who perished on September 11. John and Denise were always there, offering a smile, a kind word, a cup of coffee, a clean bandage, a game of cards, a good joke, a shoulder to cry on to everyone who came in.

On September 11, Liz Carvajal was in her late twenties, unemployed, dispirited, and unsure what to do with her life. When she saw the attacks on the World Trade Center on TV, she got in her car and drove from Flushing, Queens, to as close to the site as she could get. Talking her way in past various checkpoints, she began helping out at Ground Zero that night. Fearing that if she left the perimeter she would not get back in, she took to sleeping in doorways for a few hours each night, and working for the relief effort every waking moment. It was nearly a week before she went home for the first time, only to change her clothes, turn around and go right back in. When her path crossed after several weeks with John and Denise's, they brought her in to work full-time in the tent. By the end of the next year, once the relief effort was completed, Liz had taken and passed the New York City Police Department exam, become a private investigator, and moved in with her new boyfriend, Alex, a fireman she met and cared for at Ground Zero.

By November, 2001 the Salvation Army had erected a huge dome near the perimeter of Ground Zero where relief workers could come for a hot meal, a shower, a change of clothes, new equipment, a cup of coffee, a pack of gum -- whatever they might need. Like the Hard Hat Cafe, it was open twenty-four hours a day, seven days a week. Charlotte Leopard came to work there because her boyfriend, Gerard Baptiste, a New

York City fireman, died in the collapse of the twin towers on September 11. She wanted to be there when they found his body. Night after night, she worked in the dome, making coffee for relief workers, waiting for the dreaded news, and forming new bonds. The most significant bond she formed was with fireman Joseph "Toolie" O'Toole. Toolie was from Ladder 41/ Engine 90 in the Bronx – the same firehouse as Liz' boyfriend, Alex. For nine months following September 11, he worked at Ground Zero day after day, night after night, looking for his "brothers". Happily married, with several grown children, Toolie became like a father to Charlotte. He watched out for her, comforted her, helped her in countless ways until she became like a member of his family. Although Toolie had never met Gerard, he says of Gerard and Charlotte: "He was my brother, so she's my sister."

What makes people give everything they can of themselves in a time of crisis? What kind of lifelong bonds are formed in the intensity of communal grief? How do we find life in the wake of death? At the Hard Hat Cafe and the dome at Ground Zero, countless New Yorkers and others gave freely of their time, their hearts and their souls -- sometimes at a cost involving great personal, emotional and financial sacrifice -- to comfort the men and women in the trenches of the rescue and recovery effort. They gave everything they could of themselves, they formed unlikely and yet unbreakable bonds, they found life in the wake of death. This is their story.

PRODUCTION:

"City of Friends" will be a 60-minute documentary shot on digital video. We will film interviews with former volunteers, particularly the ones mentioned above, and many of the workers they cared for, threading their stories together into a dramatic narrative. Aside from interviews, we intend to film a dinner re-uniting volunteers and firemen at a firehouse in the Bronx; a visit by John Casalinuovo and Denise Lutrey to the site where the Hard Hat Cafe formerly stood; and the annual September 11 reunion at John and Denise's building in Chinatown, where workers and volunteers come together every year on that historic date, not in a spirit of celebration, but one of appreciation and remembrance. Weaving this together with archival footage and still photographs, we will reveal and explore a unique, as-yet-unexamined, aspect of the legacy of September 11th; the mysterious and inevitable healing process; and the enduring strength of the human spirit.

SUSANNA STYRON
Producer/Director

Susanna Styron volunteered at Ground Zero from November, 2001 to the closing of the site in May, 2002. She is the director and co-writer of the critically acclaimed Columbia Pictures feature film, SHADRACH, starring Harvey Keitel and Andie MacDowell (Venice Film Festival, Tokyo Film Festival, Los Angeles International Film Festival). For television, she wrote and directed BOTTLECAPS, an episode of A&E's 100 CENTRE STREET, created by Sidney Lumet. She directed and co-produced A DAY LIKE ANY OTHER, a half-hour film starring Richard Beymer and Ally Sheedy (Special Jury Award, San Francisco International Film Festival; Special Jury/Gold Award, Houston International Film Festival).

As a documentary film-maker, Ms. Styron co-produced, wrote, directed and edited IN OUR OWN BACKYARDS, an award-winning documentary about the nuclear industry on the Navajo Reservation (PBS; Museum of Modern Art). She has worked as an Associate Producer for Close-Up, ABC TV's documentary division. Her other documentary credits include SUSPENDED SENTENCE, which she produced, directed and edited; and AVENUE OF THE AMERICAS, on which she was assistant editor.

As a writer, Ms. Styron co-authored (with Bridget Terry) an adaptation of Ann Tyler's BACK WHEN WE WERE GROWN-UPS for Hallmark Hall of Fame; TAKING BACK OUR TOWN for Lifetime Television (2001 Christopher Award; 2002 Environmental Media Award); and CROSSING THE LINE, also for Lifetime.

As a fellow at the American Film Institute, Ms. Styron wrote and directed several short dramatic videos. She has worked in various capacities on several feature films, including assistant to the director on ALTERED STATES directed by Ken Russell, and production assistant on THAT OBSCURE OBJECT OF DESIRE directed by Luis Bunuel. She served as both Associate Producer and script supervisor on STARS ABOVE THE CITY, an Italian feature film produced by Andrew Karsch.

Ms. Styron directed and edited the video portion of TARANTULA, a multimedia theatre piece based on the book by Bob Dylan, at the Powerhouse Theater in Los Angeles; and she co-directed, with Darrell Larson, the L.A. premiere of BAD DREAMS AND BE-BOP by David Higgins at the Dynarski Theater.

Ms. Styron is the author of several screenplays, and has published articles in *Spin Magazine, The Yale Revue* and *The New York Times.* She holds a B.A. from Yale University and an M.F.A. from the American Film Institute.

JACKI OCHS
Producer

On September 11th, Jacki Ochs and her family fled their home two blocks away from the World Trade Center. Her daughter watched the towers burn from her classroom window down the street. They returned home on Thanksgiving day 2001.

Jacki Ochs' film work includes both experimental and documentary genres, which have been broadcast worldwide. Her film, "The Secret Agent" about the chemical Agent Orange received many awards including the John Grierson Award for Best New Director from the American Film Festival (1984), the Special Jury Prize from the Sundance Film Festival (1984), premieres at the New York Film Festival(1983), Mannheim Film Festival, Germany (1983) and Cinema du Reel, Paris (1984) and a Certificate of Merit from the Academy of Motion Picture Arts and Sciences. Some other awards Jacki has received for her work include a NYFA Fellowship (1987), and two MacDowell Colony Fellowships (1986,87) and the Guggenheim Fellowship (2001).

Ms. Ochs' most recent feature release, "Letters Not About Love," (1998) based on a Russian and American correspondence between two poets, received Best Documentary Feature from the SXSW Film Festival, Dziga Vertov Visionary Artist Award, Huntington International Independent Film Festival, 1998 among others. It featured Lili Taylor narrating the voice of poet Lyn Hejinian. It has been marketed to hundreds of American universities and institutions and televised internationally. It was a selected feature at INPUT '99, XXII International Public Television Screening Conference.

Articles about Ms. Ochs' work have appeared in most major US News and Film publications including the New York Times, LA Times, Plain Dealer, Film Comment, Cineaste, International Documentary Magazine and many others.

Ms. Ochs has been Executive Director of the Human Arts Association, a not for profit arts foundation, since 1976. The foundation has produced music, dance and multimedia productions as well as more than a dozen film productions. In addition Ms. Ochs taught documentary film production as an Associate Professor at SUNY Purchase from 1996 to 2001. Ms. Ochs' production experience spans over twenty years including work as an assistant director, associate director, cinematographer and producer for a number of commercial, industrial and broadcast production companies.

Currently Ms. Ochs is in post-production (Producer/Director) on a documentary about pre-adolescent girls, is producing a short tribute piece on Lenny Bruce for the ACLU and is Executive Producing a feature documentary titled "The Untold Story of Emmett Louis Till."

Ms. Ochs attended University of Pennsylvania, and received a BFA from the San Francisco Art Institute.

STEPHANIE ZESSOS
Co-Producer

Stephanie Zessos volunteered at Ground Zero for several months. Her 9/11 work also included helping downtown residents and workers receive financial assistance from the Red Cross, Salvation Army and the United Way September 11th Fund. After the official end of the recovery effort at Ground Zero in May 2002, she produced BROTHERS, a feature length documentary about men who lost their brothers on September 11th.

Prior to her years in New York, Stephanie built up her experience working for feature film directors PHILLIP NOYCE, HECTOR BABENCO and SAM SHEPARD. Some of the films she worked on during her years in Los Angeles include THE SAINT, CLEAR AND PRESENT DANGER, SILENT TONGUE, CARLITO'S WAY, THE DOORS, BRAHAM STOKERS DRACULA, POINT BREAK and BARTON FINK.

HUMAN ARTS ASSOCIATION
Non-Profit Sponsor

The Human Arts Association is a not-for-profit 501C3 foundation that supports independent productions by performers, film and video makers. It was founded in 1976 to create a structure that would ensure artists creative control of their work in addition to providing production and financial services. The foundation's purpose is to stimulate talent and nurture educational and artistic works, which can be promoted nationally and internationally. The foundation has presented several hundred performers and produced award winning films and videotapes. It sponsored ART IN GENERAL, an art gallery in lower Manhattan, from 1983 to1990 until it received its own non profit status. Other current video/film productions in development and post-production include AFTER WAR, a touring exhibition and accompanying publication by photographer Lori Grinker documenting war veterans from every major 20th century conflict, CASINO NATION, a documentary about Traditional Native American tribes and the gaming industry being sponsored by the Native American Public Television Consortium, and BEING ME, a documentary about the lives and issues of preadolescent girls.

Past films produced and/or sponsored by the Human Arts Association include FEED, a documentary about the New Hampshire primaries, BLOOD IN THE FACE, a documentary feature exploring the philosophies of the far right in the United States which opened to rave reviews at Film Forum, CONTINENTAL DRIFT, an educational film for young children about geophysics which premiered at the Museum of Natural History, and THE SECRET AGENT, an award winning film about the affects of Agent Orange on Vietnam veterans and their children, which premiered at the New York Film Festival and was the premiere feature of the Learning Channel (later to become the Discovery Network).

The Human Arts Association has been the recipient of and has served as the umbrella sponsor for many grants. A sampling of the granting agencies and foundations includes Ampex Corporation, Benneton Foundation, Crickett Foundation, Deer Creek Foundation, the Donnet Fund, the Film Fund, Global Ministries, the Joint Foundation, the Kendall Foundation, J. Roderick MacArthur Foundation, the National Endowment for the Arts, the New York City Department for Cultural Affairs, New York State Council on the Arts, the Rockefeller Foundation, SOROS Foundation, the Shumann Foundation, the Sunflower Foundation, and the United Presbyterian Church. The Human Arts Association has also raised a good portion of its funding from private individuals some of whom include Anne Roberts, Peggy Delaney, Edward and Nancy Asner, Norman and Frances Lear, Max Gail, Steve Allen, Eileen Brennan, Cristophe De Menil, Danny De Vito, Michael Farrell, Don Henley, Goldie Hawn, and Judd Hirsch.

BUDGET "CITY OF FRIENDS" (working title)

Personnel

Producer	6 mos/flat	30,000
Producer	4 mos/flat	20,000
Director	4 mos/flat	30,000
Co-Producer	6 mos/flat	20,000
Director of Photography	20 days@$450	9,000
Sound Recordist	20 days@350	7,000
Production Assistant	20 days@125	2,500
Production Assistant	20 days@125	2,500
Editor	14 wk@$2000	28,000
Assistant Editor	6 wk@$750	4,500
Sound Editor	1 wk@$4000	4,000
Office Assistant	16 wk @$600	9,600
Total Personnel		**167,100**

Production Equipment

Camera	20 days @ $150	3000
Sound	20 days @ $100	2000
Lighting	20 days @ 125	2500
Grip	20 days @ $75	1500
Batteries & Supplies	flat	500
Spare Bulbs	flat	200
Total Production Equipment		**9,700**

Stock

DV CAM stock	100 @$16	1600
Mini DV Stock (dubs)	75 @$4	300
Betacam SP stock	7@ $15	105
DigiBeta Stock	2 @ $40	80
Expendibles (Production and Post production) Flat		1000
VHS Tapes	Flat	100
CD's/Cassette Tapes	Flat	200
Total Stock		**3,385**

Production Costs

Per Diem	20 days @ 8 crew @$20	3200
Parking	$40/day, 2 NYC locations	1000
Car Rental	$100/day	2000
Gas	Flat	400
Total Production Costs		**6,600**

Post Production

Archival Rights/Clearance	5 minutes @ $2000/	10000

Edit Room Rental	16 wks @ $500/	8000
Transcripts	100 @ $60/	600
Stills Animation	8 hrs @ $300/	2400
Music Fees		6000
Graphics	Flat	4000
On Line	3 days @ 2000	6000
Sound Mix		12000
Tape Duplication		1500
Color Correction		4000
Closed Captioning		2000
Total Post Production		56,500

Office

Insurance/ General Liability		4000
Third Party Property		2000
Owned Equipment		700
Office Rental	6 mos @ 1500	9000
Phone/Fax/Cell phone	Flat	1500
Post/Messenger/Fed Ex	Flat	700
Legal	Flat	2000
Accounting	Flat	1000
DGA Pension and Health		3750
Errors and Omissions Insurance		6000
Total Office		30,650

TOTAL BUDGET   **$273,935**

IMDB.com

www.IMDB.com is an online database that lists all the credits for most films and television programs that have been produced for several decades. It is important to keep your list of screen credits up to date because often people will look you up online before meeting with you or looking at your proposal. It's a quick reference for people to do and it gives good information about your career background and what projects you have worked on, and in what capacity. Again, some advice from veteran producer/executive producer and managing partner of Emerging Pictures, Ira Deutchman, (*www.EmergingPictures.com*):

Maureen: When putting together an investor proposal, is there anything that you feel is critically important?

Ira: If you're going to put facts and figures in or references to movies and their success or paradigms of any sort, do your homework. Because anybody who is savvy about the business, when they read stuff and [find it to be clearly] exaggerated or just wrong, *it's like… close the book and move on.*

So just don't make claims that you can't back up in some way. If you're going to put numbers in, put footnotes in and tell where you got the numbers from. Unless you're dealing with dentists who are completely un-savvy, although they may ask those questions, too.

Creating a Pitch

In addition to the proposal, you'll need to work up a pitch for your film. The purpose of your **pitch** is to verbally inform, engage, and excite the person listening to your project. A pitch is a distillation of the key elements of your project and it is expressed orally. The form and length of the pitch will depend on whom you will be pitching but certain principles apply. Below I've included an insightful piece written by John McKeel (*www.SNAFUfilms.com*) about creating The Winning Pitch.

"Just the thought of standing in front of an audience scared Jim. He wasn't alone. A recent survey showed more people are afraid of public speaking than dying, so Jim worked very hard to memorize what he thought was a great speech. He wrote and re-wrote it until every word was perfect. Unfortunately, when it came time to deliver his talk, Jim was so nervous he forgot what he was going to say. He stumbled over his words. Jim stopped frequently and his eyes naturally rolled to the top of his head as he tried to remember those perfect phrases he had so meticulously constructed. He lost contact with his audience and the speech was a total bomb.

You've written a great proposal but now you have to pitch it. Never confuse the written word with the spoken word. They are two completely different forms of communication. Beautiful writing can sound stilted and pretentious when read aloud. Great literature doesn't guarantee great performance so prepare an oral presentation orally. This is so important I'm going to repeat it. Prepare an oral presentation *orally*.

How is that possible? You know your material. You've lived and breathed your project for a long time. You've talked about it with friends, family and probably perfect strangers, so your first exercise in the preparation of a great oral pitch is to sit down in a room by yourself and just start talking. Let the words come as you describe your passion. As you talk about it, certain sentences will stand out. Quickly jot it down and then keep talking. Again, remember this is an oral presentation, not a written proposal. Don't write down any more words than it will take to remind you of the thought. The key is to get back to talking as soon as possible. It's an oral presentation, so we are preparing orally for it.

If you are having trouble getting started with your talk, answer these questions *out loud*. Imagine that I am right there with you. Now let's talk:

- Your film is a jewel with many facets. Can you describe some of these facets and some of the characters or themes I will see in your final project?
- Now, if you had to choose only one theme, what is the most important facet? Why?
- Who are you making this film for?
- You seem very passionate about your project. Why?
- Tell me about some of the characters I will meet in your film.
- What do you hope people will take away from watching your film or documentary?

The three most important topics to address in your pitch are:
- For narrative — Who is the film about and what is the conflict?
- For documentaries — What is this film about?
- Why make it now?
- You have to convince us that our money (as an investment or grant) won't be wasted. Tell us why you will see this film through to completion.

After an hour you should have pages of great sentences that will trigger great thoughts. Now it's time to find your film or for a documentary — your theme.

Look over those pages of sentences you just wrote down. For the narrative — what is the most compelling way to describe your film or project. For the documentary — do you see any themes? It's time to take out more paper and write a different theme on the top of each page. Now copy all of the sentences that relate to that theme onto that page.

Take a break. Have a cup of coffee. Go for a walk. Play with the kids and then come back to your notebook. Look through all the pages. One will stand out. You've done it! That's your pitch. But how will you organize those random sentences into an organized pitch?

Try giving a four-minute talk from just the notes on that particular page. A couple of things will happen. First, a natural rhythm will develop. You'll discover you need to say this before that. A rough outline will develop. You will also find that some of the sentences aren't as powerful as the others. Discard them and you will be left with pure gold."

Producing a Trailer

Trailers created from footage that you have already been able to shoot can be a great way to raise the necessary funds for the film's full budget. It works well for narrative films when you are going after investor money but for documentary films, it is often an essential part of grant applications and pitching to a funder.

For narrative films, it can make sense to shoot a scene or two from the film if you have the resources to do that very cheaply. Often cast and crew are willing to work for a day or two on a brief section of the film if they think it will benefit them in the long run — like getting the financing to make the feature-length project. Despite limited funds for a trailer, you need to make it reflect the production values you intend for the longer film. Potential investors will be watching to see how the film looks and sounds as much as for the performances and the script. The trailer must be strong, otherwise it could be a detriment to your proposal package. Better to leave the script up to the investor's imagination, then create a poor trailer that will turn investors away from your project.

For documentaries, trailers are usually required for any application to a grant-making organization or foundation. Fernanda Rossi is an authority on creating great documentary trailers to help fund projects. She is the author of *Trailer Mechanics: A Guide to Making Your Documentary Fundraising Trailer* and she has a website at *www.documentarydoctor .com.* Here's what she has to say on the subject:

"Fundraising trailers run from 5 to 10 minutes. If you have never made a trailer before, 10 minutes probably sounds like it is nowhere near enough time to convey the depth and importance of your documentary, but once you are sitting in the cutting room you will change your mind. It will become painfully obvious, as you try to glean your best images, that a minute can be endless.

Even if you have an abundance of great images, do not indulge yourself by making a 20-minute piece. For many of the major grants over 200 trailers are submitted. Because of high volume, screeners often are unable to watch more than the first few minutes.

Your trailer is just one piece of a much bigger picture called your fundraising strategy. It will not have the entire responsibility of communicating all aspects of your future film, but it will carry the heaviest load.

Unlike your finished film, your trailer will rarely be shown on its own. If you are having a fundraising event at home, you will be there to introduce it. When submitting the trailer for grants, a proposal will accompany it. But the trailer is your kicker. It proves that you can take all your wonderful ideas and translate them into moving images. For a few minutes you can captivate your audience in a way no proposal or personal presentation can. You have to use that brief magical moment wisely and make it consistent with the rest of your fundraising plan. A good trailer can be the last straw needed to get an investor to sign a check or to make your project a finalist in a grant evaluation.

While your trailer will have a busy life visiting foundations, you should also consider using it for:

- Networks and cable outlets — some provide developing or finishing funds
- Festivals and markets — those with pitch sessions or screenings of works-in-progress
- Private investors or donors
- Corporate investors or donors
- Fundraising parties — in the comfort of your home or at another venue
- Website — for an online marketing campaign and donations
- Outreach and special programs"

Distribution Plan

You'll need a general distribution plan for your film at the outset. Of course, things will change as you progress through the steps in producing your project but it's important to make a thorough plan at the beginning. Don't just think that it will be such a great film that distributors and networks will be knocking down your door after its first screening at a major film festival. You need to research and figure out what is the best way to release, distribute, and disseminate your particular film. There is no one way to do it and with the way technology and the marketplace are changing so quickly, whatever you did on your last project doesn't necessarily pertain to your current one. You need to be constantly re-educating yourself on what works now and what will work soon and try to use an internal crystal ball to figure out what is the best strategy for your film. *Variety, Hollywood Reporter, Filmmaker* are good sources for the latest information about narrative and television. *Documentary* magazine covers the documentary industry.

There are certain markets to consider:
— Domestic theatrical
— International theatrical
— Domestic network or cable television
— International television
— DVD sales
— Internet sales and distribution
— Cell phone
— Exclusive sales through retail chains, like Starbucks, WalMart, or Amazon
— Digital downloads
— Whatever else the future provides

There are several books that detail how to distribute independent films and videos and they go into much more depth than I can here. In addition, there are many industry periodicals that are chock full of articles about the latest films and what kind of deals they made and are making. Seminars and panel discussions that occur during many of the top film festivals can also be very educational on what is the best way to distribute your film. Local film groups dedicated to offering seminars and master classes are another great resource. Check out *www.ProducerToProducer.com* for the latest information and recommendations.

Presales

Presales refers to when you sell certain rights to your film before you produce it as a way of funding the film. You could sell to a U.S. cable network and maybe an international TV network or two and might have enough money to make the film. Then you'd still have the ability to sell theatrical, DVD, and Internet rights after the film is completed. It all depends on your budget. Presales are not that easy to obtain. You usually have to have a certain known reputation as a filmmaker or producer to get a meeting with a television network or commissioning editor. There are always exceptions to the rule but the competition is tough and contacts are key. Maybe the director has a proven track record of making profitable films, or you have an A-list actress attached to your film or an Academy-nominated writer has written the script. These are the kind of things that allow you to get presales. Groundbreaking producer/executive producer and managing partner of Emerging Pictures, Ira Deutchman, (*www.EmergingPictures.com*) comments on presales:

Maureen: Is it even possible for a low-budget indie film with no recognizable talent to get presales?

Ira: Most likely not. It's always been hard because presales are always based on elements. And what are the elements? If there are no stars, or the director has never done anything before. The one thing that could save a situation like that would be if the budget is low enough and if the producer has a track record. Frankly, I would advise most people if they have that kind of a film not to think about presales. But if presales were part of your way of trying to get it financed then I would say maybe try to find a producer and godfather to give it more credibility, somebody who has a track record of working with first-time directors or whatever.

I only say that because I actually pulled that off once — I financed the film. *Kiss Me, Guido* was the film and I financed it 50% on a presale of all foreign sales rights and 50% with equity financing. But for the 50% of the foreign presale, there were no stars in the movie, the director had never made a movie before, so it was totally producer credibility and it was me and Christine Vachon who co-produced that movie. Without us attached to the movie (the budget of that film was $800,000) I don't think it would have been possible, otherwise.

So generally speaking, I think you can say that you can't think about a movie like that being sold with presales. There is one other exception I can think of which is certain genres that are considered (this is going to sound more insulting than it's meant to be) "director proof," like a slasher movie or like a really stupid teen sex comedy, or something along those lines. Even without stars, if the budget is low

> enough there may be a consideration that those films might be worth
> something on video, no matter what. So there may be some kind of a
> presale that can be done for something like that, but those are really
> the exceptions.

For documentaries, elements like the director's track record, an A-list actor who agrees to do the narration or the strength of the underlying material may be the key elements that make the project bankable for a presale. It depends. For several of the feature documentaries I have produced or co-produced, we sold a few key foreign television rights and the U.S. cable television rights and were able to fund the film entirely. It means you have to keep the budget tight but at least you know you have all the money necessary to make the film, start to finish.

Sometimes you won't be able to get a sale until after you have shot the film and have created a great rough cut. Then you might be able to get some sales. But this is a calculated risk and you should proceed with caution. I don't advise going into any kind of debt for a film. If it is a good enough project you will find the money — or wait until you have saved up the money to cover the entire budget.

For documentaries, there is the added funding option of nonprofit agencies and foundations. Development and production grants are an ideal way to get the film made if you have a film that meets the foundation's criteria and can make a strong application. This takes a lot of time and effort so make sure you and your project fit all the criteria before making the application. You'll need to plan for a long fundraising period. Often the decision from foundations takes several months after the submission deadline.

Sales Agents

Sales agents are people who specialize in selling rights to films. They have connections with the various distribution outlets and are known for the certain kinds of films that they sell. Some concentrate on narrative features, some on feature documentaries and a few sell short films.

Deliverables

Deliverables is the list of documents, masters, and other media that need to be delivered to a distributor or broadcaster when a film is bought. It is important to understand the amount of material that will need to be created for a deliverables list. It is time consuming and costly and should be factored into the postproduction timeline and budget before accepting a distribution deal. (This will be discussed, in depth, in the *Postproduction* chapter.)

Development Wrap Up

The process of getting your film from first idea to preproduction is a different adventure with each and every project. There is no way to know all the twists and turns in the road but by knowing the steps and executing them in the most efficient and logical way possible, it will be easier. By following these guidelines you should be well on your way to moving to the next level with your film.

Final Checklist Before Deciding to Produce the Film

I've put this list together as a final checklist before you take the leap and produce a film. Depending on your answers, you may decide to move forward or not:

1. Are there other films out there — in development, in production, or already released — similar to my project?

2. If so, is my project different enough so it won't be impacted negatively? For a documentary, if it is the same subject matter, is it a different enough "take" on it that it won't matter? Even the perception that it is too similar could diminish your project's viability. Make sure you research and know what has been produced and what is in the pipeline.

3. Am *I* the right person to make this film?

4. Can I devote 2–5 years of my life to this project?

5. What's the preliminary budget?

6. Can I raise all the money? Do you know exactly where you can get the financing? Or is it just wishful thinking?

7. If not, can I fund it entirely by myself (or with family and friends)? Is that something I am willing to do? Does everyone understand and accept the risks of such an investment?

8. Do I have all the rights I need in writing?

9. If making a documentary, can I afford all the archive (video and stills) that I need?

10. What format do I plan to use for shooting? What is the *exact* work-flow for the finishing of the film? What will be my deliverables? (see *Postproduction* chapter)

11. Do I trust my key collaborators? Are they people who share my values and work ethics? Will it be fun and rewarding to work with them over the long life of the project?

Depending on how you answered, you are ready to move onto the next step for your film.

RECAP:

1. **Allow 2–3 years for development.**

2. **Read great scripts to learn from the best.**

3. **Nail down the rights.**

4. **Create and memorize your log line.**

5. **Proposals differ for narratives and documentaries. They also differ depending on whom you are sending them to. Make sure it is the best it can be before sending it out.**

6. **Trailers are essential for documentary proposals. They can also be helpful for narrative projects.**

7. **Pre-sales can give you all or some of the money you need to make your film.**

8. **Acquire a sales agent or a very concrete distribution strategy.**

9. **Make sure you *really* want to make this particular film and you know the reasons why. They will sustain you during the long, dark hours.**

CHAPTER 2

SCRIPT BREAKDOWN

A SCRIPT BREAKDOWN IS LIKE a road map for your film. Preparation is very important, so what would you think if you heard this story? A friend decides that she wants to go see her favorite band play in a city that is somewhere half way across the country. She knows the name of the town and the date the band is playing. She decides to just hop in her car without directions, no knowledge of what's the best route to take, and no sense of how much it will all cost. She doesn't know if she'll need to stay at a hotel along the way and hasn't brought any additional supplies, change of clothes or even tickets to the sold out concert. What would you say to this friend?

Well, that's kind of what it's like to try to budget and schedule a film without doing a script breakdown first. You've got a great 100-page script — how do you turn that into a 25-day shooting schedule and a detailed, estimated budget? Well, the first step is the script breakdown. It's the tool the producer and/or assistant director uses to analyze a script into its specific elements that can then be turned into a plan and budget for the production. Once it is finished, you'll

> *First, have a definite, clear practical idea — a goal, an objective. Second, have the necessary means to achieve your ends — wisdom, money, materials, and methods. Third, adjust all your means to the end.*
>
> *— Aristotle*

have a way to wrap your arms around the production details and work out the first draft of the schedule and budget with a degree of ease and certainty.

Nuts and Bolts

Creating a **script breakdown** is a process that allows you to list all the characters, locations, props, special effects (SFX), costumes, etc., required by your film's script. It is usually created by the **Assistant Director (AD),** the crew person who creates the shooting schedule for the production. On a no/low-budget project, however, it is often done first by the producer because the AD has not come onto the project yet or there is no money for an assistant director yet. We'll talk more about ADs in the *Scheduling* and *Preproduction* chapters.

I put the *Script Breakdown* chapter early in this book because it is an invaluable tool when you are trying to figure out how ambitious and challenging your project will be and how best to produce it. Later in this book we will go more in-depth for the full, detailed breakdown of the final version of the shooting script in the *Scheduling* Chapter. Here we will be using a single sheet to list the major production elements of the script. You can do a breakdown by using the script breakdown template on the website *www .ProducerToProducer.com* or use computer scheduling software.

A script breakdown is not usually done for a documentary because documentaries don't normally have a traditional screenplay or require sets, production design, or costumes. The exception is for documentaries that involve historical re-creations. For *MAN ON WIRE*, a documentary I co-produced, I created a script breakdown before I budgeted or scheduled the historical re-creations shoot.

The script breakdown sheet will be used first to provide you with a snapshot of your production. After that you will use it to create a tentative production schedule laying out how many days or weeks you'll need for the preproduction, production, and postproduction phases of your film. This schedule will allow you to create an estimated budget. (As you get closer to your shoot dates you'll need to lock into a *detailed* schedule and budget — see the *Scheduling* and *Budgeting* chapters for further details.)

Finally, the script breakdown is an effective way of directing the attention of the director and/or writer to the more ambitious, expensive, and otherwise potentially problematic elements of the script at a relatively early stage in the process. As a result, they start to understand the schedule and budget ramifications of the script in a way they never could before the breakdown was created.

For instance, on *Torte Bluma*, a short film I co-produced, the other producers thought the 18-page script could be shot in six days. It's a period piece that takes place in the Treblinka death camp and we planned to shoot it all in Brooklyn, NY. Because of all the production design, props, animals, location moves, and costumed extras, the director believed that the film would require seven days to get it in the can. After I did the script breakdown it became clear that the director was right — we had to do a seven-day shooting schedule.

Breakdown Details

Creating a breakdown requires a lot of concentration and is data-entry intensive. So you may need to do it over the course of several days, depending on the length of the screenplay. Pace yourself.

Before we go over the breakdown sheet, let's define all the elements that are included in it.

Script title — script title

Page Count — list each scene in chronological order from the script. Tracking by scene numbers allows you to keep track of which elements play in which scenes. Numbering the page count allows you to build a tentative schedule later on.

Int/Ext and Day/Night — Information taken from the slug line information in the script. It will facilitate scheduling later on.

Location — Information taken from the slug line information in the script. It will facilitate scheduling later on.

Action — a short description of the action helps to keep track of what is happening in the scene.

Cast — List each actor speaking role in the scene. This allows you to track their schedules and also elements that will go with them like wardrobe, hair/makeup, and hand props.

Actors who are minors (anyone under 18 years old) are legally required to have a parent or guardian on the set at all times and can only work limited hours per day, as set by the specific state child labor laws. Keep this in mind if you have child actors in your film. You may need to add time to your schedule to accommodate the reduced work hours for the children in the cast.

Extras/Background Actors — **Extras or background actors** are the people who are in the background of a scene and do not have any script lines or specific action that requires them to take direction from the film director. List all non-speaking roles w/ approximate number of each type.

Props, Animals, Vehicles, Stunts, Weapons, EFX, Hair/Makeup — List anything in these categories for each scene.

Props — List all of the production design/art direction elements for the set. Include furnishings, hand props (things that actors hold and interact with), signs, wall decorations, etc.

Animals — List any animals required in a scene. Usually you will need animal training and a handler, as well.

Vehicles — Picture vehicles refer to the vehicles that will be seen and used by actors on camera. Vehicles that are used to transport people and things for the production itself are called production vehicles and are not counted on a breakdown sheet.

Stunts — Stunts cover fight choreography, car chases and crashes, and actor falls. You need to hire a stunt coordinator, as well.

Hair/Makeup — List any special hair/makeup considerations here.

Breakdown for *Red Flag* Script

To best illustrate how to create a script breakdown and then use it to create a tentative schedule and estimated budget, I have included the script of a short film I produced titled *Red Flag* that was written and directed by Sheila Curran Dennin. The film's log line: *Red Flag* is a comedy short that follows Tracy, a 30-something woman who endures a series of nightmare blind dates, each one worse than the last. Along the way, she has an uninvited guest — her own personal warning system — which she chooses to ignore, making her unprepared for her unexpected meeting with Mr. Right.

I am using this film as a case study because it is a good example to illustrate the process of creating a script breakdown, budget, and schedule. It's a short film but it covers a lot of the production issues we need to address. Please read the 10-page screenplay below and then look at the script breakdown sheets that follow. As you will see, I have highlighted the various elements in **CAPS** in the script that need to be transferred to the breakdown sheets; this makes it easier to keep track of the elements that will be used to fill in the sheet for each scene.

RED FLAG

written by Sheila Curran Dennin
WGA registered #1263707
Third draft

```
FADE UP ON:

1 MONTAGE:  Couples in New York City.  We see various
couples walking, talking, sitting and chatting throughout
the city streets, Central Park, etc.
Text:  On any given night in the city
MONTAGE: Continuous
TEXT:   Someone is on a blind date.
MONTAGE: Continuous
TEXT:   But are they really paying attention.
UP MUSIC:  Ho Hum's "Pretty Ugly"
MONTAGE:   The montage continues, inter-cutting the following
scenes:
A man brings FLOWERS to a doorway and rings the buzzer,
nervous and pacing, checking himself in the window,
waiting...
A man stands by a restaurant entrance, looking for
"someone"...she appears, they acknowledge each other and
shake hands...he leads her down the street on their
"date"...
A woman sits in a restaurant, waiting.  She checks her
WATCH.  Looks around again.  She then leaves, alone, stood
up...

                                           DISSOLVE TO:

2 EXT. A CITY SIDEWALK. EVENING.
A woman approaches.  She looks up at the SIGN on the
restaurant before her.  She approaches the door and opens
it, going in as we ...

                                           DISSOLVE TO:


TITLE:   RED FLAG

                                           DISSOLVE TO:

3 INT. BAR. EVENING.

We follow the woman as she walks along the BAR, clearly
looking for someone.  She sees him.


                         TRACY
                 Are you James?

                         JAMES:
```

                         I am! Tracy?

                              TRACY
          It's really nice to meet you. I'm sorry I'm a bit late.

                              JAMES
               Not a problem, not a problem. Have a seat.

We see TRACY, early 30's, and JAMES, early 30's, at the bar
settling in to their first, blind, date.   TRACY is an
attractive, put-together, professional type, a regular,
every-girl. Her date, JAMES, good looking in a relaxed kind
of way, no frills, casual attitude, has been at the bar for
a bit before her; a PLATE OF HALF-EATEN FOOD sits in front
of him, along with the remnants of a COUPLE OF DRINKS. He is
picking his teeth with a TOOTHPICK. Tracy maneuvers her way
into the BAR STOOL next to him...she stumbles a bit, acts a
little embarrassed...rights herself and sits down. James
doesn't seem to notice, or care much.

                              JAMES
                      (Through his toothpick)
                  So, you work with Natalie.

                              TRACY
          I do. I do. We've worked together for a couple years now.

                              JAMES
                    (working the toothpick hard)
          Yeah. She said. That's great. She's a good girl. A good
                               kid.

                              TRACY
          Ya. She is. She's great. She, um...(starting to notice
          the toothpick action) ...she told me that you're in real
                              estate?

                              JAMES
          I am indeed. I'm kind of waiting to see what happens with
          it. I'm not real into super hard work...but you gotta do
                         somethin, right?

Tracy stares at the toothpick in his mouth. He's twisting
it, biting it. Turning it over and over, never stopping.

                              TRACY
                  Right. That is true.

                                    JAMES
Do you want a drink?   I'm sorry I kinda started without you.

                                    TRACY
Oh God, that's fine.   I was running late anyway.   Ummm...I'd
                    love a glass of wine.

As JAMES tries to get the attention of the bartender, TRACY
can't help but stare at this man and his toothpick ... when
from out of nowhere, like a fly, something RED flies at her
face.   She bats it away, confused.   James does not seem to
notice.

                                    JAMES
                          Red or white?

                                    TRACY
                              Huh?

                                    JAMES
                    The wine.   Red or white?

                                    TRACY
            Oh!   Sorry...um, red.   Red, please.

Again, something flies in her face, bigger and redder now,
hitting her in the eye.   She bats it away again...

                                    JAMES
                 (points to the GLASS on the bar)
                          Red it is.

                                    TRACY
                Oh. That's great.   Thank you.

She takes a huge gulp of the WINE.   Again, the "fly" comes
at her, this time hanging out in front of her face, it
becomes clear that this is a RED FLAG, waving tauntingly
before her eyes.   She attempts again to bat it away as JAMES
talks and toothpicks away, his image out of focus, words
muffled, as she focuses on the flag.   She finally swats it
away as we   CUT TO:

JAMES keeps talking away, not noticing Tracy's battle with
the flag.   As he talks, Tracy blinks him in to focus.   As he
slowly becomes clearer, the toothpick has now become...the
RED FLAG...twisting and turning, being bit and swirled as
the toothpick before it.   Tracy stares with disbelief at the

Red Flag. She blinks, and it becomes the toothpick again.
She stares at JAMES keeps talking, oblivious.

                                        DISSOLVE TO:

4 INT. RESTAURANT BAR. Another evening altogether.

                    VO MALE VOICE
    It's really about paying attention, I think. Noticing
    things...clues, if you will. It's become sort of a way of
                life for me. It's how I operate.

                                        CUT TO:

We move along the bar area...it's crowded. A couple of
couples and several groups of singles hang at the bar.
Tracy sits at the BAR with another DATE, RICHARD...he is a
bit overweight, older, late 40's. He exudes self
confidence, but more of the overcompensating type. During
their conversation, whenever Tracy talks, he looks away,
just past her. At first she thinks he's really thinking
about what she's saying. But it becomes more distracting as
they go on.

                    RICHARD
    That's the only way they would have caught my Multiple
    Sclerosis...the only way I would have found out about my
wife's affair. It's been the NOTICING of things. You know?

                    TRACY
Wow. Multiple Sclerosis. If I seem surprised, it's cause
    Mandy didn't say anything. Well...I mean what would she
    say? Right? But, God. How are you dealing with it?

                    RICHARD
              (his eyes returning to her)
    I keep beautiful things around me. Only beautiful things.
Like you, you're beautiful. Keeping you around wouldn't be
                    too difficult.

RICHARD looks past her should again...intently, definitely
                    distracted.

                    TRACY
              That's really sweet. Thank you.

She goes to take a sip from her MIXED DRINK, a STIRRER
protrudes from it. She moves it out of the way. She sips
and something hits her in the eye. She pulls the drink

away. The stirrer is now...a RED FLAG! She pulls it out of
the drink, shoving it under the bar.

                        RICHARD
(Still looking behind her) My pleasure entirely. (looks at
             her) So...what's your sob story?

                        TRACY
Oh. Me. Well, no sobbing, really. Just kind of basic life
     stuff. Nothing like your story, my God. Wow.

Tracy finally can't resist, and looks over her shoulder,
looking to see what this guy is looking at...

                                                 CUT TO:

We see what he's been looking at... a beautiful, exotic
WOMAN at the end of the bar.

She turns back to him, in disbelief, and in the place where
he was waves a big fat RED FLAG. She blinks forcefully...
as we

                                            DISSOLVE TO:

5 INT. RESTAURANT. EVENING. Another evening altogether,
again.

CLOSE ON TRACY:
Tracy gives it another go, on another date. We start on
her, opening her eyes and staring ahead at:

CLOSE UP: on a very bad COMB-OVER. It is attached to what
we learn is a rather young man - way too young for a comb-
over - who is talking animatedly, on and on with passion.
We, like Tracy, hear only his muffled, distorted talking...
We cut to Tracy...she stretches a smile on her lips, trying
to be nice, to look away from the "part", to look as if
she's interested...

                     COMB-OVER MAN
           You've really never heard of them?

                        TRACY
            I'm sorry, I just haven't!

COME-OVER MAN
That AMAZES me. I mean, they're everywhere. All over TV.
Documentaries about them...they have their own *zoos*. People
do *fund-raising*. It's really kind of hip to be into them!
Really.

Tracy cannot look away from the comb-over...when from above
it a unmistakable blanket of red begins to appear, flowing
over his head. The RED FLAG has returned, larger than ever,
it flies toward her, she has to DUCK to get out of its way.
She steadies herself and tries to settle back into the
conversation ...

TRACY
(bored and rattled at the same time)
So, they're called "Meercats"?

DISSOLVE TO:

6 INT. RESTAURANT. EVNEING. Another evening altogether,
again.

Another DATE, JOE. But this one seems to be going well.

JOE
I don't think there's anything worse than blind dates.
Dating's bad enough, but blind dates?

TRACY
The stories I could tell you.

JOE
So what made you come out and meet me?

TRACY
Masocism? Boredom? I don't know...HOPE.

JOE
I'll be honest..(jokingly) because I feel I can be!
(smiles) First, I was going to cancel. Then, I figured
Anthony set this thing up as a favor so, "why not? I can
always leave after one drink". Right? Then...I walked in
and saw *you*. And...here I sit. Here I stay.

                              TRACY
                            (smiles)
          And here *I* stay. I'm having a really nice time!

                              JOE
      Me too. You're great. You really are. Almost...perfect.

JOE looks really closely at Tracy...the kind of "look" we
all yearn for - a smiling, gentle, searching...intimate
gaze. Tracy returns the gaze coyly...a bit shyly...

                              TRACY
                    (hesitatingly, playful)
                          ...what...?

He looks at her...directly now...right, at, her... nose.

                              JOE
      It's just...that nose-hair. Right there. Kinda driving me
      crazy. I've got a clipper in the car - we can take care of
                        that later.   Let's order wine!!

CLOSE UP on Tracy's completely shocked face...as the RED
FLAG drops soundly right in front of her, completely
covering frame.

                                                    CUT TO:

7 EXT PARK - DAY

Tracy walks through the Park on a beautiful Fall day. She
is talking on her CELL PHONE, checking her WATCH. Free.
Busy. Loving life. Alone.
She sees a COFFEE VENDOR CART and quickly hangs up the cell
phone, walking toward it.

                              TRACY
                          Ah...coffee!

As she moves toward the cart, she trips a little, looking
back as we all do at what "tripped" her. She giggles a bit
to herself, a tad embarrassed, as she gets to the stand.

                          TRACY (CONT'D)
                  One medium with just cream, please.

                       O.S. MALE VOICE

                    Are you a spaz?

TRACY looks around, not sure if the comment was meant for
her. She sees...MATT, a most gorgeous, stunningly
"regular", drop dead *normal* looking guy watching her. He
is, in a couple words, approachably adorable. He is stirring
SUGAR into his just-purchased COFFEE, placing the STIRRER in
his mouth when he's done. He chews on it a bit. He has a
DOG by his side and he leans on the other side of the cart,
smiling at her teasingly.

                         TRACY
                          Me?

                         MATT
                       Mm-hmm...

                         TRACY
                        A spaz?

                         MATT
                       Mm-hmm...

                         TRACY
          That's a secret only my closest friends know.

                         MATT
       Well, somebody's fooling you, cause you are one very obvious
                          "spaz".

                         TRACY
              (seeing now how cute this guy is...)
           So...is that a good thing or a bad thing.

Tracy notices the stirrer in his mouth...she stares at it
suspiciously...harkening back to "toothpick man" ...hmmm...
Throughout the rest of the dialogue, Tracy begins to look
for the inevitable RED FLAG. She looks above him, to the
side, behind him.

                         MATT
        I happen to think it's a good thing. But who am I to say.

Tracy regards him with reticence, but hopeful nonetheless.
Could this guy really be as nice, cute and normal as he
seems? Is that possible...but there *is* that stirrer in his
mouth...

                         TRACY
             OK...I'll bite...who are you?

We see what Tracy sees ...an extreme close up of his mouth
while he's talking, looking for the flag to appear
there...like in her toothpick date before.

Instead, he reaches up and throws the coffee stirrer in the
nearby TRASH CAN. No red flag comes...at least not yet.

                    MATT
              I. Am. Matt.

                    TRACY
              And I. Am. Tracy.

                    MATT
          It's very nice to meet you.

                    TRACY
          It's very nice to meet you too.
                (refers to dog)
              And who is this?

                    MATT
      This is "Miss Von Hemperton Van Dobberstein". "Dobbs" for
              short. We're walking. Want to join us?

OK - here it comes...the RED FLAG. Tracy looks around,
ready for it to POP her in the face. It doesn't.

                    TRACY
      Ummm...Well, I... (she is looking around him...for the
    "FLAG") I guess I could...(checks out behind him) for a
                  little bit...

                    MATT
  Oh - you don't have to be afraid of the Dobbs. THE kindest,
          most blast- of-a-dog you'll ever meet.

Tracy is looking everywhere for that blasted RED
FLAG......but...no flag!!

                    MATT (CONT'D)
  It's just walking...and we are a "spaz" friendly crowd here.
                Right, Dobbs?

                    DOBBS
                (barks!!)

                    TRACY

                              (laughs)
                    Well...how could I resist that?

                                                        CUT TO:

8 EXT. PARK. LATER

Tracy, Dobbs and Matt walk along the Park...talking,
laughing...Matt talks...Tracy looks for RED FLAGS...covertly
trying to be prepared for it to drop.

                                                        CUT TO:

9 EXT. PARK ENTRANCE. LATER

She and Matt and Dobbs stop walking near the entrance to the
park. Matt gestures that it's sort of time for him to go.

                              MATT
    Well, it's chow time for the Dobbs and I gotta get back to
      work. Thanks for honoring us with your "Spaz-ence".

                             TRACY
                        Happy to please!

                              MATT
                    It was nice meeting you.

    Matt starts to leave. What??? No further plan...no "let's
                    walk again sometime"???...

                             TRACY
    It was really nice meeting both of you. Really nice...

                              MATT
                   So, we'll see you later!

                             TRACY
                      OK...ummm - wait!
        Wanna walk again sometime...I'll trip over something!
                     Something really big...

                              MATT
              Can we...just...leave it at the walk. OK?

Tracy is stunned. She mumbles "OK" and stands there
watching him leave...sad and shocked.
Cut to MATT. Tracy is behind him, still staring. He senses
this, and turns to wave good bye. As he turns, we...

Cut to Tracy from his POV. To him, she is one big, huge,
RED FLAG! ...Flowing and billowing in the breeze. And she
has no clue he is seeing her this way.

Matt turns back toward camera, and breathes a heavy sigh of
relief, making a "phew" gesture with his face, and walks out
of frame.

Tracy remains on camera. She is Tracy again and we stay on
her disappointed, confused figure as we...

                                        FADE TO BLACK

Filling in the Breakdown Sheet

As mentioned earlier, you'll also need to make sure that each of your script's scenes is numbered in the order they appear in the screenplay and that you have added up the page count for each scene. Page counts are recorded in 1/8th-page increments. A quarter of a page is 2/8ths and a half page is 4/8ths, and so on. Remember to keep the numbering in eighths, don't turn 4/8ths into 1/2 or 2/8ths into 1/4. When you get over 8/8 pages you'll count it as one page. For instance, if you counted 11/8ths of a page, it will be notes as 1-3/8ths.

Below is the *Red Flag* breakdown, we have 9 scenes and they are each listed in the Script Breakdown sheet below.

Film Title: Red Flag   **Script page count: 10 3/8**

SCENE	PAGE COUNT	INT/EXT DAY/NIGHT	LOCATION	DESCRIPTION	CAST	EXTRAS	PROPS, ANIMAL, VEHICLES, STUNTS, EFX
1	4/8	EXT/Night	NYC Streets	Montage of couples meeting		5 couples - NYC Streets	flowers, wrist watch
2	2/8	EXT/Night	Bar #1	Tracy walks into bar	Tracy		sign
3	2 3/8	INT/Night	Bar #1	Tracy meet James	Tracy, James	6 bar patrons, bartender #1	half eaten food, red flag#1, remnants of a couple of drinks, bar stool, toothpick, wine, wine glass
4	1 3/8	INT/Night	Bar #2	Tracy meets Richard	Tracy, Richard	6 par patrons, bartender #2, exotic woman	mixed drink stirrer, red flag #2
5	7/8	INT/Evening	Restaurant #1	Tracy meets Comb-over man	Tracy, Comb-over man	5 background actors	red flag #3, comb-over wig
6	1 1/8	INT/Evening	Restaurant #2	Tracy meets Joe	Tracy, Joe	4 background actor couples	red flag #4
7	2 5/8	EXT/Day	Park	Tracy runs into Matt at the park	Tracy, Matt	4 park background actors, coffee vendor	coffee vendor cart, coffee cup, coffee, stirrer, Tracy's cell phone, Tracy's watch, Trash can, dog

SCENE	PAGE COUNT	INT/EXT DAY/NIGHT	LOCATION	DESCRIPTION	CAST	EXTRAS	PROPS, ANIMAL, VEHICLES, STUNTS, EFX
8	1/8	EXT/Day	Park	Tracy & Matt walk his dog	Tracy, Matt		Dog
9	1 1/8	EXT/Day	Park	Tracy & Matt say goodbye	Tracy, Matt		Dog, Tracy as red flag

Breakdown Analysis for Red Flag

By looking at each one of these factors you can determine your production requirements and discover the more challenging and expensive elements of your film. This important bit of information allows you to discuss the elements with the director and/or writer at an early stage of the development or preproduction process. By looking at this breakdown we'll discuss the specifics for the Red Flag elements.

Scene #s — *Red Flag* has 9 scenes.

Page Count — The rule of thumb for an independent low-budget production is to shoot three to four pages a day. Red Flag will tentatively be a three-day shoot.

Int/Ext and Day/Night — *Red Flag* has 5-6/8 pages of interior night scenes, 6/8 pages of exterior night scenes, and 3-7/8 pages of exterior day scenes.

Location — *Red Flag* has five locations and some pick up shots.

Cast — *Red Flag* has five principal actors. Tracy is in every scene with one other male actor each time. We did not have any need for minors as cast members — everyone is 18 years old or older.

Extras/Background Actors — *Red Flag* needed 35 extras to fill out the scenes in the bars and restaurants. For the park we would just use whatever background people were in the park at the time of shooting.

Props — *Red Flag* was able to utilize most of the decoration and interior design of each location for its art direction. We had to bring in our own food and in some cases, plates, glassware, and cutlery but, otherwise, it was pretty small and inexpensive for the art department.

Animals — For *Red Flag,* Scenes #7-9 required the character Matt to be walking his medium-size dog. The use of a dog would add some time to the schedule because animals don't always do things perfectly on the first take. Our hair/makeup artist owned an older dog with only one eye that was very mellow and perfect for our film. We only needed the dog for one day in the park and it was on a leash the whole time.

Vehicles — *Red Flag* needed a coffee vendor cart for Scene #7 in the park. We were able to rent one from a snack vendor cart company in New Jersey.

Stunts — There were no stunts in *Red Flag.*

EFX — *Red Flag* had graphic effects — the red flag that pops up in each of the five dates. We met with The Molecule graphics design group in NYC and storyboarded how they could create the graphics for the five scenes that required the red flag.

Hair/Makeup — For *Red Flag* we needed a very good wig for the Comb-over Man role. Our hair/makeup artist met with the actor and the director in preproduction to work out the correct look for this character so the make-up artist could build the wig ahead of time.

Creating a Tentative Schedule

Once you have all the elements in the breakdown, you can create your first pass at a tentative schedule from your breakdown. This is the first glimpse of how you can actually make this film. I always look forward to this step because it is the beginning of the long road to the realization of the film. There are three important criteria for determining the schedule: 1) location; 2) interior or exterior; 3) day or night.

First you need to group all the scenes together that will be shot at the same location. Then group together the scenes at each location by time of day (day or night) and interior or exterior. The result will give you an idea of how many scenes can be shot together, based on the three criteria.

For the *Red Flag* script, the grid below shows how many scenes happen in each location and whether it is Interior or Exterior and Day or Night. We have two different bar sets and two different restaurant sets — all night interiors. There are also several montage shots as exterior night shots to set up the beginning of the film. The park location is all day exterior. The red flags will be created as a graphic effect in postproduction. See the grid below:

How Many Days to Shoot?

The general rule for low-budget independent filmmaking is to shoot no more than three to four pages per day (for a 12-hour shoot day.) This script is 10 pages long, so you would normally plan for a three-day shooting schedule. We decided to do a three-day shoot with one shorter "pick-up" day. A **pick-up day** is one when you work with a reduced crew and usually no actors. The montage pick-up shots would be grabbed by the director, producer, and director of photography on a separate evening, without other crew or actors.

LOCATIONS

There are five sets and only three days to shoot, so I wanted to find a location that could work for two different sets — a restaurant *and* a bar. That way we could shoot two blind dates in a day and not have to do a company move. A **company move** requires everyone to pack up the equipment into vans and trucks, drive to the next location, unload, and set up the equipment again. It usually kills at least two hours in a shooting schedule — precious time I'd rather use for shooting purposes.

This film required four different bar or restaurant sets. We couldn't afford to construct sets so we would have to find locations. The producing challenges were: 1) We were shooting the film in New York City, a very film-savvy city. Property owners are used to getting very high location fees for their businesses. We had no money in our budget for location fees; 2) The script called for the scenes to take place at night. Almost all restaurants and bars are open during the evening hours so we couldn't shoot at night. We'd have to shoot during the day or find a day when the business was closed; 3) We needed to find one location that could work for two sets to avoid a company move on one of the days.

For *Red Flag,* to minimize company moves I found a bar location that was closed all day and night on Sunday and we could make it work as Bar #2 and Restaurant #1. On another day we would have to shoot Bar #1 and Restaurant #2 at separate locations and do a company move. On the last day we would shoot all day in a park.

LOCATION GRID – RED FLAG

Location	EXT/INT	Day/Night	# Pages
NYC Streets	EXT	NIGHT	4/8
Bar #1	EXT	NIGHT	2/8
Bar #1	INT	NIGHT	2 3/8
Bar #2	INT	NIGHT	1 3/8
Restaurant #1	INT	NIGHT	7/8
Restaurant #2	INT	NIGHT	1 1/8
Park	EXT	DAY	2 6/8
Park Entrance	EXT	DAY	1 1/8

DAY VS. NIGHT SHOOTING

I prefer to shoot during the day because it is generally easier on cast and crew. At night, people are a little more tired and you often have to use more lights.

For *Red Flag,* the two bar and two restaurant locations are supposed to take place at night. But most of these kinds of locations are open at night and I wanted to shoot during the day, if at all possible. Consequently, I found locations that would allow us to shoot during the day and have it look like night by either blocking out the daylight and/or shooting away from location's windows so the audience doesn't see the sun in the shot.

The park was day exterior, so we were able to stick with a three-day shooting schedule and didn't have to do any long nights to get the looks we needed.

WEATHER

We have one day of the shoot that is entirely exterior — the four-page shoot in the park. This situation calls for a **weather contingency**. We needed to put the exterior day early in the schedule and have a **cover set** (a different location that we could shoot at on short notice) available in case we had to switch to it on that day, if it rained. We ended up scheduling the park day for our first day of shooting and it turns out that the day before, we found out there would be torrential rainstorms. We had to switch to Bar #1 and Restaurant #2 for Day 1 and shoot the park on the last day. The weather was beautiful that day!

Final Analysis of Red Flag

Based on an analysis of all of these factors, there is a good understanding of what it will take to make this film — three shooting days, one pick-up day, five sets, four locations, five principal actors, 30 extras, a wig, weather contingency, and post graphic effects. This is an ambitious film for a low-budget, but with the script breakdown completed we knew what we had to do it and began to create a detailed production plan and schedule.

Using the Breakdown to Adjust Your Script

Now that you have completed your script breakdown, it is time to have a conversation with the director to give you more details that you will need for planning and for budgeting. The breakdown has enabled you to target the more challenging (logistically and financially) elements of the script. It's much easier to change the script *now*, if there is a cheaper and easier alternative, than to have elements in the screenplay that overload the production and may compromise the ability to get the film made. By discussing these issues early with the director and writer, some of those elements can be re-written to make the film more doable with the resources you have at your disposal. This is a critical step. If you don't engage with possible script changes now, you may put yourself at risk for not pulling off the film successfully.

For instance, if the script says "car," does it mean a cheap, beat up car that would be inexpensive and easy to get from a junk yard? If so, does it have to run or can it just be towed to the location and sit there?

If the script calls for a period vehicle — what period in history? And does it have to be an authentic period car in perfect condition? Is a car that could pass for the same time period good enough? Does it have to be a particular color? The cost of the car mentioned in the script can vary enormously according to the answer to each of these questions.

Or, after a breakdown you may realize that your film requires three days of shooting in an airport lounge — a location that is potentially very expensive and difficult to acquire for multiple days. Depending on the story, there may be another location that would work for those scenes — perhaps an abandoned warehouse — a much cheaper and easier location to procure.

I was an advisor on a low-budget production where the script called for an actor to fall off a motorcycle in the middle of a busy New York City street. The character, who is drunk, grabs the bike, drives down the block, hears a police car siren and crashes the motorcycle, after which his mother runs up and yells at him.

This would require a lot of resources: a stunt double for the actor, a motorcycle to be ridden by the actor, another motorcycle that has been "propped" to show the damage after the accident, a costume for the actor and another for the stunt person, another set of costumes that show damage to the clothes post-accident, permits to close down the street, police officers for security, and extra crew on walkie-talkies to "lock up" and control the location during filming.

Once we mapped out all the requirements for the scene, it became clear that the production could not afford it. As a result, the director and the writer rewrote the scene. In the final version of the scene, the character grabs the motorcycle and tries to start it up but it won't start.

So he jumps off the bike, runs down the street, and nearly gets hit by a cab — but gets pushed out of the way at the last minute by his mother, who was chasing him — and falls to the ground. As you can see, this is a much cheaper way to stage the scene that nevertheless preserves the dramatic action. Once you have a good script breakdown you can use the information to really tighten your script, production plan and budget.

RECAP

1. **A script breakdown is a list of all the production elements in a film's script on a scene-by-scene basis.**

2. **Download a script breakdown template from** *www.ProducerTo Producer.com* **or create your own template.**

3. **Outline all the elements for each scene on the breakdown sheet.**

4. **Once you have the script broken down, arrange the scenes according to three criteria —
a) location; b) interior/exterior; c) time of day (day/night).**

5. **Analyze the script breakdown and discuss the important elements with the director for specifics necessary to begin budgeting the film's costs. Refer to the list in this chapter.**

6. **If an element in a scene is proving to be too expensive or difficult, discuss alternatives with the director and/or writer to find out if more affordable options can be included in the next revision of the script.**

7. **Generally you can shoot 3–4 pages on a 12-hour day for scheduling purposes.**

CHAPTER 3

BUDGETING

Budgeting Overview

NOW IT'S TIME TO do a budget. Don't panic — it will be fine. It can actually be fun. In fact, budgeting is one of my favorite things to do. Seriously. It's fun, creative — even relaxing. Here are my reasons why:

1. Numbers don't lie

2. Numbers don't have attitude

3. Numbers don't have an agenda

4. Numbers can be changed easily

5. Numbers reflect the producer's vision for the film

6. Numbers lead you to concrete decisions, which are the building blocks of producing a film

7. A good producer can stretch money in a way that is deeply satisfying

I think budgeting is one of the most important skills for an indie producer to have. Limitations (i.e., a lack of money) are just an opportunity for creative problem solving. By knowing how to create and understand budgets, you can figure out how to solve the issues that the production will face.

> *Money is only a tool. It will take you wherever you wish, but it will not replace you as the driver.*
>
> *— Ayn Rand,*
> **Atlas Shrugged**

First and foremost, budgeting is a great organizing tool for your production. An estimated budget will give you a good idea of the scope — not just financial, but also logistical — of the film, which allows you to begin conceptualizing the project on many different levels. When you create an estimated budget you can begin to visualize the size of the production, the number of locations and studio days, the number of cast and crew members, as well as props, wardrobe, equipment, and so on. Without a budget, you have no idea how much to estimate for the film production costs and no concrete plans as to how to make the project happen.

For those of you who become nervous, uncomfortable, or downright terrified when interacting with numbers, have no fear — we'll go through the budget, line by line. Keep in mind that the more often you create budgets, the more facile you will become with them.

If you don't anticipate a full-time career as a producer — maybe you are a director or a screenwriter — learning how to make or, at least, read a budget is invaluable. You will be able to understand the various budget line items and discuss the budget of any film with the producer confidently. Occasionally I've encountered directors who are intimidated by budgets and are afraid to engage with the producer about their specific creative and production requirements. Knowledge is power. The more you understand the numbers, the better informed you will be about where all the money is going — and this will help you make better decisions on the creative side.

Once you have created an estimated budget, you also can begin to figure out how and where you can save money. As you'll see in the sample budget, the first draft of your budget is going to be "fat" and probably unaffordable. Don't panic. The first draft is just a benchmark for you to use as a worst-case scenario. You'll then start to whittle that down as you move through the preproduction process.

As soon as you have a script that you want to produce, you need to create a budget. Why so early in the process? You need to decide how much you will require in the way of resources, and also how much money you will have to work with — are you well financed or will this be very low-budget? You can shoot your film on digital video, 16mm film or 35mm film — all of which have very different costs. You can shoot it in your apartment or you can rent a SoHo loft for $5,000/day. There are so many variables that will determine the final budget number, and consequently, what your film will become. And they tie in directly to the creative realization of what is on the script pages.

Everything but the Kitchen Sink

There are many ways to approach budgeting. I think the best way is to create the "kitchen sink" version of the budget, first. Put "everything in but the kitchen sink." Create a budget for the most expensive format you *might* be able to shoot in. If you really would like to shoot in Super 16mm film, create a budget for that format, first. You can always create another one for a less expensive format later.

Think out everything you could possibly need and put a number to it. Don't factor in possible donations or favors in this first pass. If you know you are *definitely* getting a free camera rental then you can factor that into the budget as an assumption. But only do that if you know for sure. Put everything in there so you don't forget any possible elements. When you do the next iteration you can reduce things and tighten.

Budgeting Software

The best way to do a film/video budget is to use computer budgeting software specifically created for film/video productions. It will have a pre-formatted template that will contain all the necessary line items already listed in a numerical order.

I have enclosed a template that I've created based on the line numbers we'll discuss. It is free with the purchase of this book and can be down-loaded at *www.ProducerToProducer.com*. It is a Microsoft Excel™ spreadsheet and is a comprehensive template for indie film/video bud-geting. It is ideal for anyone who doesn't want a complicated program to learn. I recommend it for short films, music videos, documentaries, and some feature films because it is simple, user-friendly, and based on the industry standard for line-item numbers. When you get familiar with this template, you will have a good background for working on commercial productions, as well, because it uses the same AICP industry-standard line numbers. AICP stands for the Association of Independent Commercial Producers. It's an association that supports the interests of United States companies that specialize in producing commercials in various media for advertisers and agencies. One of the things that the organization did was create a standardized bid form or budget in 1984. I've used budgeting software for decades that is based on their format. I think it is a very simple and straight forward budget template. There are several compa-nies that sell software that contain this template. Some utilize Microsoft Excel™ and some use their own proprietary software for calculations.

Producer to Producer Budget Template

FILM PRODUCTION COST SUMMARY					
Date					
Title					
Length					
Client					
Production Co.					
Address					
Address					
Telephone					
Fax					
Email					
Format					
Exec. Producer					
Director					
Producer					
DP					
Editor					
Pre-Prod. Days					
Pre-Lite Days					
Studio Days					
Location Days					
Location(s)					
Dates					
	SUMMARY	ESTIMATED	ACTUAL		
1	Pre-Production and wrap costs (Totals A & C)	0	0		
2	Shooting Crew Labor (Total B)	0	0		
3	Location and travel expenses (Total D)	0	0		
4	Props. Wardrobe and animals (Total E)	0	0		
5	Studio & set construction costs (Total F/G/H)	0	0		
6	Equipment costs (Total I)	0	0		
7	Film stock/Media costs (Total J)	0	0		
8	Miscellaneous Costs (Total K)	0	0		
9	Talent costs and expenses (Total M & N)	0	0		
10	Post Production costs (Total O-T)	0	0		
	SUBTOTAL	0	0		
11	Insurance (2%)	0	0		
	SUBTOTAL Direct Costs	0	0		
12	Director/Creative Fees (Total L-Not including Direct Costs)	0	0		
13	Production Fee				
14	Contingency				
15	Weather Day				
	GRAND TOTAL	0	0		

COMMENTS

Producer to Producer Budget Template

A	PRE-PROD & WRAP LABOR	Days	Rate	OT (1.5)	OT sub	OT (2.0)	OT sub	ESTIMATED	ACTUAL
1	Producer				0		0	0	0
2	Assistant Director				0		0	0	0
3	Director of Photography				0		0	0	0
4	2nd Assistant Director				0		0	0	0
5	Assistant Camera				0		0	0	0
6	Loader				0		0	0	0
7	Production Designer				0		0	0	0
8	Art Director				0		0	0	0
9	Set Decorator				0		0	0	0
10	Props				0		0	0	0
11	Props Assistant				0		0	0	0
12	Gaffer				0		0	0	0
13	Best Boy Electrician				0		0	0	0
14	Electrician				0		0	0	0
15	Key Grip				0		0	0	0
16	Best Boy Grip				0		0	0	0
17	Grip				0		0	0	0
18	Dolly Grip				0		0	0	0
19	Swing				0		0	0	0
20	Sound Recordist				0		0	0	0
21	Boom Operator				0		0	0	0
22	Key Hair/Makeup				0		0	0	0
23	Hair/Makeup Assistant				0		0	0	0
24	Hair/Makeup Assisitant				0		0	0	0
25	Stylist				0		0	0	0
26	Costume Designer				0		0	0	0
27	Wardrobe Supervisor				0		0	0	0
28	Wardrobe Assistant				0		0	0	0
29	Script Supervisor				0		0	0	0
30	Food Stylist				0		0	0	0
31	Assistant Food Stylist				0		0	0	0
32	Video Engineer				0		0	0	0
33	Video Playback				0		0	0	0
34	Production Manager				0		0	0	0
35	Production Coordinator				0		0	0	0
36	Location Scout				0		0	0	0
37	Location Manager				0		0	0	0
38	Police				0		0	0	0
39	Fire				0		0	0	0
40	On Set Tutor				0		0	0	0
41	Motorhome Driver				0		0	0	0
42	Craft Service				0		0	0	0
43	Still Photographer				0		0	0	0
44	Production Assistant				0		0	0	0
45	Production Assistant				0		0	0	0
46	Production Assistant				0		0	0	0
47	Production Assistant				0		0	0	0
48	Production Assistant				0		0	0	0
49	Production Assistant				0		0	0	0
50	Production Assistant				0		0	0	0
	TOTAL A				0		0	0	0

Producer to Producer Budget Template

B SHOOTING LABOR	Days	Rate	OT (1.5)	OT sub	OT (2.0)	OT sub	ESTIMATED	ACTUAL
51 Producer				0		0	0	0
52 Assistant Director				0		0	0	0
53 Director of Photography				0		0	0	0
54 2nd Assistant Director				0		0	0	0
55 Assistant Camera				0		0	0	0
56 Loader				0		0	0	0
57 Production Designer				0		0	0	0
58 Art Director				0		0	0	0
59 Set Decorator				0		0	0	0
60 Props				0		0	0	0
61 Props Assistant				0		0	0	0
62 Gaffer				0		0	0	0
63 Best Boy Electrician				0		0	0	0
64 Electrician				0		0	0	0
65 Key Grip				0		0	0	0
66 Best Boy Grip				0		0	0	0
67 Grip				0		0	0	0
68 Dolly Grip				0		0	0	0
69 Swing				0		0	0	0
70 Sound Recordist				0		0	0	0
71 Boom Operator				0		0	0	0
72 Key Hair/Makeup				0		0	0	0
73 Hair/Makeup Assistant				0		0	0	0
74 Hair/Makeup Assisitant				0		0	0	0
75 Stylist				0		0	0	0
76 Costume Designer				0		0	0	0
77 Wardrobe Supervisor				0		0	0	0
78 Wardrobe Assistant				0		0	0	0
79 Script Supervisor				0		0	0	0
80 Food Stylist				0		0	0	0
81 Assistant Food Stylist				0		0	0	0
82 Video Engineer				0		0	0	0
83 Video Playback				0		0	0	0
84 Production Manager				0		0	0	0
85 Production Coordinator				0		0	0	0
86 Location Scout				0		0	0	0
87 Location Manager				0		0	0	0
88 Police				0		0	0	0
89 Fire				0		0	0	0
90 On Set Tutor				0		0	0	0
91 Motorhome Driver				0		0	0	0
92 Craft Service				0		0	0	0
93 Still Photographer				0		0	0	0
94 Production Assistant				0		0	0	0
95 Production Assistant				0		0	0	0
96 Production Assistant				0		0	0	0
97 Production Assistant				0		0	0	0
98 Production Assistant				0		0	0	0
99 Production Assistant				0		0	0	0
100 Production Assistant				0		0	0	0
TOTAL B				0		0	0	0

Producer to Producer Budget Template

C	PRE–PROD./WRAP EXPENSES	Amount	Rate	x	ESTIMATED	ACTUAL
101	Hotel				0	0
102	Air Fares				0	0
103	Per Diem				0	0
104	Auto Rentals				0	0
105	Messengers				0	0
106	Office Rental				0	0
107	Deliveries & Taxi				0	0
108	Office Supplies				0	0
109	Telephone/Fax/Cel				0	0
110	Casting Director				0	0
111	Casting Facilities				0	0
112	Working Meals				0	0
113					0	0
	TOTAL C				0	0

D	LOCATION/TRAVEL EXPENSES	Amount	Rate	x	ESTIMATED	ACTUAL
114	Location Fees				0	0
115	Permits				0	0
116	Car Rentals				0	0
117	Van Rentals				0	0
118	Winnebago				0	0
119	Parking, Tolls & Gas				0	0
120	Production Trucking				0	0
121	Other Vehicles				0	0
122	Other Trucking				0	0
123	Hotels				0	0
124	Air fares				0	0
125	Per diem				0	0
126	Train fares				0	0
127	Airport Transfers				0	0
128					0	0
129	Breakfast				0	0
130	Lunch				0	0
131	Dinner				0	0
132	Craft Service				0	0
133	Limousine/Car service				0	0
134	Cabs & Other Transport				0	0
135	Kit Rentals				0	0
136	Cel phones				0	0
137	Gratuities				0	0
138	Table & Chair rental				0	0
139					0	0
	TOTAL D				0	0

E	PROPS/RELATED EXPENSES	Amount	Rate	x	ESTIMATED	ACTUAL
140	Prop Rental				0	0
141	Prop Purchase				0	0
142	Wardrobe Rental				0	0
143	Wardrobe Purchase				0	0
144	Picture Vehicles				0	0
145	Animals & Handlers				0	0
146	Wigs				0	0
147	SFX makeup				0	0
148					0	0
	TOTAL E				0	0

Producer to Producer Budget Template

F	STUDIO RENTAL & EXPENSES	Amount	Rate	x	ESTIMATED	ACTUAL
151	Build Day Rental				0	0
152	Build Day OT				0	0
153	Pre–Lite Day Rental				0	0
154	Pre–Lite Day OT				0	0
155	Shoot Day Rental				0	0
156	Shoot Day OT				0	0
157	Strike Day Rental				0	0
158	Strike Day OT				0	0
159	Electricity/Power Charges				0	0
160	Dressing Rooms				0	0
161	Studio Parking				0	0
162	Studio Security				0	0
163	Stage Manager				0	0
164	Phone/Fax/Internet/Copies				0	0
165	Cartage/Dumpster Rental				0	0
166	Studio Painting				0	0
167	Trash Removal				0	0
	TOTAL F				**0**	**0**

G	SET CONSTRUCTION LABOR	Amount	Rate	x	ESTIMATED	ACTUAL
168	Set Designer				0	0
169	Ass't Set Designer				0	0
170	Set Decorator				0	0
171	Lead Person				0	0
172	Set Dressers				0	0
173	Effects Person				0	0
174	Carpenters				0	0
175	Grips				0	0
176	Outside Props				0	0
177	Inside Props				0	0
178	Scenics				0	0
179	Strike Crew				0	0
180	Art PAs				0	0
	TOTAL G				**0**	**0**

H	SET CONSTRUCTION MATERIALS	Amount	Rate	x	ESTIMATED	ACTUAL
181	Set Dressing/Prop Rentals				0	0
182	Set Dressing/Prop Purchases				0	0
183	Lumber				0	0
184	Paint				0	0
185	Hardware				0	0
186	Special Effects				0	0
187	Outside Construction				0	0
188	Product/Model Construction				0	0
189	Trucking				0	0
190	Messengers/Deliveries				0	0
191	Meals, Parking				0	0
192					0	0
	TOTAL H				**0**	**0**

Producer to Producer Budget Template

I EQUIPMENT/EXPENSES	Amount	Rate	x	ESTIMATED	ACTUAL
193 Camera Rental				0	0
194 Sound Rental				0	0
195 Lighting Rental				0	0
196 Grip Rental				0	0
197 Generator Rental				0	0
198 Add'l Camera Rental				0	0
199 VTR Rental				0	0
200 Walkie Talkie Rental				0	0
201 Dolly Rental				0	0
202 Dolly Accessories				0	0
203 Crane Rental				0	0
204 Production Supplies				0	0
205 Expendables				0	0
206 Camera Lens Rental				0	0
207 Jib Arm Rental				0	0
208 Camera Accessories Rental				0	0
209 Green Screen Rental				0	0
210 Underwater Housing Rental				0	0
TOTAL I				0	0

J FILM STOCK/MEDIA	Amount	Rate	x	ESTIMATED	ACTUAL
211 Purchase film stock				0	0
212 Develop film stock				0	0
213 Digital storage purchase				0	0
214 Memory card rental/purchase				0	0
215 Videotape stock				0	0
216 Audiotape stock				0	0
217				0	0
TOTAL J				0	0

K MISCELLANEOUS COSTS	Amount	Rate	x	ESTIMATED	ACTUAL
218 Petty Cash				0	0
219 Air Shipping Charges				0	0
220 Accounting Charges				0	0
221 Bank Charges				0	0
222 E & O Insurance				0	0
223 Legal fees				0	0
224 Publicity				0	0
225 Film Festival Fees/Expenses				0	0
226				0	0
TOTAL K				0	0

L CREATIVE FEES	Amount	Rate	x	ESTIMATED	ACTUAL
227 Writer Fee				0	0
228 Director Fee – Prep				0	0
229 Director Fee – Travel				0	0
230 Director Fee – Shoot				0	0
231 Director Fee – Post				0	0
232 Fringes for Labor Costs				0	0
233				0	0
TOTAL L				0	0

Producer to Producer Budget Template

M	TALENT LABOR	Days	Rate	OT (1.5)	OT sub	OT (2.0)	OT sub	ESTIMATED	ACTUAL
234	O/C Principal				0		0	0	0
235	O/C Principal				0		0	0	0
236	O/C Principal				0		0	0	0
237	O/C Principal				0		0	0	0
238	O/C Principal				0		0	0	0
239	O/C Principal				0		0	0	0
240	O/C Principal				0		0	0	0
241	O/C Principal				0		0	0	0
242	O/C Principal				0		0	0	0
243	O/C Principal				0		0	0	0
244					0		0	0	0
245	Day Player				0		0	0	0
246	Day Player				0		0	0	0
247	Day Player				0		0	0	0
248	Day Player				0		0	0	0
249					0		0	0	0
250	Background Actor				0		0	0	0
251	Background Actor				0		0	0	0
252	Background Actor				0		0	0	0
253					0		0	0	0
254	Voice Over Talent				0		0	0	0
255	Voice Over Talent				0		0	0	0
256	Voice Over Talent				0		0	0	0
257					0		0	0	0
258	Hand Model				0		0	0	0
259	Fitting fee				0		0	0	0
260					0		0	0	0
261					0		0	0	0
262	Rehearsal time				0		0	0	0
	TOTAL M							0	0

N	TALENT EXPENSES	Days	Rate	OT (1.5)	OT sub	OT (2.0)	OT sub	ESTIMATED	ACTUAL
263	Airfares				0		0	0	0
264	Hotel				0		0	0	0
265	Per diem				0		0	0	0
266	Cabs and transportation				0		0	0	0
267	Extras casting director				0		0	0	0
268					0		0	0	0
269					0		0	0	0
270					0		0	0	0
271					0		0	0	0
272					0		0	0	0
273					0		0	0	0
274	Talent Agency fee (10%)				0		0	0	0
275	Pension & Health				0		0	0	0
276					0		0	0	0
	TOTAL N							0	0

Producer to Producer Budget Template

O	EDITORIAL	Amount	Rate	X	ESTIMATED	ACTUAL
277	Post Production Supervisor				0	0
278	Editor				0	0
279	Assistant Editor				0	0
280	Assistant Editor				0	0
281	Transcription				0	0
282	Edit equipment rental				0	0
283	Hard drive purchase				0	0
284					0	0
	TOTAL O				0	0

P	FILM TRANSFER	Amount	Rate	X	ESTIMATED	ACTUAL
285	Film to Tape Transfer				0	0
286	Tape to Tape Color Correct				0	0
287	Videotape Downconversion				0	0
288	DVD/Videotape Stock				0	0
289	Film to Tape Transfer				0	0
290	Tape to Tape Color Correct				0	0
291	Videotape Downconversion				0	0
292	DVD/Videotape Stock				0	0
293					0	0
	TOTAL P				0	0

Q	AUDIO	Amount	Rate	X	ESTIMATED	ACTUAL
294	Audio Sweetening				0	0
295	Audio Edit				0	0
296	Audio Mix				0	0
297	Audio Load In/Load Out				0	0
298	Sound Effects Library				0	0
299	Back-Up Audio files				0	0
	TOTAL Q				0	0

R	MUSIC	Amount	Rate	X	ESTIMATED	ACTUAL
300	Music Composition				0	0
301	Music Rights/Clearance				0	0
302	Music Recording				0	0
303	Music Supervisor				0	0
304	Audiotape Stock/Files				0	0
	TOTAL R				0	0

S	FILM FINISHING	Amount	Rate	X	ESTIMATED	ACTUAL
305	Negative Cutting				0	0
306	1st Answer Print				0	0
307	2nd Answer Print				0	0
308	Additional Print(s)				0	0
309	Blow up to 35mm				0	0
310	Film Out				0	0
311	Screening Room Rental				0	0
312	Screening Room Equip. Rental				0	0
	TOTAL S				0	0

T	MISCELLANEOUS	Amount	Rate	X	ESTIMATED	ACTUAL
313	Stock Footage Researcher				0	0
314	Stock Footage Licensing				0	0
315	Screener Copies				0	0
316	Misc. Equipment Rental				0	0
317	Shipping				0	0
318	Messengers				0	0
319	Post Working Meals				0	0
320	DVD/Videotape stock				0	0
321	DVD Duplication				0	0
322	DVD Authoring				0	0
	TOTAL T				0	0
	TOTAL POST PRODUCTION			0	0	0

Many of them also have Purchase Order logs, Petty Cash logs and other important documents that are used during the actualization process (to be discussed in the *Wrap* Chapter).

Movie Magic Budgeting is software specifically created for budgeting feature films. It is the industry standard and has templates in it that correspond to various film studios and television networks. It is proprietary software (*www.entertainmentpartners.com*) that does not allow multiple people to share one application. *Movie Magic Budgeting* is companion software to *Final Draft* (screenplay software) and *Movie Magic Scheduling* (discussed in the *Scheduling* Chapter), so you can break down a feature script written in *Final Draft*, put it into a schedule with *Movie Magic Scheduling* and then import directly into *Movie Magic Budgeting*. Naturally, this can save you time transferring info from one format and stage to the next. This is a robust piece of software which also allows you to create budgets with various currencies, globals and in-depth fringe rates (see later in this chapter).

For short films, music videos or documentaries, I would not use *Movie Magic Budgeting* — it's a little cumbersome, has a longer learning curve and is rather expensive. But it is indispensable for feature films, television series, or anything that requires more line items and additional customization. Other software packages include *Showbiz Budgeting, Budget Forms Pro* and *Auto Actuals.* Go to *www.ProducerToProducer.com* for more information.

Budget Breakdown

A budget breakdown starts with the information you have created in the script breakdown and elaborates on it so that you have enough details to be able to put a price on each aspect required to complete the project.

So go back to the script and the script breakdown and figure out the following:

1. How many days to shoot? The rule of thumb is three to four pages per day for a low-budget indie production.

2. How many days to scout?

3. What crew positions do you need? What will you be paying each of them? (This can range from nothing to deferred compensation to a daily or weekly rate.). We'll discuss these options later in this chapter.

4. How many cast? SAG or non-union? What agreement will you be working under? Does it require pay or deferred pay? If pay, does it require the payment of a flat fee (with deferred for OT) or does it require OT to be factored in? (We'll discuss the different SAG agreements in the *Casting/SAG* Chapter)

5. Set build or locations? If you need to build a set — how elaborate? You'll need to budget for a studio, as well. If locations, list them in detail. If both, you'll need to know what you will build and what you will shoot on location and how many days for each.

6. Cast and crew numbers — How many cast and crew do you plan to hire for the film? This is a unique number for each film project and depends on what is required to accomplish your particular production and its ambitions. Also — how many days do you require for each actor and crew person for preproduction, rehearsal, shoot, and wrap?

7. Travel and transportation costs — do you have to hire vans and travel the cast and crew? Do you have to fly people to certain places and budget for airfare? What about accommodations? Do you need to put cast/crew up overnight? Do you need to hire vans and trucks for equipment, props, and costume departments?

8. Catering/food costs — Lunch and craft service for how many people and how many shoot days? If people are staying overnight you'll need to budget for a per diem or for breakfast and dinner, as well.

9. Props/art/picture vehicles — What will you need to purchase/rent for these elements in the film?

10. Equipment: what format? For film: Super 35mm film, Super 16mm film, Super 8mm film. For video: HD (High Definition) or SD (Standard Definition). Which camera and accessories for which technology? Do you need a dolly, crane, underwater housing, or Steadicam? What is required for grip and lighting equipment? Do you need audio recording or audio/video playback? Are walkie talkies needed?

11. Sync Sound? Or MOS (without sync sound recording)? Audio and/or video playback?

12. Shooting Ratio — how much film or videotape or digital media storage drives do you need to budget for? Each format requires a

different amount of material to capture the footage on that format. The first thing you need to figure out is your estimated shooting ratio (will discuss later in this chapter) and then use that to budget properly for your medium. Remember that film requires three steps in budgeting — film stock purchase, development, and then transfer of film to video/digital files. Also keep in mind that digital video may need to be down converted, backed up, and archived and that will have a cost, as well.

13. Postproduction — how do you plan to finish? Finish in 35mm film? Create a digital intermediate? Film print? Shoot video? Finish in video? Create an HD or SD master? You may need to budget for a tape-to-tape color correct session or a film-to-tape re-transfer of selected material. Audio mixing and sweetening will also be considered.

14. Music: composer or licensing music? You'll need to have some sense of what the music needs will be. If it is a composer, do you know the rate charged? If it is music licensing, will it be easy to get and at a reasonable cost? Is there flexibility in this area?

15. Film festivals? Marketing and PR? Film festival application fees, posters or postcards are the bare minimum that you need to put in the budget. Depending on your marketing plan, there may be costs involved.

16. Legal costs, overhead costs like office rental, office equipment, office labor, insurance, and accounting also need to be factored in.

Before creating a budget, answer these questions on a piece of paper and refer to it as you work your way through all the budget sections.

Estimated Budget

Now you are ready to create a first draft of your estimated budget. Just like a writer, you need to get it all down on paper and then start to revise. You also should decide whether to do two or more budgets based on different film/video format choices in production or postproduction. You or the director may want to compare costs on shooting Super 16mm vs. HD, or to compare two different digital video formats. Or, you may decide to budget for Super 16mm but would like to see the cost difference between finishing to a HD master vs. 35mm film print. Be prepared to do a full budget one way, then duplicate it and make some format changes to see the cost differences.

As I said above, always start with your most realistic "kitchen sink" budget. Decide what is the highest-quality format that you can realistically afford to shoot in, and budget for that format first.

So let's build a budget. The easiest way to do that is to go through each line item on the *ProducerToProducer.com* budget template and plug in realistic numbers for each.

Spreadsheet Mechanics

The *ProducerToProducer.com* budget template utilizes Microsoft Excel™, so you will need to make sure you have that software on your computer and that you have a basic proficiency in that program. There are formulas (mathematical equations) across each line item to create subtotals and totals throughout the document. Each line has a number on the far left side that is called a line number. To the right of that number is a name, and there are some columns to the right of that. You should not change the names of the line items because they are standardized for the film industry and are rather comprehensive. If you want to add something, look for a line item in the correct section that is empty and type in a new name.

Each subtotal column has a formula. It is important to keep the integrity of each formula, so don't change them or it will corrupt the mathematics of the spreadsheet. Each row uses certain columns to allow you to add up multiple elements for computation. For instance — Amount column **x** Rate column = Salary Total. Or Days column **x** Rate column = Rental Total.

Geography of the Budget

This budget is eight pages long. It is organized as follows:

Page 1 — Referred to as the **Top Sheet** — is divided into three sections. The top section contains the contact details, lists the shooting format, number and types of locations, and the number of shooting days. The **middle** section contains the subtotals for each of the sections later in the budget. It also has line items for the insurance fee, production fee, and other contractual fees. The **bottom** section is for the Comments/ Assumptions — a place to state what assumptions the budget is based

on, i.e., a union or non-union crew, what is included or not included in
the budget.

Page 2 — Preproduction and Wrap Crew Labor costs

Page 3 — Production/Shooting Crew Labor costs

Page 4 — Preproduction costs, Location costs, and Props/Wardrobe/
Hair/Makeup costs

Page 5 — Studio costs, Set Construction costs

Page 6 — Equipment costs, Film/Video stock costs, Overhead costs,
Writer's and Director's fee costs

Page 7 — Actor's salary costs and Actor expenses

Page 8 — Postproduction costs

Let's go through it page by page:

Top Sheet

On the Top Sheet, fill in the following pertinent info:

Date: This will allow you to keep track of this budget with respect to
others created at different times.

Title/Length: Title and total running time of project.

Name, address, phone, fax, address, and email address: Put all
your contact information here.

Number of studio shoot days: The total number of days that you plan
to shoot on a stage.

Number of location shoot days: The total number of days that you
plan to shoot on location.

Format: Film or video and specific type.

Director: Name, if known.

Producer: Your name.

Director of Photography: Name, if known.

Editor: Name, if known.

Shoot dates: The inclusive dates of the shoot.

It's important to put all this info here so that anyone who reads the
budget will understand the parameters you have set for this estimated
budget and the production. If you have planned for a 24-day shoot, then
when someone looks at the labor sections, most of the labor costs will
reflect 24 days for shooting and some time for prep and wrap.

Don't touch the middle part of the Top Sheet! As you enter in
numbers on the subsequent budget pages, the subtotals will be automatically totaled and transferred to the front, section by section. The only

formulas you will use/change in this section will be for the insurance fees, the production fees, and any other contractual fees that you need to compute. The final total is posted at the bottom of this middle section.

The bottom part of the Top Sheet is the place for your comments/assumptions. Here you should write sentences that explain your reasoning for creating the budget (i.e., "the budget assumes that the DP fee includes the use of his/her own camera as part of the total fee"). This explains to the reader why there will not be any money for camera rental on line 193. It should also include details about what guild contracts you are using ("Production will be working under the Modified Low-Budget SAG agreement" or "All labor will be non-union"). Any other details regarding postproduction should be outlined here (i.e., "Budget does not contain money for color correction. Will be done by editor on FCP editing system").

Creating the Estimated Budget

When you begin making your budget, go through each line item and decide if you need to put a cost there. For this first pass, if you are not sure exactly how much something costs, put a good guesstimate there (you can always take it out later). There will be some (or many) line items that you won't be sure about, so you can either guess or leave the item blank for now. But keep a piece of paper next to you with a list of all the line items that you will need to research so you can fill in next. That way you can go back to the budget and insert the correct numbers when you obtain them.

Let's say your film takes place in an art gallery and a house. For the house, you can shoot for free at a friend's place. (The director and DP have seen it and think it will work fine.) For the art gallery, though, you'll need to location scout. If you are shooting in New York City, you might go to Chelsea or SoHo one afternoon with a digital still/video camera and shoot a few galleries that look right for the scene. Then you show them to the director, who picks two options. You call the galleries and discuss what kind of fee they would charge you to shoot on a Sunday (when the gallery is usually closed.) One gallery says $3,000 (including a security person to watch you and the art during the shoot) and the other says $1,000 plus $500 for a security guard for 10 hours. Put down $3,000 for now, on that line item. That way you know that you have enough in the budget to rent either place. Later, when you need to tighten the budget you can reduce down to $1,500 if you need to. Continue line by line in this way.

When creating an estimated budget, everything goes in the Estimated columns only. The Actual column is used once you start spending money and need to start entering your real costs from your production's receipts. (See the *Actualization* section later in this chapter.)

Detailed Line Items

In this portion of the chapter we will go through the budget, line by line (with line numbers corresponding to the Producer To Producer template) and give you all the info you need to know to budget for your film. We'll use the *Red Flag* script breakdown that we did in the last chapter to help with the budgeting now.

I am going to use the short film *Red Flag* for this *Budgeting* chapter case study. If you recall, we planned for a three-day shoot with one pick-up day. It represents many of the things that a typical indie feature would have to grapple with but it is a shorter production timeline. If you multiply the number of shooting days by eight, you'd have a feature-length film. Of course, it's a bit more complicated than that but I think the short-film format will allow us to go through the budget, line by line with concision. We did the film as a no/low-budget project — it means that no crew was paid and SAG actors work deferred under the Short-Film agreement. Only production costs were budgeted.

Producer to Producer Budget Template

	FILM PRODUCTION COST SUMMARY					
Title	Red Flag					
Length	10 min. short film					
Client						
Production Co.	Hands On Productions, Inc.					
Address						
Address						
Telephone						
Fax						
Email						
Job #						
Writer	Sheila Curran Dennin					
Director	Sheila Curran Dennin					
Producer	Maureen Ryan					
DP						
Editor						
Pre-Prod. Days						
Pre-Lite Days						
Studio Days						
Location Days	3.5					
Location(s)	NYC					
Dates	September 2008					
	SUMMARY	ESTIMATED	ACTUAL			
1	Pre-Production and wrap costs (Totals A & C)	$0				
2	Shooting Crew Labor (Total B)	$0				
3	Location and travel expenses (Total D)	$4,385				
4	Props. Wardrobe and animals (Total E)	$725				
5	Studio & set construction costs (Total F/G/H)	$0				
6	Equipment costs (Total I)	$6,100				
7	Film stock/Media costs (Total J)	$0				
8	Miscellaneous Costs (Total K)	$200				
9	Talent costs and expenses (Total M & N)	$0				
10	Post Production costs (Total O–T)	$1,765				
	SUBTOTAL	$13,175	$0			
11	Insurance (2%)		$0			
	SUBTOTAL Direct Costs	$13,175	$0			
12	Director/Creative Fees (Total L–Not including Direct Costs)	$0				
13	Production Fee					
14	Contingency					
15	Weather Day					
	GRAND TOTAL	$13,175	$0			

COMMENTS						
	Shot on Sony EX1 camera – free rental from producer.					
	Budget includes sfx for red flag.					
	SAG short film agreement in place for this production.					
	Edited on FCP w/ post effects.					
	Production insurance in place – free from prod. company.					

Producer to Producer Budget Template

A	PRE–PROD & WRAP LABOR	Days	Rate	OT (1.5)	OT sub	OT (2.0)	OT sub	ESTIMATED	ACTUAL
1	Producer				0		0	0	0
2	Assistant Director				0		0	0	0
3	Director of Photography				0		0	0	0
4	2nd Assistant Director				0		0	0	0
5	Assistant Camera				0		0	0	0
6	Loader				0		0	0	0
7	Production Designer				0		0	0	0
8	Art Director				0		0	0	0
9	Set Decorator				0		0	0	0
10	Props				0		0	0	0
11	Props Assistant				0		0	0	0
12	Gaffer				0		0	0	0
13	Best Boy Electrician				0		0	0	0
14	Electrician				0		0	0	0
15	Key Grip				0		0	0	0
16	Best Boy Grip				0		0	0	0
17	Grip				0		0	0	0
18	Dolly Grip				0		0	0	0
19	Swing				0		0	0	0
20	Sound Recordist				0		0	0	0
21	Boom Operator				0		0	0	0
22	Key Hair/Makeup				0		0	0	0
23	Hair/Makeup Assistant				0		0	0	0
24	Hair/Makeup Assisitant				0		0	0	0
25	Stylist				0		0	0	0
26	Costume Designer				0		0	0	0
27	Wardrobe Supervisor				0		0	0	0
28	Wardrobe Assistant				0		0	0	0
29	Script Supervisor				0		0	0	0
30	Food Stylist				0		0	0	0
31	Assistant Food Stylist				0		0	0	0
32	Video Engineer				0		0	0	0
33	Video Playback				0		0	0	0
34	Production Manager				0		0	0	0
35	Production Coordinator				0		0	0	0
36	Location Scout				0		0	0	0
37	Location Manager				0		0	0	0
38	Police				0		0	0	0
39	Fire				0		0	0	0
40	On Set Tutor				0		0	0	0
41	Motorhome Driver				0		0	0	0
42	Craft Service				0		0	0	0
43	Still Photographer				0		0	0	0
44	Production Assistant				0		0	0	0
45	Production Assistant				0		0	0	0
46	Production Assistant				0		0	0	0
47	Production Assistant				0		0	0	0
48	Production Assistant				0		0	0	0
49	Production Assistant				0		0	0	0
50	Production Assistant				0		0	0	0
	TOTAL A				0		0	0	0

Producer to Producer Budget Template

B	SHOOTING LABOR	Days	Rate	OT (1.5)	OT sub	OT (2.0)	OT sub	ESTIMATED	ACTUAL
51	Producer				0		0	0	0
52	Assistant Director				0		0	0	0
53	Director of Photography				0		0	0	0
54	2nd Assistant Director				0		0	0	0
55	Assistant Camera				0		0	0	0
56	Loader				0		0	0	0
57	Production Designer				0		0	0	0
58	Art Director				0		0	0	0
59	Set Decorator				0		0	0	0
60	Props				0		0	0	0
61	Props Assistant				0		0	0	0
62	Gaffer				0		0	0	0
63	Best Boy Electrician				0		0	0	0
64	Electrician				0		0	0	0
65	Key Grip				0		0	0	0
66	Best Boy Grip				0		0	0	0
67	Grip				0		0	0	0
68	Dolly Grip				0		0	0	0
69	Swing				0		0	0	0
70	Sound Recordist				0		0	0	0
71	Boom Operator				0		0	0	0
72	Key Hair/Makeup				0		0	0	0
73	Hair/Makeup Assistant				0		0	0	0
74	Hair/Makeup Assisitant				0		0	0	0
75	Stylist				0		0	0	0
76	Costume Designer				0		0	0	0
77	Wardrobe Supervisor				0		0	0	0
78	Wardrobe Assistant				0		0	0	0
79	Script Supervisor				0		0	0	0
80	Food Stylist				0		0	0	0
81	Assistant Food Stylist				0		0	0	0
82	Video Engineer				0		0	0	0
83	Video Playback				0		0	0	0
84	Production Manager				0		0	0	0
85	Production Coordinator				0		0	0	0
86	Location Scout				0		0	0	0
87	Location Manager				0		0	0	0
88	Police				0		0	0	0
89	Fire				0		0	0	0
90	On Set Tutor				0		0	0	0
91	Motorhome Driver				0		0	0	0
92	Craft Service				0		0	0	0
93	Still Photographer				0		0	0	0
94	Production Assistant				0		0	0	0
95	Production Assistant				0		0	0	0
96	Production Assistant				0		0	0	0
97	Production Assistant				0		0	0	0
98	Production Assistant				0		0	0	0
99	Production Assistant				0		0	0	0
100	Production Assistant				0		0	0	0
	TOTAL B				0		0	0	0

Producer to Producer Budget Template

C	PRE-PROD./WRAP EXPENSES		Amount	Rate	x	ESTIMATED	ACTUAL
101	Hotel					0	0
102	Air Fares					0	0
103	Per Diem					0	0
104	Auto Rentals					0	0
105	Messengers					0	0
106	Office Rental					0	0
107	Deliveries & Taxi					0	0
108	Office Supplies					0	0
109	Telephone/Fax/Cel					0	0
110	Casting Director					0	0
111	Casting Facilities					0	0
112	Working Meals					0	0
113						0	0
	TOTAL C					**0**	**0**

D	LOCATION/TRAVEL EXPENSES		Amount	Rate	x	ESTIMATED	ACTUAL
114	Location Fees		1	900	1	900	0
115	Permits	bathroom	1	125	1	125	0
116	Car Rentals					0	0
117	Van Rentals	15 passenger	1	140	1	140	0
118	Winnebago					0	0
119	Parking, Tolls & Gas		1	400	1	400	0
120	Production Trucking					0	0
121	Other Vehicles					0	0
122	Other Trucking	14 ft. grip truck	5	140	1	700	0
123	Hotels					0	0
124	Air fares					0	0
125	Per diem					0	0
126	Train fares					0	0
127	Airport Transfers					0	0
128						0	0
129	Breakfast					0	0
130	Lunch	25 people x 3 days	3	17	25	1275	0
131	Dinner					0	0
132	Craft Service	25 people x 3 days	3	150	1	450	0
133	Limousine/Car service					0	0
134	Cabs & Other Transport		1	75	1	75	0
135	Kit Rentals					0	0
136	Cel phones					0	0
137	Gratuities					0	0
138	Table & Chair rental					0	0
139	Extras craft service		1	8	40	320	0
	TOTAL D					**4385**	**0**

E	PROPS/RELATED EXPENSES		Amount	Rate	x	ESTIMATED	ACTUAL
140	Prop Rental					0	0
141	Prop Purchase		1	325	1	325	0
142	Wardrobe Rental					0	0
143	Wardrobe Purchase		1	250	1	250	0
144	Picture Vehicles					0	0
145	Animals & Handlers					0	0
146	Wigs					0	0
147	SFX makeup					0	0
148	Coffee cart rental		1	150	1	150	0
	TOTAL E					**725**	**0**

Producer to Producer Budget Template

F STUDIO RENTAL & EXPENSES	Amount	Rate	x	ESTIMATED	ACTUAL
151 Build Day Rental				0	0
152 Build Day OT				0	0
153 Pre-Lite Day Rental				0	0
154 Pre-Lite Day OT				0	0
155 Shoot Day Rental				0	0
156 Shoot Day OT				0	0
157 Strike Day Rental				0	0
158 Strike Day OT				0	0
159 Electricity/Power Charges				0	0
160 Dressing Rooms				0	0
161 Studio Parking				0	0
162 Studio Security				0	0
163 Stage Manager				0	0
164 Phone/Fax/Internet/Copies				0	0
165 Cartage/Dumpster Rental				0	0
166 Studio Painting				0	0
167 Trash Removal				0	0
TOTAL F				0	0

G SET CONSTRUCTION LABOR	Amount	Rate	x	ESTIMATED	ACTUAL
168 Art Director				0	0
169 Ass't Art Director				0	0
170 Set Decorator				0	0
171 Lead Person				0	0
172 Set Dressers				0	0
173 Effects Person				0	0
174 Effects				0	0
175 Lead Scenic				0	0
176 Scenics				0	0
177 Painters				0	0
178 Construction Coordinator				0	0
179 Art Dept. Supervisor				0	0
180 Art PA's				0	0
TOTAL G				0	0

H SET CONSTRUCTION MATERIALS	Amount	Rate	x	ESTIMATED	ACTUAL
181 Set Dressing/Prop Rentals				0	0
182 Set Dressing/Prop Purchases				0	0
183 Lumber				0	0
184 Paint				0	0
185 Hardware				0	0
186 Special Effects				0	0
187 Construction Labor				0	0
188 Art Trucking				0	0
189 Art Supplies				0	0
190 Meals, Parking				0	0
191 Prop Purchase				0	0
192 Wardrobe Rental				0	0
TOTAL H				0	0

Producer to Producer Budget Template

I	EQUIPMENT/EXPENSES		Amount	Rate	x	ESTIMATED	ACTUAL		
193	Camera Rental					0	0		
194	Sound Rental					0	0		
195	Lighting Rental		1	650	3	1950	0		
196	Grip Rental		1	650	3	1950	0		
197	Generator Rental					0	0		
198	Add'l Camera Rental					0	0		
199	VTR Rental					0	0		
200	Walkie Talkie Rental					0	0		
201	Dolly Rental					0	0		
202	Dolly Accessories					0	0		
203	Crane Rental					0	0		
204	Production Supplies		1	100	1	100	0		
205	Expendables		1	100	1	100	0		
206	Camera Lens Rental		1	2000	1	2000	0		
207	Jib Arm Rental					0	0		
208	Camera Accessories Rental					0	0		
209	Green Screen Rental					0	0		
210	Underwater Housing Rental					0	0		
	TOTAL I					6100	0		

J	FILM STOCK/MEDIA		Amount	Rate	x	ESTIMATED	ACTUAL		
211	Purchase film stock					0	0		
212	Develop film stock					0	0		
213	Digital storage purchase					0	0		
214	Memory card rental/purchase					0	0		
215	Videotape stock					0	0		
216	Audiotape stock					0	0		
217						0	0		
	TOTAL J					0	0		

K	MISCELLANEOUS COSTS		Amount	Rate	x	ESTIMATED	ACTUAL		
218	Petty Cash					0	0		
219	Air Shipping/Carriers		1	100	1	100	0		
220	Phones & Cables					0	0		
221	Bank Charges					0	0		
222	E & O Insurance					0	0		
223	Legal fees					0	0		
224	Still Photography					0	0		
225	Film Festival Fees/Expenses					0	0		
226	Pop Up tent + chairs		1	100	1	100	0		
	TOTAL K					200	0		

L	CREATIVE FEES		Amount	Rate	x	ESTIMATED	ACTUAL		
227	Writer Fee					0	0		
228	Director Fee – Prep					0	0		
229	Director Fee – Travel					0	0		
230	Director Fee – Shoot					0	0		
231	Director Fee – Post					0	0		
232	Fringes for Labor Costs					0	0		
233						0	0		
	TOTAL L					0	0		

Producer to Producer Budget Template

M	TALENT LABOR	Days	Rate	OT (1.5)	OT sub	OT (2.0)	OT sub	ESTIMATED	ACTUAL
234	O/C Principal				0		0	0	0
235	O/C Principal				0		0	0	0
236	O/C Principal				0		0	0	0
237	O/C Principal				0		0	0	0
238	O/C Principal				0		0	0	0
239	O/C Principal				0		0	0	0
240	O/C Principal				0		0	0	0
241	O/C Principal				0		0	0	0
242	O/C Principal				0		0	0	0
243	O/C Principal				0		0	0	0
244					0		0	0	0
245	Day Player				0		0	0	0
246	Day Player				0		0	0	0
247	Day Player				0		0	0	0
248	Day Player				0		0	0	0
249					0		0	0	0
250	Background Actor				0		0	0	0
251	Background Actor				0		0	0	0
252	Background Actor				0		0	0	0
253					0		0	0	0
254	Voice Over Talent				0		0	0	0
255	Voice Over Talent				0		0	0	0
256	Voice Over Talent				0		0	0	0
257					0		0	0	0
258	Hand Model				0		0	0	0
259	Fitting fee				0		0	0	0
260					0		0	0	0
261	Pension & Health				0		0	0	0
262	Rehearsal time				0		0	0	0
	TOTAL M							**0**	**0**

N	TALENT EXPENSES	Days	Rate	OT (1.5)	OT sub	OT (2.0)	OT sub	ESTIMATED	ACTUAL
263	Airfares				0		0	0	0
264	Hotel				0		0	0	0
265	Per diem				0		0	0	0
266	Cabs and transportation				0		0	0	0
267	Extras casting director				0		0	0	0
268					0		0	0	0
269					0		0	0	0
270					0		0	0	0
271					0		0	0	0
272					0		0	0	0
273					0		0	0	0
274	Talent Agency fee (10%)				0		0	0	0
275					0		0	0	0
276					0		0	0	0
	TOTAL N							**0**	**0**

Producer to Producer Budget Template

O	EDITORIAL	Amount	Rate	X	ESTIMATED	ACTUAL
277	Post Production Supervisor				0	
278	Editor				0	
279	Assistant Editor				0	
280	Assistant Editor				0	
281	Transcription				0	
282	Edit equipment rental				0	
283	Hard drive purchase				0	
284	Visual SFX	1	1500	1	1500	
	TOTAL O				1500	0

P	FILM TRANSFER	Amount	Rate	X	ESTIMATED	ACTUAL
285	Film to Tape Transfer				0	
286	Tape to Tape Color Correct				0	
287	Videotape Downconversion				0	
288	DVD/Videotape Stock				0	
289	Film to Tape Transfer				0	
290	Tape to Tape Color Correct				0	
291	Videotape Downconversion				0	
292	DVD/Videotape Stock				0	
293					0	
	TOTAL P				0	0

Q	AUDIO	Amount	Rate	X	ESTIMATED	ACTUAL
294	Audio Sweetening				0	
295	Audio Edit				0	
296	Audio Mix				0	
297	Audio Load In/Load Out				0	
298	Sound Effects Library				0	
299	Back-Up Audio files				0	
	TOTAL Q				0	0

R	MUSIC	Amount	Rate	X	ESTIMATED	ACTUAL
300	Music Composition				0	
301	Music Rights/Clearance				0	
302	Music Recording				0	
303	Music Supervisor				0	
304	Audiotape Stock/Files				0	
	TOTAL R				0	0

S	FILM FINISHING	Amount	Rate	X	ESTIMATED	ACTUAL
305	Negative Cutting				0	
306	1st Answer Print				0	
307	2nd Answer Print				0	
308	Additional Print(s)				0	
309	Blow up to 35mm				0	
310	Film Out				0	
311	Screening Room Rental				0	
312	Screening Room Equip. Rental				0	
	TOTAL S				0	0

T	MISCELLANEOUS	Amount	Rate	X	ESTIMATED	ACTUAL
313	Stock Footage Researcher				0	
314	Stock Footage Licensing				0	
315	Screener Copies				0	
316	Editor – transportation	1	265	1	265	
317	Shipping				0	
318	Messengers				0	
319	Post Working Meals				0	
320	DVD/Videotape stock				0	
321	DVD Duplication				0	
322	DVD Authoring				0	
	TOTAL T				265	0
	TOTAL POST PRODUCTION			0	1765	0

LABOR CONSIDERATIONS

This section is for labor costs for your shoot days only. Please note that at the bottom of each of these two Labor pages there is a P&W line below the Labor subtotal line. P&W stands for Pension and Welfare and it is where you put your Fringe rate if you are going through a payroll service for your crew payments. **Fringes** is the word used for the total amount of federal tax, state tax, city tax, unemployment tax, social security tax, Medicaid tax, union pension charges, and payroll fees that need to be computed and paid for each employee on your production. Check with your accountant to determine if you will be required to pay out fringes/ P&W. If so, contact a payroll service to find out what the rate should be — usually between 19-22% of labor costs on top of the day-rate salaries. Overtime is computed in the 1.5X column or 2X column for the two different overtime computation rates.

Regarding labor costs, these are the deals you can make with your crew (from the least expensive to the most):

1. Everyone works for free or deferred.

2. Pay only certain key crew/skilled crew positions, and everyone else works for free or deferred.

3. Pay all crew a small stipend per day.

4. Pay all crew a flat day rate.

5. Pay all crew (union or non-union) a day rate plus overtime (OT) (and if union, then add the union P&W charge, as well).

Your labor costs (along with travel costs, food, office rental, and phone charges) will account for a big chunk of your budget. So try to keep your labor costs down as much as possible. This is not done to exploit the people who are going to help make the film, but it's one of the few areas where you can save money. It's important to be able to get the best people you can afford, but there are other ways to compensate someone besides money.

I've done many productions on which very skilled crews have worked for free or for a small stipend (a fraction of what they would normally receive) because they believed in the project and wanted to be a part of it. So if you have a great script, or if a crew person will get to do something he or she doesn't normally get to do, then that can be the "payment." To the right person, that's enough. Because it is *not* always about the money.

On the other hand, don't be penny wise and pound foolish. I co-produced a short film a few years ago — a very ambitious project with a very tight budget. We paid the skilled labor but we didn't have the money to pay the production assistants, so I decided to recruit PAs who could work for free. We advertised online and received many resumes from people with little or no production experience. We interviewed many people and picked the best of the bunch. They were enthusiastic and helpful. But you get what you pay for. The volunteer PAs lacked the experience of veteran PAs that would have cost us money. On our fifth day of shooting, one of the PAs drove a production truck into a low-hanging heater in a parking garage and we had to pay $2,500 to fix it. I often think of how many experienced PAs I could have hired for that amount of money.

Keep in mind that on shorter-term projects (less than six shooting days) you can often find a DP to shoot your project for free because lots of people use short films or music videos as a way to build their reels. More often, you'll have to pay their assistant camerapersons, gaffers, and/or key grips. You usually will have to pay for a sound person, but you can often get a production designer, props, and hair/makeup for free. A production manager could be someone who usually works as a production coordinator and wants to do the job to try to move up the ladder. You should be able to find PAs by referrals, contacting local film schools and so forth. One of the best PAs I have ever worked with was a 15-year-old high school sophomore — he was smart, highly motivated, and had energy to burn. He was the son of one of the executive producers and was a delight to work with.

LABOR RATES AND MOST FAVORED NATION

These A & B sections are for labor costs only. Depending on the budget version you use there may or may not be overtime or fringes computed. Labor rates are open to negotiation with each individual crew person, but most of the time it is done on a most favored nation basis.

Most favored nation is a legal term used to describe the universal pay rate that each corresponding labor rank is paid. So each department head (i.e., DP, Production Designer, Costume Designer, Head Hair/Makeup) are paid the same rate. Then the next level in each department gets the same rate (i.e., AD, Ass't Camera, Gaffer, Key Grip, Sound Recordist, Script Supervisor). Then the next level gets paid the same rate (Best Boy Electric, Best Boy Grip, Costume Ass't, Hair/Makeup Ass't, 2nd AC), etc.

This creates universality across each corresponding position in each department. That way everyone at the same level in the crew hierarchy gets the same rate. This industry standard is based on fairness and fosters harmony among the ranks. I do all of my productions this way and it keeps things easy and clean. If you don't pay crew on a most favored nation basis, it will lead to anger and resentment. If you make a side deal with some and expect them to keep the secret, forget about it! Crews talk to each other and compare rates all the time. Your secret will be shared and it will run through the ranks like a wild fire and you'll have trouble to contend with. I highly recommend most favored nation for all productions.

Below is a breakdown by budget section of what to include in each section:

SECTIONS A & B (LINE #1-50, #51-100)

Section A is used to estimate labor costs for Prep and Wrap. Section B is for labor costs for Production. This section consists of the line items for your labor costs for all of your crew. Each line item breaks down by the number of days and rate per day. This Section A includes time and money for crew during location scouting, tech scouting, set build, shopping, pre-light and wrap. Section B includes time and money for all shoot days. Computed by # of days **x** day rate. Overtime is computed in the 1.5x (1.5x the hourly rate) column or 2x (2x the hourly rate) column for the two different overtime computation rates.

Below are the key crew positions to consider for your production:

Producer
Director
Director of Photography
AD
2nd AD
Assistant Camera
Gaffer
Electrics
Key Grip
Grips
Sound Recordist/Production Mixer
Production Designer

Art Director
Props
Props Ass't
Video Engineer or Digital Imaging Technician (DIT)
Audio Playback (for music videos or musicals only)
Video Playback
Location Scout
Script Supervisor (scriptie)
Production Manager
Production Coordinator
Production Assistants (preferably with their own cars)
Police
Fire
Tutor

Depending on the size of your production and your project's specific needs, this list may expand or contract.

Once you decide on the configuration of your crew, you'll pick what kind of pay scale you can afford and start entering the number of days and hours in each line. Remember to factor in the costs for a tech scout for your crew in Section A (we'll discuss tech scout in the *Preproduction* chapter). Usually you'll need the Producer, Director, DP, AD, Production Designer, Sound, Gaffer, Key Grip, Location Manager, and Production Manager on the tech scout. You'll also need to hire various departments to prep and wrap for the film, i.e., Production Designer, Art Dept., Set Dressers, Costume Designer, Hair and Makeup, Location Scout, UPM, Production Coordinator and PAs. In Section A you'll need to estimate how many people and how much time for prep and wrap in these departments. In Section B you'll estimate the number of shoot days and if you'll need to put in for overtime. Most non-union crews will work on a 10-hour day so overtime (OT) will start after 10 hours. Usually the 11th and 12th hours are computed at 1.5x the per-hour rate of the day rate. After 12 hours, it is 2x the per-hour rate of the day rate. For instance, if the pay rate is $500/10 hr. then the per hour rate is $50; 1.5x = $75/hr; 2x = $100/ hr. A 10-hour day = $500, 12-hour day = $650 and a 13-hour day = $750.

If you are paying fringes (federal, state, city taxes, social security tax, etc.), it's best to contact a payroll company and they can tell you what it will cost to pay for each person. They will also charge a small fee for the work they do. The rates are generally 19-22% on top of each person's gross salary.

SECTION C #101-113 PREPRODUCTION/SCOUTING EXPENSES

Hotel — Costs for hotel nights when scouting and prepping. Call or go online to get prices. Computed by # of nights **x** cost/night **x** # of rooms.

Air/Train/Bus fare(s) — Costs for air, train, or bus fares for scouting and prepping. Computed by # of people **x** cost/round trip (RT).

Per Diem — (Latin for "by the day") — Costs to reimburse crew for out-of-town costs when shooting overnight away from home, (e.g., meals, phone charges, and laundry costs); Costs for per diem for each person during scouting and prepping when out of town. Computed by # of days **x** cost/day **x** # of people. Cost/day depends on what city you are visiting. Certain cities (domestic or international) are more expensive than others and per diem will reflect the relative costs.

Car Rental(s) — Costs for car rentals for scouting and prepping. Can be computed as daily, weekly, or monthly rentals. Depending on your production insurance coverage, you may need to budget for the daily Collision Damage Waiver (CDW) fee to cover the vehicle in case of any accident. Check your policy and make sure you are covered or supplemented through the rental company. There are other kinds of insurance you can purchase from the car rental agencies. Read the fine print ahead of time on their websites so you can make the decision quickly when the car is picked up. Car rental on an hourly basis is another option. If you only need the car for a few hours, it might be more cost effective. Computed by # of days **x** cost/day **x** # of cars.

Taxis — Costs for taxis for scouting and prepping. Computed by estimated total.

Messengers — Costs for messengers for scouting and prepping. Computed by estimated total.

Office Supplies — Costs for binders, paper reams, pens, pencils, markers, staples, rubber bands, envelopes, stationery, fax machine, etc. Computed by estimated total.

Copies — Costs for copying scripts and production related papers. Computed by estimated total.

Telephone/Fax/Cell — Costs for telephone, fax and cell phone charges for scouting and prepping. May include phone installation costs, Skype, and international calls. Computed by estimated total.

Casting Director — Costs to hire a casting director. Computed by # days **x** cost/day.

Casting Expenses — Costs for audition facilities rental, videotaping expenses, etc. Computed by # days **x** cost/day.

Working Meals — Costs for lunches or coffee with people for meetings related to the film. Computed by estimated total.

SECTION D #114-139 LOCATION EXPENSES

Location fees — Put in your high estimate for all locations. Don't forget to base all figures on how many hours you plan to shoot at a location. Some locations have a flat rate for 10 hours, then overtime (OT) after that, at time and a half. (Divide the rate by 10 hours and then multiply by 1.5 to get the hourly overtime rate.) Don't forget to budget for a Minder for each location. Most places will want you to pay for a person to stay with you and your cast/crew at the location for the entire shooting period. You will want them, too. Someone familiar with the location can answer questions, has keys to all the doors and closets and knows how to turn off the noisy air conditioner when you are shooting sound takes. You'll need to pay for this person, in addition to a location rental fee but they are usually worth the expense. Computed by # of locations **x** cost/location.

Permits — Some municipalities or locations will require a permit fee or fees. (We'll discuss this further in the *Locations* Chapter). Computed by estimated total.

Car rental(s) — Costs for car rentals needed for transporting people to and from the shoot. Can be computed as daily, weekly, or monthly rentals. Depending on your production insurance coverage, you may need to budget for the daily Collision Damage Waiver (CDW) fee to cover the vehicle in case of any accident. Check your policy and make sure you are covered or supplemented through the rental company. There are other kinds of insurance you can purchase from the rental agencies. Read the fine print ahead of time on their websites so you can make the decision quickly when the car is picked up. Car rental on an hourly basis is another option. If you only need the car for a few hours, it might be more cost effective. Computed by # of days **x** cost/day **x** # of cars.

Van rental(s) — Costs for van rentals needed for transporting people in minivans or 15-passenger vans, or transporting equipment, wardrobe, production supplies, and craft service in cargo vans. Some larger cities have companies that cater to film companies. They allow PAs to pick up the vans easily and will take the back seats out of the vans without a hassle. See Car Rental(s) above for additional info.

Winnebago — Costs for Winnebago/RV vehicles. Computed by # of days **x** cost/day **x** # of vehicles.

Parking/Tolls/Gas — Costs for transportation, costs for parking, tolls, and gas. Computed by estimated total.

Truck rental(s) — Costs for truck rentals needed by art department for transporting set pieces, building material, and other big items. See Car Rental(s) above for additional info.

Air/Train/Bus fare — Call or go online to get prices. Computed by # of roundtrips (RT) **x** cost/trip **x** # of people.

Hotel — Costs for hotel for cast and crew during the shooting period. Call or go online to get prices. Computed by # of nights **x** cost/night **x** # of rooms.

Per Diem — (Latin for "by the day") — Costs to reimburse crew for out-of-town costs when shooting overnight away from home, (e.g., meals, phone charges, and laundry costs); Costs for per diem for each person during scouting and prepping when out of town. Computed by # of days **x** cost/day **x** # of people. Cost/day depends on what city you are visiting. Certain cities (domestic or international) are more expensive than others and per diem will reflect the relative costs.

Breakfast, Lunch, Dinner Catering — Number of days **x** rate per person **x** number of people for breakfast, lunch, and/or dinner. **You have to feed your crew every six hours.** For a 12-hour day, ideally you'd serve a hot breakfast at call time then work six hours; have a hot lunch, then work six hours and complete the wrap. Then the crew would be done for the day and you wouldn't have to serve dinner (discussed further in the *Production* Chapter).

If you work past six hours after finishing the lunch meal, then you'll have to serve dinner, as well. I usually budget for breakfast and lunch for each shoot day and maybe a few dinners, if I think we might go over 12 hours on a few days (depending on how many total days/weeks for the entire shooting period). If there are any set build or pre-light days you can decide to have a catered lunch or ask people to go off set and obtain their own. Depending on budget, I'll give the crew money for meal costs offsite. (Have lots of money in paper bill form to give out to the crew.)

Craft service — This is for the food you have available for people to munch on throughout the day. Generally it consists of coffee, tea, juice, soda, and water for beverages. In the morning, fruit, muffins, bagels, croissants with butter and cream cheese are served. Then bite size sandwiches — or, if you have access to a stove or microwave, little quiches, spring rolls, etc. In addition, you might have crudités, cheese and crackers, munchies, gum, mints, cookies, and candy (there is a full Craft Service list in the *Preproduction* Chapter).

You can make your Craft Service table as minimal or as lavish as your budget allows. If you shop at a discount warehouse, you will stretch your dollars much further.

Taxi — This is for the charges to transport people to and from airports if they need to travel by plane. It also includes charges for taxi travel if you are working in a city where that mode of transportation is used (e.g., New York, NY, Washington, D.C., etc.). Calculate the number of rides **x** rate per ride **x** number of people — and remember to count each trip separately, so a roundtrip equals two rides.

Kit Rentals — Costs for kit rentals for hair/makeup kits and grip/electric kits. Computed by # of days **x** cost/day **x** # of kits.

Gratuities — Tips at hotels, for skycaps at airports, janitors, etc.

Cell phone — You should make deals with production staff (including PAs, who will need to communicate with the Production office when they are out on runs) to compensate them for the costs they incur while working on the project. Work the deal out ahead of time, make it the same across the board on a most favored nation basis (see above for explanation) and be clear about what you will and will not pay for. It's best to make it a flat deal so you can keep the costs manageable. I usually ask PAs to increase their monthly plans if they are going to be on a shoot for multiple days and I will pay the difference in their monthly costs for that month. Do the same for text-messaging plans.

Another way to do it is to purchase Pay-As-You-Go mobile phones and give them out to the crew members who need them. That way the production can keep track of the charges and recharge the minutes during the prep, production, and wrap periods. Then, when the production is over, the crew person returns it to the production. No annual fees are involved and they can be used for the next production you produce.

SECTION E #140-148 PROPS/WARDROBE/SFX

Prop Rental/Prop Purchase — Costs to rent and purchase props and other scenic elements for all the sets and locations.

Wardrobe Rental/Wardrobe Purchase — Costs to rent or buy the costumes/wardrobe.

Picture Vehicle Rentals — Costs to rent any vehicles that appear or are driven *on camera* in the film.

Animals and Handlers — Costs to rent a trained animal, the time for the animal prep and trainings, and the trainer/handler's costs.

Wigs — Costs to rent or purchase wigs and materials to build them.

Special Effects (SFX) Expenses — The costs of any effects like fires, explosions, or gun-firing. Depending on the effect, you may need to obtain a permit from the local fire department. (See *Preproduction* Chapter for more information.) (The SFX operator will be in the Labor costs in Section B.)

SECTION F #151-167 STUDIO RENTAL AND EXPENSES

Studio Rental — Compute how many days you'll need to shoot in a studio, if any. There are usually different rates for Build, Pre-Light, Shoot and Wrap days. There is usually overtime after 10 or 12 hours, but make sure you check to find out the rules for the studio you are using.

Studio Manager — Some studios charge for managers to be on duty during your work time or sometimes there is only a charge for overtime.

Electricity — Studios usually have an additional charge for the Pre-Light and Shoot days to cover the cost of using lights.

Phone/Fax/Internet/Copies — There is usually a charge for these services. Often they are flat fees with the copier on a *pay-as-used* basis.

Parking — Some studios have a charge for cast/crew parking.

Miscellaneous Equipment — If you need to rent additional equipment like a scissor lift or ladders you should put them here.

Cartage/Dumpster Rentals — Costs to rent dumpster(s) for discarding set construction materials and other debris.

Studio Painting — Your production may need to paint the studio walls and/or floor a different color than that it is. Usually the studio will charge a fee to have it painted to your color and then to paint it back to the regular color.

Trash Removal — costs for daily trash removal and pick up studio personnel.

SECTION G #168-180 SET CONSTRUCTION LABOR

Set Designer — Fees for a designer to create the set and construction plans.

Carpenters — Costs for skilled crew to build the set # of days **x** day rate **x** # of people.

Grips — The grips who work on the construction crew.

Outside Props — The crew who shops for props in stores and prop houses.

Inside Props — The crew who works with props on set and on location.

Scenics — The crew who paint the set and create scenic effects # of days **x** day rate **x** # of people.

Strike Crew — Crew members that come in for the *strike* of the set only. They dismantle it safely and dispose of it. Sometimes you need to hire a different crew than the one that put it up. Especially when there is a **turnaround** issue. (Turnaround refers to the minimum amount of time that can transpire between the wrap time for an individual cast or crew member and the call time for the next day. This is usually 10 or 12 hours.) A strike crew can be a lower day rate because it does not require the same skill level of those who built the set # of days **x** day rate **x** # of people.

Production Assistant — Specific PAs to work in the set construction department # of days **x** day rate **x** # of people.

SECTION H #181-192 SET CONSTRUCTION MATERIALS

Set Dressing Purchase and Rental — Materials to dress the set, i.e., furniture, artwork, lamps, wallpaper, etc.

Lumber — Material to build the set.

Paint — Necessary to cover the set surfaces.

Hardware — Whatever needs to be purchased to build the set.

Special Effects Construction/Person — If your production requires a special effect that needs to be constructed, it will be entered here. This includes water tanks, air guns, pumps, etc.

Outside Construction and Trucking — If something needs to be built off site and moved to the set.

Product/Model Construction — If you need to have a product created for a shoot — perhaps a product that does not exist in the marketplace or needs to be created in a specific way that is not purchasable off the shelf.

Trucking — Costs associated with trucking something for the set.

Messengers/Deliveries — Costs for deliveries for the set.

SECTION I #193-210 EQUIPMENT RENTAL

NOTE: If you are shooting more than two consecutive days, usually you can get a deal from the rental house for equipment rentals. It is common to get a "2- or 3-day week" for equipment that is being rented for longer. If you are renting for a total of three consecutive days, you can ask for a two-day rental. If you are picking up on a Friday and returning on a

Monday, you should only be charged for a one-day rental # of days/weeks **x** daily/weekly rate.

Camera Rental — Costs to rent the camera equipment. This includes the camera body, lens, and tripod. Additional accessories are listed in separate line items # of days/weeks **x** daily/weekly rate.

Sound Rental — Costs to rent the sound equipment. This includes microphones, digital audio recorder, boom pole, audio mixer, back-up audio recorder, etc. # of days/weeks **x** daily/weekly rate.

Lighting Rental — Costs to rent the lighting and electrical equipment. This includes light fixtures, light stands, electrical cable, electric distribution boxes. and ballasts # of days/weeks **x** daily/weekly rate.

Grip Rental — Costs to rent the grip equipment. This includes grip stands, heads & arms, flags & nets, reflector boards, grip clips, and apple boxes, etc. # of days/weeks **x** daily/weekly rate.

Generator Rental — Costs to rent an electric generator. Generators can be as small as a 45 amp "putt putt" genny that you can rent from a hardware store or it can be a large truck with enough gasoline to power 750 amps. They come in different sizes and are priced accordingly. If you rent a truck you'll need to hire a generator operator who will drive the truck to location, hook up the electrical cables and monitor the electrical power situation throughout the shoot day. Their fee would be computed in *Section B — Crew Shoot Labor.*

Dolly Rental — Costs to rent a dolly. There are several different kinds with different price points # of days/weeks **x** daily/weekly rate.

Dolly Accessories — Costs to rent a dolly track and various dolly accessories # of days/weeks **x** daily/weekly rate.

Crane Rental — Costs to rent a crane and track # of days/weeks **x** daily/weekly rate.

Jib Arm Rental — Costs to rent a jib arm # of days/weeks **x** daily/weekly rate.

Walkie Talkie Rental — Costs to rent walkie talkies. Walkies should be rented for any shoot that requires communication between crew members over long distances. This includes most exterior shoots, shoots in large studios and interior shoots that require communication with people at vehicles that are parked far away # of walkies **x** # of days/weeks **x** dailiy/weekly rate.

Production Supplies — Costs for miscellaneous supplies like batteries, garbage bags, traffic cones, cleaning supplies, tissues, padlocks to secure equipment trucks, etc.

Expendables — Costs for supplies for the grip, electrical, and camera departments. Gaffer's tape, gels, clothespins, sash cord, etc. Can be charged on a **Pay as Used** basis whereby you only pay for the amount that you consume.

Camera Lenses — Costs to rent additional lenses for the camera # of days/weeks **x** daily/weekly rate.

Camera Accessories Rental — Costs to rent video tap, monitor, cables, etc. # of days/weeks **x** daily/weekly rate.

Green Screen Rental — Costs to rent a green screen. # of days/weeks **x** daily/weekly rate.

Underwater Housing Rental — Costs to rent underwater housing for the camera # of days/weeks **x** daily/weekly rate.

SECTION J #211-217 FILM STOCK, VIDEOTAPE STOCK AND DIGITAL MEDIA

Purchase Film Stock 16mm — Costs to purchase 16mm film stock. Amount of footage **x** cost/ft.

Develop Film Stock 16mm — Costs to develop 16mm film stock. Amount of footage **x** cost/ft.

Purchase Film Stock 35mm — Costs to purchase 35mm film stock. Amount of footage **x** cost/ft.

Develop Film Stock 35mm — Costs to develop 35mm film stock. Amount of footage **x** cost/ft.

Digital Storage Purchase — Costs to purchase additional digital storage like hard drives. NOTE: Research how many MB of memory you will need for the digital camera on the setting that you intend to use. Many cameras can run at different "rates" and use different amounts of memory for a fixed amount of minutes. Estimate accordingly.

Memory Card Rental/Purchase — Costs to rent or purchase memory cards for the camera.

Videotape Stock — Costs to purchase videotape stock for the camera... # of videotapes **x** cost/tape. NOTE: Some video cameras run at a faster speed than the # of minutes stated on a videotape. Make sure you understand the running time for your camera and estimate accordingly # of videotapes **x** cost/tape.

Audiotape Stock — Costs to purchase audiotape stock for the audio recording device or back up system # of audiotapes **x** cost/tape.

HOW TO COMPUTE SHOOTING RATIO

Shooting ratio is an important concept because it impacts the budget exponentially. Once you know the shooting ratio that you plan to use for the film, you can create a solid estimate of how much film or digital media memory and storage drives you will require for the whole project.

The shooting ratio is the total number of minutes of footage acquired vs. the final total running time of your film. That formula is expressed as two numbers — like 10:1 or 15:1. That means, on average, you plan to shoot 10 or 15 times the material for that one moment in the film. If the final TRT of your film is 100 minutes, then for a 10:1 shooting ratio, you would plan to shoot 1,000 minutes of material. At 15:1 you will budget for 1,500 minutes of material. For a low-budget film, a 10:1 or 15:1 is usually the norm. Higher-budget films can often afford higher shooting ratios.

SECTION K #218-226 MISCELLANEOUS COSTS

Air Shipping Charges — Costs for using air courier services.

Accounting Charges — Costs for accounting services.

Bank charges — Costs for bank transfers and other fees.

Legal Charges — Costs for legal services and fees.

Errors and Omissions Insurance — Costs for E&O insurance.

Publicity — Costs to hire or create publicity for the project.

Film Festival Fees/Expenses — Costs for film festival applications and travel expenses.

SECTION L #227-233 CREATIVE FEES

Writer Fee — Fee for writer.

Director Fee — Prep — Fee for director's prep days.

Director Fee — Travel — Fee for director's travel days.

Director Fee — Shoot — Fee for director's shoot days.

Director Fee — Post — Fee for director's postproduction days.

Fringes for labor costs — Payroll taxes/fees for the above labor costs.

SECTION M #234-270 TALENT FEES

O/C Principal — Salary for on-camera principal actors # of actors **x** # of days **x** day rate.

Background Actors — Salary for background actors (extras) # of actors **x** # of days **x** day rate.

Voice Over Talent — Salary for voice over talent. Computed by the hour or half hour # of actors **x** # of days **x** hourly rate.

Fitting Fee — Additional fee for a costume fitting.

Rehearsal Fee — Additional fee for rehearsal time.

Wardrobe Fee — Additional fee for wardrobe rental from the actor.

SECTION N #271-276 TALENT EXPENSES

Air Fare — Costs for actor airfares.

Hotel — Costs for actor hotel charges.

Per Diem — Costs for actor per diem.

Cabs and Transportation — Costs for transportation for actors.

Agent Fee — Usually a 10% markup paid to the agent for each actor. Total cost = All actors total salary **x** 10%.

Pension & Health — a percentage charge multiplied to the total amount of Talent salaries. Computed by total of talent salaries **x** percentage for the P&H for the actors guild (usually SAG or AFTRA).

SECTION P #277-322 POSTPRODUCTION

EDITORIAL

Postproduction Supervisor — # of days/weeks **x** day/weekly rate.

Editor — # of days/weeks **x** day/weekly rate.

Assistant Editor — # of days/weeks **x** day/weekly rate.

Transcription — Computed per minute of running time of audio material.

Edit System Rental — # of weeks **x** weekly rate.

Hard drive purchase(s) — Costs for purchases of data storage and memory back up. NOTE: Buy enough so you have a back up of all your original material and save each cut on two or more separate drives, as well.

DVD/Videotape stock — # of DVDs/tapes **x** cost per DVD/tape.

DVD Duplication — costs to create DVD copies.

DVD Authoring — Costs to author a DVD.

FILM TRANSFER

Film-to-Tape Transfer — # of feet **x** cost/foot. Varies by the type of transfer — Unsupervised, One Light, Best Light, or Supervised. (Will discuss further in *Postproduction* chapter). Each has a different rate. Get a bid in writing from the facility you plan to use.

Tape-to-Tape Color Correct — # of feet **x** cost/foot. Either done on a desktop editing system or at a postproduction facility. Rates and the level of expertise vary greatly. Get a bid in writing from the facility you plan to use.

Videotape Downconversion — Costs to downconvert digital formats to another format... # of tapes (and running time of each tape) **x** cost/tape.

Videotape Stock — Costs to purchase videotape stock # of videotape **x** cost/tape.

AUDIO

Audio Sweetening — Costs to add sound effects and sweeten the audio tracks # of hours/days **x** hourly/daily rate.

Audio Edit — Costs to edit the audio tracks and prepare for audio mix # of hours/days **x** hourly/daily rate.

Audio Mix — Costs for audio mix # of hours/days **x** hourly/daily rate.

Audio Load in/Load out — Costs for time to load in and load out the audio files # of hours/days **x** hourly/daily rate.

Sound Effects Library — Costs to use a sound effects library and any rights required.

Back-Up Audio Files — Costs to back up and archive audio files. Usually based on # of minutes of material.

MUSIC

Music Composition — For musical composer fee.

Music Rights/Clearance — Costs for the rights to clear and purchase the rights to music for the audio track. Rights need to match the usage you require for the project. (see *Music* chapter).

Music Recording — Costs to record the musical composition. Includes studio rental, audio recording personnel, and musician fees.

Music Supervisor — Computed by # of weeks **x** weekly rate or a flat fee.

Audiotape Stock/Files — Costs for audiotape stock or computer drives for files and copies.

FILM FINISHING

Negative Cutting — Computed on a cost per cut and the number of dissolves in the film negative.

1st Answer Print — Computed by cost/foot.

2nd Answer Print — Computed by cost/foot.

Additional Print(s) — Computed by cost/foot.

Blow up to 35mm — Computed by cost/foot.

Film Out — Digital scan to film negative or film print. Computed by cost/foot or running time.

Screening Room Rental — Costs to rent a screening room. Computed by # of hours **x** cost/hour.

Screening Room Equipment Rental — Costs to rent equipment for screening room.

MISCELLANEOUS

Stock Footage Researcher — Computed by # of days/weeks **x** daily/weekly rate or a flat rate.

Stock Footage Licensing — Costs to license the stock footage used in your project.

Stock Footage Screener Copies — Costs to purchase screener copies to look at the material.

Miscellaneous Equipment Rental — Computed by # of days/weeks **x** daily/weekly rate.

Shipping — Costs for air shipping and/or postage costs.

Messengers — Costs for messenger services.

Working Meals — Costs for postproduction working meals.

DVD/Videotape Duplication and Stock — Computed by # of DVD/videotapes **x** cost/DVD/tape and/or duplication costs.

Cash Flow

Once you have created your estimated budget, you need to create a **cash-flow schedule** to match that budget. A cash-flow schedule states when you are going to need certain amounts of money to cover the specific costs tied to the prep, production, and postproduction stages of the film. You'll need option money and writer's fees early in the process, then scouting/casting costs, next will be salary costs, as you hire cast and crew. After that, you'll have equipment rental costs, location fees, production and costume design expenses, catering, etc. These stages usually happen in a particular and predictable order. Once you know your shoot dates, you can create a cash-flow schedule that dictates how much money needs to be available in any given week to cover the costs for those line items.

Working Budget

Once you begin preproduction you will start to get a true sense of how much things will really cost for your project. Up until now you have put estimated numbers into your budget based on preliminary research, past experience, and knowledge of what things cost. Once you start to finalize your choices such as specific locations and final equipment lists you will start to get final numbers on what things will really cost. It's imperative that you input these new, and more accurate, numbers into a **working budget**. Some budget templates have a button you can push that allows the software to switch to a working budget format. If the one you are using doesn't have this feature, then make a copy of your official estimated budget and rename it as the working budget and start moving the numbers around to reflect the new numbers you are getting for your actual needs.

This step is essential to be able to keep a running tally of how your estimated budget is being adjusted in a concrete way. You'll start to see very quickly if you are over or under in individual line items and budget sections. You may have estimated that you'd need $3,000 for location costs to rent a house for a few days. But then your parents give you permission to use their home and you now have a $3,000 savings on that line #. But then the director of photography does the tech scout and realizes that your parents' home is very dark with little ambient light and will need additional lighting equipment, so your lighting order goes up by $1,000. You can see how things start to really shift around once you lock in and make final decisions on how and where the money will need to be dispersed on the film.

Padding and Contingency

Although your budget is based on what you think it will take to make your film, you can never know for sure until you have completed the project. That's why it is always good to pad or put in a contingency to cover any overages that may occur during the production. A **pad** refers to areas or line items in the budget that you know you have overestimated and you can go to if you need to pay for additional costs in other areas. I always do this so I know I have a little extra in case things change. A **contingency** is a line item on the top sheet that is usually set at 10% of the total budget that is added just in case things go over budget. The funder understands to expect that the budget could go up to the amount of the estimated budget and the contingency combined.

Budget Actualization

I wanted to mention **budget actualization** here but will go into more depth in the *Wrap* chapter later in the book.

Budget actualization occurs when you enter each paid or payable invoice into the budget in the ACTUAL column (next to the ESTIMATE column) in your budget. Each invoice is entered onto the line item that it matches, i.e., airfares are on the airfare line item, lighting rental is on the lighting line item. This process should be done as soon as you begin to receive invoices to be paid. Each one should be entered into the budget and it will start to total up for you what the actuals are for the budget. You now know what the real final costs are for your film.

Once this process is completed and all of your invoices have been entered into the budget you can compare the difference between individual line items and subtotaled sections of the budget. Sometimes you are over in certain sections and under in others and they offset each other. This is to be expected. The goal is to come in under in the overall budget.

Tax Resale Certificates

Each state allows for production companies to use resale certificates when purchasing goods or services that contribute to the production of a film. This allows the production company to avoid paying sales tax on these items at the time of purchase if they are used to make the film. This is because when the film is completed and sold, sales tax will paid at that time and the government realizes that would be a double tax situation. You can obtain the resale certificate form for each state's tax authority. Fill it out and give to the vendor you are purchasing goods or services from and they will not charge sales tax for your transaction.

Tax Incentives/Credits

Many states in the U.S. have tax incentives or tax credits for film productions that are produced in their states. They are usually between 5%-25% of the monies spent in the specific state and the rules and regulations vary widely from state to state. Some give you tax credits that are used against the production company's tax returns for several years and some states actually give you money back that you can use to offset costs. Some states allow productions to be exempt from hotel sales taxes for nights at hotels for cast/crew. Some tax credits you can sell through a tax credit broker and turn them into cash instead of waiting to use them in your upcoming tax returns over the next few years.

There are very specific rules that you need to follow in order to be assured that you are eligible for the tax credit. The best place to start to research is the film commission for the state you are interested in shooting in. They often have the information on the state film commission website and the contact info for follow-up queries.

You'll need to meet with the entity in charge of the tax credit system to learn the eligibility requirements and accounting procedures necessary to get the money. They will also advise you on what the timeline will be once you apply for the credit. It is usually based on the amount of money that you actually spend in the state, but that can vary. Not all line item expenses are covered and depending on the state rules, the money may come in the form of tax rebates or money rebates that pay out over a couple of years. If you sell your tax credits through a broker you usually receive them sooner.

RECAP

1. Don't be intimidated about budgeting. Follow the steps in this chapter and go line by line through the budget.

2. Use a budgeting software template to help you estimate each element of the production and put it in an organized form.

3. Overestimate on the first pass by creating the "kitchen sink" version, so you don't forget any projected need.

4. After you have completed the first draft of the budget, discuss your assumptions with the director and key department heads for any questions about the production requirements. Refine and tighten the budget according to what is needed and what you anticipate your total funding will be.

5. Once you have a realistic budget, create a cash-flow schedule so you know when you need money in the bank in order to fund the key phases of filmmaking — development, pre-production, production, and postproduction.

6. Continue to revise the budget as assumptions and reality change to create updated "working" budgets.

7. Explore tax incentive programs throughout the U.S. to maximize your funding.

CHAPTER 4

FUNDING

NOW THAT YOU KNOW how much it will take to produce your film, you need to find the money to fund it. Financing your film is one of the hardest (maybe *the* hardest) aspects of making your film. There are many funding and fundraising possibilities. You will have a unique strategy for each film you produce that is dictated by the type of film you are making. This chapter will give an overview of the most common ways producers fund their independent productions. This is not an exhaustive list and should be used as an overall guide only.

Pre-sales

We discussed this in the *Development* chapter earlier in this book. It's helpful to review here.

Pre-sales refers to when you sell certain rights to your film before you produce it as a way of funding the film. You could sell to a U.S. cable network and maybe an international television network or two and might have enough money to make the film. Then you'd still have the ability to sell theatrical, DVD, and Internet rights after the film is completed. It

I think there's only one or two films where I've had all the financial support I needed. All the rest, I wish I'd had the money to shoot another 10 days.

— Martin Scorsese

all depends on your budget. Pre-sales are not that easy to obtain. You usually have to have a certain known reputation as a filmmaker or producer to get a meeting with a television network or commissioning editor. There are always exceptions to the rule but the competition is tough and contacts are key. Maybe the director has a proven track record of making profitable films, or you have an A-list actress attached to your film or an Academy-nominated writer has written the script. These are the kind of things that allow you to get pre-sales.

For documentaries, elements like the director's track record, an A-list actor who agrees to do the narration or the strength of the underlying material may be the key element that makes the project bankable for a pre-sale. It depends. For several of the feature documentaries I have produced, we sold a few key foreign television rights and the U.S. cable television rights and were able to fund the films entirely. It means you have to keep the budget tight but at least you know you have all the money necessary to make the film from start to finish. Any additional rights you sell after the film premieres goes back to you and the investors.

Often you won't be able to get a sale until after you have shot the film and created a great rough cut. Then you might be able to get some sales. But this is a calculated risk and you should proceed with caution. I don't advise going into any kind of debt for a film. If it is a good enough project, you will find the money — or wait until you have saved up the money to cover the entire budget.

For documentaries, there is the added funding option of nonprofit agencies and foundations. Development and production grants are ideal ways to get the film made if you have a film that meets the foundation's criteria and can make a strong application. This takes a lot of time and effort, so make sure you and your project fit all the criteria before making the application.

Sales Agents

Sales Agents are people who specialize in selling rights to films. They have connections with the various distribution outlets and are known for the certain kinds of films that they sell. Some concentrate on narrative features, some on feature documentaries and some also do short films.

If you do not get any or enough pre-sales then you will need to raise money through additional funding sources. The following is a list of potential rights you could sell before, during, or after you have produced the film.

U.S. (domestic) television rights — These can be to television networks like ABC, CBS, NBC, and Fox or to cable networks like HBO, TLC, IFC, and Sundance Channel.

International (foreign) television rights — These would be networks like the BBC (British Broadcasting Corporation), CBC (Canadian Broadcasting Corporation), ZDF (Germany), ARTE (France).

Domestic DVD rights — Rights to license the DVD for the U.S. market.

International DVD rights — Rights to license the DVD for the international markets — usually a separate deal for each country.

U.S. theatrical rights — Rights for a run in theaters in the U.S.

International theatrical rights — Rights for a run in theaters, internationally.

Internet rights — Rights to broadcast the film on specific Internet sites.

"Viral" rights (IPods, cell phones, etc.) — Rights to broadcast via cell phones, etc.

Equity Investors

If you can't get any pre-sales or not enough for your budget, you can look into Equity financing. Equity financing is when you get investors to put up cash for your film in exchange for a repayment deal if the film ever becomes profitable.

NOTE: Whenever creating an investment deal make sure you contact an attorney who can advise you on the legalities and any Security and Exchange Commission (S.E.C.) rules or regulations that you need to follow.

Generally, an equity investment deal would have a formula for people who are investing money to the entity that is producing the film. For a certain amount of money they will get a certain number of Points. **Points** are usually divided into Producer points and Investor points — two different "pots" of investment within the ownership structure. Investor points are usually paid back up to 125% of the original investment initially. After that repayment, then the Producer Points holders are paid back and then if there is more profit after that, everyone receives profits on a **pari passu** basis. The Latin phrase means "of equal step" and signifies that each entity is paid back with the same rights as every other entity.

Producer points are usually divided according to the producer(s) deals with various cast, crew, and other important people who helped get the film made. Sometimes points are given out to the cast and crew who work for free or deferred as a way of sharing profit participation on the "back end."

Deferred Payment Deals

Another deal that can help make your film possible is a deferred payment deal for cast and/or crew. This means that you are paying cast/crew less than what they would normally work for and the rest is deferred and will be paid if the film becomes profitable. You can make a deal that is completely deferred (cast/crew working for free) or partially deferred (cast/crew are paid something now and paid the rest of their salary later if the film becomes profitable).

Like equity investments, it should be made very clear to the cast and crew that there is a good chance that they may never see any more money. Chances that a film makes a profit are slim. I always advise everyone that they should never expect to see a dime and if they do, it's a bonus. Remember that they don't get paid until all the costs to make and market the film are recouped. The lower these total costs, the better chance that cast/crew will be paid their deferments.

Payment of deferments is usually done on a pari passu basis, as well. So if you have $10,000 worth of deferred salaries but only $5,000 worth of profit, then everyone is paid 50% of the money owed to them. Then if you make another $5,000 of profit a year later, the rest of the money is paid back to the cast/crew.

Union Signatory Film Agreements

SAG Indie is a section of the Screen Actors Guild (SAG) that facilitates several low-budget agreements for films that are made with budgets from $50,000–$2.5 million. There are four of them — short film ($50,000), ultra low-budget ($200,000), modified low-budget ($625,000) and low-budget ($2,500,000). Each agreement outlines a reduced salary for each union actor and the short-film agreement allows for salary deferments for the actors. When working under a salary deferment deal, the producer only pays the actors' salaries if the film is sold. The SAG agreements put the union actors in **first position** to be paid. That means that whatever money comes in, they need to be paid before all others. All the information can be found at *www.SAGIndie.com.*

The American Federation of Television and Radio Artists (AFTRA) is another talent union that covers actors for projects that originate on video. You can find information about the rules for their members at *www.aftra.com.*

Other Funding Options

There are other funding options to explore for your film. These can be done in conjunction with pre-sales and equity investment or they can be the sole way of funding your project.

FISCAL SPONSORSHIP

Perhaps your grandmother wants to donate money to support your film project and writes you a check for that amount. You can take that money and say "THANK YOU." Or you can also take steps to set up a tax exempt sponsorship for your film so your grandma can also get a tax deduction for her generous contribution.

To be able to have your donors take advantage of a tax deduction, you need to obtain fiscal sponsorship with a nonprofit institution that has this option for films. Certain nonprofits (also called a 501(c)3 institution because of the numbers and letters that it refers to in the U.S. tax code) allow you to apply for fiscal sponsorship for your project. They usually request information about the film — the storyline, the production plan, the schedule, and the budget. If it meets with their guidelines then you will be approved and can set up an account with them. Each nonprofit has its specific rules for donations and the administration of the account. Be sure to read them carefully and follow them so you can access your donated money in a timely manner.

In order for your donor to receive a tax deduction, he or she will need to write the check to the nonprofit institution that will earmark the donation for your film. Then you put in a withdrawal request to the fiscal sponsor to receive your funds. Each fiscal sponsor charges an administrative fee of 5-8% that is deducted from any monies that come into your account. If they have a 5% charge and you receive a $1,000 donation, you'll be able to use $950 and the institution will keep $50 for administrative and accounting costs.

For donors who give money to your project, ask if they work for companies that have matching contribution policies for employees who make charitable donations. If the corporation does, they may match the dona-tion, dollar for dollar. A $1,000 donation can equal $2,000.

Not all fiscal sponsorships are the same. You'll need to research which organization would best fit with your project. Some groups have specific criteria geared toward their missions or areas of interest, such as films made by women or Jewish-themed projects, etc. Check *www.ProducerToProducer.com* for more information.

IN-KIND DONATIONS

Another kind of donation is called an **in-kind donation**. An in-kind donation is goods or services, not money. Some fiscal sponsors accept in-kind donations and give a donor a tax deduction for an amount equal to what they gave you. So if a costume rental company gives you clothing that equals $500 worth of rental fees for free, they can get a deduction for the $500. Check with the individual fiscal sponsor to find out their specific rules and regulations.

On my last short film we needed two dozen cupcakes for a scene we were shooting. I live around the corner from one of NYC's famous cup-cake emporiums. I contacted the manager and sent my request in an email and promised that they would get a screen credit at the end of the film. He approved my request and we got $60 worth of cupcakes for free. After we shot the scene we gave all the cupcakes to our crew for dessert after lunch that day.

Many years ago, I produced a two-day music video shoot in Super 16mm for $256 total. Everyone donated everything (we only needed to pay for lunch for two days) and we all had a blast. We really believed in the musical artist and his indie music label and we all wanted to help them by making a great music video that was worth at least $60,000. We asked lots of favors of people and they all said "yes." It can be done but it takes a lot of time and effort to get donations so give yourself enough time in preproduction.

Lastly, when you receive fiscal sponsorship from organizations, check to see if they have any discount arrangements with certain vendors in your area. Some require you to become a member and you are extended the negotiated discounts that the membership includes. This can be helpful in stretching your donated dollars.

Community Involvement

Fostering community involvement is another way to get much needed assistance (financial and logistical) for your film. If your film's script revolves around a certain ethnic group or a specific theme or political cause you should contact the communities that would be in support of the film. There are often mutual benefits for creating outreach to specific groups.

Several years ago one of my students produced a film that had an Armenian protagonist and a major scene takes place during an Armenian American wedding ceremony. That is an ethnic group that is under represented in American films. If you live in a city with a local Armenian community, you could contact them and involve them in your film. They could provide extras for a specific scene or donate props or costumes. You'd be amazed how helpful groups could be if they want to see your project get made.

Alternatively, you may have a documentary about a specific subject that complements a nonprofit organization's mission. They may be able to do a fundraiser for your film and help get the word out to the people who would be most interested in your project.

There's a real craft to asking for donations and discounts. Below are ideas to keep in mind to increase your chances of success.

How to Ask for Donations and Discounts

WHAT: KNOW WHAT YOU ARE ASKING FOR

Do the math. Figure out how much film stock (or whatever you require) you really need to shoot your project. You only get one opportunity to ask for a deal so make sure it is the right amount. You don't want to ask for too much or too little. Be very specific with your request and see what response you receive.

For people who are giving you a donation (cash or in-kind) make sure they know what/how their money is being used. Be specific about what their donations are buying — the costumes or food for the crew for one day or the film stock, etc. It makes them feel more connected to the project and they know how their donations will benefit your project.

WHY: KNOW WHY YOU ARE ASKING

Be specific. "I'm asking for the film stock because I believe this film needs to be shot on film and not video for very specific reasons...." "I'm

‍ing to borrow a dolly for the weekend because we are shooting the climax of the movie and it will make a huge difference on the impact of that scene in the film." "I'm asking for a cash donation because we have already raised x\$ and just need another x\$ to be able to fully finance the film." "I'm asking for a donation because I am a student and this is part of my education." You need to be clear about why you need it and make sure you let the potential donor know why it is so important to you and your project.

HOW: KNOW WHAT THEY WILL GET IN RETURN

Once again, be specific. Here are some options:

1. A screen credit at the end of the film

2. A sponsorship credit in all advertising and press releases

3. A DVD for promo uses

4. A promise to shoot their child's bat mitzvah party the following March

5. An offer for their sister to be an extra in the film

6. A promise of your undying devotion forever

7. A commitment to tell everyone to rent from them in the future or eat at their restaurant

8. An understanding that you will rent from them when you do a commercial shoot with a bigger budget next month

9. Keep the person or company informed about the progress of the film through periodic emails or an invite to the premiere

You may not have a lot of money but there are many ways of "paying" someone back. Let them know what you plan to do and then make sure you do it. Putting it in writing is even better. I often use a donation sheet so I can keep track of who gave what, when it needs to be returned, and the contact details for that person. That way I have all the info on one sheet and I can refer back to it later. It also helps to track the "thank you" screen credits at the end of the film.

WHO: FIND OUT WHOM YOU NEED TO ASK

The receptionist at the rental house probably does not have the authority to give out a free camera package for four days. The person in the rental department probably doesn't either. But you should pitch to them to gauge their reaction. "We are booked for the next three weeks but after the 1st of the month we don't have anything on reserve." Or "the owner got burned last time because the filmmaker didn't return it on time and we lost out on a rental for the next day." So now you know a bunch of details that will help you modify your pitch when you do get to the owner — change your shoot dates to after the 1st of the month and make sure you make it clear that you will put down a deposit for the cost of the rental so if it comes back late they won't lose money. Already you are ahead of the game and addressing some of the obstacles that might make the owner reluctant to say "yes."

HOW: CREATE YOUR BEST PITCH

Rehearse your pitch ahead of time so you have your best chance of getting what you are asking for. Then just ask. Then be silent and wait for the response. If they are not sure and hesitate, offer to follow up with a letter, proposal, or email. Then follow up after that. As long as you don't get a "no," you still have a chance for a "yes."

Carole Dean has written a great book that includes important information about film fundraising titled *The Art of Funding Your Film: Alternate Financing Concepts.* She created the Roy W. Dean grant in 1992 and has given away over $2 million in goods and services to deserving filmmakers over the last two decades. Information about the grant can be found at *www.fromtheheartproductions.com.* When discussing this subject of fundraising she advises: "Filmmakers usually get up to 70% of their donations from individuals and company owners and about 30% from grant organizations and other places. That's about a 3:1 ratio. I think it's important to figure out what percentage of your budget can come from which kind of donor and then put the appropriate amount of time and energy in each area. Divide the budget pie up and then go after the different pieces of the pie."

Grants

There are many organizations out there that give grants to film projects. Most are nonprofit and their application criteria is tied to their mission for the organization. This is particularly useful for documentary filmmakers. Depending on your film's theme or subject matter, there may be grant opportunities. You can do research by reading industry magazines and going to industry websites. Also check out the Foundation Center (*www.foundationcenter.org*) which is a clearinghouse for information about nonprofit foundations across the country. They have comprehensive databases on foundations and their giving history and the Center offers workshops on how to research and apply for grants.

Fundraising Trailers

As discussed in the *Development* chapter, trailers are often required for grant applications and are a very helpful fundraising tool whether your film is a narrative or a documentary. Trailers are usually six to eight minutes long and are edited from footage that you already have acquired and that accurately reflect what kind of film you plan to make. Like writing a strong proposal for your film, it is a real challenge to create a good trailer that will get investors and grant organizations to give you money. But a good trailer can allow you to raise all the money you need for your film. According to grant-maker Carole Dean: "80% of my applicants have trailers. If you don't have a trailer, it is much more difficult to win. With the trailer, the judges can see your filmmaking talents as opposed to just reading a proposal only. It puts you ahead of solely the written word."

Find a Mentor or Executive Producer

Another way to fundraise for your film is to get a mentor or someone who wants to support your project to come on board to help you get funding. If you can get a well-known producer or director to take you under their wing it can be very helpful. Back in the mid 1990s, film director Greg Mottola (*Adventureland, Super Bad*) was a few years out of Columbia University's Graduate Film Program and he befriended Steven Soderbergh. Steven was impressed with Greg's talent, and served as one of the producers to help him make his first feature. With Steven's name behind the project, Greg and his producer Jonathan Stern were able to raise enough money to produce the low-budget indie film *The Daytrippers*.

Beware of Credit Cards as a Way of Funding Your Film's Budget

We've all heard the stories about maverick filmmakers who make their first feature for $50,000 and put it all on their credit cards and then sell it at Sundance for $300,000. Great for them, but the odds of being able to pull that off are extremely low (the cinematic version of winning the lottery).

It's even more competitive to get your feature, short, or documentary sold in the marketplace. The distribution paradigm is constantly shifting and it's very difficult to get your money back and make a profit on any film — even a really good one. I'm not trying to discourage you from making a film, but it's important to have realistic expectations so you don't get into an accumulated debt that could haunt you long after your film is completed.

If you put your production costs on credit cards, you'll be paying them off for years. DON'T DO IT. Find another way. Postpone your production until you have raised all the money and then shoot.

I wrote ALL the money. Lots of people decide to go forward with a film based on having enough money "to get it in and out of the lab" — basically enough money to shoot it (and process the film and transfer to video if necessary) and get to an edited rough cut. They expect to edit the film on their own with their FCP (Final Cut Pro) or a borrowed edit system and then figure out how to finish it after that. Finishing costs for the audio work, mix, soundtrack creation, color correct, additional editing, and mastering can be quite a hefty number. It can be very hard to raise this money after the production has been completed. There are so many unfinished films out there. You can get yourself into a horrible Catch 22 — you don't have enough to finish the film and you can't make any money from the film until you do. Make sure your have a solid plan on how to finish your project completely and properly before you start your production.

RECAP

1. **If you can get pre-sales for various rights to your film, it's a great way to fund your film.**

2. **There are many deals you can create to attract equity investment in your film. Define investor points, producer points, and deferment deals clearly in legal contracts.**

3. **Explore what SAG actor agreements your film can qualify for and apply to SAG for approval.**

4. **Fiscal sponsorship is a good way to attract tax deductible donations to your film. Some organizations facilitate in-kind donations, as well, for use on your film.**

5. Know "who, what, when, how, and why" before you approach vendors for free or discounted goods and services.

6. Consider applying for grants if your film meets the criteria.

7. Do not use credit cards to finance your film. There are other ways to make a film — don't take on personal debt — it's only a movie.

CHAPTER 5
CASTING

CASTING IS AN EXTREMELY important part of your film. You can have a fabulous script but if it isn't well acted and cast with the right actor for each role, you won't have a good film. Getting the best possible actor for each role is essential and you should never go into production unless you have the best actors for each role, for your film. If that means postponing production until you have the right cast, then you might need to do that. It is that important.

As discussed in the *Development* chapter, casting is often a key factor in raising funds for your film. Well-known actors or stars can cinch the deal with investors. Distribution is impacted by what recognizable talent you have in your film. A star's name and picture on the cover of the DVD can make all the difference when someone is making the decision to buy, rent, or download your film.

Hiring a Casting Director

As discussed above, a well-known actor(s) can make all the difference when seeking funding for your project. Ideally you would bring a casting director on board to help you attach talent to your film. Sometimes

"90% of directing is casting."

— *Milos Forman*

"Casting is everything."

— *Albert Maysles*

a casting director will work on a deferred basis – do the work during the development phase and then get paid when the funding is in place. Other casting directors will require payment to come on board during this period.

Once you decide which casting directors you'd like to work with, contact them and discuss the project. *Imdb.com* is a great place to research who cast your favorite films. Look up those films and see who the casting director was. Make a short list of your top casting directors and contact them, one by one. If a director is attached to the project, he or she will want to be a part of the decision making process, as well. If they are interested, then send them the script. Once they have had time to read the script, follow up and find out if they liked the script and want to work on the project.

If they are interested then it's time to make sure you are both on the same creative wavelength. Ask them who they imagine for the lead roles. Listen to which actors they suggest. Do those match the ones on your short list? Are you both in sync? Do you have the same vision for the tone of the project? This is a very subjective area and it is critical that you are both on the same page regarding the actor choices. Good casting directors have the ability to read the dialogue and extrapolate who that character is and who the best actors are to realize that role.

Make sure you feel comfortable and don't just go with a casting director who is willing to work on your film. If you don't share the same creative vision, you should look for a different casting director who is better suited to your particular film.

Once you have determined that you are both on the same page, creatively, then you'll need to discuss schedule and expectations. At that point the casting directors will decide, based on interest and workload, if they want to do the project. Some of the bigger casting directors may like your project but may be too busy to do it themselves. They could offer to have one of their assistants do the job. That can be a good deal because the assistant will be calling agents and actors with the clout and name recognition of the lead casting director, but you will get direct contact with the assistant who can give you and your film more time and attention. It's up to you to weigh all the factors and decide if it is the right situation for you. Once you have a verbal agreement, you should create a written agreement stating the casting fees, timeline, and payment schedule.

If you don't know whom you'd like to cast the film you can get a list of casting directors from your local film commission. Depending on the size of your city, there will be various people available in your area. Research what kind of casting they do. Some specialize in certain areas like children or extras or maybe a certain type of project — like commercials. If you don't personally know their work, get a reel and look it over. If you like what you see, start the process that I outlined above.

Keep in mind that, when attaching talent in the development phase, you do not necessarily have to work with a casting director in your city because it will not usually require any auditions. Your choices will be based on the actor's previous work in other films. So you could hire a Los Angeles- or New York-based casting director to work on your project even if you live in a different city. If you did attach an out-of-town actor to your film, you'd need to be prepared to pay for travel costs, per diem, and hotel for the production period. Be mindful of the ethnic makeup of your cast, as well. Certain cities have larger populations of specific ethnic groups and it might require you to cast from that particular city to get the right actors.

Attaching an Actor or "Star" to Your Film

Casting often takes place at two phases in the process of producing a film. It happens at the development stage and the preproduction stage. When you cast during the development stage you are looking to **attach an actor** to your film. Depending on the recognition factor, it can be very helpful in getting domestic or international financing. If you can attach a well-known actor(s) it often gets investors interested in funding or purchasing pre-sale rights to your film.

Attaching an actor to your film is different from casting all the roles during preproduction for your film. Attaching an actor is when you want to get a verbal and/or written agreement with a recognizable actor that says he or she will play one of the roles, if you get the specified financing for the film. This allows you to shop your film around to potential investors with the knowledge that you have that specific actor(s) attached to your project. For independent filmmakers, a talented and well-known actor can make a big difference regarding your ability to fund the film.

Pay-or-Play Deal

Depending on the level of the stars, they may want a pay-or-play deal to attach their names to your project. In a **pay-or-play deal** you are agreeing to pay them a certain fee, regardless of whether or not the film gets made. In such a deal, the star would agree to receive a specific payment by a certain date that would not depend on the ultimate fate of the film financing. For certain stars, this may be a good deal for you because their names bring enough to the table that it is worth the investment. Most other actors will attach themselves to a project without a pay-or-play deal because they really like it and want to help get it made so they can play the role.

To attach an actor to your film you'll need to draw up a short list of the actors you'd like for the various roles in your film. Discuss with your casting director to get a reality check on which actors might be available and interested in your film. For a cameo role that only requires a day or two of work you might be able to go for a bigger name because it won't require a long time commitment. Short films often can cast well-known actors because they only shoot for a few days.

Once you come up with the game plan for whom you want to go after, you need to work out the offer to the actor. If you are working under one of the talent union contracts (see later in this chapter) the minimum salary for an actor will be dictated by the agreement. You and the casting director may decide that is all that you will pay or you may decide to pay a higher fee to the actor. Whatever the deal, put it in a brief deal memo so it can be sent out to the actor's agent. Depending on each individual actor's recognition factor you may increase or decrease the offer.

Once you have decided which actor you want to make an offer to, your casting director will contact the actor's agent or the actor, directly (if he doesn't have an agent), and send the script, the offer, and a deadline for a response. The actor would not be asked to audition for the role. At this level, there are enough examples of the actor's past work in other films that you already know he'd do a brilliant job. You just offer it to the actor.

For each role, you need to wait until you have gotten a response from that actor before moving on to the next actor on the list. It can be a slow process and that is why the response deadline is important. The casting director will stay in touch with the agent to find out if the actor has read the script and what the reaction to it is. If the actor is interested, the agent will also be able to let you know what dates the actor would be available, based on the current schedule. This is important information to have. If you plan to shoot in the spring but the actor will be in production on another film all spring, it could be a deal breaker. You need to weigh how important that actor is to the project vs. how locked in you are to the shoot dates. Sometimes you can change your production timeline to accommodate an actor's schedule.

Attaching Talent and Casting Without a Casting Director

If you can't hire a casting director, you can cast a film yourself. It means that you will do the process outlined below, yourself, and you won't have the benefit of a casting director's reputation when contacting actors' agents. On the other hand, going through agents can sometimes be a hindrance if you have a very low budget. Agents are paid based on a percentage of their clients' salaries. If an actor takes a no or low-budget project, the agent might not receive any money because the actor isn't earning anything from the project. Depending on the agent and his or her vision for the client's career, this may be a disincentive for the agent to champion your project to the actor.

In this case, it might be better to get the script and offer it directly to the actor if you can. For instance, maybe the screenwriter wrote the script and had Edie Falco in mind for the female lead, the whole time she was writing it. You decide that you'd like to offer Edie Falco the lead role. Without a casting director, the best way to put an offer into an actor is to get a script directly into her hands. Maybe you have a friend, who has a friend who is Edie's hair stylist on her films. Maybe this person would be willing to get it to the hair stylist. The hair stylist reads it and thinks Edie would like it and then passes it to Edie. She may or may not read it. If she reads it and likes it, you may get a phone call or her agent may phone you. The chances are very, very slim. But it's worth a try. Sometimes a star may be interested in a project for other reasons besides money.

As discussed before, when you put out an offer like the above example, you need to wait to hear back from that actor before you can move onto offering it to another actor. This can take up valuable time, but that is the protocol. You'll need to decide if you have the time to wait for a response before your film goes into production. It may be better to put in an offer, do a casting session for all the roles so you have a great cast, regardless of the star's answer and then decide when you need to move on if you haven't received answer. If you decide to do that, make sure to make the actor's agent aware, so there is a chance to get a final answer before you move on.

The Casting Process

For those roles that need to be cast through casting sessions, the process is fairly straight forward. You will first want to create a **casting breakdown sheet** for your film. It is a list of each role and a brief description of the age, gender, ethnicity, and physical attributes of each one. For instance – "24-year-old, Caucasian male, fit condition, and must be able to ride a mountain bike." Once you have the breakdown, the casting director will send it to appropriate agents and also post it to the local actor populations via ads in certain trade newspapers and online casting sites. If you are casting outside of your home city, contact the local film commission for recommendations about the best places to publish your casting notice to get the greatest response to your ad.

If you plan to work under one of the guild contracts (more later in this chapter), then you will need to register your production with the union and get approval of your application. Once approved, the guild will give you a registration number — many of the casting publications will need this number before they will post your casting breakdown for union actors to read/view. Make sure you give yourself enough lead time to apply and register your project with the union before you plan to post your casting breakdown.

Once the ad is up or online, actors and agents will submit headshots and resumes for consideration for a particular role. A **headshot** is an 8x10 photograph of the actor, with a resume usually attached to the other side of the photo. This information allows the casting director to make decisions about who would be right for an audition for each role. Photos can be deceiving, so if you think someone might be right for the role, bring her in for an audition if you have time in the schedule. Depending on the amount of good actors to be seen and the number of roles to be cast, your audition/casting schedule may be multiple days or weeks.

Auditions/Casting Sessions

Casting sessions or auditions are usually held in a space that is either in the casting director's office or in a space that is rented or borrowed for that purpose. The space needs to be big enough to accommodate an actor or two, casting director, director, producer, and casting assistant. The room should have a video camera on a tripod with a monitor and it should have soundproofing so conversations can't be heard out in the hallway. Ideally there are several chairs outside the room for actors who are waiting, reading the sides, and prepping before their turns.

"Sides" is the term used for a portion or scene from the film's screenplay that is copied and given to actors before they audition for the role. Often there is a side for each role – something that, when performed, will give the casting director, director, and producer an idea of the talent and appropriateness of the actor who is auditioning. Usually the copies are put out on a table where the actors sign in, outside the audition room. Each actor reads and prepares before going into the audition. It's a good idea to fax or email the sides to actors before the audition day. It gives them time to prepare so they can give their best performances. If you used an online breakdown service, they often have an email component or the ability to post the sides and then the actors can access them through the website.

The director, casting director, and/or producer, and casting assistant are usually present for each casting session. Sometimes the first session is only with the casting director and is videotaped so the director can look at the tape afterward and make decisions. For a videotaping, each actor is given a consecutive number written on a card and there is a log taken by the assistant. Once the video camera is rolling, the actors say their names, their phone numbers or agencies and hold up the numbers on the cards so the camera can see them. This allows a person to scroll the videotape quickly afterwards, to locate a specific performer. After the session, the tape, log, and all the headshots are sent to the director, along with the casting director's notes. I usually make a copy of the log and DVD for me to keep and refer to, as well. The headshot is helpful because it gives other pictures of the actors, their resumes, and their training – info that is helpful in making a decision. The director will look at the tape and make notes using the log to keep track of which actors he or she likes enough to pick for callbacks.

Callbacks

Creating a callback list is a process that is usually done by the director in consultation with the producer and the casting director. **Callbacks** are second auditions where you can see the actor work more in-depth with the material, allowing for more interaction between director and actor. Asking actors to come in for callbacks means that they are among the finalists in the search for that particular role. Sometimes the director will pair up one actor with another in a callback to see how they look or work together. Directors may pair certain actors with several different partners to see how different pairs play out. Callbacks are used to give directors enough information so they can make their final selections for each role.

Extras Casting

Extras or **Background actors** are any roles that do not require speaking lines or very detailed action that would require specific direction from the director. They are the people sitting at tables in a restaurant behind the table where the principal action is taking place – thus background actors. They are the people walking down the street, standing in line at the hot dog stand, and sitting in the bleachers when you are shooting a scene that takes place at a ball game. There are casting agencies and casting directors that specialize in extras casting — creating the background action to look and work well is a specific skill.

Casting for extras is usually done closer to the shooting dates, not when you are doing the principal-actor casting. As you get close to the production dates, the director will be able to quantify and describe what kind of actors she wants. Extras casting is usually done completely from headshots unless you are in a remote filming area that does not have a ready-made pool of extras who are available to work on your film. In that case, you can do an open call and announce that you are doing a casting session to the local community. An **open call** means that anyone can show up and be auditioned. An article in the local newspaper is a great way to get the word out. Then you can schedule a time and place for people to show up.

On the film *BOMBER*, we shot the film on location in Bad Zwischenahn, Germany. It's a very small town near Oldenburg and they had never had a film shot there before. We were able to get an article in the local newspaper and then set up casting sessions at a room in a nearby hotel. People arrived and they filled out information cards and had their pictures taken. Then they met with the director, Paul Cotter, and he got a sense of how they might work in the various scenes in the film that required extras. Those notes were put on the cards and he used them later to determine whom he wanted in the background for specific scenes in the movie.

Casting, scheduling, feeding, and coordinating background actors is a bit of a job. But for independent filmmaking, nothing says low-budget more then to have a restaurant scene with only your two principal actors in the restaurant. You need to fill the frame with enough people to make it believable. It's important to invest the time and money to get the right people for your scenes.

Casting Schedule

You want to cast as far in advance as possible before your first day of shooting. Ideally, for a feature, you'd want to have a minimum of one month to spend time rehearsing and doing a wardrobe fitting and hair/makeup tests. You want to start the audition weeks or months before scheduled rehearsals so you have enough time to find the best actor for each role.

To Be Union or Not to Be Union...

Screen Actors Guild (SAG) is a guild or union organization whose members are film and television actors. American Federation of Television and Radio Artists (AFTRA) is another acting guild. Both guilds include voice over talent and on screen stunt performers. SAG and AFTRA negotiate a new contract with motion picture and television producers every three years. That contract outlines the minimum payment for each kind of acting job, residual payments, and the conditions and rules that must be followed by all signatories to the contract. A **signatory** is a company or individual who signs the contract and agrees to all the conditions of the contract for all of their productions during the contract period.

If you are a signatory or are working with a signatory company, all the actors need to be in the union. There is one exception called a **Taft Hartley waiver** (named after the Taft-Hartley Labor Act of 1947) that allows a producer to petition to the union to use a specific person who is not yet in the union for very specific reasons. Those reasons allow for people who have not yet joined the union to work on a union film – such as children who are just starting out in the acting business, specific ethnic requirements that cause you to cast outside of the union ranks, or shooting in a remote area of the country where there are no union actors in the local population.

If you want to cast union actors in your film, you'll need to sign and follow the union contract. SAG and AFTRA have created several low-budget contracts specifically geared to independent film productions. The agreements are tied to the size of your film budget.

As mentioned in the *Funding* chapter, SAG Indie is a section of the Screen Actors Guild (SAG) that facilitates several low-budget agreements for films that are made with budgets from $50,000-$2.5 million. There are four of them – short film ($50,000), ultra low-budget ($200,000), modified low-budget ($625,000) and low-budget ($2,500,000). Each agreement outlines a reduced salary for each union actor and the short-film agreement allows for salary deferments for the actors. When working under a salary deferment deal, the producer only pays the actor's salary if the film is sold. The SAG agreements put the union actors in **first position** to be paid. That means that whatever money comes in they need to be paid before all others.

Go to *www.SAGIndie.org* to check out the various contracts and determine which one is right for your production. Keep in mind that it takes some time to file the proper paperwork/application for the SAG contracts. Give yourself some time to fill out the application and get it to the local SAG office, so they can process and get it approved. As mentioned above, some breakdown services, papers and Internet sites require proof of your SAG registration before they will allow you to send out your listing to SAG actors. If that is the case, make sure you give yourself enough time to get registered before you posting your actor breakdown.

As a producer you have a choice to make regarding whether you want to make your film union or non-union for actors. If you decide to work under a union contract you will need to abide by the contract rules and salary specifications. It's your choice and generally union actors have more experience than non-union talent. For actors to join the union they have to work on at least two union projects before they can apply for membership. That means they generally have a certain level of proficiency and talent because that's not the easiest thing to do. This is not to denigrate non-union actors. There are lots of fantastic non-union actors. If you do get Edie Falco to be in your film, she will definitely be a union member and you will need to be a signatory in order to work with her.

Depending on your film, you will decide whether to work under a union contract or not. In smaller cities and markets, most of the available talent may be non-union so that is something to consider, as well. A few of the SAG Indie contracts allow you to mix union and non-union actors in your cast so it might behoove you to sign up, so you have both options when casting.

AFTRA covers actors for projects that originate on video. You can find information about the rules for their members at *www.aftra.com*.

Union Paperwork

If you decide to produce your film under a union agreement, once you register and are approved, you will be given a bunch of paperwork to use during preproduction, production, and the wrap of your film. There will be a form that will list the hours worked by each actor on each day of production. The actors need to approve and sign for each day's work schedule when they are wrapped at the end of each work day. There are also individual short-form actor contracts that need to be signed by each actor and copies given to the actors, their agents, and the union. After you wrap you need to send back the paperwork to your local guild office so they can check it over and keep it on file. Any payments you make to your actors should be paid within 14 days of their work on your project.

RECAP

1. **Hire casting directors based on their reputation and their vision for the roles in your film.**

2. **Attaching a name actor to your film can be a critical factor in attracting investors to your project.**

3. **Pay-or-Play deals allow you to lock in an actor to your film based on specific contractual elements like salary and schedule.**

4. **Creating a casting breakdown sheet allows you to post ads for the roles you are looking for. Auditions and callbacks allow the director to decide which actor is best for each role.**

5. **Extras casting is an important step in making your film the best it can be. Make sure to give this process the time and attention it requires.**

6. **If you wish to work with union actors, you'll need to become a signatory to a guild contract. There are some deferred salary agreements at *www.SAGIndie.org and at www.aftra.com*.**

CHAPTER 6

PRE-PRODUCTION

N ow that you have a great script that is ready to shoot and all the necessary funding for the entire film, you are ready to start preproduction on your film. Practically speaking, preproduction begins the moment you decide to do a film. From that point on, everything you do is, in some way, prepping for the film.

But for the purposes of this chapter, the preproduction phase begins when enough funding is in place to begin scouting, setting up a production office, hiring cast and crew — the final countdown weeks or months when you are taking concrete and specific steps to make your film happen. Your timeline will depend on what needs to be done and how much time and help you have to do it. The preproduction phase ends on the last day before the start of principal photography.

Production Triangle

Preproduction is the most important period in the life of a film. It can make or break your film. So many films have gone off the rails because they didn't have enough preproduction time or didn't get everything accomplished

Eye, mind and heart —

you need the balance of

all three.

— Henri Cartier-Bresson

150

that they needed to do during that period. Now is the time to discuss the one of those immutable laws of nature, like Murphy's Law or the 80/20 Rule. It's called the **Production Triangle** and it is one of those undeniable Truths.

THE PRODUCTION TRIANGLE — You only get 2 out of 3

Good   Fast

Cheap

Most independent films want to be **Good and Cheap** so that means you **can't** have the third side of the triangle — **Fast**. If you want it **Good and Fast,** it **won't** be **Cheap** and if you want it **Fast and Cheap,** it **won't** be any **Good.**

Make sure you get as much time as you can for preproduction. If the schedule is unrealistic, then push back your shooting dates and take more time for preproduction. It is one of the most essential things that help to ensure a successful production. If there is one regret that I have heard over the years, it's the lack of preproduction time — "I wish I hadn't rushed into production." "I wish I had waited longer to find a better actor for the lead." "If I had only taken more time to wait until the DP I really wanted became available...."

You only get one shot, so make it count and take the time and get the help you need to prep your film properly — because you can't make excuses for the film after it is completed. It costs more to repair or cover up a mistake, then to get it right the first time.

Don't get me wrong. I'm not advocating to prep forever and never make the film. At some point you must "pull the trigger" and decide on your shoot dates. Just make sure you've done everything in your power to maximize your film's resources. Because every day spent on good preproduction adds up to a better film in the end.

Need to Get the Money in the Bank

As mentioned earlier, you need to have a final version of the script (no changes to production but there may be additional dialogue changes) and a *locked* budget before you begin final preproduction. You need to know what your film's needs are and you need to know when all the money to fully fund the budget will become available.

It's important to figure out what date you need the majority of the money by (often the postproduction money can be delayed until the editing phase, because much of it will happen a few weeks or months later) and let the director and/or funders know. As the producer you'll need to be clear that if you don't have that sum available (i.e., in a checking account) on that day, you'll have to delay the shoot until the money has arrived.

This is a tough position to take but as the producer it is your job to do it. It is also *your* reputation at stake and the deals that *you* have agreed to for the sake of the production. If you can't follow through on your commitments, then you can't move forward. It's very important to maintain your integrity and the trust of your cast, crew, and vendors.

Preproduction Countdown

This is a general guide on a timeline for doing various preproduction tasks. Your film may require less time or more depending on its unique parameters. Below is a quick reference list. Later in the chapter, each one is explained in detail.

12-9 WEEKS BEFORE PRINCIPAL PHOTOGRAPHY

- Obtain demo reels for all key department heads — director of photography, assistant director, production designer, costume designer, and sound
- Create shot lists and storyboard the film
- Scout for locations and studio space
- Do final script revisions
- Purchase domain name and create initial website for the film
- Begin to create the Production Book

8 WEEKS BEFORE PRINCIPAL PHOTOGRAPHY

- Fill out the SAG application/paperwork for the production and submit to SAG
- Place ads for cast and/or hire casting director and begin auditions
- Hire key department heads (listed above)
- Finalize and lock all locations
- Lock script

- Purchase production cell phones for the director, key department heads and staff or work out a flat monthly rate plan to reimburse them for their cell phone use
- Obtain insurance package quotes
- Test the workflow for the film/video format(s) you are considering for the production

7 WEEKS BEFORE PRINCIPAL PHOTOGRAPHY

- Hold auditions for all roles
- Have DP generate tentative camera, lighting, and grip list for the production
- Negotiate location fees
- Find out about what permits you will need
- Production designer creates props lists and creates set-build designs
- Begin shopping for props

6 WEEKS BEFORE PRINCIPAL PHOTOGRAPHY

- Hold Callbacks
- Put out ads for crew positions/begin calling people for crew positions
- Begin signing location deal memos and release forms
- Finalize bond with SAG and any other completion bonds, if necessary
- Create first draft of the production book

5 WEEKS BEFORE PRINCIPAL PHOTOGRAPHY

- Hire cast and negotiate with agents
- Put out equipment lists to vendors for bids
- Get bids for studio rentals
- Go over wardrobe budget estimate with costume designer
- Go over production design/props budget estimate with production designer
- Hire a still photographer and/or videographer to create set publicity photos, electronic press kit (EPK) and/or "making of" video

4 WEEKS BEFORE PRINCIPAL PHOTOGRAPHY

- Sign/finalize SAG contract paperwork
- Start actor rehearsals
- Sign cast deal memos
- Obtain caterer bids
- Hire assistant camera or video engineer
- Begin wardrobe purchases/rentals

- Pick studio facility
- Pick equipment vendors
- Assistant director creates first draft of production schedule

3 WEEKS BEFORE PRINCIPAL PHOTOGRAPHY
- Sign crew deal memos
- Finalize equipment deals and details
- Obtain insurance certificates for locations and equipment and fax/ email to certificate holders
- Obtain location permits
- Hire transportation vehicles
- Pick caterer or figure out how you will feed your crew good meals
- Do tech scout
- Coordinate extras casting

2 WEEKS BEFORE PRINCIPAL PHOTOGRAPHY
- Fax credit card authorization to vendors for equipment, props, and costumes

1 WEEK BEFORE PRINCIPAL PHOTOGRAPHY
- Buy craft service food and supplies
- Finalize the production book
- Copy final scripts
- Have final preproduction meeting with key department heads
- Create transportation personnel lists
- Work out who's-doing-what lists

FINAL WEEK COUNTDOWN
- Create pick-up/runs lists
- Finalize call times and directions for 1st day of shooting and give out to all cast and crew

Preproduction Countdown Explanations

12-9 weeks before principal photography
- **Obtain demo reels for all key department heads — director of photography, assistant director, production designer, costume designer and sound**

  You will want to obtain reels for key department heads in advance, so you and the director have time to find good people. In larger cities, there are agents that specialize in representing DPs, costume designers, production designers, hair/makeup people, and editors. Get in touch with them and tell them about your project and which positions you are looking to fill. They will ask about shoot dates (some of their clients may be on long-term projects and not available for your dates) and what you have to pay. Depending on the pay scale, the agent will be able to recommend clients. If it is very low pay or no pay, the agent may not have any clients who would accept non-paying gigs, but they may be able to recommend an assistant costume designer who would be willing to work for free to "move up" and get more experience.

You also can put online ads on websites that cater to the local production community where you will be shooting. It's also helpful to watch other independent films and independent features that you admire and check out the credits for anyone you want to contact for your film. Consult colleagues and your mentor to get introductions to talented key department heads whom you are interested in for your project. These collaborators are essential to making a great film. For the producer, this is how you "cast" your crew. It's important to spend the time and energy to get the right people for each key position.

● **Create shot list and storyboard the film**

The director and the director of photography will create the shot list for the film. Many directors like to create storyboards to work out how the film will look on paper when cut together. **Storyboards** are drawings that illustrate the director's shot list in the narrative order of the film. Each drawing is created within a box that is the approximate ratio of the framing of your film. You can read them like a comic strip to see how each shot would cut together to make up each scene. The drawings in each frame are very specific in terms of the film language the director and DP envision for each shot, i.e., medium shot, wide shot, close up, over the shoulder shot, etc.

You can hire a storyboard artist or purchase a storyboard computer software program for the director's use or for someone else to use to create the storyboards. Some programs can allow for 3D dimensionality and camera movements to more closely approximate how the camera would move on the frame. Go to *www.ProducerToProducer.com* for more information.

Some directors like to use a storyboard artist who draws each frame according to the director's description. This works well but, depending on the artist's rate, it may be expensive for your budget. Check out art schools and art programs where you may be able to find an art student who would be willing to do it for an affordable rate. And there is also the old "stick figure" option. As long as the director and DP can communicate the exact shot they have in mind to each other and the rest of the crew, it doesn't need to be fancy.

● **Scout for locations and studio space**
This will be discussed at length in the *Locations* Chapter.

● **Final script revisions**
It's extremely important to get the final changes to the script written as soon as possible. Minor dialogue changes can happen up until the final minutes before shooting, if necessary.

But getting to a final script from a production perspective means the following:

— Locations should be locked. If your script calls for a suburban house, a high school, a restaurant, and an office building… at this stage, you want to lock those in and only be concentrating on *which* one of each type you will choose to meet the aesthetic and production demands.
— You know what happens in each scene and the general action will not change
— Principal roles are locked in the screenplay
— Costume needs for all characters are locked
— Time of day or night is locked
— The majority of equipment needs are locked
— Production design concepts are locked

It's important for you, the director and the writer to have these elements locked in the screenplay before you start approaching key department heads. When they start reading the script they will be assessing the potential of the script creatively and from a production point of view. They need to decide if they are interested in the project on both counts and will have lots of questions for you and the director.

From the director they will want to know what the look and feel of the film is. What are the time period, the characters' motivations, and the creative vision for the film? From there, the key department heads will have questions for the producer regarding schedule and budget. On *MAN ON WIRE,* many of the historical recreation scenes take place on the roof of the World Trade Center where the tightrope walk occurred. A long-running discussion in preproduction between the director, the DP and the production designer was whether or not we would shoot those scenes on top of an actual roof, 50 or more stories in the sky or build it in a studio. This decision would have a big impact on the production designer's schedule and budget and those of the lighting and grip departments.

● **Purchase domain name and create initial website for the film**
Decide what web domain name you wish to purchase for the film. Most films are using *www."title"themovie.com* or *www."title"thefilm.com.* Then create an inexpensive website that you can add on to as the film progresses. You can use it for publicity, for donations, for blogging and for dissemination of information to the cast and crew.

● **Begin to create production book**
The production book is the "bible" for the film. It contains all the contact info (names, phone numbers, email addresses) for the cast and crew, the schedule, vendor information, and driving directions. Start to create it now and add to it as more information is gathered. Below is the template I used for the short film *Red Flag*.

Red Flag

Job

Production Book

New York, NY

Production cell phone #

CONTACT LIST

PRODUCTION COMPANY   **Name**
                          Address
                          Phone
                          Fax
                          Celll
                          Email address

CREW LIST

Producer	Name	Cell Email address
Writer/Director	Name	Cell Email address
Director of Photography	Name	Cell Email address
Assistant Camera	Name	Cell Email address
Gaffer	Name	Cell Email address
Key Grip	Name	Cell Email address
Grip/Electric	Name	Cell Email address
Grip/Electric	Name	Cell Email address
Sound/DIT	Name	Cell Email address
Script Supervisor	Name	Cell Email address
Production Designer	Name	Cell Email address
Art Director	Name	Cell Email address
Costume Designer	Name	Cell Email address
Hair/Makeup/Wig creator	Name	Cell Email address
Casting Director	Name	Cell Email address

Red Flag
4

Editor	Name	Cell Email address
SFX	Name	Cell Email address
Prod. Ass't	Name	Cell Email address
Prod. Ass't	Name	Cell Email address
Prod. Ass't	Name	Cell Email address

SCHEDULE

Friday, September 26, 2008

Shoot day – NYC 4 pages

AM   Location Name
            Address
            Phone

PM   Location Name
            Address
            Phone

Scene #2 – James – 2 6/8 pages
Scene #6 – Joe – 1 2/8 pages

7.00am   Crew call time at Location. Load in and set up
                equipment

9.00am   Begin videotaping Sc. 2 – Date with James

1.00pm   LUNCH

1.45pm   Wrap out equipment.

2.45pm   Drive to next location

3.30pm   Arrive at location. Load in and set up equipment

5.00pm   Begin videotaping Sc. 6 – Date with Joe

6.30pm   Wrap

7.30pm   Drive away

SCHEDULE

Saturday, September 27, 2008

Pick up shots

4.30pm	Begin videotaping extras + exteriors
7.30pm	End videotaping extras + exteriors. Wrap
8.00pm	Walk away

SCHEDULE

Sunday, September 28, 2008

Shoot day – NYC 3 3/8 pages

Location Name
Address
Phone

Scene #4 – Richard – 1 5/8 pages
Scene #5 – Comb Over Man – 6/8 page

6.00am	Crew call time at Bar. Load in and set up equipment
8.00am	Begin videotaping Sc. 4 – Date with Richard
11.30am	Reset for Sc. 5
12.00pm	LUNCH
12.45pm	Final prep
1.30pm	Begin videotaping Sc. 5 – Date with Comb Over Man
4.00pm	Wrap
5.00pm	Drive away

SCHEDULE

Monday, September 29, 2008

NYC Shoot – 4 pages

Location
Address
phone

Scene #7 – Matt – 2 5/8 pages
Scene #8 – Matt – 1/8 page
Scene #9 – Matt – 1 1/8 pages

7.00am	Crew call time at Location. Load in and set up equipment. Coffee vendor cart arrives and sets up
9.00am	Begin videotaping Sc. #7 – Matt + Coffee vendor
12.00pm	End videotaping Sc. #7. Reset for Sc. #8
12.30pm	Begin videotaping Sc. #8 – Matt
1.00pm	LUNCH
1.45pm	Resume videotaping Sc. #8 – Matt
2.30pm	End videotaping Sc. #8. Reset for Sc. #9 at Park entrance
3.00pm	Begin videotaping Sc. #9 – Matt
4.00pm	End videotaping Sc. #9. Reset for Sc. #10
4.30pm	Begin videotaping Sc. #10 – Matt
5.30pm	WRAP
6.30pm	Drive away

Red Flag
9

SCHEDULE

Tuesday, September 30, 2008

Wrap
Editing begins

VENDOR LIST

BATHROOM (PARK)   **Name**
Address
Phone
Fax
Contact name
Email address

CAMERA   **Name**
Address
Phone
Fax
Contact name
Email address

CAMERA LENSES   **Name**
Address
Phone
Fax
Contact name
Email address

COFFEE CART   **Name**
Address
Phone
Fax
Contact name
Email address

FILM COMMISSION   **Name**
Address
Phone
Fax
Contact name
Email address

INSURANCE   **Name**
Address
Phone

Red Flag
11
—

Fax
Contact name
Email address

LIGHTING/GRIP   **Name**
Address
Phone
Fax
Contact name
Email address

LUNCH   **Name**
Address
Phone
Fax
Contact name
Email address

TRAIN   **Name**
Address
Phone
Fax
Contact name
Email address

VAN   **Name**
Address
Phone
Fax
Contact name
Email address

8 weeks before principal photography

● **Place ads for cast/hire casting director and begin auditions**

See *Casting* Chapter for how to hire a casting director, advertise for the roles, and begin auditions.

● **Hire key department heads**

You want to pick the department heads as early as possible because they will have a big impact on the vision for the film and estimated budgets for their departments. So this is where the "casting" of your crew begins. Here's a short list of criteria:

1. Talent

2. Experience

3. Availability for prep and shooting period

4. Interest and vision for the project

5. Work ethic

6. Good connections for potential vendor discounts and favors

7. Good contacts for other crew members for the department

8. Compatibility with director

9. Plays well with others

10. References

11. No yelling and treats everyone with mutual respect

12. Does not lie

13. Communicates effectively

You can place the emphasis anywhere you'd like in this list. But, for me, # 8-13 are high up on my list. Personality, work ethic, and honesty pretty much trump talent and experience for me, every time.

I'm not saying I'd hire someone who was not right for the job but I'm saying that other factors are just as important — and even more so — when you have limited resources and everyone has to pull together to create a miracle. I've changed my feelings about this over the years — I used to tolerate a—holes more, earlier in my career. But I've gotten older and I try not to do that anymore. Life really is too short. I'd rather give the job to a talented, experienced decent person. The nice people need to be rewarded for their decency and I try to do that, one production at a time.

So enough proselytizing. Two last bits of advice — 1) Don't get seduced by a resume or demo reel and 2) ALWAYS CHECK REFERENCES. Almost all of my bad crew hires over the years happened when I was too desperate or felt I didn't have enough time to check references. Learn from my pain. Check them out. Call up and talk to the producer or director on at least two (three is better) of their more recent productions and ask how they were to work with, what their strengths and weaknesses are and would they hire or recommend them in the future. Wait for the answers, listen, and read between the lines, if need be. Follow up with a question if you feel it's important but try not to take too much of the person's time and thank him when you are finished. I always call people back when they ask for references on crew people. Because if they are good, I want to help get them more work and if they are bad, I want to save some other producer from a painful fate.

Here's a good list of questions when you call for a reference:

1. How long have you known him?
2. What position did the person fill on your film? What kind of job did she do — great, good, bad?
3. Would you hire him again? If so, why? If not, why not?
4. What are her strengths?
5. What are his weaknesses?
6. Anything else I should know? Any insights regarding working with this person?

● **Finalize and lock all locations**
See the *Locations* Chapter.

● **Lock script**
As described earlier, you need to lock the script from the production point of view (except for dialogue changes), as soon as you can. If you make major changes after a certain point, it can cause big problems for each department, create delays in the schedule, and add cost overruns for the budget.

● **Purchase production cell phones for the director, key department heads and staff or work out a flat monthly rate plan to reimburse them for their cell phone use**
Often it is cost effective to purchase cell phones on a pay-as-you-go basis for the crew people who need to use cell phones on your production. They are relatively inexpensive and then the production staff can add minutes to the cell phone and control costs for each person.

Another way to do it is to have a crew person get the highest-minute plan for the cell phone and then work out a flat monthly rate that you agree to pay for the added minutes to the phone plan. Do this for text plans, as well.

Have the crew person check out the cell phone company's rules ahead of time. Sometimes the change doesn't take effect until the next billing cycle, so you might need to call sooner if you need to make the change by a certain date, to take advantage of the cost savings.

Invest in a headset or earbuds for your cell and land line phones. As the producer you can save your neck and shoulders a lot of strain if you get one. It also allows you to have your hands free when you need to write or carry something. In many states it is illegal to drive without a headset so you'll need to get one if you will be doing any driving during the prep or production periods of the film. But I make it a rule to not text or call whenever I am driving. It's too dangerous. Either pull over to use the phone or ask someone else to drive if you need to be on the phone.

- **Test the workflow for the film/video format(s) you are considering for the production**

It's very important to test the workflow for production and postproduction for whatever format you decide to shoot your film on. You need to know what all the steps are and if it all works smoothly down the line – i.e., down conversion, duplication, codec, editing system, audio plan and final output to masters. Shoot some material and run it through the various steps so you know it works and what the cost implications are.

7 weeks before principal photography
- **Hold auditions for all roles**

See the *Casting* Chapter.

- **Have DP generate tentative camera, lighting, and grip list for the production**

At this point you should have picked your best two choices for each location and the DP has been able to visit them all with the director. The DP knows what format you are shooting in and the general size of the production. You should be able to get general equipment orders from the DP. Later, when you have your tech scout with the director, DP, gaffer, and key grip, you can get the final, exact lists. But the DP should be able to ball park enough for you now so you can send the list to vendors for bids.

● **Negotiate location fees**

Now that you have your first and second choices for each location in your script, it's important to negotiate your best rate. The *Locations* Chapter goes into detail. Don't forget to negotiate access for your key department heads to visit the locations soon after you have finalized the deals. They will need to visit the locations to take measurements and photos for the prep work they need to do. You'll also want to be able to go back for a tech scout, at a later date.

● **Find out about what permits you will need**

See *Locations* Chapter. Each town, city, county, and state has its own rules about shooting on public property. Make sure you do the proper research and paperwork for any locations that require permits or other paperwork.

● **Update script breakdown**

See *Script Breakdown* Chapter.

● **Production designer creates props lists and creates set-build designs**

At this point, with close-to-finalized locations and an updated script breakdown, the production designer can now finalize the production design budget with an estimate for costs to rent and buy what is needed for the production design, props, landscaping, and set construction. As the producer you want to get this list so you can compare it to the estimate you have in your overall production budget, to see where you stand. If any set building is required, the production designer should have drawings for the design and several bids from builders for how much it will cost.

You then take all these estimates and figure out if you have enough money to pay for it all. Often you won't, so you'll need to discuss with the director and PD ways that you can do things more cheaply. Maybe you decide to shoot in a smaller space so the PD doesn't have to procure so many things for the space and it's more affordable, etc. The discussions are ongoing until you all come up with a plan that works for the creative team and for your budget.

● **Begin shopping for props**

The props master, in consultation with the production designer (PD), will need to begin shopping for props. They will go to prop rental shops, flea markets, furniture stores, discount stores, retail stores, and everything in between to source what is required for the film. By now, they will have discussed the look in minute detail with the director and DP. Is it a period piece or does it take place in the present day? Does it have a look that is very upscale or does it take place in a dingy, low-rent world? They will take lots of digital photos to show the director and DP, to determine what the right props are. Once the director indicates her preference, the props master will price out those items to come up with an estimated budget.

6 weeks before principal photography
● Hold Callbacks
See *Casting* Chapter

● Put out ads for crew positions/begin calling people for crew positions
You can never start too soon looking for crew for your film. I look at it as the "other" casting that you have to do. You cast your crew as much as you cast the actors. And it's just as important.

You need to consider experience, talent, personality, and availability (see list under the department heads list). Because you have limited resources, there are other factors, as well. For instance, one gaffer may have his own lighting/grip truck but the other one is easier to work with. Or one assistant director (AD) is available for the shoot dates but not the tech scout and the other one is usually a 2nd AD and wants to move up and get experience as a 1st AD. Or the best key grip who is willing to work for the rate you can afford is a real pain and will bring down the rest of the crew's morale. Your alternate choice is a grip with less experience but who doesn't have an attitude problem. These are the kind of decisions that you have to grapple with.

The other thing to keep in mind about hiring a crew for an independent film is that most of the time you'll be asking crew members to work for very much below their normal rates. This is where you'll have to *sell* the film to each and every potential crew member. And this is where it is important to be clear about the strengths and merits of the film.

If Edie Falco is going to be the lead actor, then tell the potential crew member as soon as you get on the phone. If the screenplay was picked as a finalist for a screenplay competition at a film festival recently, then mention it. If you've got a well-known DP on the project, that should be of interest to assistant camera people, video engineers, grips, and electrics. So much of putting a great crew together on an independent film is a sales job. But you also need to know if the crew person is good for your project. As mentioned earlier, read their resumes and call their references. A bad or uncooperative crew member is a liability to your production and you need to work hard to insure against it.

Ultimately it is a numbers game. Sometimes you have to call five people to fill a position and sometimes you have to call 50 (no joke). Once I get people on the phone, even if they aren't interested or available for the shoot dates, I always ask them for at least two names and numbers for other people who might be interested. That way, you never run out of people to call. Eventually you'll get to the "yes."

When hiring crew, *always* go with your gut. Even on the phone, you'll pick up on a vibe or get an inkling about a person. I always ask enough questions to make sure I know if they know what they are doing. You can often tell, by *how* they answer the questions, if they have enough experience. Even if you are desperate, don't hire someone you don't feel confident about.

Lastly, there are several crew positions that are notoriously hard to fill with great people. They are 1st AD, AC, DIT, and Sound Recordist. You may have to pay them more than you originally budgeted, to fill the position, but they are crucial and if you don't pay now, you'll end up paying more later.

● **Sign location deal memos and release forms**
See *Locations* Chapter

5 weeks before principal photography
● **Hire cast/negotiate with agents**
Once the director makes his final casting choices, you'll need to book the actors. It's fun to make the phone calls to the final cast picks, but don't forget to call the ones who were in callbacks, but who didn't get the roles. If you have a casting director, she usually takes care of this job. If you don't have one, as the producer, you will need to do it. It's not so easy to do because you are delivering disappointing news, but make sure you make the effort and contact the actors or their agents. Remember that the actors took the time to prepare for the auditions and callbacks and deserve an answer, one way or the other. Thank them for their time and talent and let them know that you have gone with someone else for the role. No need to get into specifics and no need to give false hope. Just inform them and thank them. There may come a time when your first choice has to drop out of the production due to any number of unforeseen circumstances and you may have to recast with someone from your callback list.

Most of the time, whether you are working under the SAG Indie film contract or as a fully non-union production, you will not be paying any of the actors during the production period (they will be working for deferred pay). But that doesn't mean there won't be a negotiation regarding some of your actors. If you have cast a "name" talent to your project or if the actor's agent has some deal points to discuss, you'll want to get the negotiations going as soon as possible. You don't want it to be a week before you shoot and still not have a signed deal memo with your lead actors.

Remember that *everything* is negotiable, so don't despair if the star talent's agent wants lots of potentially expensive conditions for the actor in order to work with him/her. That's an agent's job — to get the most for his or her client. Your job is to figure out what your production can and cannot afford to do for the actor and let the agent know. For instance, you may not be able to give them their own Winnebagos for the length of the shoot, but you can offer them a room at the back of the townhouse you'll be shooting in to be used as a special, dedicated room for their peace and quiet. You can make sure it has a couch, fresh fruit, bottled water, and the actor's favorite magazines, while you are shooting at that location. It doesn't cost the production anything extra but it gives actors the privacy they were asking for.

Remember to keep your eye on the final outcome you want — to work with that actor for your film. The negotiating process may be a bit trying, but if you keep focused on the outcome, it will be easier for you and best for the production.

● **Put out equipment lists to vendors for bids**

As mentioned earlier, you will have researched equipment rental houses and the DP may have some recommendations or places she rents from on a regular basis. Send out the list to the person in charge of the rental department at each place. They may want it faxed or emailed. Then they will take your list and "bid it out." Usually their computer will spit out the list price and then in a separate column or on the bottom they will discount the price 5, 10, 15, 20 or 30%. No one ever pays the list price, but it's the size of the discount that is most important. If you have a personal connection or if the director or DP does, let the rental agent know before they do the estimate, that way they can give you a good discount before they send it to you.

Depending on the format you are shooting in, you may think about buying a camera, tripod, or other piece of equipment. Prices for video equipment are getting more and more affordable and sometimes it's cheaper to buy and resell afterwards or rent it out to others after you are finished shooting your project. Think about it, do the research and get bids for purchases if you think it might make financial sense.

THE IMPORTANCE OF VENDOR RELATIONSHIPS

Having good long-term relationships with the people and companies that rent equipment, locations, vehicles, props, etc., is extremely important to being able to do your best for your production. Vendors are partners with you in the making of the film in the same way as the cast and crew. If you have a good working and respectful relationship, vendors can really help you regarding service and budget.

It's important to be loyal to vendors who help you out. I've been working with the same vendors for decades and we have an ebb and flow to what kind of deals I make for each project. There are some projects that I can pay full rate for, and I do. There are other projects that I do for "love" not money, and that's when I can ask the vendor for a favor and deep discount in order to get the things we need to make the project happen properly.

Another way to pay back such a favor is to recommend the vendor to other producers for their productions. If you like the vendors, it's easy to recommend them and I also tell the other producers to let the vendors know that I told them to call. That shows the vendors that I am serious about helping them out in any way I can to build up their businesses.

You can't ask for a favor EVERY time or vendors will get resentful and balk. But if you rent from them over the long term, you build up a trust and understanding that you both need each other and you help each other out.

● Get bids for studio rentals

At this point you'll know if you will need to shoot in a studio or on location, or a combination of the two. If you need to do a set build, you'll need to rent a studio. Once again, get a few bids from several studios so you can compare estimates.

● Go over wardrobe budget estimate with costume designer

By now the costume designer will have priced out all the wardrobe for the film. If the film is not a period piece then, hopefully, the costume designer can augment the costume list with clothing that the actors bring to set from their closets. This will save you wardrobe rentals/purchases and it means that the clothes will already fit the actor well. Note: the SAG contract requires nominal fees to be paid to an actor for each outfit you rent. With non-SAG actors you may pay them fees or they may allow you to borrow their clothing for the shoot at no charge.

Double check to see if you need "multiples" for any pieces of clothing. Anything that is going to get damaged or altered during a scene will require you to have more than one for multiple takes.

Anything that can't be acquired from the actors' closets will need to be purchased or rented. The costume designer will do the research and send you a line-by-line estimated budget for clothes, shoes, accessories, and cleaning to cover all of the outfits needed for the entire production.

● **Go over production design/props budget estimate with production designer, props master, and set designer (if applicable)**

Like the costume designer, you'll need a line-by-line estimate from the production designer. This master budget will include any prop rental and purchases and set construction costs. Once you have the estimate you can start brainstorming on how to lower the dollar amount — either through discounts and donations or any cheaper alternatives that the PD and director can approve.

The production design section of the budget is often a large percentage of your total costs. Anything you can do to reduce costs in this area will have a big impact on the rest of the budget. Creative solutions in the production design/props/set departments are also possible because there can be some flexibility on how something looks on screen. How that is achieved is often open to various options for the director and the production designer to consider and work out.

On the feature documentary *Wisconsin Death Trip*, the film recreates stories from a newspaper that was published in the 1890s. It was a period film and we had a very low budget. One of our smart solutions was to shoot almost entirely at historic sites throughout the state of Wisconsin. Every state has many historic homes and locations that have been preserved by local, state, and federal entities. They are visited by thousands of people per year and are filled with historically correct, and sometimes priceless, antiques. We were granted permission to shoot at almost every site that we requested, usually for a very small donation fee.

● **Hire a still photographer and/or videographer to create set publicity photos, electronic press kits (EPK) and/or "making of" video**

Most distributors will expect 50+ high resolution (300 dpi or higher) still photos from the set of your film. It's important for publicity purposes to have photos that show the director, DP, crew, and actors working on the set. Some deliverables lists may ask for an EPK or a "making of" video.

These are not usually required for low-budget productions but, if you have the resources, now would be the time to hire a photographer and videographer so they can visit your set for a few days during the production period.

4 weeks before principal photography

• Sign cast deal memos

After you have negotiated your talent contracts, you'll draw up deal memos that reflect the understanding you have with your actors. You can download a template at *www.ProducerToProducer.com* that can be customized for your use. Usually talent agreements are negotiated on a most favored nation basis (see *Budgeting* chapter). That means whatever you negotiate for one actor, the other actors will receive the same deal. Make sure you are clear about each deal with your actors.

If you are working under a union agreement you will use a union work contract for each actor. This contract is tied to the guild agreement you would have signed previously (see *Casting* chapter) and will cover the rights to the use of their appearances in your film. If you are using non-union actors they will sign a talent-appearance release form in addition to the deal memo, so you have the proper rights to use their images in your film.

• Start actor rehearsals

Once the proper paperwork is signed, you'll be free to schedule rehearsals. Talk to the director to find out how often she would like to rehearse with the actors and how. What kind of space would she like — an apartment or "black box" rehearsal space? You can rent a space but to save money you can often borrow a space or classroom. You can use friends' apartments if they work during the day and you keep your hours between 9 a.m. — 5 p.m. Another possibility would be to borrow an office conference room, if you decide to do rehearsals on a weekend.

As you get closer to shooting, it may be helpful to rehearse in the actual locations. If that's not possible, you can put tape on the floor of a studio to mark off the space. The director may decide to work separately with each actor and then bring them together later in the process. Check with the director and find out how she likes to do it. Remember to not let them *over* rehearse. That can be as bad as not having enough rehearsal time.

• Hire Assistant Camera or Video Engineer

You'll want to have the assistant cameraperson (AC), digital imaging technician (DIT) or video engineer locked in by now. These positions are critical to the look of the film and directly interact with the DP. Often the DP will recommend good and trusted crew people and give you names and numbers to call. Make sure you check references and that the DP approves whom you finally decide to hire.

Every crew person is critical but department heads are particularly important as key collaborators and managers of the crew who work in their departments.

● Begin Wardrobe Purchases/Rentals

Once you have approved the wardrobe budget you need to communicate the bottom line number to the costume designer and make sure he agrees to keep to that budget. It's very important to be clear about what you expect. Let him know that you are signing off on a specific amount of money for costume rentals/purchases to clothe everyone in the film and it will not cost more than $XYZ. The costume designer should sign off on this amount and agree that if he thinks he may be going above this amount for any reason, he has to let you know *immediately* because *only you* can authorize him to spend any more money.

In each crew person's deal memo there should be a section that outlines this procedure. You never want to be in the position of getting handed a bunch of receipts that any department head expects to be reimbursed for but that exceed the allotted budget.

Keep in mind that sometimes things change. Maybe there are additional costumes added to the list or a certain (cheaper) costume rental was on hold — but when the costume designer went to pick it up from the rental company it was still out to another production and he now has to rent a more expensive alternative. These things need to be discussed as soon as the costume designer finds out so you can be aware of potential overages. You, the director, and the costume designer can discuss it and decide what to do.

● Credit card/cash deposits for Production Design and Costume Design rentals

When production designers, props masters, or costume designers need to rent things, they will have to put down cash or credit card deposits, usually for the value of the props/costumes rented. That way, if anything happens to the rentals, the rental houses are assured they will be covered for their losses. Depending on how many rental companies are used, you will need to fax or scan/email over credit-card authorization sheets to the stores. These are usually forms that the stores send for you to fill out with production company/credit card info, for the deposit and/ or rental charges. They also usually require a copy of the front and back of the credit card and a copy of the credit card holder's driver's license. This is to avoid fraud. I suggest that you make copies and/or scan copies of the front and back of the credit card with the driver's license. Keep these in a safe place — they will save you time when you have to send the documents to various rental companies. Remember to confirm that all the paperwork is in order, a few days before the production design or costume design departments have to pick up the clothes. This will save time on pick-up day, so there is no delay for the departments in procuring the rentals.

● **Sign out petty cash to key department heads**
At this point in preproduction, the production design and costume design departments will need petty cash for their purchases, as well. They will "sign out" on a Petty Cash Sign Out Sheet for the amount of money they are given. The department heads will make the purchases and keep all the receipts. Anything they do not use for the shoot can be returned and refunded back to the production. Throughout the shoot the department head will reconcile all the petty cash on a Petty Cash Sheet, using all of the receipts.

You want to keep a revolving line of petty cash for each department. Once a certain amount of money has been reconciled, a new infusion of cash can be given out. That way there is never a large amount of unaccounted cash out at any given time. It allows you to track spending and keep on top of your actualized budget so you know where you stand.

Wardrobe purchases and rentals will happen all the way up to, and sometimes during, a shoot. It's best to organize it ahead of time but sometimes there are last-minute changes due to script changes or a casting change.

HOW TO RECONCILE PETTY CASH

Reconciling petty cash is an important skill to have. It may seem like an easy thing to do but I can't tell you how many people have trouble with it. Here are the steps for the crew person you are giving the petty cash to:

1. Count out the money that you are given and then sign out for that amount with the producer.

2. Keep petty cash separate from your own personal money.

3. Pay for production-related expenses with cash and obtain a receipt for everything you pay for. If you can't get a receipt (i.e., parking meters, gratuities), write down the amount on a piece of paper with the date, the amount and what it was used for.

4. When you are ready to give the money back to the producer, tape up each receipt on scrap paper and number them.

5. Get a petty cash reconciliation envelope from the producer and fill in the info for each receipt.

6. Add up each receipt and total it for the receipt total.

7. Add up the total cash you have on hand for the cash-on-hand total.

8. The receipt total and the cash-on-hand total should equal the total amount you were given.

9. If the amounts do not total correctly, go back and check your math or find missing receipts until the totals are correct.

10. Hand in all the paperwork, receipts, and cash to the producer and make sure the producer takes your name off the petty cash sign-out sheet and closes out the amount.

● **Pick studio/stage facility**

Once you have bid your job out to several studios you'll have an idea of the various costs. Make sure to go over the bids thoroughly. One studio may charge a flat fee for 10 hours and another stage may charge a higher fee for 12 hours. But when you add in the two hours of overtime (OT) for the first facility, you realize it is more expensive if you plan to go for 12 hours or more.

Remember to factor in the other costs for **green rooms** (holding areas for actors), tables and chairs, hair, makeup and wardrobe rooms, electricity, dumpster fee, cartage, and studio manager rates, so you know you are not comparing "apples and oranges" between the three bids.

There are also other factors to consider — how far a distance do cast and crew have to travel? Are there tolls? Once you multiply several vehicles times $7 RT for tolls, you may find the studio is not such a great bargain. Or the travel time to get there and back adds two hours onto each shoot day and blows your tight shooting schedule. Once you have analyzed the bids, discuss with the director and key department heads to find out if there are any other mitigating factors that concern them.

Then make your decision. And then negotiate the best rate you can. Use the other bids you received as leverage in your negotiation. If it's a multiple-day shoot, maybe you can get them to not charge you for the build day or the strike day. Always put the studio "on hold" but don't "confirm" until you must and you know you are definitely going to use it.

HOLD/CONFIRMATION PROTOCOL

Reserving studios, equipments, and locations all work on a **hold, confirm,** and **challenge** system. You need to know these terms and understand them so you don't put yourself on the hook for commitments you can't keep.

If you confirm, then you have "bought it" and if the shoot gets cancelled or postponed you still owe the studio or equipment house for the rental costs for the days that you confirmed, because the studio couldn't rent it out to another company for those days.

So the best thing to do is put a hold on the facility for all the dates you need. Ask if you have a 1st or 2nd hold. If you are reserving far enough in advance you'll probably have a 1st hold. The next person/company that wants the same dates will have a 2nd hold. As the dates get closer, the other production many decide to confirm and will put in a challenge for that date(s). The studio will then call you and give you 24 hours to confirm or you lose the date(s). If you confirm, then you "own" the dates and will need to pay for them whether you shoot or not.

This is the way it works for equipment rentals, studios, locations, and freelance personnel. It's a pretty fair system and it's important to understand and follow the rules of the game. Your word is your bond in this business. Make sure you honor your commitments.

● Pick equipment vendors

Picking equipment vendors is very similar to picking a studio/stage. You'll be making the decision based on price, availability of what you need and also other factors like reputation for service, quality, and reliability.

Consider this — you are out on location and a light stops working on the set and the vendor can't come out with another unit until the next day. Is that the best vendor for you? Maybe another vendor will charge a bit more, but give you a back up light and cable in case there is an equipment problem at a far away location. It may be a better deal in the long run. Those are the kind of things that make a big difference and need to be factored into your decision on whom to hire. Remember when shooting at a studio, the facility usually has its own equipment and usually insists that you rent lighting and grip equipment from it, during your shoot.

● Assistant director creates first draft of production schedule

The 1st assistant director is the person who should create the production schedule for the film. If money is tight and you as the producer know how to create a production schedule, it might make sense to do the first draft yourself.

The schedule will be based on the latest draft of the script. Each scene will have a number that will be locked in from this point forward. If scenes are added or subtracted they will receive scene numbers like 1A or 2A, then 2B. The AD will break them down into the smartest and most efficient way of shooting the film. Shooting chronologically (according to what happens in the script) rarely is the most efficient way to shoot a film. You will most likely be shooting the film out of sequence, based on factors like location availability, weather conditions, geographic considerations, actor availability, technical requirements, etc.

Once the first breakdown is completed, it is disseminated to the key department heads and they will go through it and make comments about the feasibility of it for their departments' schedules. Maybe a set needs to be built and it won't be completed until the second week of principal photography. The AD will have to reschedule those scenes for after the set construction completion date. On *MAN ON WIRE,* we had a seven-day shoot for our NYC historical recreations. Our interior apartment location was not available at the beginning of our shooting period because another film was shooting in it. We had a two-day shoot schedule for 7 World Trade Center and that had to happen on a weekend. So it meant that we HAD to shoot the big set construction in a studio as our first shoot day. We would have much preferred to shoot that later in the schedule, but we were forced to make it our first day of principal photography by default.

3 Weeks before principal photography
● Sign crew deal memos

At *www.ProducerToProducer.com* you'll find a sample crew deal memo. You can amend that one or create your own. At the very least, it should state the crewperson's name, address, phone, social security number, paid rate for the job, dates of employment, title, screen credit, and rules of employment.

● Finalize equipment deals and details

Make sure to finalize your deals for equipment now. Be clear about what you need and let the vendors know if you may be changing some of the order as you get into the final week of prep. Work out your money deal at this point so you know what to expect.

Also discuss what the insurance certificate should read so you can request one for each vendor now. Make sure to work out *how* you will pay for it, too. If this is your first rental with this company you will probably have to pay on a C.O.D. (cash on delivery) basis. Find out if they need a check ahead of time. Some companies will only accept a company or certified check. Some will allow you to pay via credit card. Work out these details now and make sure you have done all the proper paperwork for each vendor so there are no problems when your crew picks up the equipment, props, etc., closer to the production period.

● Obtain location permits

Depending on where you are shooting for your exteriors and certain other buildings, you may need to acquire location permits. Contact the film commission that has jurisdiction for the towns, cities and/or states that you will be shooting in. *www.afci.org* has the listings for U.S. and international film commissions. See the *Locations* Chapter for more information.

● Obtain insurance certificates for locations and equipment

Insurance is a critical part of producing any film production. The *Insurance* Chapter has a wealth of information. Please read that over before proceeding. Any individual or company can obtain insurance for a production and there are many insurance brokers that cater to the film business. Some of them allow you to fill out a form online and then get a quote via email. Go to *www.ProducerToProducer.com* to get a list of insurance companies/brokers.

At this point in preproduction, you want to send out the insurance certificates to all your vendors and any locations at which you may be shooting. You'll need to obtain the information for each location and vendor and then forward it to your insurance broker who will create an insurance certificate that you can give to the location owner or vendor. This certificate assures them that your general liability and production insurance are in effect and will cover any loss or damage due to your production, less the deductible that your policy dictates.

● Hire transportation vehicles

At this point you'll need to figure out how many vehicles you have to rent for the production. Certain departments may need their own vehicle(s) such as the art, camera, grip & lighting, and wardrobe departments.

These may need passenger vans, cargo vans, and/or trucks. Depending on your studio or locations, you may need to transport cast and crew to/from the set each day. Add up how many people you need to transport and then put the appropriate number of vehicles on hold.

Remember that not all cast and crew will have the same call times, so you have to figure out how many people will travel at the same time. Perhaps you can do two "runs" to the set in the morning in the same vehicles if there is enough turnaround time but, generally, that is not possible. Also keep in mind that you'll need to rent vehicles for errands, pick ups, or runs. Sometimes the cheapest way to cover this situation is to get production assistants who have their own cars and pay them for the mileage they put on their cars on a per-mile basis or pay for gas and tolls during the production period.

Regarding the vehicles you rent (vans and trucks), be sure to have enough *qualified* people to drive them. Make sure the PA (or other crew person) has experience and is comfortable driving a van or truck — 14-foot trucks can be a daunting challenge for uninitiated drivers. You don't want an accident or damage to the rental caused by a driver's inexperience. You may need to hire professional drivers for some of the vehicles.

Early in my career, on the first shoot day of the first short film I produced, we had to drive 45 minutes across the Lake Pontchartrain Causeway Bridge out of New Orleans, LA. I had worked out, with all the PAs, who was picking up which cast and crew member and driving which vehicle, the night before. We all set out at 5 a.m. the next morning, crossed the bridge and arrived at the location right on time at 6 a.m. As we were setting up, we realized that our lead actor was not on set. I queried the assigned PA/driver and she let out a gasp when she realized she had picked up the other two actors but had forgotten the lead who was still waiting for her back in his apartment in downtown New Orleans. It was going to be at least an hour-and-a-half roundtrip for the PA to go pick him up and get him to set. We had already blown our first day's shooting schedule before the day had even begun.

● **Pick caterer or figure out how you will feed your crew good meals**

I almost titled this book, "Feed Your Crew Every 6 Hours" because I believe that is one of the most important things to do as a producer on any film. I wasn't kidding and I'll tell you why.

Any production runs on the stomachs of the crew. It's very important. Sometimes your crew is not being paid at all or very little, so the only thing they are getting each day for their labors on your film is food. So make it really good. It also shows that you value and respect their contribution to your project and you want to honor that by serving good food at meal time and on the craft service table. It isn't going to be cheap but it will be the best money you spend on your film. A well-fed crew is a happy crew. And a happy crew gives its all to you and your project.

If you choose not to hire a caterer you can hire a friend or family member who is a great cook to buy all the ingredients at a discount warehouse store and make home-cooked meals for your crew. Explain to them that they will need a place to prepare the food for a cast and crew of 20-40 people and will have to serve the food at the specific time and keep it hot until then.

The other thing I have done for crew meals is to canvas the neighborhood I'm shooting in a few weeks ahead of time and find out what kind of restaurants can make platters of food that we can bring to the set for lunch or dinner and serve to the crew. Lots of ethnic foods work well this way, but make sure it is high quality and does not have any MSG, in case crew members have reactions to that ingredient.

Lastly, remember to poll your crew prior to finalizing the menu to find out about food allergies, vegetarianism, and any kind of special diet requirements you need to be aware of. You don't want anyone to get ill and you don't want to have to send a PA to run out to get a "special meal" for someone who can't eat what you have ordered for lunch that day.

● **Do tech scout**

The **tech scout** is when the director, producer, and department heads go to each location and work out all the logistics for each shoot day. The crew should include the director, producer, DP, 1st AD, gaffer, key grip, sound recordist/production mixer, production designer, location manager, production manager, and PA/driver.

The director and DP will have the close-to-final shot list and will "walk through" what will happen in each space. The DP will discuss lighting and grip requirements with the gaffer and key grip. The production designer will go over the plans for what will be in each space and how it will look.

If you have a location manager, he will be there and will discuss the rules for shooting in the space — i.e., no smoking, garbage disposal, what entrance can be used, shooting times, parking, etc. If you don't have a location manager, the producer should have all the details.

The sound recordist will be listening to the space and deciding if there are any problems that need to be discussed, such as turning off central air conditioning or refrigeration. If there is a construction project across the street, it may impact your shoot there from 7:00 a.m. to 4:00 p.m. Try to go to the location on the same day of the week that you plan to shoot so you can learn if there are certain things that might affect your shoot on that day of the week. Discuss with the location owner anything that might have consequences for your production — garbage pick-up schedule, landscaping, building construction, apartment renovations, school children playing in a nearby playground, freight elevator operation schedule, parking regulations, etc.

The producer and the production manager will be listening to all of these issues and concerns and taking copious notes. Each key department head will have his or her own specific questions, concerns, and requests that you will need to follow up on. Don't worry, at some point your head will want to explode with all the specific requests and details that each department head is bringing up. But it's OK because you want to know about all these things NOW. This will allow you to address them and work them out so they do not plague you on the shoot day when you have scores of people, lots of pressure, a tight shooting schedule, and a lot of money at stake.

HOW TO DO A TECH SCOUT

1. Schedule the tech scout far enough in advance so that you can have all the key department heads there — director, producer, production manager, 1st AD, DP, camera assistant/video engineer, gaffer, key grip, sound recordist/production mixer, production designer, and PA/driver.

2. Arrange the scout in the most time-saving way. Start south and move north or start east and move west — whatever makes sense for the city or town you are scouting. Keep in mind traffic patterns — don't schedule the scout to start in the middle of rush hour — and avoid as much of it as you can with canny scheduling.

3. Create a schedule on paper that reflects travel time and how much time you'll need to go through each location properly. If you are shooting at a house and will be using four different rooms and the backyard, it will take more time to scout than a small Manhattan apartment. Make sure to give enough time for a full discussion in each location with the director. The crew will need to take measurements and notes so they can have all the info they need to plan for their departments.

4. Check with each location owner and make sure they can accommodate the date and time that you wish to scout. Tell them that you will have a small posse in tow so they don't freak out when you arrive with so many people. Non-film people are always surprised that it takes a small army to make a film and it's best to prep them so they are not overwhelmed by the crew's arrival.

5. If there is a house electrician or maintenance person who will be a key interface for the location, ask the owner if that person can be available for you to meet with during your visit. The gaffer will need to talk to the electrician and many others may have questions of a technical nature for the maintenance person. Some office buildings have HVAC personnel (Heating, Ventilation, and Air Conditioning) and it would be good for the sound recordist to talk to them about sound that may be emitted by these systems.

6. Schedule enough travel time between each location or you will fall behind in your schedule.

7. After six hours, schedule a lunch break. With a crew of about 10 people you'll need to make a reservation somewhere so you can get in and out easily. Keep in mind the crew's food preferences/allergies and choose a restaurant/diner that can accommodate them. Don't do drive-thru at a fast-food restaurant. Everyone needs to sit down and have a proper meal to fuel themselves for the rest of the day.

8. For a crew this size, rent a 15-passenger van and get a PA/driver if you can afford to do it. It will keep everyone together so you all arrive at each location at the same time and allow people to discuss questions with each other while in transit.

9. Make sure to bring bottled water for everyone so no one gets dehydrated. You may decide to do a coffee run sometime during the day, too — it keeps everyone's energy up.

10. Once you arrive at the locations, meet with the owners and introduce them to the crew. Then move to the first area/room you plan to shoot in and start the tech-scout discussions.

11. The director will go through the shot list for the area with the DP so everyone knows what will happen in the scene, where actors will move to, where the camera will be and what shots are planned for the scene(s). The 1st AD may add info that is relevant for the crew, like the sequence of scenes that are scheduled for that day.

12. After the director has taken everyone through the sequence, the crew will quickly and succinctly ask pertinent questions. Certain issues/problems will come up and often they can be solved right there on the spot. If the discussion gets too long, you may suggest that it be tabled until another time so you can keep on schedule. Play it by ear.

13. Continue in this way until you complete all the locations scheduled for the day.

14. If you fall behind, call the next location to inform them of your delay.

● **Obtain final equipment lists and send to your vendor**

After the tech scout, the gaffer, key grip, and assistant camera/video tech, within 24 hours, will send you their final detailed equipment lists. Hopefully, they are not too different from the original guestimates. Take the lists and forward them on to your equipment vendors. The vendors will tweak their bids and you will negotiate the final deals for all of your equipment.

● **Coordinate extras casting**

If your film requires **extras** (non-speaking actors who appear in the background), you will need to cast and coordinate them. Depending on how many you need for each shoot day and how specific they need to look, this often is a separate casting job.

Ideally, you'd have an extras casting director. If that is not possible, you'll need to get a coordinator to take on this challenge. The key is to find a very organized person in charge of this job. (See *Casting* Chapter)

2 Weeks before principal photography

● **Fax credit card authorization to vendors for equipment, props, and costumes**

You want to finish up as much paperwork as you can two weeks before principal photography. Make sure you have sent in all your paperwork to the vendors at this time. Call every vendor to confirm receipt of the paperwork. Nothing can destroy a tightly packed pick-up schedule the day before you start shooting faster than PAs waiting at the rental house for the correct paperwork to be faxed over.

When you do get confirmation of your order and the paperwork make sure to get the name of the person you spoke to. When you give the PA all the pick-up info two weeks later you should include the contact person's name and phone number, as well.

● **Fax insurance certificates to vendors, etc.**

For all the above reasons, you want to get this paperwork into the vendors now so you have less to do during the final two-week crunch period. Coordinate with your insurance company so that each location and rental place that requires an insurance certificate has received it.

● **Fill out tax resale certificates and send to vendors**

As mentioned in the *Budgeting* chapter, each state allows for production companies to use resale certificates when purchasing goods or services that contribute to the production of a film. This allows the production company to avoid paying sales tax on these items at the time of purchase if they are used to make the film. This is because when the film is completed and sold, sales tax will paid at that time and the government realizes that would be a double-tax situation. You can obtain the resale certificate form for each state's tax authority. Fill it out and give to the vendor you are purchasing goods or services from and they will not charge sales tax for your transaction.

● **Create transportation personnel lists**
Transportation of cast, crew, equipment, props, and costumes can be a surprisingly complex task for your production. If the location and/or studio are not easily accessible by reliable and cheap public transportation or if your crew don't have access to their own vehicles, you will be responsible for getting them to and from set every day. If you have a transportation captain, he will coordinate the schedules and vehicles for the daily production. If you don't have a dedicated crew person, then the job falls under the production staff duties. This is a critical job and needs to be taken care of properly. Transportation problems are the number one reason why schedules get delayed on shoot days. Make sure someone is on top of this job on a daily basis.

Keep in mind the individual cast and crew call times for each shoot day. One actor may need to be on set at 7:00 a.m. and another one has a call time of 12:00 p.m. You'll have to make separate arrangements for each actor. For people (cast and crew) who have the same call times, it works best to have a central place where everyone meets and then have a seven- or 15-passenger van take them to the location. Depending on the size of your cast/crew you may need more than one van. Also remember that you will need to have a competent and experienced driver armed with accurate driving instructions to set for every shoot day. You don't want the production's driver to get lost on the way to set.

The other vehicles you need to coordinate are the vans and trucks that will be used for picking up and delivering equipment, props, set pieces, and wardrobe. Certain departments (art, camera, wardrobe, construction) may rent vehicles for exclusive use by their departments. But the production department will need at least one van for pre-shoot day pick ups and errands throughout the production. Figure out who will be driving it each day and make a schedule with all the necessary driving directions, addresses, phone numbers, and contact personnel.

In many cities there are two designations of license plates — commercial and personal. If you own a car, you'll have a personal license plate. If you own a truck or van and use it for transporting produce, equipment, or materials, the state will designate it as a commercial vehicle and there will be different regulations that pertain to that vehicle when on the road. In certain cities, commercial vehicles can park in certain areas on the street that allow for loading and unloading to do business. Sometimes there are also different tolls that are charged to commercial plate vehicles on roads and bridges. In most states, 15-passenger vans, cargo vans, and trucks have commercial license plates. Make sure you know the rules of the road for commercial vehicles in the area that you will be driving for your production.

For productions that need to transport people and equipment in and around the greater New York City area, there are special rules for vehicles that have commercial plates. Commercial plate vehicles are NOT allowed to drive on certain roads in NYC. In other cities and states, vehicles can be banned from using certain roads or bridges due to license designation or weight limits. Make sure all production drivers know and follow these rules. Otherwise you'll get a very expensive citation and in some cases, a truck could get stuck under a low underpass — an absolute nightmare.

1 Week before principal photography
● Buy craft service food and supplies

Craft service refers to the food and beverages that are provided to the hard-working crew and extras throughout the shoot day. The origin comes from the term to provide "services for the crafts." Usually, it is laid out on a table and it can be anything from elaborate and expensive (handmade gourmet treats and made-to-order cappuccinos) to minimal (coffee, tea, water, fruit and bagels). Your budget will probably be more along the lines of the latter but it's still important to have craft service and keep it stocked during every day of shooting. Crew and cast work very hard and need to have snacks and beverages available throughout the day for energy and hydration.

When affordable, a professional craft service person can be hired to buy, prepare, and service craft service. On tighter-budget films, a PA may be assigned to purchase the craft service food and supplies and to set it up as a self-service table.

GREEN PRACTICES IN FILM PRODUCTION:

Following green and eco-friendly practices when producing a film is good for the environment. The Producer's Guild of America (PGA) has been working to address this issue and there is good information provided on the website *www.pgagreen.org*.

There are several ways green practices impact craft service. Providing water to everyone throughout the day is an important job for the production team. Dehydration is a serious issue and it's important to make sure everyone has enough water to stay hydrated. Providing disposable individual bottles of water is expensive and adds a lot of plastic to landfills over the course of a production. I prefer to give everyone bottles for water on the first day of production and put their names on them with a sharpie pen. Then I provide large containers of chilled water on the craft service table and people can fill up their bottles throughout the day.

For coffee and tea, productions often use disposable paper or plastic coffee cups. This can really add up on your budget and in the landfills. On *BOMBER*, a recent feature I worked on in Germany, we got hot beverage cups for each cast and crew member and put their names on them with a sharpie pen. They used their cups throughout the day and then, each night, the cups were washed and put back on the craft service table.

ESSENTIAL CRAFT SERVICE SUPPLIES LIST

Coffee
Tea
Water
Juice
Soda
Breakfast snacks — i.e., bagels, muffins, croissants
Butter
Cream cheese
Jam
Milk/Half and Half
Sugar
Fruit
Trail mix/energy bars
Cheese and crackers
Hummus and pita bread slices
Chips and Salsa
Small vegetables and dip
Small chocolate candies (never put out on the craft service table until
     after lunch)
Cookies
Nuts and raisin mix
Gum
Small fire extinguisher
First Aid kit
Aspirin, Ibuprofen
Sunscreen
Hand sanitizer

Shopping for craft service is best done at a discount warehouse store — you can buy in bulk to save money and reduce packaging. Fruits and veggies and other items may need to be bought elsewhere. But it is good to go to the warehouse first and then a local supermarket to fill in on the things you weren't able to get. In many cities you can get the supplies delivered for a nominal charge.

● **Finalize production book**
Now it's time to finalize the production book with the schedule, the names and contact info for all cast and crew, the vendor information list and location contact information. You can email this to all the cast and crew or post it online at a website that is secure and can only be accessed by cast and crew. This is an important document that gives everyone the important information they need to do their jobs well.

● **Buy production supplies/expendables**
Unlike office supplies, production supplies and expendables are the materials you'll need for the production phase of the project. It will include office supplies but also much more. You should check with department heads to find out if they need anything that should be ordered/acquired by the production department.

Grip and Lighting department expendables
Various rolls of adhesive tape (gaffer's, camera, double stick, paper tape, etc.) various colors and sizes
Gels and Diffusions (for gelling lights and windows)
Show cards
Dust off/canned air
Clothespins
Rope
Twine
Monofilament
Fabrics
Rubber matting

Camera department expendables
Various adhesive tapes
Dust off/canned air
Empty film cans and bags (if shooting film)
Eyepiece covers
Written camera reports (in triplicate)

Script Supervisor
Digital camera for continuity photos
Copies of his/her reports

Wardrobe/Costume
Digital still camera
Hangers
Steam iron
Wardrobe racks

Production design/art/props
Tarps to protect floors
Paper tape
Bubble wrap to protect props

Sound
Batteries

AD
Pads of paper
Portable printer
Printer paper

Production
Portable file boxes
File folders
Pens
Pencils
Office supplies
Stapler + staples
Sharpies
Petty cash receipt book
Rubber bands
Paper clips
Stationery
Envelopes
Reams of white recycled printing paper
Reams of colored recycled printing paper
Portable printer
Locks for securing the back door of any rental trucks

● Copy final scripts
It's time to make multiple copies of the script for all department heads, actors, etc. If changes are made after this time they should be made on colored paper and given out to all department heads and actors each day that there are script changes. One color will be used for each revision so that everyone can keep track of the changes and add them to their scripts.

● Send out final equipment lists/create pick-up day instructions
This is the time to amend any equipment lists with your vendors. The department head should confirm the list. Then you can lock the list and make copies that will be used by the PAs on the pick-up day. This

will reduce confusion at the equipment house on pick-up day, as well. Remember to call your contact at each rental house to confirm that all paperwork is in order.

Create one document that contains all necessary information — vendor addresses, phone numbers, contact names, driving directions and a list of what needs to be done or picked up at each location. Include any paperwork (i.e., credit card authorizations, etc.) that need to be given to the vendors. Then hand a copy to each of the PAs who are going to be doing the pick-ups in the rental van or truck. If there is a exterior locking mechanism on the back of the trucks, make sure to give the PAs locks with keys so they can lock them up between pick-ups.

You need two PAs for every van/truck on the road. One needs to stay with the vehicle at all times and the other will go into the company and pick up or deliver whatever is necessary. The PA who stays with the rental vehicle will also be able to move the vehicle if required, being careful to park only in legal spots to avoid parking tickets.

● **Have final preproduction meeting with key department heads**
This is a very important meeting to schedule the week before principal photography begins. There should be an agenda and you'll want to move through the entire shooting plan for the film. For a feature film you'll only be able to go through the first day or two but if there are any potential conflicts with the extended shooting schedule they can be addressed in the meeting.

Go through the first day's schedule in detail. Transportation, how to get to the location, set-up times, etc. Department heads will bring up any specific questions, concerns, problems they may have in their departments. People from all departments can discuss and problem solve and come up with final solutions. This is the last time to sit down and discuss together in detail before the hectic pace of the shoot starts. By this point most questions will have been answered but use this meeting to finalize any remaining questions.

● **Create accurate driving directions for all locations and stages**
Accurate driving directions for all locations and stages are essential. I can't stress this enough. Many a shooting schedule has been destroyed because production vehicles got lost on the way to location and the whole shoot was impacted. The location manager should create the driving directions. If you do not have a location manager then have a trusted member of the production team (someone with a good sense of

direction) drive to each location and write down detailed directions with the correct mileage. Online directions (like *www.googlemaps.com* and *www.mapquest.com*) are good back-ups but do not always take you the best way for the cast and crew that will be driving.

Remember that some roadways and bridges may have restrictions on what kind of vehicles can drive on which roadway. In that case, you'll have two sets of driving directions — one for cars and small vans and one for trucks. In certain locations, there may be limits to how big or heavy a truck can be. There have been times where I've had to cross a bridge and our grip truck is too big or heavy. In that case you'll need to have a different way to get the truck to that location or need to have multiple smaller/lighter vehicles to get the equipment to the location. The alternate directions may take longer for the journey, so do the research and give those vehicles an earlier departure time for the location.

In some cities, public transportation may be the best way for the cast and crew to travel to the shooting location. This can save you a lot of time and money but if there is a problem with the subway or metro on the morning of your shoot, your production could be delayed by late arrivals. In this case, I often have the key cast and crew driven to set and the other production personnel take public transportation.

● **Pre-visualize/create "who's-doing-what" lists**
There are so many details that need to be attended to for a successful production. It's important to make sure you don't forget any of them or it can have a perilous impact on the film. To avoid this predicament I sit down with the production manager periodically throughout preproduction and a week before our first day of principal photography and pre-visualize the entire first few days of production to make sure we have not forgotten anything.

I "see" every step in the process for the final prepro day and the first day of shooting — the PAs arriving at the van rental place and picking up the vehicles and driving to the location, the production and craft service people arriving at the location and setting up, next the DP and other departments arrive and begin setting up equipment, the hair/makeup crew move into their trailers or rooms and set up their departments, next the cast with the first call time arrive and check in with the AD and the director and then head to the hair/makeup and wardrobe rooms to get ready, etc.

The reason for this is that by going step by step, the production manager and I pick up on things we may have forgotten and have time to make sure we take care of them. For instance, we may realize that we are short on the number of PAs we need for the first shoot day. Or the hair/makeup crew doesn't have a designated room at the first location and we need to rectify that before we start shooting. Or we forgot to schedule a car to pick up the actors for the early call time. It's incredibly helpful and a great way to catch potentially catastrophic mistakes. We have a week to deal with them and make any adjustments we need to beforehand.

Pre-visualization also allows you to "see" the whole day in your mind and that process makes it seem as if you have already "lived" it. On the actual shoot day, you are able to stay present because you have already seen how the day is supposed to happen and now you can concentrate on what is happening in the moment. This may sound "new-agey" but I've been doing it for years and find it to be a very helpful tool.

Final Week Countdown
● **Create pick-up/runs lists**
The day before the start of principal photography is the day for the pick-up of all equipment, props, etc. Depending on all that you have to do, you'll need two production assistants for each vehicle you rent. One person needs to sit in the van while the other PA does the pick-ups at the rental house. Someone is *always* in the vehicle, so the equipment, props, etc. can't be stolen and in case the vehicle needs to be moved while the other PA is on the run.

At this point I want to mention a disturbing scam that has happened in NYC in the past. This happened to a student of mine a few years ago and with some quick thinking and fast running he was able to foil the robbers. Here's out it worked: The robbers loitered outside of known equipment rental houses and waited while the PA returning equipment brought in the first load. While the other PA was up front in the driver's seat, they opened the back door of the van and took the camera cases before the other PA had returned. It's so important to have one of the PAs guarding the equipment between trips to the rental house or make sure the van doors are locked between trips. You can never be too careful. Make sure you go over this protocol with all of your production assistants before they go out on their runs.

For the pick up/runs list create a realistic schedule based on the start time and end time for the work day. That way you can time out how long it will take to get from one place to another and to load in the equipment/props. This list should have the name of the businesses, the addresses (with cross streets), phone numbers and the contact names. Include a

comprehensive list of everything that needs to be picked up at each location. This allows the PAs to check off each item on the list before leaving
the rental house. If they have any questions (is it OK to replace one kind
of tripod for another because it is not available on pick up day?) They
should call you to double check. Make sure you have taken care of payment (cash, credit card, on account) ahead of time so there are no delays.

Organize everything in the most efficient and streamlined way. Start
from where the PAs will pick up the van/truck/car. Also remember to
check ahead of time that they have their driver's licenses and are old
enough to drive the rental vehicles according to the company rules.
Some rental companies require the driver to be at least 25 years old to
rent a vehicle. Also find out if you need to register each person who will
be driving the vehicle or if the company allows any employee on the
shoot to use the vehicle and receive insurance coverage.

Schedule the pickups so they are doing runs closest to the vehicle
rental place, fanning outward from there. Usually the equipment houses
don't allow pick-ups until later in the afternoon (remember to check their
rules) so often it's best to purchase/pick up food, craft service, expendables, film stock or videotape, props, and other supplies that can be done
earlier in the day.

When picking up equipment make sure you have determined that the
van/truck will have enough time and space to get it all done. If not, you'll
need to alter your plan and maybe rent an additional vehicle and hire
two more PAs to get it all done in one day. The pick-up day is a critical
day — it's the day that you put together all the means of production that
you need for the next day — the first day of principal photography.

● **Call times and directions**

The AD will create a call sheet for the production. A **call sheet** is one
sheet that lists the name, phone number, and email address for each cast
and crew member. It also lists the call time for each cast/crew. The AD
or a member of the production staff will need to call and/or email each
cast/crew member with the call time and directions for the first shoot
day. This needs to be done no later than 24 hours before the call time the
next day. It should be clear on the email that everyone needs to email
back or call a specific phone number to confirm. For those cast/crew
members who have not confirmed by early afternoon, then the AD/pro-
duction person will call them and follow up to get a verbal confirmation.
The AD will keep a written list of each person who has confirmed and
shouldn't stop until everyone has been contacted and been confirmed.

For future shoot days, the call time/directions info will be given out at the end of the shoot day via the new call sheet, so you only need to do this on the day before principal photography or for any cast/crew members who are coming in to work after the first day of shooting. For cast members, the call times and directions are usually given to their agents and confirmed through them. If actors don't have agents/managers, then they are contacted directly. I also recommend that you call the cast personally on the day before the first shoot day just to be assured that they got the message from their agents.

RECAP

1. **Remember the Production Triangle — Fast, Good, and Cheap — you only get two out of three.**

2. **Make sure to get the funding into a bank account based on the cash-flow schedule so you can stay on schedule for preproduction.**

3. **Follow the detailed preproduction schedule for the months leading up to the start of principal photography.**

CHAPTER 7

LOCATIONS

Finding Locations

FINDING THE RIGHT LOCATIONS for your film is always a big challenge. Ideally, you will hire a location scout to help you find places to shoot. They have the contacts and experience to help you find the locations your production requires. If you are on a tight budget, you may need to devise other strategies to find your locations.

Create Location Lists

Go to your script breakdown and determine how many sets you require for your film. Then discuss with the director, DP, and production designer whether the set will be built in a studio or shot on location. It is often cheaper to shoot in a location than to build a set and rent a stage. In some cases there may be flexibility — the preference may be to shoot on a stage but if the right location is found then it would be acceptable.

Discuss if other locations could be used to replicate the real thing. For instance, it is usually very difficult to procure a working hospital room for a shoot day but a hospital-like room in a nursing home may be more doable

> *The essential thing 'in heaven and earth' is... that there should be a long obedience in the same direction; there thereby results, and has always resulted in the long run, something which has made life worth living.*
>
> *— Friedrich Nietzsche*

and affordable. Talk out these kind of options ahead of time so the location scout has as much flexibility as possible when scouting.

Discuss what the visual and logistical priorities are for each location. Explain to the scout that you'll need certain things, for instance — a bathroom for cast and crew, running water, a place to set up the table and chairs for the crew meals, nearby parking, a freight elevator to load in equipment, etc.

The scout will request a tentative budget — the amount you can pay for each shoot day. Depending on the kind of money you can afford the scout will plan accordingly. For example, if you are looking for a luxury loft space and can't afford a fully furnished, luxury condo in the trendy part of town, you might be able to dress an artist's loft in the up-and-coming section of town and bring in all your own props and a coat of paint. A strategy will start to emerge.

The Specifics of Location Scouting

Once you have the list, you and the location scout should come up with a game plan for scouting locations to maximize time and money. Consult with them on where they have filmed in the past that may work for your film. Decide which locations are the priority — some will be more important than others to find. You may decide that you could use a friend's apartment if you don't find the "bedroom set" that was on the list. The office location may be the most important one for the scout to start on because it will be used for the most amount of shooting days.

The location scout you hire will have a day rate (the rate may include the use of her car or it may be additional) and will charge for expenses as well — printing costs and travel expenses (gas, tolls, parking).

Remember to give all the vital information you can to the scout before she begins her work. Include info like: 1) day or night; 2) tentative shoot dates; 3) how many cast & crew; 4) the need for a place to feed crew; 5) do you need running water or electricity?; 6) bathroom (or are you bringing a Winnebago?; 7) specific looks or shots that are required (i.e., what you see when looking out a window); 8) sync sound or MOS (no sound recording).

Based on how many days you can afford a scout, you should agree to a timeline – how many sites to be scouted and photographed per day and when you'll receive the location photos (usually each night or the next morning). As you receive the photos you will show them to the director,

DP, and production designer and get notes. Give the feedback to the scout so she can refine her search as she goes. It's amazing how helpful it is to the creative process to get photos of actual locations so the creative teams can start to make specific plans.

Location Folders

Every location scout has his or her own particular style for creating location folders. Some still paste them up in a legal-size manila folder. But most of the time it is done digitally through a website that everyone can access. The scout will take the digital photos and combine them to create a 360° picture of the room. Specific angles and elements of the location will be photographed and uploaded or emailed to you. Other pertinent info should also be provided:

1. The address, phone number, email address, and contact person name

2. Time of day when photo was taken

3. Notes describing what direction the location windows are facing — north, south, east, and west. This helps the DP to determine where the light would be at a specific time on a specific day

4. The usual location fee (You may nor may not want the scout to inquire about the rental fee.)

5. Any restrictions or caveats that are important to know when considering that particular location (i.e., it's not available on Sundays or only available weekdays from 6:00 a.m.–2:00 p.m.)

Once you receive the first batch of photos you can determine if the scout is on the right track. Discuss with the creative teams and then give specific feedback to the scout for the next day of scouting. It will allow her to be more accurate in what you are looking for and how to find it. You'll repeat this process until all of the locations are found for your film.

Check with Local Film Commissions for Leads

Every state has a film commission and most large cities and regions have one, as well. They are a great resource for many things and can be very helpful in giving you leads and information about potential locations. They often have a photographic archive of locations in the area that are available for viewing either in their offices or on their websites.

To find the local city/region and state film commissions go to the Association of Film Commissioners International at *www.afci.org*. They list all the domestic and international film commissions on their website.

Once you have your local film commission's URL, go to the website and see what information is provided on the Internet. Also call and briefly explain your project to the appropriate people at the office. Tell them when you plan to shoot and what locations you need to find. They will ask you questions and then let you know what may be available. Often they can email you photos or you may decide to go to their office.

Use the film commission — your tax dollars pay for it and they are there to help you. I've had great experiences with many film commissions over the years. They are usually very knowledgeable and are a big help if you are shooting in an area that you are not familiar with. Once you do find your locations, they will give you the rules and regulations for the area and help coordinate your permit application and issuance if required.

City parks, public housing, and other local governmental land are often free or almost free for filming purposes. The film commission will have the contact info for the various agencies and contact people so you can follow up on those possibilities. On the short film, *Torte Bluma*, the film takes place during the Holocaust in the Treblinka concentration camp. For several scenes, we chose to shoot it in Brooklyn, NY at the Floyd Bennett Field at Gateway National Park. The permit was very affordable and we where able to get the looks we needed.

Federal, state, and location historical societies are another affordable way to find great locations with built-in production design. They often charge a nominal rental fee and all of the furnishings are historically correct and in good condition. As mentioned before, we shot the majority of *Wisconsin Death Trip* at Wisconsin historical sites. My favorite one was the 19th century steam locomotive restored by the community of Eagle, WI. They were kind enough to let us shoot on it for two different scenes.

Alternatives to Hiring a Location Scout

If your budget is too tight to hire a location scout, I suggest two other options: 1) pay a fee to a profession location scout to open up his or her location files to you; 2) you and the director scout for yourselves. Many scouts maintain comprehensive picture files of the thousands of locations they have scouted over the years and will go through their databases and make copies of the ones that might work for your project. Each location file will contain photos of all angles of the site, address, contact name and number, and the requested location fee. This can jump start your scouting and save a lot of time.

Often, your budget may not allow such a luxury, so the task will fall to the producer and director to find the locations on their own. This is where resourcefulness, serendipity, negotiating experience, and good people skills come into play.

Send out an email to family and friends with the specifics of what you are looking for. Be as specific as you can about what/where/when you plan to shoot. You'd be surprised how helpful they can be. It's easy for them to forward your email to other family and friends and so on. I've gotten great leads this way and often people think of places that you might not have considered. Sometimes people are willing to let you use their country homes or their apartments if they are out of town, for free. Many people find the prospect of having a movie shot at their places an exciting idea.

The other thing to remember is the power of production design. An available and affordable location may not look like the right place but with some paint, props, and clever art direction, it could work very nicely.

Writer/director Paul Cotter (*BOMBER, Estes Avenue*) likes to be flexible when scouting for low-budget productions. He advises:

"Don't be too precious about your locations. If the script calls for a cafe, but you can only get a bar, it's great if you can adapt the script to allow a location change. On *BOMBER*, I had written a pivotal scene to be shot in the European equivalent of a Dollar Store — a "Euro Markt." It would have been great because the cheap, kitschy vibe of the store would have worked as a wonderful dramatic counter-point to what was a really heavy scene. But, try as I might, I couldn't get a suitable Euro Markt to agree to let us shoot there. On my travels, however, I found a vast, and importantly WILLING, furniture store — so I changed the scene to be set there. Sure it was too bad it didn't work out to be a Euro Markt, but did the scene suffer? No. The essential dramatic thrust of the scene remained the same, just in a different place with its own sense of character."

Finalizing Location Decisions

Once you have several good location possibilities and you have narrowed down your choices, you need to make some decisions. You'll want to go visit your first and second choices with the director (and DP if possible) to see if those choices will really work for the film. It's always good to look at no less than two places for each location in your film. That way you'll have a back-up option.

When you go for the in-person visit, you are looking at all the possibilities of the location. Ask the location owner or supervisor if there is any new or ongoing construction in the area that could impact your shoot. Also ask the owner/supervisor about availability — days and times you can have access.

When you look at the property you need to consider many things at once. Here's a checklist:

1. Is this the right "look" for the film?

2. Is it big enough for your shooting purposes?

3. Does it have all the props you need or will you have to buy/rent more or different ones?

4. Are there bathroom facilities that cast and crew can use?

5. Is there a holding area for talent? A place for hair/makeup and wardrobe to set up and work?

6. Where will cast and crew be able to sit and eat for lunch? Do you need to bring in tables and chairs? Or procure a separate nearby location for the catered meal?

7. Where can you park the trucks and/or vans for the production? Is it safe or will you need a security person to watch the vehicles all day/night long?

8. Is there room to stage equipment when it's not in use?

9. Is there an Internet connection for the production staff's laptop computers? Do you get good cell phone service?

10. Are there any sound issues with the location — noisy radiators or ventilation systems that can't be turned off or quieted or is there an active construction site across the street?

11. Is the location affordable for your budget?

12. If it is a "period" production, does the location have any attributes that will be problematic for the historical period you are shooting for?

Once you have all the answers for each location, you can make your decision. A location may look perfect and be affordable but if there are no bathroom facilities, you may have to rent an RV/Winnebago for the shoot day and that may add money to the total rental price. The location you want may not be available for the shoot dates you had in mind — can you change the schedule so you can shoot there? If you have flexibility you may be able to change your dates so you can shoot there. What if you and the director love a location but the rental rate is beyond your budget? Negotiation is the next step in the process.

Negotiating the Deal

Everything is open to negotiation. If both parties in a negotiation want it to happen and can get enough of what they want, then it can happen. If you are asking for a reduction (sometimes, a significant reduction) in a rental price then you need to come up with other ways to compensate for the requested discount. These can be many things and it depends on what would be useful and meaningful to the owner. For instance:

1. A credit in the screen credits of the film.

2. A DVD copy of the finished project.

3. The owner's son wants to be in a film — do you have a role for an extra that he could fill?

4. The owner's daughter wants to get into film school — can she work on your film as a PA to get some experience?

5. Advertise for the location for a few hours. One of my students bartered with a restaurant that was near campus. For a free 1/2 day shoot in the restaurant, he put up flyers around campus one afternoon to advertise the restaurant to students.

6. Offer to pay for the location's employee to stay with you overnight during the shoot to make sure everything runs smoothly.

7. If the location serves food, promise to pay them for the cast and crew lunches for each shoot day — that will add to their bottom line.

8. Offer to shoot some footage of the location for promo purposes to use on their website. Another one of my students shot some promotional 35mm film of a location after they wrapped production one night. For using the location for free, it took him and the DP an hour and 300 feet of film that they developed and transferred and gave to the location owner for future promotional use. It was a win-win for both of them.

9. You offer to shoot the owner's niece's wedding video the following summer in exchange for a free location now.

10. Get creative — there are many ways to provide compensation other than money.

Back-up Locations

Having a back-up location for all of your top choices is essential. I always negotiate a good deal with the back-up location first. Once that is in place I then negotiate with the first choice to get the best deal possible. Having the back-up one in your "back pocket" gives you confidence and leverage when trying to make a deal with your number one choice. Having a back-up location is also essential in case the first choice owner changes his mind and pulls out of the deal. This happens more often than one would like, so you always need to be prepared.

Paperwork

Once you have agreed to the terms you'll need to do some paperwork with the owner. You'll want to sign a location release form, obtain an insurance certificate, and work out the payment schedule.

Location Release Form

A location release form should state the shoot dates (and back-up dates), address, rental rate per hour, number of hours (i.e., $1,000 for a 12-hr./day, then $150/hr. after 12 hours). The form will include other information, like whether you have to hire someone to oversee the production, liability issues, a hold-harmless clause (see *Legal* chapter), who has responsibility for what, a payment schedule, access to certain areas at the location including a freight elevator and parking, and when the key department heads can have access to the location prior to the shoot date(s). Put everything you have discussed and negotiated with the owner in writing. Email or fax it to the owner and get it signed as soon as possible. You want to make sure you have a firm deal and that the deal points are acceptable to both parties before you get too close to shooting.

Sometimes owners change their minds or try to change the deal. If you get the papers to them quickly and get them signed you'll know that you have that location locked. If they hesitate or fail to sign in a timely manner, then it is a warning sign that you may not have a completed deal and you may need to go with your back-up location. The more lead time you have, the better able you will be to switch to another location, if necessary.

Notice that I keep referring to the *owner* of the location. You must get the owner's signature (not a manager or relative or employee) because that is the only person who has the legally binding authority to sign the agreement.

General Liability Insurance Certificate

Insurance is a critical part of covering your liability for all of the locations at which you decide to shoot. (See *Insurance* Chapter). **Liability** is another word for things that you and the production are responsible for, legally. Each location will require a general liability insurance certificate before they will let you onto their premises. Often the owners will have specific language as to how they want the certificate to read. This is often the case when you shoot in a city, state, or federal property and they require you to write a certificate out to the public authority. You'll need to obtain the proper language and forward it to your insurance agent so he or she can write out the certificate correctly.

Sometimes the owner specifies a certain dollar amount for the limitations (usually between $1–2 million) and the agent should check to make sure your policy meets the requirements. If your policy does not and the owner insists on a certain amount, you will have to decide to either buy an additional amount of insurance (a rider) or you will need to find another location that will accept your insurance coverage.

Co-ops and Condos

While we are talking about property ownership we should also cover the issue of co-op and condos and their boards. In many U.S. cities, apartment owners live in buildings that are run as co-ops or condominiums. For these types of properties, there are **co-op and condo boards or associations** that run the management of the buildings and uphold the buildings' rules and regulations.

In these cases, the co-op or condo owner is not the only entity you need to get permission from to enter and film on the premises. You'll need to contact the boards/associations to get approvals, as well. Usually co-op/condo boards meet once a month, so you should contact them *at least six weeks* before you plan to shoot so you get on the schedule for the next board meeting. They may ask you to submit a letter, budget, script, and production plan or they may have a specific application for you to fill out. You may or may not be required to appear in person, as well. They will then tell you when they next convene and how long it will take to receive an answer.

If you get approval, they usually will require an insurance certificate for the co-op/condo association as well as the individual homeowner. They also may have a list of rules you must agree to follow and/or a fee that is required for the co-op/condo association. If you agree to the terms, then make sure to get a signed permission letter from the co-op/condo board for your files.

There are also some "gated" communities or developments in the U.S. which have associations that oversee a certain area of homes. It's important to do your research to find out if the location you plan to shoot at has such a governing body. Sometimes the homeowners don't even understand that there are rules that they have to follow for a film-shoot request, so it's best for you to do the research yourself.

One of my students shot a short film at her uncle's home in Maryland. His home was in a development outside of Washington, D.C. She asked if she needed any other approvals to shoot in his home and he said no. On the morning of the film shoot, as the production van and assorted cars descended upon her uncle's home, she was promptly visited by two condo association board members who tried to shut her down because she didn't get their permission! She explained that she was told that she didn't have to and it was her uncle who got in trouble. They worked it all out but it was a stressful way to start the production.

Permits

Filming permits are often required when you shoot in U.S. cities and towns. Permits are usually required for public exteriors in many cities/towns (i.e., sidewalks, roadways, public parks). It's also a way for municipalities to track what productions are shooting in a certain area and to make sure that the production crew is following the local regulations. As discussed earlier in this chapter, film commissions will provide you with this information. Go to the website and call the office to discuss your specific production needs and how to apply for a permit.

Some cities require a fee for a permit and others do not. Los Angeles has a rather expensive fee structure for filming permits and New York does not have a permit fee at all.

Police/Fire/Sheriff's Departments

Depending on your production needs for your exterior shooting, you may need to involve the police, fire, or sheriff's departments of the municipality in which you are shooting. If you need to stop traffic, block off a street or shoot with equipment on the outside of a vehicle, you'll need to contact the police or the sheriff for permission and coordination. You also will need to pay for officer(s) to be on your shoot. The work and fees will be determined by the local authority. An exception is New York's Police Department's Film and TV unit which provides police officers for free, per their discretion.

If you need to open a hydrant to access water for a **wet down** (watering down a street) or if you are planning to use pyrotechnics you will need permission and in most cases, pay a fee to the local fire department. Give yourself several weeks to do the application process.

Tech Scout

We discussed this in depth in the *Preproduction* chapter. Please refer to that section.

Shoot-day Protocol

On the shoot day, the location manager (if you don't have one, then the 1st Assistant Director will usually perform this role) will arrive 1/2 hour prior to anyone else's call time. She will have decided where each vehicle will be parked, where to load in and where each department will be set up at the location. Each crew/cast person will check in with the location manager/PM and follow their instructions — otherwise anarchy will reign.

Run Through with Owner

At the beginning of the shoot day or the day before, the location manager (or producer) will do a "run through" of the location with the owner. The location manager will take digital photos or video of the various areas of the location and close-ups of any details that show prior damage. They will write up a short list describing any pre-existing damage to the location and both the owner and location manager should sign it.

Remind each department that it is important to treat the location with utmost care. Protective boards should be put down on the floors if necessary, sound blankets should be wrapped around fragile furniture and show cards should be affixed to walls to protect them. Grips and art department crew should be knowledgeable of what kind of tape they can use on certain surfaces and they should check with the AD if there are any questions or concerns.

Crew should be reminded to report any problems or damage to the location as soon as it occurs so the location manager/producer is aware of it immediately. It's vital to know about damage as soon as it happens than to find out about it afterwards or to have the owner point it out later. Also it gives the production staff time to come up with a solution or fix it immediately, if it is possible.

Leave It Better Than You Found It

The best mantra for location shooting is "Leave it better than you found it." Have the crew pick up all trash as they go along and have the location manager inform everyone of the rules for proper disposal at the location. The location manager will have worked this out ahead of time with the owner so there are no problems about trash disposal. Most locations will require you to take all of your garbage with you when you leave (or they may allow you to use their dumpster for a fee). Film production normally creates a lot of trash and you should expect to make arrangements to take it away. In most cities it is illegal to dump your garbage in public garbage cans on the street.

Idiot Check

An **idiot check** is when you go around a location (every nook and cranny) looking for any equipment or materials that have been left behind. Forgetting equipment is a nuisance at the least and expensive at the most. You'll have to send someone to pick it up the next day or you'll have to pay to replace it. Best to find it all and put it back where it belongs with the proper department before you leave the location.

At the end of the shoot day after the crew has wrapped, the owner and location manager will do the same "run through" together again. The owner will point out any new damage caused by the filming. If there is any damage, it will be noted on the sheet, pictures will be taken to document it for any kind of insurance claim. If it is slight damage, the owner may accept it or request repairs to be done or a small payment from the production company as compensation. If so, this deal can be added to the sheet and signed by the owner and producer.

If the damage is extensive, then an insurance claim will be necessary. The producer should arrange to make a claim the next day and begin the paperwork process with the insurance company (See *Insurance* Chapter). Photos and descriptions will be needed and an explanation provided to the insurance agent to begin the process. Remember that each insurance policy has a deductible, so find out about the amount before you put in the claim to make sure that it will be over the deductible limit.

The Day After the Location Shoot

Always remember to call and thank the owners the next day. Make sure they are satisfied with how everything turned out and follow up on any outstanding issues. You want to leave a good impression and do the right thing. You may want to shoot there again some day and if you leave on good terms, you'll be able to come back again. It's not just your reputation but also the film industry's reputation that is at stake. There have been many times in the past when I approached a location that would be perfect for a project and they refused because they had a bad experience with another film production a few months before. It's horrible to have a good location ruined by inept and unprofessional productions. It's important to be courteous and responsible when you shoot.

Tax Incentive Programs

As mentioned in the *Funding* chapter, many states and cities in the U.S. have tax incentive programs to entice film productions to film in their area. Having a film produced in your state can bring in a lot of money and jobs, so many states have created rebates ranging from 5–25%. Some states give cash back at the end of the production and other states give a tax rebate to the production company over a period of year(s). Some require you to shoot a certain portion of the budget in the state and others have less rigid regulations. Go to *www.ProducerToProducer.com* to learn about the various film tax incentive programs in the area(s) you are interested in for your production.

RECAP

1. **Create your list of required locations and hire a location scout in the area you are looking. If you can't hire a scout, the scouting will be done by the production staff.**

2. **Have the scout put digital photos online so the producer, director, and other key department heads can look at them and give back notes to the producer.**

3. **Check with local film commissions for information about possible locations and permits.**

4. **Finalize your location choices. Secure a deal for your back-up location first and then negotiate for your first choice to secure a deal.**

5. **Make sure to get a signed location release form and obtain an insurance certificate for your general liability coverage for the locations.**

6. **Have the location manager coordinate the cast/crew/equipment on the shoot day for parking issues, etc.**

7. **Contact the local police and fire departments if you have any production issues that fall under their jurisdictions.**

8. **Utilize tax incentive programs for the areas you are shooting in to stretch your production dollars.**

CHAPTER 8

LEGAL

WHEN MOST PEOPLE ARE confronted with a 20-page legal document, it can be overwhelming — leading to feelings of anxiety, frustration, or outright fear. If you are not a trained lawyer, the language and concepts can be confusing, frustrating, even intimidating. As the producer, it is your job to deal with various legal concepts and documents, so it's important to learn them. But you don't have to be an attorney to understand them. As with all things, the more you learn, the easier it becomes.

For this chapter, I've asked George Rush, an entertainment attorney and sales agent based in San Francisco, to share his expertise and guidance (*www.gmrush.com*). We will break down the most common legal concepts that you will encounter in the documents that come your way. Then we'll outline the specific documents that are most often used in film productions. At the end of the chapter we'll go over additional documents that may be of use to you in specific cases. You'll find templates for some of these documents at *www .ProducerToProducer.com* to help when creating your own forms, deal

Determine the thing that can and shall be done and then we shall find a way.

— Abraham Lincoln

214

memos, and contracts for your production. And now for the legal disclaimer: **This chapter is for informational purposes only and is not intended as legal advice.**

It's All About Rights

As discussed in the *Development* chapter, one of the tenets of film producing revolves around the understanding, negotiation, and acquisition of rights. **Rights** is a derivative of the word "copyright" and copyright refers to the "right to copy." Copyright is exactly what it sounds like — rights pertaining to the copying of something someone owns. For example, if one were to copy this book, you would need the rights from me, the owner/author. The producer needs to have the rights to the property (i.e., novel, comic book, play, etc.) he wishes to develop *before* moving forward with the project. Generally, this is done by acquiring an option to purchase the rights. This is usually a nominal sum that gives you the exclusive rights to purchase the motion picture rights to a property for a fixed period of time. Do not spend a lot of resources developing a story unless you are certain you can obtain the rights. Work with an attorney to make sure you have all the signed legal documents for the rights you require before you look for financing or talent attachments.

It's All About Liability

Another major aspect of a producer's responsibilities has to do with liability. **Liability** is your legal risk and exposure. As a producer, you need to eliminate or mitigate the circumstances under which you may be liable or at risk for an occurrence. For instance, a distributor will not be interested in your film (regardless of its merits) unless there is zero or next-to-no liability.

This is done in several ways:

1. Written agreements that seek to eliminate or set limits on liability for the producer/production entity. This ranges from contracts with your cast and crew to music/archival licenses to financial agreements with your investors. You want a written agreement for everything you can think of, where there may be liability.

2. Incorporation to shield a producer and the film's personnel from any damages if a liability arises during the producing of a film. You, as an individual, do not want to be party to any of these agreements.

If there is a dispute about an agreement, that means they would go after you, and if you lose, your personal assets. You want the party to these agreements to be your company, which will be the legally responsible party and whose only asset will be this one film.

3. Acquisition of proper insurance so the production and its cast, crew, and resources are covered for possible risk factors. We will discuss this in detail in the *Insurance* chapter.

In this chapter we will discuss general legal concepts and then outline specific legal documents. At the end of the chapter, we'll go over incorporation and how to do that for a film production.

Breakdown of a Legal Document

Most legal documents related to film producing contain specific legal components. Below is a breakdown of those concepts that you will find in the various kinds of documents you will come across.

PARTIES

State who/what are the two or more parties that are signing the agreement.

TERM

State the date that the agreement commences and the period of time that the contract covers.

RIGHTS

If it is an agreement covering rights, state which rights are being covered by the document. Examples include broadcast rights (right to broadcast on TV), music composition rights (rights to a piece of music), theatrical distribution rights (rights to distribute a film/video in theaters), DVD rights (rights to create and sell a DVD of a work).

SERVICES

What exactly are you obligated to do, and what exactly is the other party obligated to do.

FEES

For lawyers, this is often called consideration — the benefit of the bargain. The amount of money paid for the purchase, usage, or rental of something, This could be a location rental fee — how much will be paid for the use of a location for a certain period of time or acquisition fee

— money paid for a period of time for certain rights to a project. It could also be the day rate of a cast or crew member.

LIABILITY
Who/what is responsible for any problem or damage that may occur during a production.

LIMITATIONS
What the document does and does not cover regarding the agreement.

RIGHT TO ENTER INTO AGREEMENT
All parties signing agreements must verify that they are legally responsible for the parties they are signing for.

CAN OR CANNOT ASSIGN TO OTHERS
Need to state if the parties can or cannot assign rights in the agreement to others.

RECOURSE OR REMEDY
How and where the parties will be able to go to remedy a situation if they have problems with an outcome, or if something has changed.

CONTACT INFORMATION
How and where each party can be contacted in the future, usually via written and/or delivered mail.

Legal Concepts
There are several concepts or legal language that play a role in some of the legal documents in the film industry. Here's a short list:

FAIR USE
Two good websites for more information are at *www.fairuse.stanford .edu* and *www.centerforsocialmedia.org*. This is a definition from the Stanford website — "fair use is a copyright principle based on the belief that the public is entitled to freely use portions of copyrighted materials for purposes of commentary and criticism. For example, if you wish to criticize a novelist, you should have the freedom to quote a portion of the novelist's work without asking permission. Absent this freedom, copyright owners could stifle any negative comments about their work." Fair Use is a defense against someone suing you for copyright infringement. It is a shield, not a sword. There are a lot of grey areas and misconceptions

regarding fair use. In a very basic sense, you need to be commenting on a copyrighted work for it to even be considered fair use.

Unfortunately for filmmakers, there is not an easy, bright-line test for what is or is not fair use. There is not a lot of case law that makes things clear for independent filmmakers. There are a number of legal/academic groups (including Stanford University and American University) that advocate best practices for fair use and/or advocate a broadening of fair use. If you are consulting with one of these group's websites, read their information very carefully, since it is usually pretty cautious. Don't get carried away because, usually, those who sue for copyright infringement have deep pockets. Unless you have deep pockets yourself, you do not want to be the guinea pig to create a new precedent in fair use copyright law.

Generally, copyrighted matter that you have not licensed, that is being used in a fictional narrative film, will not be fair use. However, as more narratives incorporate elements of documentary, it does come up. One of the deliverables that most distributors require is a copyright report. Distributors will want to see that you have licensed all copyrighted material and if something is not licensed, they will want to know if it is fair use.

PARI PASSU
This means "at the same time, at the same rate."

MOST FAVORED NATION
This means that the party will receive the same terms for a particular thing as any other party. For example, if the definition of "net profits" is most favored nation, the definition will be as good as that which everyone else on the film receives.

List of Agreements During Each Phase
Below is a list of individual agreements that are most often used in the course of producing a film. Each document is used during a specific phase in the filmmaking process, as outlined below:

DEVELOPMENT
Option Agreement
As discussed in the *Development* chapter, an option agreement is used when you wish to have an "option" to own the rights to creative material that has been previously produced, i.e., book, short story, play, or screen-

play. It will be for a fixed period of time for a certain fee and usually there is a renewal feature built into the agreement.

Signature by Creator of the Work and the Purchaser of the Work

Writer's Contract

This agreement commissions a writer to write a screenplay — either original or based on other material. If the screenwriter is a member of Writer's Guild of America (WGA), it will be a WGA contract. If the writer is non-union, then it will be a specific agreement drawn up by the purchaser. It will contain the writing schedule, the payment schedule, re-writes, details about the ownership of the work, and how long the rights are owned by the purchaser before they revert back to the screenwriter.

Signature by Screenwriter and Purchaser of the Script

Non-Disclosure Agreement

This agreement is between two parties to treat information confidentially and to not share it with third parties. It is often used by companies when reading unsolicited scripts and treatments and is used to limit liability in regard to producing work that is similar to a past submitted proposal.

Investor's Agreement

This proposal is the document that you send out to interest investors in your project. Because its purpose is to inform potential investors about the project, it must also be in compliance with Security and Exchange Commission (SEC) regulations. The document states all of the potential risks involved for those investing in the film in clear detail. Attorney George Rush advises: "Independent film, unlike investing in other businesses, is the worst business. The likelihood of the investors making their money back are like slim to none, and because of that you need to give them full disclosure about the risks, in particular. It is absolutely necessary to disclose that. So, if they sign on the dotted line, they know what they're getting into."

Also if you accept money from an individual outside the state in which you are incorporated, then you have to make sure you are complying with that particular state's security laws. This is an area in which you need an attorney to make sure you are compliant with relevant security laws. **Do not try this on your own, as one of your biggest liabilities will be the money received from investors.**

PREPRODUCTION

Crew Deal Memo

As discussed in the *Preproduction* chapter, this document covers the employment details for each crew person. It should state screen credit, payment, time period, job responsibility, and work rules & regulations.

Signature by Producer and Crewperson

Location Release Form

This form (as discussed in the *Locations* Chapter) covers the deal for each location you use during the production of your project. It should state the fee, the rental time period, the liability for the producer and for the location's owner.

Signature by Producer and Property owner

Appearance Release Form

This form is signed by non-union talent who appear in your project. (If the production company is a signatory to a union contract, the actors will sign the guild paperwork.) The form allows you to use their images in your film (usually in perpetuity, worldwide, in any current and future media).

Signature by Person on Screen

Producer/Director Agreement

This may be a "work for hire" agreement or some other document between the producer and the director of the project. The document should solidify the expectations and responsibilities that you and the director agree to meet during each phase of the project. Areas to be covered should include: 1) funding; 2) screen credit; 3) responsibilities; 4) cash flow; 5) ownership of the project and ownership of the work done by the producer and the director; and 6) "points" or profit participation on the film.

Signed by Producer and Director

PRODUCTION

Union contracts — crew and cast

If your production company is a signatory to any crew or cast unions, you will sign the negotiated union contract. The union will have paperwork for each cast or crew member to sign for employment.

Signed by Producer and Union cast/crew member

Non-union Crew Deal Memo

If your production is non-union for crew, this document will detail the employment details such as salary, payment, work period, screen credit, kit rental fees, rules and regulations, and profit participation.

Signed by Producer and Non-union crew member

Music License Agreement

Most films/videos use some kind of music for the soundtracks — either previously recorded compositions that they want to use in the soundtrack or original work composed specifically for the project. There are two kinds of music rights that you need to obtain with regards to music — Synchronization license (publishing) and Master Use license (recording) (see *Music* Chapter).

Make sure to get both rights for each composition and the correct usage that you need, i.e., film festival, DVD, theatrical, television, online, etc.

Signed by Producer and Music Rights holder or representative

Logo Release Form

To be signed when you use the logo or brand of a product on screen in your film. These logos are trademarked so you need to look into the ownership and obtain the trademark holder's permission to use them. The rights holder may want to read the script before giving permission. However, if a trademark is used as it is intended to be used, clearance is not required.

Signature by Producer and Trademark Holder or representative

Legal Corporate Entities

A producer wants to limit any kind of damages that could arise from a liability issue on a film for the producer, the production entity, and the rest of the film's personnel. On a shoot, if a ladder falls on a picture vehicle and causes $25,000 worth of damage, the insurance policy will cover the cost of repairs, minus the deductible. But if the car's owner decides to sue for loss of rental income while the car is being repaired, the producer could be responsible for the legal costs and the monetary award for the owner, if he or she wins the suit. In such a situation, you want to make sure a legal judgment can't come after your personal money or assets (like your home or car). Consequently, it is wise to set up a corporate entity to protect yourself and the film. The most common options are either a corporation or a limited liability company (LLC). The key points of each entity are outlined below.

CORPORATION

A corporation is a business entity that acts as a legal person. Corporations provide structure so that groups of individuals may conduct business as an individual entity. The most common corporations for film are limited partnerships and limited liability companies. These entities, for the most part, shield their members from liability.

LIMITED PARTNERSHIP (LP)

A limited partnership is made up of a general partner, usually the producer, and limited partners, usually the investors. The investors have limited liability, while the general partner has all the liability. George suggests a limited liability company for films.

LIMITED LIABILITY CORPORATION (LLC)

An LLC is almost like a hybrid of corporation and partnership, and as the name suggests, limits your liability. The terms of the LLC are analogous to that of a corporation — instead of articles of incorporation, you have articles of organization. Instead of stockholders, an LLC has members. In charge of the LLC is the manager who, more often than not, is you, the filmmaker. This currently is the most common structure. Usually, it is set up just for this one film, isolating it for any other asset.

Never Sign Anything Without Proper Legal Advice

Legal counsel is essential when making a film. Reading this chapter of *Producer To Producer* does not eliminate your need to obtain proper legal counsel. If anyone gives you a document to sign, you should hire a knowledgeable lawyer to look it over and give approval before you sign. For most film documents I suggest you get an entertainment lawyer who specializes in film. There are many different areas of specialty in law. Real estate law is very different from corporate law or divorce law, etc. An entertainment attorney will be familiar with issues specific to the film industry.

Talk to fellow filmmakers to get recommendations for good lawyers. Go to legal seminars offered by local film organizations. Take meetings with several candidates before you select your attorney. Lawyers charge by the hour or 1/10th of an hour. But most attorneys will give you a 20- to 30-minute, free consultation, so you can find out about them before you decide.

If you cannot afford an attorney, there are organizations that provide legal counsel for reduced fees to artists throughout the country. Volunteer Lawyers for the Arts (VLA) is a organization that offers pro bono services to low-income artists and non-profit organizations that provides such services. Go to *www.vlany.org* for more information.

Your Lawyer Is an Extension of You

Remember that your attorney represents you, particularly when negotiating on your behalf. Your attorney's interaction and behavior in each negotiation reflects directly on you. Factor that into your selection criteria. What kind of person do you want out there working on your behalf?

There is a businesswoman I know who had four different lawyers whom she used to help run her business. Carole Dean ran three locations of Studio Film & Tape, selling short ends of film and reprocessed tape. During her 33 years in business she used four specialized attorneys. She had a mean, bulldog attorney to collect monies from late-to-pay clients and also a corporate attorney for leases, business dealings, and contracts. In addition, she had a liability attorney to protect her against liability for selling short ends of film and to create and keep current her invoice disclaimer, and she had an accident attorney to analyze and collect on other people's insurance policies and handle accident suits. She found that by choosing a professional in each field, she saved money and had excellent results.

I picked my attorney because she's intelligent, experienced, steady-as-a-rock, fearless, and a good negotiator. I know she will negotiate hard on my behalf but she is reasonable and forthright. She's not a bully and doesn't play games. I also like the way she writes. Her legal writing style is clear — not overblown with too much legalese — and it's efficient.

People who know me might say that I just described myself and they probably are not that far off the mark. I want my attorney to reflect my style and values. Hey, but that's me. Some people feel you should get someone who is the opposite of you. If you are kind and decent, then get a shark to negotiate for you. That's your choice. Keep it in mind when you are making the hiring decision.

Attorney As Financier/Executive Producer/ Producer's Rep

This chapter has been discussing the legal issues and legal documents used to produce a film. There is another area in entertainment law that concentrates on film financing and packaging. Some attorneys work in that area as producer's reps. This is a natural extension of the work they do and you should look into these kinds of services if appropriate for your project. There are many individual attorneys and law firms that have film financing and packaging services.

RECAP

1. **Negotiate, sign, and keep copies of all necessary legal documents throughout each phase of producing the film. You'll need to keep them on file and include copies of the agreements as part of your deliverables list.**

2. **Create a corporate entity for your film to protect yourself and others from liability.**

3. **Learn about legal terms and concepts for negotiation purposes.**

4. **Hire a good entertainment lawyer to review and amend any legal documents before they are signed.**

5. **Your lawyer is an extension of you. Pick one who represents you in the way you wish to be seen.**

CHAPTER 9

INSURANCE

Why Do You Need Insurance?

THE SHORT ANSWER IS SO you and your collaborators can financially transfer the liability for any accidents, mishaps, or damage that may occur to a person or thing during your production to an insurance company. That's not to say that you don't have *responsibility* for all aspects of your production. But if a grip breaks her leg while stepping off a ladder and you have workers compensation insurance coverage in place, the insurance will be able to pay for her medical bills for a cast, rehabilitation, and a percentage of her lost wages, since she cannot work for several weeks. It's also against the law, in all 50 states, not to have this coverage and while the fines for failure to have this are different in all 50 states, in New York State the current fines are $2,000 for each 10-day period that coverage was not in place!

It's your responsibility to obtain all the necessary insurance policies, such as General Liability, Hired or Non-owned Auto Liability, Auto Physical Damage, Workers Compensation and

Doubt is not an agreeable condition but certainty is absurd.

— Voltaire

in some states you also need DBL (Disability Benefits Law), Production Insurance (covering the master, props, sets, wardrobe, equipment, locations), Umbrella Liability, Travel Accident Insurance and Errors & Omissions Insurance. From a legal standpoint, you protect yourself and the production through legal contracts. From the insurance standpoint, this is done by acquiring the proper insurance coverage for your film.

DO NOT PRODUCE A FILM OR VIDEO UNLESS YOU HAVE THE PROPER INSURANCE. No film is worth the potential financial ruin a lawsuit could cause you and your fellow collaborators.

For this chapter I enlisted Christine Sadofsky, the president of Ventura Insurance (*www.venturainsurance.com*) to illuminate the world of production insurance coverage.

Common Insurance Policies

COMMERCIAL GENERAL LIABILITY INSURANCE

This coverage will protect you from claims alleging bodily injury, property damage, personal injury, and advertising injury that you cause to a third party. A third party is someone other than your employees, unpaid volunteers, independent contractors, or freelancers. An example would be if you were shooting in a city park and a jogger tripped over an electrical cable. This basic coverage will be required to obtain permits, to rent locations, and to rent equipment. The premium for this coverage will be based on Gross Production Costs for the policy period for film, TV, and video producers. A **premium** is the fee you pay for your insurance to the insurance company. Insurance brokers are paid a commission by the insurance company when they sell you the policies. Since a premium is an estimated number, many insurers will audit the figures and require that at the end of the 12 months (the policy term), you provide the actual Gross Production Costs, and the deposit-premium paid when you bought the policy will be adjusted accordingly.

Limits are typically $1,000,000/Each Occurrence with a $2,000,000 General Aggregate (maximum the policy will pay). Higher limits are available by purchasing an Umbrella Policy. The reasons for higher limits will be discussed in the Umbrella Liability section that follows.

Deductibles are not usually found on General Liability policies issued to producers. A **deductible** is the amount of money you need to pay before the insurance company will pay an approved claim.

WORKER'S COMPENSATION INSURANCE

This insurance covers workers (cast and crew) both freelancers and independent contractors who do not have their own policies, in case they have an accident on a job that requires medical attention. The policy provides for full reimbursement of all medical costs and a percentage of lost wages if the employee cannot work. There is a minimum number of days that the employee must be out of work for lost wages to kick in.

This policy also provides Employer's Liability coverage to protect the production company/employer for third party claims against the production company/employer arising out of an injury to an employee (a spouse who brings a lawsuit against the employer). It's important to note that if you decide to use a payroll service company which becomes the employer of record for the production, you still should obtain a basic workers compensation policy for the minimum premium, since the Employer's Liability coverage under the payroll service company DOES NOT extend to your company, leaving you exposed. Also, if you have a volunteer or someone you pay cash to and this person is injured while working for you, the payroll service company will not cover that loss, since they have no record of this person.

The premium for this policy is based on the actual compensation you will pay to all full-time employees, freelancers, and independent contractors. This compensation is multiplied by a rate for a certain class of employee (the rate is higher for a gaffer than it is for an production office coordinator). Then there are taxes and fees that are calculated to develop the final deposit premium. This policy is auditable at the end of the policy period because the compensation given upfront most likely was an estimate and will need to be adjusted at the end of the 12 months. It's important to keep good bank records and accounts payables so you know how much you spent on Gross Production Costs during that 12-month period.

DISABILITY INSURANCE

This policy is also **statutory** (required by law) and employers need to provide coverage for employees for injuries that occur off the job. The current benefit is only $170 per week for up to 26 weeks, and the cost of this policy is very inexpensive. Failure to have this policy will also result in a fine. There are five states (NY, NJ, RI, CT and CA) that require disability insurance for employees.

AUTO INSURANCE

Whether you own, rent, borrow, or hire an automobile, you will need Auto Liability to protect you from claims alleging bodily injury and/or property damage that you may have caused while operating an automobile. In addition, most owners of the vehicles want you to protect their vehicles from physical damage in case of accidents.

The primary limit of liability found under an auto policy is $1,000,000 and the coverage for physical damage will vary by insurance company. This damage to the auto will also be subject to a deductible, for example $1,000. Therefore if you damage the auto and the total cost to repair the auto is $3,500, you will be responsible for the first $1,000 and the insurance company will pay the rest of the claim.

The premium for this type of insurance will depend upon whether you own, lease, or rent the vehicle. If you own or lease the vehicle, you will need to provide the year, make, model, VIN# (Vehicle Identification Number), cost new, garaging location, and the driver information. If you are renting the vehicles, you will need to provide the total cost of rental charges you expect to incur during the 12-month policy period.

PRODUCTION INSURANCE

This policy covers many aspects of the production and depending upon the size of the production, you should never shoot without it.

NEGATIVE FILM/VIDEOTAPE PRODUCTION COVERAGE

The policy starts with coverage to protect your "master" whether this is film, video, or HD. After shooting for the entire 15-hour day, if this "master" is destroyed, lost, or stolen, the policy will give you the funds to reshoot the work. Example: If someone leaves the laptop computer with the only copy of the film's digital footage at the airport by accident, the insurance will pay for the reshoot costs.

FAULTY STOCK, CAMERA, & PROCESSING COVERAGE

If the camera has a cracked lens, or the lab destroys your film or the raw stock you purchased was damaged, you will need to reshoot the segments and the coverage will provide the funds to do so, less your deductible. Example: If the AC removes a camera lens out of a lens case and discovers there is a crack and you can't shoot the scene.

EXTRA EXPENSE COVERAGE

If any of the property being used for the production is damaged or destroyed and you have to cancel or postpone the production, you may incur extra expenses because of this loss. The policy will reimburse you for any EXTRA EXPENSE you incur as a result, less your deductible. Example: If there is a fire at your location the night before your shoot.

PROPS, SETS, & WARDROBES COVERAGE

If the production either owns or rents props, sets, or wardrobe, the policy will provide coverage in case there is a loss and these items have to be replaced, less the deductible. Example: If someone drops and breaks a prop and it needs to be replaced.

THIRD-PARTY PROPERTY DAMAGE COVERAGE

Provides protection to the production company in case someone working for the production damages the location they are working in, less the deductible. Example: A grip accidentally ruins a location's wooden floor by using the wrong tape and destroying the finish.

CAST INSURANCE COVERAGE

If a declared cast member has an accident or becomes ill and cannot work, this coverage will reimburse the production company for any extra expense that is incurred due to the interruption, postponement, or cancellation of the production, less the deductible. In order to have sickness coverage apply, each declared person must undergo a medical exam by a CAST doctor and after the underwriter approves the medical, then full cast coverage can be included. This coverage is not an automatic part of the policy so this must be discussed with your broker. This kind of coverage is usually purchased for a television series and $3-million, or higher, film productions.

FAMILY BEREAVEMENT COVERAGE

This coverage extends the coverage to include reimbursement to the production company in case a declared cast member must leave the production due to the death of an immediate family member, subject to a limit per loss and/or a specified numbers of days and less the deductible.

UMBRELLA INSURANCE

This policy will provide higher limits of liability over several policies. If you decide to purchase a $5,000,000 Umbrella, this limit will be available for claims over and above the primary General Liability, Employer's

Liability, and Auto Liability (as discussed above). The reasons for this coverage will vary but sometimes you are contractually required to have more than $1,000,000; or you have a big production with many autos, cast, crew, and hazardous activities and you want the higher limits to give you better protection.

The premium for this is actually based on the premiums for the coverage that "sit underneath" this policy. So they will look at what the premium is for General Liability, Auto Liability and, sometimes, Employer's Liability charges and price it accordingly.

ERRORS & OMISSION (E&O) INSURANCE

This insurance provides defense and indemnity from claims alleging copyright infringement, trademark infringement, plagiarism, libel, slander, defamation, and other media perils that arise from the CONTENT OF YOUR MEDIA. This coverage can start the moment your project starts shooting but typically, unless there is a definitive distribution agreement in place, a producer would not purchase this coverage until it is required by the distribution company. The premium is based on the entities — both domestic and international — where your film will be screened. Worldwide distribution is higher than if the film is only playing on a domestic cable television network.

The limits will start at $1,000,000/Each Occurrence and will go as high as $5,000,000/Each Occurrence — this will depend upon your contract with your distributor. The policy period is usually longer than one year and/or will include a rights period endorsement so that the distributor is covered throughout the contract period. The premium for this type of policy will depend upon the size of the budget, the length of the production, the territory for distribution, the type of production (for example: a documentary vs. a reality TV show), and the answers to the questions in the application. This coverage will require a completed Media application and the answers in this application become a **warranty** under the policy, so it's critical that the application be completed accurately. If you fill out the form and say you have certain signed releases and licenses, but you don't, if there is a claim, it will not be covered. This policy can also be extended to cover the title of the production, music, film clips, and merchandise.

UNION TRAVEL ACCIDENT INSURANCE

When productions employ various union personnel there will be requirements that the production company provide travel/accident insurance for its members. This coverage and the benefits paid are in addition to the workers' compensation policy. The premium is based on the total number of union vs. non-union personnel, their travel plans (if any), and the type of hazard/work they will be performing. The limit for the insurance will be determined by the various union contracts.

FOREIGN PACKAGE POLICY

If the production requires traveling outside of the U.S., Canada, Puerto Rico, or any of the U.S. territories, you will need to obtain a foreign policy in order to have all the same coverage you had here follow you, wherever you may go. This policy provides Foreign General Liability, Foreign Excess Auto Liability (excess over the coverage on the auto you are renting) and Foreign Workers' Compensation. The premium for this is based upon the foreign budget figures, the number of cast and crew traveling, the duration of the trip, and the concentration of people traveling together. The more individuals you have traveling together on the same aircraft, the higher the premium for the foreign workers compensation.

Workers' compensation does not exist in other countries. Many countries have national health care coverage but it will not cover U.S. citizens. You'll need to extend your coverage for the U.S. crew when they travel and shoot abroad.

To cover the local crew in a foreign country, you may want to hire a local production services' company that will hire the local crew and the production can use their insurance, as well.

OTHER SPECIALTY COVERAGE

I. Stunts and hazardous activities need to be discussed, upfront, with your insurance company so that they can fully understand the nature of the hazard and work with you to control the potential for loss.

II. Animals can be a part of your production and you will need to have your production policy amended to include coverage for any extra expenses you may incur if the animals cannot perform, causing you to shut down your production. In addition, you may be required to have Animal Mortality insurance in case the animal dies during the production while in your case, custody, and control.

III. Railroad Protective liability is required by most municipal public transport operations if you need to film on the platforms or in the actual train cars. This is a separate policy that requires extra time to obtain the insurance and this insurance is usually for the benefit of the municipal authority.

IV. Watercraft insurance is required if you rent watercraft to be used in the production. You will need non-owned watercraft liability and hull coverage (for damage to the boat) and this, too, is a separate policy so give yourself enough time to arrange for this.

V. Aircraft insurance is more common than you think. If you have aerial photography as part of your production, you will need to obtain quotes for non-owned aircraft liability insurance. Most times, you can request a Waiver of Subrogation on the aircraft hull (the body of the plane) because trying to obtain coverage for this hull is cost prohibitive. Again, this takes some time to arrange, so plan ahead. Don't just work under the pilot's insurance for your production because it won't protect you if someone is hurt by something that your production did to the aircraft.

VI. Weather insurance is very important if you are filming live outdoor events. Certainly unexpected bad weather will cause the event to be cancelled and without this coverage, you will incur costs for the shooting day(s) and will not have any means of reimbursement unless you buy weather insurance. The premium is determined by the number of hours you need the protection and by the type of weather you are either insuring against or insuring for. (For example, if you need complete sunshine in Seattle, WA, it will cost more than if you plan to shoot in Florida.)

Completion Bond/Guaranty

A completion bond is a written agreement that guarantees that a film will be completed on time and on budget. It is for the benefit of the investors and is usually not required for low-budget, independent films. If your investors require a completion bond you will need to contact a bond company and go through a rigorous process to get approval. The bond company will want to see the script, the schedule, the budget, resumes of key department heads and cast and information about the investors and their financial commitments. They will also want to meet with the director and the key prodction team to determine their experience to deliver the film as promised. The fee for a bond (usually about 3% of the total budget) may be a flat fee on a low-budget film.

How Do You Obtain Insurance?

A production program, including all of the insurance discussed above, is usually purchased through an insurance company that specializes in this kind of insurance coverage. Go the *www.ProducerToProducer.com* for more information about insurance companies.

When you are ready to purchase a policy, you need to work with an insurance broker who also specializes in production insurance. He will ask you to fill out a production application. You'll need to decide on how many months you will want to have coverage (up to a year), what kind of coverage you require, what deductibles you wish to have and what limits of coverage you need. It's best to ask for a bid for small deductibles and high limits and find out what that will cost — you can always adjust those factors to decrease the premium cost later. The longer the duration of the policy, the cheaper it will cost on a per-month basis. Getting a one-month policy is the least cost effective option but if you will only need it for one month, it will be cheaper than an annual policy. But if you think you will have more than one project over the course of the coming year, an annual policy may be the best option. You can amortize it across the 12 months. It pays to have the broker **market** (bid out) your insurance to all the insurance companies that he works with so you can see what the best deal is for you and your company. Some brokers have an online quote system which allows you to answer questions online and then receive an estimate via email. Some insurance companies also allow you to finance the payments over a longer period of time.

Based upon the information in the production application, you may also be asked for resumes of the principals or key employees, a list of projects that you have worked on in the past and whether or not you have had insurance before. If you are actually **remarketing** (bidding out for a renewal) your insurance, you will also be asked for a **loss run**, which is a report that your insurance company produces that will show whether or not you have had claims.

Once the broker has all the information and receives quotes from the various insurance companies, you will receive a formal proposal with all the options and at that time, you and the broker can decide which is the best program for you.

How Insurance Brokers Work

Each bid may be different regarding the limits and some of the exemptions so make sure you read them carefully. Don't just go with the cheapest quote — it needs to be the right coverage and your broker will advise you.

Once you have decided to purchase the policy, the broker will take your full payment for the premium or offer you a financing plan with a monthly payment schedule after you provide an initial down payment. Upon receipt of the payment and written approval from you, the agency will **bind** (make it effective) your policy and issue you the certificates as proof of coverage.

Agents will answer any questions you have during the process of buying the policy or any questions that arise during the period that you carry the coverage. Agents will also facilitate any claims that may occur during the policy period.

Once the insurance is in place, the broker's job isn't finished. Throughout your policy period, you may have questions, or you may need to adjust your policy to reflect a new project or you may have a claim and need to report the loss to the insurance company. The servicing of your insurance is one factor that distinguishes brokers from one another. Determining which brokers are right for you means deciding on location, so that you are in the same time zone, whether or not they are readily available to assist you when you call, how fast they turn around requests, and how much they truly understand your business.

Certificate Issuance

When renting equipment or a location, you'll need to provide proof of your insurance coverage to the vendor or owner. This will be done by obtaining certificates for vendors with the correct language and sending to them via email or fax. Once the vendors or owners receive the certificates, they know they are covered and will allow you to pick up the equipment or enter the location premises.

Your insurance broker will explain the procedure for obtaining certificates. Some require you to fill out an online form or send an email. They will then type up the certificates and send them to you via email or fax. Others have an online system that they give you access to and you simply type in the name and address of the company requesting the certificate, click the print button and email or fax the certificate yourself.

When you are adding an entity to your insurance as an **Additional Insured,** you are actually offering to protect them in case your employees cause an injury to a third party and, in that situation, the entity is also sued with you. They want your insurance company to defend them since "you" caused the claim.

When you are adding an entity to your insurance as a **Loss Payee**, you are recognizing that you have their property in your care, custody, and control and if you damage it, you will be responsible to them for its replacement.

There are several types of certificates that can be requested:

Evidence Only — this certificate simply shows the coverage you have purchased as proof only.

Equipment Rental Certificates — where the certificate will include your general liability and equipment coverage and it will include the rental company as an Additional Insured and Loss Payee.

Location Certificate — where the certificate will include your general liability and workers' compensation and it will include the owner of the location as an Additional Insured on the general liability policy.

Permit Certificate — can be a very specific form issued by the municipality, or a standard certificate, but with specific wording. In most cases, brokers must issue these certificates even if they have online systems. The certificate will list your general liability policy and sometimes, the auto, workers' compensation and umbrella, depending upon who is asking, and the municipality will be added as an Additional Insured.

Auto Certificates — are issued for the rental of equipment vans, honey wagons, prop cars, etc. These companies also want to be listed as Additional Insured and Loss Payee, too.

Insurance Audits

Unlike an audit from the IRS, an insurance audit is a way for the insurance company to obtain the actual exposure and change the premium accordingly. Since some of the policies are based on production costs and compensation, and each of these figures will change throughout the 12-month policy period, the audit simply adjusts the premium to reflect the actual exposure. So, for example, if you estimated $1,000,000 of production costs and you actually had $1,500,000, you will owe more premium for the additional $500,000. Conversely if you only had $800,000 at the end of the policy term, then you would receive a return premium for the extra $200,000.

An insurance audit occurs at the end of your policy's coverage period. The insurance company will have you answer a questionnaire about how much money you spent on cast/crew salaries and production costs throughout the policy period. It's important to keep accurate records of all of your financial transactions so you can answer the questions quickly and accurately.

What to Do When You Have a Claim?

Insurance brokers play a key role if you ever have an insurance **claim**. As soon as an accident occurs or something is lost, stolen, or damaged, you will need to notify your insurance broker. She will ask you specific questions and let you know how to proceed. You'll need to fill out a claim report, giving very specific details (i.e., how/where the accident occurred, what piece of equipment (with serial #s) was stolen or how/what damage was done to a location). You many need to file a police report, substantiate the equipment's value, send in copies of medical reports, take photos, etc., and she will advise you on what is needed to submit the claim.

Insurance brokers also determine if the claim equals an amount that is higher than your deductible. If the cost of replacement is less than your policy's deductible, then you don't have a claim to report, since this portion is your responsibility. But if the costs exceed the deductible amount, it will probably be worthwhile. One caveat — once you put in a claim on a policy, it will be noted the next time you go to renew your policy. Insurance carriers may determine that your company is a higher risk and your premium may be more expensive next time because of the former claim. Keep that in mind when you are deciding what to do but always discuss all the options with your broker.

Things You Should Know

1. You can't "sell" or "rent" your insurance policy to anyone else. The coverage afforded under the policy was issued to you and it was based on the information about you and your company. Coverage will not respond in a claim if you try to allow another production company to "use your insurance."

2. You can't cover your equipment rental business (something you just started to do because producing was slow) using your production

policy. A production policy is not going to cover the operations of a rental facility — you must call your broker.

3. You can't change a certificate of insurance, once it was issued, to reflect higher limits, or coverage that you forgot to buy, since this evidence of insurance is on record with the broker and in a claim situation, the parties will realize the certificate was illegally modified.

4. You can't buy coverage today and then put it a claim for something that already happened. A known loss is not going to be covered unless the loss occurs after you first buy the insurance.

5. Your homeowner's or tenant's coverage won't cover your business.

6. There is no insurance to cover the investors if the production does not do well in theaters or during distribution.

7. You can't cover the personal effects (i.e., jewelry, jackets, laptops) of your employees.

Never Go into Production Without Insurance

It is vitally important that you obtain the proper insurance coverage for any of your films. If you don't have insurance, it will be virtually impossible to rent equipment, props, or a location for your production. But even if you don't have those immediate considerations, there are greater liability issues that are of concern for you and everyone involved on your production. You don't want to take the chance that someone gets hurt or a very expensive piece of equipment gets broken and your future personal financial health is at serious risk because of a lawsuit or because a collection agency has decided to go after you. It's only a film and nothing is ever worth the risk. It's important to sleep well at night.

RECAP

1. **Do not go into production without the proper insurance coverage.**

2. **Plan to obtain insurance many weeks before you plan to shoot so you can discuss your production needs with your insurance broker.**

3. The insurance broker will bid out to insurance companies for your needs and make recommendations about what coverage to purchase.

4. Commercial General Liability, Worker's compensation, Disability, Auto, Production, Umbrella, E&O, Union Travel Accident, Foreign Package, and Specialty insurance are all options for your production needs.

5. Certificates are issued by the insurance broker when you send the correct information for each certificate holder request.

6. When the insurance policy expires you will send in total gross production costs to the insurance company to comply with the audit.

7. Your insurance broker will assist you if you have a claim.

CHAPTER 10

SCHEDULING

Overview

SCHEDULING FOR A FILM is one of the most critical steps in the preproduction process. It's the road map for the film. Once you have a solid working draft of the shooting schedule, the various departments can start to plan when they need to do certain work or acquire equipment or props for certain days. The schedule will also dictate which actors work on which days and that affects the schedule for the costume, hair and makeup departments.

Scheduling is a paradox — a fixed set of plans and assumptions that the entire production works with, but a schedule can never be locked in stone because it must be fluid enough to react to real time changes and adjustments. For instance, you plan on shooting a day of exterior scenes in the local park but if, 24 hours before the call time, the weather forecast calls for torrential rain, you are going to have to change the schedule. It will have to switch to the cover set and the shoot will be inside all day. All departments must be alerted to the change so they can prep the new scenes for the revised schedule.

> *"No matter. Try again.*
>
> *Fail again. Fail better."*
>
> *— Samuel Becket,*
>
> **Worstward Ho**

The shooting schedule for your film is usually created by the film's assistant director. On very low-budget projects you may not be able to afford to hire an AD or you may only be able to have someone on the production for the shoot dates and not for any prep time. In that case, the producer usually creates the first pass at the shooting schedule. That's what we did on *MAN ON WIRE* — I created the first draft of the schedule so we could get a general idea of how to plan for the film. Then, a week before we started production, 1st AD Curtis Smith and 2nd AD Eric Berkal came on board and finalized the schedule. Thankfully, my original plan was close to what Curtis created, so we were able to move forward quickly in the final prep for the film. For the purposes of this chapter, we will assume you have an AD who will come on board early in the preproduction phase of the film.

Script Breakdown

Earlier in the book we discussed the script breakdown. If you created an initial script breakdown, now the AD will do the final breakdown several weeks before commencement of principal photography. The script should be locked at this point — any additional changes should be only dialogue/word changes and nothing that affects locations, props, wardrobe, lighting, and hair/makeup.

To create a script breakdown, the AD can use computer software programs or do it with custom-made forms. There are many film-scheduling computer software programs on the market today. One of the most common scheduling programs is EP Scheduling™ and that is what I have used here for the *Red Flag* examples. It is easy to learn and will allow you to create a script breakdown, shooting schedule and all of the other forms that the AD needs to distribute to the cast and crew.

Element Sheet Creation

With a computer software program, each scene will have a separate breakdown elements sheet. The AD will enter all of the elements from each scene in the script into the breakdown elements sheet (similar to the one in the *Script Breakdown* chapter). The elements that are entered on the breakdown sheet are the following: cast; background actors (extras); vehicles; stunts; SFX; props; wardrobe; hair/makeup; animals; locations; and set.

The following is the set of sheets for the case study film *Red Flag*. The short film has 9 scenes and there are 9 sheets, one for each scene. All of the element sheets and stripboards utilize Movie Magic Scheduling software.[1]

[1.] Screen shot created using Movie Magic Scheduling software owned by Entertainment Partners. For more information, http://www.entertainmentpartners.com/Content/Products/Scheduling.aspx

Scene #:   1   Sheet #:   1
                              Breakdown Sheet   Int/Ext: EXT
Script Page: Day/Night: Evening
Page Count: 4/8

Scene Description: Montage of couples meeting on NYC streets
Settings: NYC streets
Location: NYC streets
Sequence: Script Day:

	Background Actors 5 couples-NYC streets	**Props** Store bought flowers Wrist watch

Scene #:	2	Breakdown Sheet	Sheet #:	2
			Int/Ext:	EXT
Script Page:			Day/Night:	Evening
Page Count:	2/8			

Scene Description: Tracy walks into bar.

Settings: Bar #1

Location: NYC Bar

Sequence: Script Day:

Cast Members Tracy		
	Wardrobe Tracy - Day 1	

Scene #:   3

Script Page:

Page Count: 2 3/8

Breakdown Sheet

Sheet #:   11

Int/Ext: INT

Day/Night: Evening

Scene Description: Tracy meets James for blind date #1

Settings: Bar #1

Location: 1260 Bar

Sequence: Script Day:

Cast Members	Background Actors	Props
James Tracy	6 extras at bar Bartender #1	Half eaten food Red Flag #1 Remnants of a couple of drinks Toothpick wine glass
	Wardrobe James - Day 1 Tracy - Day 1	

Scene #:   4

Breakdown Sheet

Sheet #:   4

Int/Ext: INT

Script Page:

Day/Night: Evening

Page Count: 1 3/8

Scene Description: Tracy has blind date with Richard who reveals he has MS.

Settings: Bar #2

Location: The White Rabbit nightclub

Sequence: Script Day:

Cast Members	Background Actors	Props
Tracy	6 bar extras	Mixed drink w/ stirrer
Richard	Bartender #2	Red Flag #2
	Exotic woman at bar	
	Wardrobe	
	Richard - Day 2	
	Tracy - Day 2	

Scene #:	5		Sheet #:	5

Breakdown Sheet

Int/Ext: INT

Script Page:

Day/Night: Evening

Page Count: 7/8

Scene Description: Tracy goes on blind date with Comb-over Man and talks about Meercats.

Settings: Restaurant #1

Location: The White Rabbit nightclub

Sequence: Script Day:

Cast Members	Background Actors	Props
Tracy Comb-over Man	5 background actors	Red Flag #3
	Wardrobe Comb-over Man - Day 3 Tracy - Day 3	**Makeup/Hair** Comb-Over wig

Scene #:	6		Sheet #:	6

Breakdown Sheet

Int/Ext: INT

Script Page:

Day/Night: Evening

Page Count: 1 1/8

Scene Description: Tracy goes on blind date with Joe.

Settings: Restaurant #2

Location: ARIUM cafe

Sequence: Script Day:

Cast Members	Background Actors	Props
Tracy Joe	4 background actor couples	2 wine glasses Red Flag #4
	Wardrobe Joe - Day 4 Tracy - Day 4	

Scene #:	7	Breakdown Sheet	Sheet #:	7
			Int/Ext:	EXT
Script Page:			Day/Night:	Day
Page Count:	2 5/8			

Scene Description: Tracy runs into Matt in the park and thinks she has found Mr. Right.

Settings: Park

Location: Central Park

Sequence: Script Day:

Cast Members	Background Actors	Props
Matt	4 park background actors	Coffee in cup
Tracy	Coffee vendor	Coffee stirrer
		Coffee vendor cart
		Tracy's cel phone
		Tracy's watch
		Trash can

Vehicles
   Coffee vendor cart

Wardrobe
   Matt - Day 5
   Tracy - Day 5

Scene #: 8	Breakdown Sheet	Sheet #: 8
Script Page:		Int/Ext: EXT
Page Count: 1/8		Day/Night: Day

Scene Description: Tracy, Matt and Dobbs walk through the park.

Settings: Park

Location: Central Park

Sequence: Script Day:

Cast Members
  Matt
  Tracy		

	Wardrobe
	  Matt - Day 5
	  Tracy - Day 5	

Scene #: 9

Script Page:

Page Count: 1 1/8

Breakdown Sheet

Sheet #: 9

Int/Ext: EXT

Day/Night: Day

Scene Description: They all finish walking and Tracy asks to meet again, Matt says no. He turns to leave and Tracy

Settings: Park entrance

Location: Central Park

Sequence: Script Day:

Cast Members Matt Tracy		**Props** Tracy as a Red Flag
	Wardrobe Matt - Day 5 Tracy - Day 5	

Creating the Shooting Schedule

The elements sheets are usually entered into the software program in chronological order — how they occur in the script. When placed in strips, they become the **stripboard**. Below is the stripboard in chronological order.

RED FLAG CHRONOLOGICAL SCHEDULE				
1 4/8 pgs	1	EXT	NYC streets Montage of couples meeting on NYC streets	Evening
2 2/8 pgs	2	EXT	Bar #1 Tracy walks into bar.	Evening
11 2 3/8 pgs	3	INT	Bar #1 Tracy meets James for blind date #1	Evening
4 1 3/8 pgs	4	INT	Bar #2 Tracy has blind date with Richard who reveals he has MS.	Evening
5 7/8 pgs	5	INT	Restaurant #1 Tracy goes on blind date with Comb-over Man and talks about Meercats.	Evening
6 1 1/8 pgs	6	INT	Restaurant #2 Tracy goes on blind date with Joe.	Evening
7 2 5/8 pgs	7	EXT	Park Tracy runs into Matt in the park and thinks she has found Mr. Right.	Day
8 1/8 pgs	8	EXT	Park Tracy, Matt and Dobbs walk through the park.	Day
9 1 1/8 pgs	9	EXT	Park entrance They all finish walking and Tracy asks to meet again, Matt says no. He turns to leave an	Day

End Day # 1 Friday, September 19, 2008 -- Total Pages: 10 3/8

End Day # 2 Saturday, September 20, 2008 -- Total Pages:

End Day # 3 Sunday, September 21, 2008 -- Total Pages:

End Day # 4 Monday, September 22, 2008 -- Total Pages:

The first pass on creating a stripboard or shooting schedule is created by looking at the stripboard and following several scheduling principles to organize the scenes in the most cost effective and rational way.

Scheduling Principles

These are general strategies that are used as a guideline for film scheduling. Many of these were discussed in the *Script Breakdown* chapter.

1. Generally, on independent films you plan to shoot three to four script pages per day for a 12-hour day. The elements sheet contains the script-page length so, as each day's shoot is created, you can track how many pages it adds up to.

2. Schedule exterior shoots early in the production schedule, in case of inclement weather. This allows you to change the schedule and switch to a **cover set** — an interior location that is not affected by bad weather.

3. Schedule day shoots first in a schedule and switch to night shoots later. This way, you'll wrap your final day shoot in the evening and then everyone will get that night and the entire next day off before having to arrive on set that evening for the next shoot "day."

4. If at all possible, don't schedule a love scene or a very difficult or complicated scene for the first day of shooting. Put it later in the schedule when the cast and crew have gotten to know each other better and are in a groove before you tackle the more challenging scenes.

5. Also avoid shooting the beginning of the film on the first few days of shooting if possible. The beginning of a film is the most critical section of a film — audiences are trying to decide how they feel about your project. You want to start as strong as possible, at the beginning. It's best to shoot the opening scenes of a film later in the schedule. That way the director and the crew have gotten into a groove, the actors have established their characters for themselves and the look of the film as been figured out and is consistent. The corollary to this principle is to *not* shoot the last few scenes on the first day, either. The ending is the next most important section of a film and you want the director and the actors to figure out the character arcs ahead of time.

6. Try to make the first day of shooting a relatively easy day, so you have a better chance of it going well. It allows the cast/crew to gather information after the first day of principal photography.

7. If possible, shoot out individual actors on one or two days, if they only play in a few scenes. **Shooting out an actor** means that you group all the their scenes together in the schedule so you pay them for the least amount of time. If an actor only has work in four scenes out of total of 20, try to schedule them so they can all be shot in one or two days. That will save you from having to shoot four different partial days, if at all possible.

8. When using elderly actors, or actors with limits to their stamina, try to keep their shoot days shorter.

9. When shooting with children, consult the labor regulations for minors (children under 18 years old) in the U.S. state you are shooting in. Depending on the regulations, the children's ages will limit the amount of hours per day they can shoot on set. The regulations may also limit which hours of the day they can shoot (perhaps no night shooting) and may require an on-set tutor for school study purposes, during the academic year. Go to *www.ProducerToProducer.com* to get more information.

10. When shooting any special effects (SFX), weapons, pyrotechnics, or choreography (fight or dance) consult with the SFX coordinator, weapons specialist, pyrotechnics person or choreographer to find out if they have any special needs and how it will impact the schedule.

11. The same goes for any scene that requires an animal. Consult the animal trainer or handler to find out what to expect and how it may impact the schedule for any given scene.

12. In general, when scheduling the shooting order of specific shots for any scene, schedule the wide shot first, then medium shots, then close-ups. It helps with continuity.

13. Hardly ever, will you shoot the script in chronological order. Although, it may be helpful or comforting to the director and/or actors to do so, it is almost never the most efficient or cost effective way to shoot the film. Film actors and crew are used to doing this and learn how to achieve continuity in their performances and across all the departments. Keep continuity with the assistance of a good script supervisor.

14. Keep company moves to a minimum because they eat up a lot of non-filming time. A **company move** is when you have to pack up everything — cast, crew, equipment, props, etc., and move to another separate location. This is not the same as when you move from shooting in the bedroom to the living room in the same house location.

15. Keep in mind any location specifics, i.e., if you can't shoot on weekends or a certain location is only available during specific times. That will need to be factored into the scheduling.

Once you and the AD understand the previous scheduling principles, the AD can get started making the first pass at the schedule. Break out all the scenes at one location on the same day. If there are too many for one day, then put them on multiple days.

Once the AD has laid out the schedule in a form that makes sense, send it out to the director for comments and change requests. After approval, send it to all the department heads. You'll find out quickly if there are any scheduling issues that affect the various departments. Then it's time to adjust and make final decisions.

If the director does not have a final shot list, there should be a conversation about how many shots and setups the director is thinking about for each scene. Will there be a need to set up a dolly or crane? Will a Steadicam be used for shooting any of the scenes? Any important (and time-consuming) set ups that the DP needs for a location? Gelling of windows, big lighting set ups? What about the art department — they need to prep for a specific scene or location? Do they have to get to the location a day or two ahead of time to set dress? Hair/makeup — what do they estimate for their work on the actors at the beginning of the day? Do they have to create specific horror makeup that takes longer for one of the characters? What about costumes — any special circumstances? The AD will discuss with each department head so they know if there is anything that will add more time to the schedule.

Scheduling Steps

Creating a schedule has many steps and paperwork documents that emanate from those steps. The first step is to create a stripboard. From the stripboard, you can create many other forms that different departments require. We'll go through the steps here and use the short film *Red Flag* from earlier in this book to illustrate the steps. I used the EP

Scheduling software application so you'll see the paperwork generated by the application and how it all fits together.

Stripboard Creation

Once I saw all the issues for the film laid out in the elements sheets, I grouped the scenes based on each location we needed. We had a total of six locations but wanted to shoot in three days. So we had to double up on one day and do a company move to another location in the afternoon to make our schedule work. Below is the Stripboard schedule that was created using Movie Magic Scheduling software:

RED FLAG CHRONOLOGICAL SCHEDULE

11 2 3/8 pgs	3	INT	Bar #1 Tracy meets James for blind date #1	Evening
6 1 1/8 pgs	6	INT	Restaurant #2 Tracy goes on blind date with Joe.	Evening
End Day # 1 Friday, September 19, 2008 -- Total Pages: 3 4/8				
1 4/8 pgs	1	EXT	NYC streets Montage of couples meeting on NYC streets	Evening
2 2/8 pgs	2	EXT	Bar #1 Tracy walks into bar.	Evening
End Day # 2 Saturday, September 20, 2008 -- Total Pages: 6/8				
5 7/8 pgs	5	INT	Restaurant #1 Tracy goes on blind date with Comb-over Man and talks about Meercats.	Evening
4 1 3/8 pgs	4	INT	Bar #2 Tracy has blind date with Richard who reveals he has MS.	Evening
End Day # 3 Sunday, September 21, 2008 -- Total Pages: 2 2/8				
7 2 5/8 pgs	7	EXT	Park Tracy runs into Matt in the park and thinks she has found Mr. Right.	Day
8 1/8 pgs	8	EXT	Park Tracy, Matt and Dobbs walk through the park.	Day
9 1 1/8 pgs	9	EXT	Park entrance They all finish walking and Tracy asks to meet again, Matt says no. He turns to leave an	Day
End Day # 4 Monday, September 22, 2008 -- Total Pages: 3 7/8				

Several other points to note:

1. *Red Flag* is an 11-page script. Based on the three to five pages per day, we planned to shoot the film in three days. Everyone on the crew was donating his or her time. This was a big donation from a very professional crew so I wanted to keep the shooting time down to the absolute minimum. It would be tight, but doable.

2. All of our scenes were interiors except for the end of the film where all the scenes take place outside in Central Park in NYC. We were shooting in late September so I knew rain was a possibility. I scheduled the Central Park day as our first day in the schedule. Even though these scenes are the final scenes of the film I put them first because it was a full day of exteriors. If we found out that it was going to rain, I could always switch to one of the other cover sets and rearrange the schedule. In fact, that is what happened — 24 hours before our first day of shooting the forecast called for torrential rain and we switched to the Day 4 schedule for the bar and the restaurant.

3. We didn't have any night shooting so everything was scheduled for typical 12-hour work days — usually 6:00 a.m. – 6.30 p.m. On our last day in Central Park we used available light, so we started a little earlier to make sure we maximized all the daylight for a shoot in September in NYC.

4. We didn't have any problematic acting scenes in the script (no nudity, violence, or extreme emotional distress) and we had very strong actors so I didn't have to worry about what scene to schedule first.

5. Because of the rain on the first day, we ended up shooting the first scene in the film as the first scene in our schedule. It was not ideal — we had to work out some technical issues and everyone was getting up to speed. If I could have changed it I would have, but there was no choice.

6. Our first day of shooting was a doable day — not the easiest, but no harder than any others.

7. We were able to shoot out our actors. Our lead character was Tracy and she was in every scene. All the scenes were blind dates

so it was easy to schedule each male actor for only one day or half day and not require them to return for another day of shooting.

8. We did not have any elderly actors or anything that required additional time for the schedule.

9. We did not have any minors in the film.

10. We had a special effect that played in each scene in the film — the red flag that was added in postproduction. I met with the director, DP, and the visual effects producer to discuss what we'd need to do when we were shooting the film to make sure we had everything the effects producer would need in post to create the graphics of the red flag. We needed to be mindful of framing and timing on certain shots. Otherwise we had nothing that would require additional time to the schedule.

11. We had one dog that played in all the scenes that were shot in Central Park. Our make up artist had an older dog that he knew would be mellow and just sit on the end of the leash for the particular scenes. No additional time was required. Central Park has a dog-friendly policy that requires dogs on leashes between 9:00 a.m. – 9:00 p.m.

12. The film language (the kind of camera shots that were devised for this film) for *Red Flag* was fairly straightforward. We shot everything either on a tripod or handheld. We usually shot in close ups and medium shots with a few wider shots.

13. We shot the beginning of the film first, then mixed up the middle scenes and shot the end of the film last. This worked out nicely, but if we had had good weather on the first day we would have shot the end of the film first. Our talented script supervisor was on top of all the continuity.

14. Location schedules impacted our schedule quite a bit. We were shooting 75% of the film in restaurants and cafes — most of which are open early and closed late, seven days per week. Here is the list: Bar #1 — I found a bar that opened at 4:00 p.m. every day and was willing to let us come in at 7:00 a.m. and pay the bar's cleaner to stay with us until we left at 3:00 p.m.
Bar #2 and Restaurant #1 — I found a nightclub that was closed on Sundays and big enough to double as two different spaces. We

used it for Bar #2 and for Restaurant #1 which we turned into the "cupcake café" that plays for the 3rd blind date in the film.

Restaurant #2 — I found an upscale café that was closed in the evening and let us do a half-day shoot there.

Park — It was early autumn in NYC so I knew that Central Park would be packed on the weekend. We planned to shoot on one of the weekdays to avoid the crowds.

Our shoot ended up being on a Friday, Sunday, and Monday with a few pick-up shots for the montage and the exterior walking-into-the-bar shot on Saturday with only the DP, the director, the actress playing Tracy, a few extras, and me.

Day-Out-of-Days Schedule

After you have entered all of your elements in the script breakdown and then created your stripboard, you will then create several Day-Out-of-Days schedules that track the various production elements so each production department can plan for its elements on a day-by-day basis. These are the elements: cast, background actors (extras), vehicles, props, wardrobe, hair/makeup, animals, locations, and set.

The Day-Out-of-Days schedules focus on one element only and track it for each shooting day of the production schedule. It comes in the form of a very stripped down calendar with a "short hand" for when each element "starts and stops work" on the film. Here's the Cast Day-Out-of-Days for *Red Flag:*

Feb 7, 2010
8:00 PM   **Day Out of Days Report for Cast Members**

Month/Day	09/19	09/20	09/21	09/22	Co.						
Day of Week	Fri	Sat	Sun	Mon	Travel	Work	Hold	Holiday	Start	Finish	TOTAL
Shooting Day	1	2	3	4							
Matt				SWF		1			09/22	09/22	1
Tracy	SW	W	W	WF		4			09/19	09/22	4
Comb-over Man			SWF			1			09/21	09/21	1
Richard			SWF			1			09/21	09/21	1
James	SWF					1			09/19	09/19	1
Joe	SWF					1			09/19	09/19	1

Each cast member is listed in the left-hand column. The rest of the columns refer to the shoot dates and work schedule.

SW — Start Work — The first day that the character works on the film

W — Work — Each day that the character works on the film

WF — Work Finish — The last day that the character works on the film

SWF — Start Work Finish — The first and last day that the character works on the film

Travel — Refers to the total number of travel days for the character

Work — Refers to the total number of work days for the character

Holiday — Refers to the total number of holidays for the character

Start — The date that the character begins work on the film

Finish — The date that the character finishes work on the film

Total — The total number of travel, work, and holidays the character has in the film's work schedule

Below is the rest of the Day-Out-of-Days schedules for the rest of the departments for *Red Flag:*

Feb 7, 2010
8:00 PM   **Day Out of Days Report for Location**

	Month/Day	09/19	09/20	09/21	09/22	Co.						
	Day of Week	Fri	Sat	Sun	Mon	Travel	Work	Hold	Holiday	Start	Finish	TOTAL
	Shooting Day	1	2	3	4							
NYC Bar			SWF				1			09/20	09/20	1
NYC streets			SWF				1			09/20	09/20	1
1260 Bar		SWF					1			09/19	09/19	1
ARIUM cafe		SWF					1			09/19	09/19	1
The White Rabbit nightclub				SWF			1			09/21	09/21	1
Central Park					SWF		1			09/22	09/22	1

Feb 7, 2010
8:00 PM   **Day Out of Days Report for Background Actors**

	Month/Day	09/19	09/20	09/21	09/22	Co.							
	Day of Week	Fri	Sat	Sun	Mon	Travel	Work	Hold	Holiday	Start	Finish	TOTAL
	Shooting Day	1	2	3	4							
4 background actor couples		SWF					1			09/19	09/19	1
4 park background actors					SWF		1			09/22	09/22	1
5 background actors				SWF			1			09/21	09/21	1
5 couples-NYC streets			SWF				1			09/20	09/20	1
6 bar extras				SWF			1			09/21	09/21	1
6 extras at bar		SWF					1			09/19	09/19	1
Bartender #1		SWF					1			09/19	09/19	1
Bartender #2				SWF			1			09/21	09/21	1
Coffee vendor					SWF		1			09/22	09/22	1
Exotic woman at bar				SWF			1			09/21	09/21	1

Feb 7, 2010
8:00 PM   **Day Out of Days Report for Props**

	Month/Day	09/19	09/20	09/21	09/22	Co.							
	Day of Week	Fri	Sat	Sun	Mon	Travel	Work	Hold	Holiday	Start	Finish	TOTAL
	Shooting Day	1	2	3	4							
2 wine glasses		SWF					1			09/19	09/19	1
Coffee in cup					SWF		1			09/22	09/22	1
Coffee stirrer					SWF		1			09/22	09/22	1
Coffee vendor cart					SWF		1			09/22	09/22	1
Half eaten food		SWF					1			09/19	09/19	1
Mixed drink w/ stirrer				SWF			1			09/21	09/21	1
Red Flag #1		SWF					1			09/19	09/19	1
Red Flag #2				SWF			1			09/21	09/21	1
Red Flag #3				SWF			1			09/21	09/21	1
Red Flag #4		SWF					1			09/19	09/19	1
Remnants of a couple of drinks		SWF					1			09/19	09/19	1
Store bought flowers			SWF				1			09/20	09/20	1
Toothpick		SWF					1			09/19	09/19	1
Tracy as a Red Flag					SWF		1			09/22	09/22	1
Tracy's cel phone					SWF		1			09/22	09/22	1
Tracy's watch					SWF		1			09/22	09/22	1
Trash can					SWF		1			09/22	09/22	1
wine glass		SWF					1			09/19	09/19	1
Wrist watch			SWF				1			09/20	09/20	1

Feb 7, 2010
8:00 PM   Day Out of Days Report for Makeup/Hair

Month/Day	09/19	09/20	09/21	09/22	Co.						
Day of Week	Fri	Sat	Sun	Mon	Travel	Work	Hold	Holiday	Start	Finish	TOTAL
Shooting Day	1	2	3	4							
Comb-Over wig			SWF			1			09/21	09/21	1

Feb 7, 2010
8:00 PM   Day Out of Days Report for Set

Month/Day	09/19	09/20	09/21	09/22	Co.						
Day of Week	Fri	Sat	Sun	Mon	Travel	Work	Hold	Holiday	Start	Finish	TOTAL
Shooting Day	1	2	3	4							
Bar #1	SW	WF				2			09/19	09/20	2
Bar #2			SWF			1			09/21	09/21	1
NYC streets		SWF				1			09/20	09/20	1
Park				SWF		1			09/22	09/22	1
Park entrance				SWF		1			09/22	09/22	1
Restaurant #1			SWF			1			09/21	09/21	1
Restaurant #2	SWF					1			09/19	09/19	1
Restaurant #3											0
Restaurant #4											0
Studio											0

Feb 7, 2010
8:00 PM   Day Out of Days Report for Animals

Month/Day	09/19	09/20	09/21	09/22	Co.						
Day of Week	Fri	Sat	Sun	Mon	Travel	Work	Hold	Holiday	Start	Finish	TOTAL
Shooting Day	1	2	3	4							
Dog				SWF		1			09/22	09/22	1

Feb 7, 2010
8:00 PM   **Day Out of Days Report for Wardrobe**

Month/Day	09/19	09/20	09/21	09/22	Co.						
Day of Week	Fri	Sat	Sun	Mon	Travel	Work	Hold	Holiday	Start	Finish	TOTAL
Shooting Day	1	2	3	4							
Comb-over Man - Day 3			SWF			1			09/21	09/21	1
James - Day 1	SWF					1			09/19	09/19	1
Joe - Day 4	SWF					1			09/19	09/19	1
Matt - Day 5				SWF		1			09/22	09/22	1
Richard - Day 2			SWF			1			09/21	09/21	1
Tracy - Day 1	SWF					1			09/19	09/19	1
Tracy - Day 2			SWF			1			09/21	09/21	1
Tracy - Day 3			SWF			1			09/21	09/21	1
Tracy - Day 4	SWF					1			09/19	09/19	1
Tracy - Day 5				SWF		1			09/22	09/22	1

As you can see, all of this information is distilled from the initial Elements sheets that were created for each scene. Inputting all the elements accurately is vital so you can track each one, day-by-day and department by department. If done correctly, there shouldn't ever be a missing prop or the wrong vehicle for a particular set up on a specific shoot day.

Scheduling each shoot day — how do you know how long something will take to shoot?

Scheduling for a film is not a science, it's an art. Those who do it well have a unique combination of traits — an understanding of the big picture, the medium-sized reality and the specific minutia that factor into the ever-evolving state of a film schedule.

To schedule a shoot day, you have to base it on the size of the crew, the number of company moves, the location or studio set up time, how fast the crew can load in and set up, how fast the cast can get in and out of hair and makeup and wardrobe, and any other technical issues that could impact the schedule, i.e., setting up a crane or dolly shot.

When working on a low-budget shoot on location I usually schedule two hours from the call time at the location before I expect to get the first shot off of the day. I put that on the schedule and know that it could be 2.5 hours before we get the first shot. But that is a good rule of thumb. Then, depending on the shot list and the amount of set ups, the AD can schedule the rest of the day.

Feed your crew every 6 hours and other union regulations that affect the day's schedule

There are several rules that are part of a union contract that directly impact how to create the day's schedule. Often you will be using a non-union crew but working under a union contract for the actors. Or maybe you are working with a union camera depart and grip/electric department but everyone else is non-union. If you are working under any union contract you need to know the rules for meals and meal penalties, travel time, overtime, and the studio zone. Consult the union contract for the regulations.

Meal time — The first rule, whether or not you are working under a union contract, is to **feed your crew a hot meal every six hours.** If your call time is 7:00 a.m., then you have to break for lunch no later than 1:00 p.m. The lunch break has to be at least 30 minutes long and the "clock starts ticking" after all have received their food. If you have a lunch line for a buffet meal, you wait until each person has gotten a plate of food before you start counting the 30 minutes for the meal period. Once the crew is back up and working the clock resets and you have to provide another hot meal six hours later.

Meal penalty — **Meal penalties** are levied under a union contract when you don't feed the crew after six hours. The charge is usually added onto the hourly rate at 15-minute intervals. So if you go past the lunch period by a half hour, you'll need to pay two times the meal penalty as stipulated in the contract.

Turnaround time — **Turnaround time** is the amount of time from the end of work on one shoot day to the call time for the next consecutive shoot day. It needs to be 12 hours for actors working under a union contract. For non-union cast and crew it should be at least 10 hours to make sure the cast/crew is working under safe conditions. Anything less than 10 hours is a very unsafe situation.

Overtime — Cast and crew are paid an hourly rate based on either an 8-hour, 10-hour or 12-hour day. For union actors their rates are always based on an 8-hour day. Union contracts for crew are usually for a 10-hour day. Sometimes you negotiate a rate base on 12 hours. The meal period is often "off the clock" so it's a "free" half hour. After the cast/crew work the entire day-rate period, an hourly overtime rate is calculated at 1.5 x for usually 2 or 4 hours and then it goes up to 2 x the rate.

Studio Zone — This refers to the area around a major city that is considered "in the studio zone." It means that if you shoot inside the zone, the cast and crew do not get paid for their travel time to the set/location. Once they arrive on set for the call time, the clock starts ticking for their day rate. If you shoot outside of the studio zone then you will have to pay cast and crew travel time before they get to set and after they leave set to get home.

Travel time — Travel time refers to the time from when they leave home and get to the set and the same thing at the end of the day when traveling home. If the set is outside the studio zone then you'll have to pay them "from portal to portal." That means that the clock starts ticking from the time that they leave their homes to the time they arrive home — the travel time is "on the clock" and you have to calculate it accordingly. Sometimes you'll need to provide a van to transport cast/crew from a central meeting point and drive them to the location. In that case, the clock starts ticking from the time the van departs from the meeting point until the cast/crew is returned after the shoot is over.

Portrait of an Assistant Director

The 1st assistant director is one of the pivotal positions on any film. Like the director and producer, they set the tone for how the production operates on a week-by-week, day-by-day and hour-by-hour basis. I've worked with Ads who are tyrants and screamers. I have also worked with those who are the most competent humans on the planet. It's a tough position but for those who do it well, it's a revelation to watch them work. The best ADs operate and make decisions based on years of experience, intuition, split-second analysis, and mutual respect for others. They need to be master observers of human nature, be great negotiators (how do you get a diva starlet out of the Winnebago when she's having a tantrum?), have amazing stamina and be able to move groups (sometimes very large) of people from one place to another quickly and efficiently. In addition, they should have a deep knowledge of a director's film language and the ability to suggest shots or ways of getting a scene in the bag when the sun is setting and you are losing the light at the end of a long shoot day. It's a pretty tall order. But they are out there and when you find them and get to work with them, it's an amazing thing to watch.

HOW BEST TO WORK WITH AN ASSISTANT DIRECTOR:

ADs are the linchpins of the crew. They report to the producer and the director and it's important to keep the lines of communication clear. You need to keep them up to date on any schedule changes from the production side and they need to be reacting to the needs of the director at the same time. This can be a delicate balancing act. As producer, you want to get the director's vision on screen but you also want to stay on schedule and on budget. A good AD can help accomplish both.

Depending on the director, when we are shooting, I often only communicate with the director through the AD. I don't want to distract the director and if all communication goes through the AD, it often makes it easier. The AD is most intimately aware of what is happening on a minute-by-minute basis and can deliver the message at the right time to the director.

Often I will only speak to the director at lunch. We'll spend some time doing a reality check about the day's schedule and discuss any other pressing matters. If we are behind schedule, lunchtime is when the director, AD, and producer can strategize and decide how best to get back on track. This may be the time to discuss dropping some shots or set ups to make up time. It needs to be a gentle negotiation because no director wants to lose anything from the day's shot list. But you do need to walk away from the lunch table with a plan that everyone can live with. If you don't, the afternoon will devolve and overtime will be looming.

Consensus is key in the lunchtime discussion and as the producer you have your opinions about what is essential and what can be cut. The AD can be invaluable by helping to problem solve the situation.

Locking the Schedule

You need to lock the schedule at least a week before you plan to begin principal photography. Each department and all cast/crew need to know when to prepare for each scene. If you keep changing things around, it will really undermine the cast/crew's ability to be fully prepared for each shoot day and will have a negative impact on the film and your ability to do the best job possible.

RECAP

1. **Hire an AD several weeks before you begin principal photography to put together the final script breakdown and schedule.**

2. **Follow the scheduling principles when determining what is the best schedule for your film.**

3. After all elements are entered into the elements sheets, you'll have a stripboard in script order. The next step is to move the strips around to create the schedule in shooting order.

4. Create day-out-of-days schedules for all production elements and departments.

5. Follow all union contract rules for overtime, meal penalties, and turnaround times.

6. Work in sync with the AD to maximize the efficiency of the production department.

CHAPTER 11
PRODUCTION

N OW THAT YOU HAVE accomplished all the things discussed in the *Preproduction* chapter you are ready for the first day of principal photography. This is the moment you have been working toward for weeks/ months. It's a great feeling finally to be *making* the film, instead of just *talking about* making the film. I've never gotten over the feeling of excitement and teamwork that occurs during this phase — it's a fascinating and fulfilling process. Finally, now is the time to take a leap into the deep end of the pool.

The night before your first day of principal photography

1. VISUALIZE THE DAY TO COME
As I mentioned in the *Preproduction* chapter, pre-visualization is a key tool for me and I recommend it. Sit down and visualize the entire day to come, from the moment you awake until you go home, exhausted, after the shoot. No detail is too small to see in your mind's eye. I do this for every production I've been involved with, and it is an absolutely indispensable

Caretake this moment. Immerse yourself in its particulars. Respond to this person, this challenge, this deed. Quit the evasions. Stop giving yourself needless trouble. It is time to really live; to fully inhabit the situation you happen to be in now.

— Epictetus

tool. Though this might sound new age-y, I can't tell you how many times it has saved me, allowing me to catch an oversight the day before that would have adversely affected the next day's shoot.

I begin at the beginning: I visualize myself hearing the alarm clock, turning it off and getting up to take a shower. I visualize what I am going to wear. I see myself having breakfast and packing up my computer and printer. Then I hear the doorbell ring as the PA arrives right on time to pick me up to drive to set. We have a call time that falls within the rush hour, so I have researched where construction hot spots will be that morning — we avoid them and sail through to the location.

I visualize arriving on set at the same time as the AD and the craft service call. I make sure that we have the home phone and cell phone numbers for the stage manager of the studio (just in case she is a little late). The craft service person is setting up the coffee, and the AD and I have time to go over a few last-minute scheduling questions. Now it's time for the crew to arrive — in my mind, that is. Here we go — off to the races!

You get the idea. I do this for every moment of the day… literally. While visualizing, I often "see" things that may become problems or that have been forgotten. Oops, I forgot to call the driver for the actor to let him know to pick up 15 minutes sooner. Or, we didn't tell the location manager that we have added another van to the production vehicle list. Or the production manager needs to remind the costume designer that we have switched to the blue dress for the lead actress to wear for the first scene. Since it is still the day before, I have time to address those issues. Once I have "seen" the entire day to come, I can relax. In my mind's eye, I have done it all already — tomorrow I will be doing it for the second time. And everything's easier the second time around.

2. CONFIRM ALL CALL TIMES AND PICK-UPS

No later than 6:00 p.m. the night before the shoot day, make sure that you check in with the person who has given out all the cast and crew call times (usually the AD or production manager) and confirm that they have heard back from everyone. If there are any outstanding confirmations, make sure this person calls again until they receive confirmation from every cast and crew person. For the drivers, they need to remind them of whom or what they will be picking up in the morning.

3. GO TO BED EARLY — AND MAKE SURE THE DIRECTOR DOES, AS WELL

This is so important. Make sure you have taken care of everything ahead of time so you can get some good sleep the night before shooting begins. If you can, make sure the director gets enough sleep, as well. You'll both be running on adrenaline, but that will only get you so far. Film production is a marathon, not a sprint, so you need to pace yourself accordingly.

4. SET TWO SEPARATE BATTERY-POWERED ALARM CLOCKS

I can't tell you how many people have over slept for call times. Either the electrical power goes out overnight and their alarm clocks don't go off or they rely on wake-up calls from the front desk of a hotel and they never happen.

I strongly advise getting two battery-powered clocks (they cost as little as $10). Set one for five minutes after the other, in case you fall back to sleep. Never rely on a wake-up call from the front desk of the hotel you may be staying in. The night staff of a hotel can be unreliable and you shouldn't put your shoot day's fate in their hands. Many a time have I stood in a hotel lobby waiting for a crew person to come down for our departure in the van. A phone call reveals a startled crew member who was not awakened by the hotel "wake-up" call. When shooting out of town, I usually travel with an extra alarm clock in case someone forgets to bring one along.

First Day of Principal Photography

The shooting period of a film or video with the main unit of crew and actors is called principal photography. Photography without the actors (establishing exterior shots or drive-by shots) is called **second unit photography**. In this section I will only be discussing production for principal photography. It's important that everything goes as smoothly as possible on the first day — you want to create momentum and win over the cast and crew.

Producer's To Do list for the first day:

• *Leave your cell phone on.* From the moment you wake up until you go to sleep, keep your cell phone on. You need to be available to solve any last-minute problems.

• *Arrive on set ahead of time.* Watch how things start to unfold. Check in with the assistant director to make sure everyone is on set on time. The AD, the production staff, and the craft service person should have been on set 30 minutes before everyone else's call time. Having coffee, tea, and bagels set up for when the crew arrives is very important.

• *Pitch in.* It's good for the crew to see you as a hands-on producer — someone who is dedicated to making the production go well. The same thing goes for the production staff. Be sure that all production personnel are organized and informed so they can support all that is going on with every department.

• *Set the proper tone.* It is crucial at this time to set a tone of mutual respect and support for the entire shoot. You want to instill the values of communication, collaboration, and FUN from the very beginning. When I visit other producers' sets I can tell within 10 minutes if there's a good vibe or one of fear and resentment. Cast and crew pick up on the cues quickly so if you are respectful, supportive, communicative, and positive, the rest of the production will follow suit. Be strong and steadfast. Be the quiet leader.

• *Check in with the talent.* Find out if the actors are comfortable and happy, and let them know you are thinking of them and appreciate their contribution.

• *Check in with the director.* Is everything okay? Is she getting what she needs? Does she have the support she requires? Does she need to discuss any creative or logistical issues?

• *Watch the assistant director.* Is the AD keeping things moving? Is the AD communicating well with the cast and crew, and establishing the proper tone, as discussed above?

• *Get the first shot of the day off on time.* Remember in the *Scheduling* chapter how we discussed putting an "easy" setup on the morning of the first day? It's important to get that first shot off as close to the scheduled time as possible. You want to build momentum. It is demoralizing to the cast and crew if you get to the lunch break and you haven't shot the first scene yet.

• *Serve a late-morning snack.* It's good to pass around a little snack, mid morning, if you can afford it. It makes people feel taken care of and gives them energy. Don't have chocolate or candy out on the craft service table until after lunch. The sugar highs and lows wreak havoc on cast/crew energy levels.

• *Keep everyone hydrated.* Make sure the PAs go around and offer water to cast and crew. The director, DP, and AD often don't have time to go get some more water if they run out. Keep an eye out for anyone who needs to have more liquids.

• *Serve lunch on time* (no more than six hours after the first call time for cast/crew). Serving lunch late is against the rules (see *Scheduling* chapter) and demonstrates a lack of caring and/or organization. Poll the crew ahead of time to find out if there are any food allergies or food specifications (like vegetarianism). If you have any vegetarians, you will need to serve vegetarian options at each meal (not just salad).

The order for the food line is usually 1) crew, 2) cast, 3) production staff. Begin counting the 30 minutes for the lunch period when the last person has gone through the line. Usually this works out to be about 40 or 45 minutes from the lunch call until the "back on set" call.

• *Maintain momentum after lunch.* The AD will give the "back on set" call. If you have served good, healthy food, people should be energized rather than sleepy and can pick up where they left off before eating.

• *Serve another snack later in the day.* It's great if you can have a little snack served a few hours after the lunch meal. Now is the time to put chocolate/candy out on the craft service table for people who want it. Also, a fresh pot of coffee is usually a good idea.

• *Watch out for problems.* Is the art department ready when it needs to be? Is the director consistently waiting on the costume department? Is the key grip able to keep his or her crew working together, or do they seem to be at cross purposes? Do the actors know their lines? Are they getting along with the director? Is the director getting the shots that are planned or is it clear that you don't have enough time to get everything on the shot list? What's the vibe?

As the producer you need to be monitoring all of this so you can spot any problems or potential issues that need to be resolved. It's best to keep your "finger on the pulse" so you can anticipate any issues before they become big problems. I also rely on the production manager to spot concerns ahead of time and check in, often, throughout the day.

• *Stick to a 12-hour day.* As discussed in the *Scheduling* Chapter, you do not want to go past a 12-hour day schedule. This keeps costs down because you don't need to budget for a second meal. It also gives the cast and crew a 10- to 12-hour turnaround time without causing you to have to push back the call time for the next day. This keeps them from burning out and allows them the time to get enough sleep before the following shoot day. It's an important safety issue.

• *Make safety a priority.* Make sure everyone is working safely and properly. Watch that the production equipment is operated in a safe manner and that everyone understands that safety comes first on the set.

You set the tone for the rest of the production. If they understand that safety is the most important thing, they will work accordingly.

• *Determine the next day's schedule.* In consultation with the assistant director, figure out the schedule and call times for the next day of shooting. I like to discuss this at lunch with the AD and get a tentative game plan together for the following day. If you didn't shoot all the scenes you had planned for the first day, you may decide to add them to the next day (if you are on the same set or location) and shuffle the schedule a bit. The AD should prepare a call sheet, which will give the details for the next day's call times, locations, and what scenes will be shot. Discuss and finalize this information together. Then have the call sheet printed out so you and the AD can initialize it and copies can be distributed to the cast and crew when you call "wrap."

• *Call "wrap" on time.* Sometimes this is impossible. If you think you will go past six hours after returning from lunch, start making plans for a second meal. Order something that is healthy and hot, and pizza is usually not acceptable — the crew will grumble. Check with department heads about what you are thinking of ordering and make sure you have it ready on time. Discuss with the department heads whether they want a 30-minute sit-down meal or a walking meal. A **walking meal** means that they will all take about 10 minutes to grab some food when it arrives and then keep working. (If it looks like you'll be done with your shooting day within about an hour of the meal call, often they will opt for a walking meal.) Note that cast and crew will not be "off the clock" for a walking meal as they would be for a sit down meal — the walking meal will be computed as work time.

• *Plan for at least a 10- to 12-hour turnaround time.* As discussed in the *Scheduling* chapter, **turnaround time** is the number of hours between the end of work on one shoot day and the call time for the next shoot day. It is paramount for your cast and crew to have at least this period of time to get home, relax, sleep and get to set for the next day. For safety's sake, you should never give a call time any earlier than 10 hours from the time cast/crew finished work the night before. For instance, if everyone finished work at 8:00 p.m., you can't have a call time any earlier than 6:00 the next morning. Most union contracts require a 12-hour turnaround time. Make sure to schedule accordingly.

WHO SAYS WHAT AND IN WHAT ORDER ON SET

PHRASE	WHO SAYS IT	WHY
"Quiet on set"	AD	To get everyone quiet and to let them know you are going for a take
"Roll Sound"	AD	To have the Sound Recordist begin rolling sound
"Sound Rolling"	Sound Recordist	To let everyone know sound is recording properly
"Roll Film/Video"	AD	To have the AC or DP turn on the camera
"Speed"	AC or DP	To let everyone know that the camera is on and recording properly
"Action"	Director	To let everyone know to begin the acting, etc.
"Cut"	Director	To let everyone know that the take is over
"Background Action"	AD	*If there is a need to give an audio cue to Extras before the Director says "Action"

Note: If the sound is being recorded in camera, there doesn't have to be "Roll Sound/Sound Rolling" cues

Wrap Checklist

Wrap is called by the AD when the last take of the last shot is completed and everyone is assured (usually by the assistant cameraperson) that the take is technically good or "clean." Once you call "wrap" there are several things that need to be done to "wrap out the day":

1. Confirm that the actors have changed back into their street clothes and returned their costumes to the wardrobe department. Never allow an actor to leave the set with a costume — they could forget a piece of it the next day, destroying your continuity.

2. Leave the location in better shape than when you arrived. Make sure the cast and crew report any damage to the location to you or the production manager so you can take care of it immediately.

3. Dispose of garbage properly. The location manager will know where to put the garbage if you are on location. If in a studio, consult the studio manager and follow the proper procedures.

4. Get all cast and crew out the door as soon as they have completed their work. You want them "off the clock" as soon as possible so you won't have to pay overtime.

5. If you are shooting on film: collect the exposed film (organized by the camera assistant), the camera reports (which say how much film and what stocks were shot, and what the developing and print instructions are), and the recorded audio material. Create a purchase order for the material including the vendor's name, address and phone number, the information in the camera reports, and film-to-tape transfer/telecine instructions. All of this information will be given to you by the camera assistant, who will have double-checked it with the director of photography.

6. If you are shooting on video you'll either have shot digitally or on videotape. For digital, you'll have transferred the material during the day or at the end of the day to at least two separate hard drives. One should be sent over to the editors so they can begin editing. The other drive should be kept in a separate, safe place in case something goes wrong with the first drive.

If you shot on videotape, you'll want to get back-up dubs made. If the dub house is open they should be taken directly there. If not, take the recorded tapes to a secure place like a locked room in a well-protected office or keep them at your home overnight until they can be stored at a secure office. Also make sure that the red safety tab on the front right side of each tape has been pushed to the "save" side. Even if you did not fully finish recording on a tape, take it with the others and start with a new tape on the next shoot day. The next day, have these tapes dubbed onto back-up videotape stock or digitized to a hard drive (and make sure that is backed up, as well).

You must protect the camera originals and create backup copies for every frame of film or video shot. Send a trusted PA to the lab or postproduction facility. Remind the PA to go *directly* to the facility without any stop offs. The material must never be left unattended in a vehicle, not even for a moment. Everyone in the business has heard the horror stories of PAs stopping to get gas and having the film stolen out of the passenger side of the van. Make sure you explain this to the PAs so they understand the importance of their mission.

7. Make several copies of the script notes from the script supervisor (usually one copy for the producer, the editor, and the script supervisor, as well as a backup copy), then send one set to the editor who will be assembling the rough cut of the project. The editor will use these notes to create the assembly cut, looking for the takes the director has identified as the best.

8. Confirm that each department has taken care of the required clean-up chores, like cleaning any necessary wardrobe overnight, finishing touches on a set piece, etc.

9. Confirm that the production manager has prepared the production report for the day. The **daily production report** will state all the wrap times, the amount of film or videotape shot (with roll numbers), and other pertinent information.

10. Show **dailies** (the material that was shot a day or two before) each night after the shoot. If you are shooting on film, dailies must be developed overnight, then transferred to video to be viewed at least a day later. If you are shooting in video, you'll need to arrange for a way to project the footage digitally. Watching dailies in a screening room or auditorium is the best way to view them if you can afford it. Otherwise you can arrange for the director and DP to view them on a large computer or TV monitor.

   Who watches daily varies with each project. Usually it is the director, producer, and department heads who screen them together. They check to see how things are progressing in general, as well as the look of the film, how the performances are coming across, and so forth. Actors are usually not shown dailies during production. Discuss with the director what they prefer.

11. Get something good to eat.

12. Go to sleep as early as you can. Get up and do it all over again.

Budget Actualization

Originally you created the estimated budget for the amount of money that the production had available. In preproduction you locked it and then you created a working budget that reflected exactly where you stood with the budget as you led up to principal photography. You may have originally budgeted $2,000 for the lighting and grip order but you were able to get a deal and it only cost $1,750. At first you thought you'd need $3,000 for location fees but you end up spending $3,500 (and so on). Once invoices start coming in, you create the third and final version of the budget — the actualized budget. We'll discuss this further in the *Wrap* chapter.

Second Day Disasters

Beware of the Second Day Disasters phenomenon. I've been on shoots where everything goes like clockwork on the first day of shooting. Then the second day is an unmitigated disaster. The PA oversleeps and arrives 45 minutes late with the lead actor; the caterer gets lost and misses the lunch meal call time by half an hour; the assistant wardrobe person forgets the handbag that an actor needed in the third set up of the day, and so on.

Why? Because everyone was so busy gearing up for Day 1 that they didn't prepare properly for Day 2. Day 1 went well because the adrenaline was pumping and everyone was so focused, but on Day 2 the adrenaline has been spent and people are now feeling how tired they really are. On the second day the crew is making mistakes and letting things fall through the cracks. This is not intentional. Everyone wants to do a great job every day. But a film production is a marathon, not a sprint. You have to pace yourself and set up the production so it can sustain a high level of efficiency and professionalism from day to day, week after week.

I am often amazed at how well a shoot can go because every day could so easily be a disaster. There are so many little and big things that have to go right every minute of every day. So you need to be mindful and always watching to keep the production on track.

Enemy of the Production

There is another potential problem that you need to be aware of while you are in production. Veteran producer Richard Brick (*Sweet and Lowdown, Hangin' with the Homeboys*) refers to this problem as the

Enemy of the Production (EOP) and you need to be on the look out for him or her on the set. The **EOP** is the person who, for whatever reason, tries to sabotage the production in overt or covert ways.

It can be the person who complains about everything — the food, the pay, the long hours, etc., and starts to infect the work environment with a bad attitude. Or they are the people who try to hijack the production by denigrating one of the key positions like the director or producer, undermining their leadership and trying to take control of the cast and crew. Or they are the actors who battle with the director in front of everyone on set and try to destroy the director's relationship and trust with the rest of the cast.

If you spot an EOP among your cast or crew, it is best to discuss with the director your concerns about the person before taking action. Once you and the director are on the same page, you need to act swiftly to take care of the problem. It's a two-step process. First, try to have an honest discussion with the EOP. State what you have witnessed and observed about their attitude, behavior, or work style and explain why you have grave concerns about its negative effects on the cast and crew. Then ask the EOP what he or she thinks and feels.

Make sure your really listen to what they are saying. Do they have legitimate complaints or it is coming from a place of malice and discontent that cannot be fixed through discussion and compromise? If you can, try to come to a mutual compromise about moving forward, working together. Then make it clear that you expect them to change their ways and treat the production with respect. Let them know that you will not tolerate any of the past attitudes or behaviors.

Be watchful and see if it resolves over the next day. If you cannot come to a mutual compromise then you must terminate the person immediately.

You should have a back-up person ready to step in so there will be minimal impact on the film. But the bottom line is, the production will be better off without that person on the crew. In addition, it sends an immediate message to the rest of the crew about your intolerance for that kind of behavior.

Now the only caveat to this rule is if the person is one of the actors already filmed for your production. Then it becomes a much more complicated issue that may not be resolved by termination but may only be dealt with by discussion and negotiation. It's best to discuss with the director before you contact the individual actor so you are both clear about what kind of action can be taken.

Cigars and Fine Chocolates

Often it's the little things that can make all the difference with your production. It's about taking care of the people you work with and letting them know that you appreciate their assistance with your project.

This can be summed up by an experience a lighting designer (LD) friend had on a production a few summers ago in North Dakota. He was trying to get some important information from the director of the music festival so he could do his job of designing the lighting for the show. The festival director would not return phone calls or emails and generally ignored all requests for assistance from the LD during the preproduction phase. At one point when the LD was out in North Dakota on a location scout he met the fest director. They got to talking and he found out that he was a cigar smoker and they had a little chat about cigars. The director mentioned that he liked a certain cigar brand but they were too expensive, so he smoked this cheaper kind.

Two weeks later when the LD returned to North Dakota for the prelight day, he presented the director with a box of Partegas Anniversary 1926 cigars that he had purchased in NYC. The festival director was shocked at the unexpected present and clearly moved by the gesture. No one had ever done something like that for him before. That afternoon everything changed — the LD got everything he asked for and the gig went off without a hitch. It was a $250 box of cigars and it was the difference between success or failure.

I tell that story to illustrate that a small act of appreciation can go a long way to making a film production a smoother and nicer experience for all. Think about the different ways you can show your gratitude for those who are helpful and important to your film.

DIRECTOR'S THROUGH-LINE:

The collaboration between a producer and director is a vital relationship. I have the pleasure of having long-term working relationships with several highly talented directors and it is a source of great satisfaction to help bring their visions to the screen. Each one is a unique personality and requires specific strategies to help us work best together. As a producer, any insight into the director's psyche or personality can be incredibly helpful.

Early in my career I realized that it would be advantageous if I could "predict" how they would react to any given situation as a way for me to know how best to handle their reactions throughout the often stressful filmmaking process. I decided to use a technique that I was taught in a Directing the Actors class in film school — it's called creating the character's "spine" or "through-line." For actors, if you can figure out the lead character's spine then you could predict how he or she would react to any circumstance in the play or script that you were directing. So I adapted it and made it a tool for collaborating with directors.

Now when I start to work with a director I haven't worked with I figure out his through-line. Some of the ones I've come up with — "to never be bored," "to always feel free and never boxed in," "to please others," "to always feel in control." Once you know the director's spine, your life as a producer becomes much easier!

RECAP

1. **Visualize the first day of principal photography at least one day before your shooting begins so you can make sure you have covered all the tasks that need to be accomplished.**

2. **Confirm all call times and pick-ups so everyone arrives on time and at the right location.**

3. **Go to bed early so you are well rested.**

4. **Set two battery-powered alarm clocks so you wake up on time for the shoot day.**

5. **Arrive on set early the first day and make sure all is running smoothly. Check in with all the key department heads and actors and troubleshoot any problems as they arise.**

6. **Set a good working tone of mutual respect.**

7. **Feed your crew every 6 hours.**

8. Call wrap no later than 12 hours from the call time. Make sure everyone has a 10- to 12-hour turnaround time (12-hour turnaround for union cast/crew) for the next day's production.

9. Leave the location better than when you arrived.

10. Avoid second day disasters and make sure all are prepared for the next day's shoot before they leave set.

11. Keep alert for EOPs and make sure to confront them as soon as they make themselves known. If necessary, fire them so they cannot "infect" the rest of the production.

12. Remember to demonstrate gratitude to those who help your production. Without everyone working together, you wouldn't be able to make the film.

CHAPTER 12

WRAP

C ALLING "WRAP" FOR THE last time on the last day of principal photography is a joyous moment. Congratulations! You have pulled off a minor miracle and you should be proud of yourself. Enjoy the sensation but not for too long because you, the production staff and crew have to spend the next few days "wrapping out the job."

Wrapping Out

Wrapping out is almost like doing everything you did leading up to the shoot but now in reverse order. Equipment, sets, props, costumes, etc., need to be packed up and returned to where they came from. Things that were rented will be sent back to the rental houses. Things that were purchased will either be stored, sold, recycled, or donated.

While you were shooting, each department was returning things that they no longer needed. But much of what was needed was used until the last day of shooting, so now there is a lot to do. Each department is in charge of what it was using. But you need to be checking in with them to make sure it is being done properly and in a timely manner.

If one advances confidently in the direction of his dreams, and endeavors to live the life he has imagined, he will meet with a success unexpected in common hours.

— Henry David Thoreau

Some guidelines:

1. Things that have been rented need to be returned the next day *by a certain time* or else the production will be charged an additional rental day.

2. Rental costumes need to be dry cleaned before being returned.

3. Wardrobe that was purchased may need to be stored until there is confirmation that there will be no need for re-shoots.

4. Set construction pieces and purchased props may need to be stored, as well. If there is a chance that there could be a re-shoot, the production should put things that are too expensive to recreate into storage for the time being.

5. Anything that was purchased and will be used again should be given to the production company for future use.

6. Anything that can't be put to good use can be donated so someone else can use it. It keeps it out of the landfill and the production can get a tax deduction. Thrift stores can take donations. There are other organizations geared toward artists or film productions in certain cities that recycle the materials you donate for use by other artists and films. Go to *www.ProducerToProducer.com* for more information.

Lost/Missing/Damaged

L & D refers to loss and damage. These are dreaded words for any producer. You work so hard to come in under budget and it could all be blown away when a crew person loses an expensive walkie talkie or if someone breaks a piece of expensive video equipment while shooting. You'll have to pay to replace the items or to have them repaired. It's a good idea to budget for these costs in your estimated budget. The best way to minimize these costs is to hire a responsible crew so those kind of mistakes are kept to a minimum.

Deposit Checks and Credit Card Authorizations

For many of the equipment, prop, and costume rentals, the production had to put down a deposit check or a "hold" on a credit card to secure the rental transaction. When the departments are making their returns, they need to make sure to get the deposit check and credit card paperwork back to you so you can make a note of it and dispose of it properly. Especially with all the identity theft that goes on today, you need to make sure you take care of this paperwork when closing out the job.

Actualized Budget

As discussed in the *Production* chapter, the **actualized budget** is the version that contains all the actual invoices, petty cash, and payroll that has been paid or will be paid to produce the film. The actual numbers will be entered and totaled up in the Actual column of the budget, which is located to the right of the Estimated column.

To create an actualized budget you will need to make a purchase order for each invoice and give it a consecutive purchase order number. A **purchase order** is a document that signifies that the production company agrees to pay the amount that is stated on the order. Once you have issued a PO for a certain invoice, you have entered into an agreement with the vendor or payee that the production company will pay the full amount according to a specific payment schedule (usually within 30 days of invoice date). The PO will state the following info: vendor address, phone, fax, email address, invoice #, invoice date, company tax ID#, what was purchased, invoice amount, budget line item #, payment method (on account, check # or credit card payment) and payment due date.

Once you have entered this information onto the purchase order you will transfer some of the key details to the purchase order log. This log will use one line for each PO. You'll enter the Budget line item #, date, PO#, vendor name, amount, payment status (paid or unpaid) and payment method. Once this is completed, you'll also add in all the money paid out for petty cash receipts in a petty cash log. All this information will be entered into the budget computer software so it can add up the actuals. Some software allows you to enter the information on a purchase order log within the budget template and then push a "send actuals" button and have all the numbers automatically transferred and totaled in the Actual column of the budget.

As you move through the production, you will keep adding to the list of invoices paid and to be paid. You will not know the final budget number until every invoice has been entered. But you can keep comparing it to the estimated budget to see if you are on track as you go. This is important so you can anticipate any overages and figure out ways to mitigate them by saving money in other areas, so you can still come in under budget.

Here is the final actualized budget for *Red Flag*. I originally estimated $13,175 for *Red Flag*. The final actualized number came to $11,548. Below is the final budget. You can see the side-by-side comparison of what I had estimated and where we actually spent the money. We came in under budget by $1,627.

Producer to Producer Budget Template

FILM PRODUCTION COST SUMMARY							
Title	Red Flag						
Length	10 min. short film						
Client							
Production Co.	Hands On Productions, Inc.						
Address							
Address							
Telephone							
Fax							
Email							
Job #							
Writer	Sheila Curran Dennin						
Director	Sheila Curran Dennin						
Producer	Maureen Ryan						
DP							
Editor							
Pre-Prod. Days							
Pre-Lite Days							
Studio Days							
Location Days	3.5						
Location(s)	NYC						
Dates	September 2008						
	SUMMARY	ESTIMATED	ACTUAL	VARIANCE			
1	Pre-Production and wrap costs (Totals A & C)	$0	$106.91	106.91			
2	Shooting Crew Labor (Total B)	$0	$0.00				
3	Location and travel expenses (Total D)	$4,385	$3,781.04	(603.96)			
4	Props. Wardrobe and animals (Total E)	$725	$663.72	(61.28)			
5	Studio & set construction costs (Total F/G/H)	$0	$0.00				
6	Equipment costs (Total I)	$6,100	$5,528.57	(571.43)			
7	Film stock/Media costs (Total J)	$0	$0.00	0.00			
8	Miscellaneous Costs (Total K)	$200	$125.00	(75.00)			
9	Talent costs and expenses (Total M & N)	$0	$0.00	0.00			
10	Post Production costs (Total O–T)	$1,765	$1,343.50	(421.50)			
	SUBTOTAL	$13,175	$11,548.74	(1,626.26)			
11	Insurance (2%)						
	SUBTOTAL Direct Costs	$13,175	$11,548.74	(1,626.26)			
12	Director/Creative Fees (Total L–Not including Direct Costs)	$0	$0.00				
13	Production Fee						
14	Contingency						
15	Weather Day						
	GRAND TOTAL	$13,175	$11,548.74	(1,626.26)			

COMMENTS							
	Shot on Sony FX1 camera – free rental from producer.						
	Budget includes sfx for red flag.						
	SAG short film agreement in place for this production.						
	Edited on FCP w/ post effects.						
	Production insurance in place – free from prod. company.						

Producer To Producer Budget Template

A PRE-PROD & WRAP LABOR	Days	Rate	OT (1.5)	OT sub	OT (2.0)	OT sub	ESTIMATED	ACTUAL
1 Producer				0		0	0	0
2 Assistant Director				0		0	0	0
3 Director of Photography				0		0	0	0
4 2nd Assistant Director				0		0	0	0
5 Assistant Camera				0		0	0	0
6 Loader				0		0	0	0
7 Production Designer				0		0	0	0
8 Art Director				0		0	0	0
9 Set Decorator				0		0	0	0
10 Props				0		0	0	0
11 Props Assistant				0		0	0	0
12 Gaffer				0		0	0	0
13 Best Boy Electrician				0		0	0	0
14 Electrician				0		0	0	0
15 Key Grip				0		0	0	0
16 Best Boy Grip				0		0	0	0
17 Grip				0		0	0	0
18 Dolly Grip				0		0	0	0
19 Swing				0		0	0	0
20 Sound Recordist				0		0	0	0
21 Boom Operator				0		0	0	0
22 Key Hair/Makeup				0		0	0	0
23 Hair/Makeup Assistant				0		0	0	0
24 Hair/Makeup Assisitant				0		0	0	0
25 Stylist				0		0	0	0
26 Costume Designer				0		0	0	0
27 Wardrobe Supervisor				0		0	0	0
28 Wardrobe Assistant				0		0	0	0
29 Script Supervisor				0		0	0	0
30 Food Stylist				0		0	0	0
31 Assistant Food Stylist				0		0	0	0
32 Video Engineer				0		0	0	0
33 Video Playback				0		0	0	0
34 Production Manager				0		0	0	0
35 Production Coordinator				0		0	0	0
36 Location Scout				0		0	0	0
37 Location Manager				0		0	0	0
38 Police				0		0	0	0
39 Fire				0		0	0	0
40 On Set Tutor				0		0	0	0
41 Motorhome Driver				0		0	0	0
42 Craft Service				0		0	0	0
43 Still Photographer				0		0	0	0
44 Production Assistant				0		0	0	0
45 Production Assistant				0		0	0	0
46 Production Assistant				0		0	0	0
47 Production Assistant				0		0	0	0
48 Production Assistant				0		0	0	0
49 Production Assistant				0		0	0	0
50 Production Assistant				0		0	0	0
TOTAL A				0		0	0	0

Producer To Producer Budget Template

B	SHOOTING LABOR	Days	Rate	OT (1.5)	OT sub	OT (2.0)	OT sub	ESTIMATED	ACTUAL
51	Producer				0		0	0	0
52	Assistant Director				0		0	0	0
53	Director of Photography				0		0	0	0
54	2nd Assistant Director				0		0	0	0
55	Assistant Camera				0		0	0	0
56	Loader				0		0	0	0
57	Production Designer				0		0	0	0
58	Art Director				0		0	0	0
59	Set Decorator				0		0	0	0
60	Props				0		0	0	0
61	Props Assistant				0		0	0	0
62	Gaffer				0		0	0	0
63	Best Boy Electrician				0		0	0	0
64	Electrician				0		0	0	0
65	Key Grip				0		0	0	0
66	Best Boy Grip				0		0	0	0
67	Grip				0		0	0	0
68	Dolly Grip				0		0	0	0
69	Swing				0		0	0	0
70	Sound Recordist				0		0	0	0
71	Boom Operator				0		0	0	0
72	Key Hair/Makeup				0		0	0	0
73	Hair/Makeup Assistant				0		0	0	0
74	Hair/Makeup Assisitant				0		0	0	0
75	Stylist				0		0	0	0
76	Costume Designer				0		0	0	0
77	Wardrobe Supervisor				0		0	0	0
78	Wardrobe Assistant				0		0	0	0
79	Script Supervisor				0		0	0	0
80	Food Stylist				0		0	0	0
81	Assistant Food Stylist				0		0	0	0
82	Video Engineer				0		0	0	0
83	Video Playback				0		0	0	0
84	Production Manager				0		0	0	0
85	Production Coordinator				0		0	0	0
86	Location Scout				0		0	0	0
87	Location Manager				0		0	0	0
88	Police				0		0	0	0
89	Fire				0		0	0	0
90	On Set Tutor				0		0	0	0
91	Motorhome Driver				0		0	0	0
92	Craft Service				0		0	0	0
93	Still Photographer				0		0	0	0
94	Production Assistant				0		0	0	0
95	Production Assistant				0		0	0	0
96	Production Assistant				0		0	0	0
97	Production Assistant				0		0	0	0
98	Production Assistant				0		0	0	0
99	Production Assistant				0		0	0	0
100	Production Assistant				0		0	0	0
	TOTAL B				0		0	0	0

Producer To Producer Budget Template

C	PRE–PROD./WRAP EXPENSES		Amount	Rate	x	ESTIMATED	ACTUAL
101	Hotel					0	0
102	Air Fares					0	0
103	Per Diem					0	0
104	Auto Rentals					0	0
105	Messengers					0	12.25
106	Office Rental					0	0
107	Deliveries & Taxi					0	0
108	Office Supplies					0	0
109	Telephone/Fax/Cel					0	0
110	Casting Director					0	0
111	Casting Facilities					0	0
112	Working Meals					0	94.66
113						0	0
	TOTAL C					0	106.91

D	LOCATION/TRAVEL EXPENSES		Amount	Rate	x	ESTIMATED	ACTUAL
114	Location Fees		1	900	1	900	500
115	Permits	bathroom	1	125	1	125	0
116	Car Rentals					0	0
117	Van Rentals	15 passenger	1	140	1	140	134.92
118	Winnebago					0	0
119	Parking, Tolls & Gas		1	400	1	400	523.5
120	Production Trucking					0	0
121	Other Vehicles					0	0
122	Other Trucking	14 ft. grip truck	5	140	1	700	841.77
123	Hotels					0	0
124	Air fares					0	0
125	Per diem					0	0
126	Train fares					0	0
127	Airport Transfers					0	0
128						0	0
129	Breakfast					0	0
130	Lunch	25 people x 3 days	3	17	25	1275	995.98
131	Dinner					0	0
132	Craft Service	25 people x 3 days	3	150	1	450	567.07
133	Limousine/Car service					0	0
134	Cabs & Other Transport		1	75	1	75	217.8
135	Kit Rentals					0	0
136	Cel phones					0	0
137	Gratuities					0	0
138	Table & Chair rental					0	0
139	Extras craft service		1	8	40	320	0
	TOTAL D					4385	3781.04

E	PROPS/RELATED EXPENSES		Amount	Rate	x	ESTIMATED	ACTUAL
140	Prop Rental					0	0
141	Prop Purchase		1	325	1	325	238.85
142	Wardrobe Rental					0	0
143	Wardrobe Purchase		1	250	1	250	210.87
144	Picture Vehicles					0	0
145	Animals & Handlers					0	0
146	Wigs					0	0
147	SFX makeup					0	0
148	Coffee cart rental		1	150	1	150	214
	TOTAL E					725	663.72

Producer To Producer Budget Template

F STUDIO RENTAL & EXPENSES	Amount	Rate	x	ESTIMATED	ACTUAL
151 Build Day Rental				0	0
152 Build Day OT				0	0
153 Pre–Lite Day Rental				0	0
154 Pre–Lite Day OT				0	0
155 Shoot Day Rental				0	0
156 Shoot Day OT				0	0
157 Strike Day Rental				0	0
158 Strike Day OT				0	0
159 Electricity/Power Charges				0	0
160 Dressing Rooms				0	0
161 Studio Parking				0	0
162 Studio Security				0	0
163 Stage Manager				0	0
164 Phone/Fax/Internet/Copies				0	0
165 Cartage/Dumpster Rental				0	0
166 Studio Painting				0	0
167 Trash Removal				0	0
TOTAL F				0	0

G SET CONSTRUCTION LABOR	Amount	Rate	x	ESTIMATED	ACTUAL
168 Set Designer				0	0
169 Ass't Set Designer				0	0
170 Set Decorator				0	0
171 Lead Person				0	0
172 Set Dressers				0	0
173 Effects Person				0	0
174 Carpenters				0	0
175 Grips				0	0
176 Outside Props				0	0
177 Inside Props				0	0
178 Scenics				0	0
179 Strike Crew				0	0
180 Art PAs				0	0
TOTAL G				0	0

H SET CONSTRUCTION MATERIALS	Amount	Rate	x	ESTIMATED	ACTUAL
181 Set Dressing/Prop Rentals				0	0
182 Set Dressing/Prop Purchases				0	0
183 Lumber				0	0
184 Paint				0	0
185 Hardware				0	0
186 Special Effects				0	0
187 Outside Construction				0	0
188 Product/Model Construction				0	0
189 Trucking				0	0
190 Messengers/Deliveries				0	0
191 Meals, Parking				0	0
192				0	0
TOTAL H				0	0

Producer To Producer Budget Template

I EQUIPMENT/EXPENSES		Amount	Rate	x	ESTIMATED	ACTUAL
193 Camera Rental					0	0
194 Sound Rental					0	0
195 Lighting Rental		1	650	3	1950	1800.5
196 Grip Rental		1	650	3	1950	1321.05
197 Generator Rental					0	0
198 Add'l Camera Rental					0	0
199 VTR Rental					0	0
200 Walkie Talkie Rental					0	185
201 Dolly Rental					0	0
202 Dolly Accessories					0	0
203 Crane Rental					0	0
204 Production Supplies		1	100	1	100	363.35
205 Expendables		1	100	1	100	45.87
206 Camera Lens Rental		1	2000	1	2000	1812.8
207 Jib Arm Rental					0	0
208 Camera Accessories Rental					0	0
209 Green Screen Rental					0	0
210 Underwater Housing Rental					0	0
TOTAL I					6100	5528.57

J FILM STOCK/MEDIA		Amount	Rate	x	ESTIMATED	ACTUAL
211 Purchase film stock					0	0
212 Develop film stock					0	0
213 Digital storage purchase					0	0
214 Memory card rental/purchase					0	0
215 Videotape stock					0	0
216 Audiotape stock					0	0
217					0	0
TOTAL J					0	0

K MISCELLANEOUS COSTS		Amount	Rate	x	ESTIMATED	ACTUAL
218 Petty Cash					0	0
219 Air Shipping Charges		1	100	1	100	0
220 Accounting Charges					0	0
221 Bank Charges					0	0
222 E & O Insurance					0	0
223 Legal fees					0	0
224 Publicity					0	0
225 Film Festival Fees/Expenses					0	125
226 Pop Up tent + chairs		1	100	1	100	0
TOTAL K					200	125.00

L CREATIVE FEES		Amount	Rate	x	ESTIMATED	ACTUAL
227 Writer Fee					0	0
228 Director Fee – Prep					0	0
229 Director Fee – Travel					0	0
230 Director Fee – Shoot					0	0
231 Director Fee – Post					0	0
232 Fringes for Labor Costs					0	0
233					0	0
TOTAL L					0	0

Producer To Producer Budget Template

M TALENT LABOR	Days	Rate	OT (1.5)	OT sub	OT (2.0)	OT sub	ESTIMATED	ACTUAL
234 O/C Principal				0		0	0	0
235 O/C Principal				0		0	0	0
236 O/C Principal				0		0	0	0
237 O/C Principal				0		0	0	0
238 O/C Principal				0		0	0	0
239 O/C Principal				0		0	0	0
240 O/C Principal				0		0	0	0
241 O/C Principal				0		0	0	0
242 O/C Principal				0		0	0	0
243 O/C Principal				0		0	0	0
244				0		0	0	0
245 Day Player				0		0	0	0
246 Day Player				0		0	0	0
247 Day Player				0		0	0	0
248 Day Player				0		0	0	0
249				0		0	0	0
250 Background Actor				0		0	0	0
251 Background Actor				0		0	0	0
252 Background Actor				0		0	0	0
253				0		0	0	0
254 Voice Over Talent				0		0	0	0
255 Voice Over Talent				0		0	0	0
256 Voice Over Talent				0		0	0	0
257				0		0	0	0
258 Hand Model				0		0	0	0
259 Fitting fee				0		0	0	0
260				0		0	0	0
261				0		0	0	0
262 Rehearsal time				0		0	0	0
TOTAL M							0	0

N TALENT EXPENSES	Days	Rate	OT (1.5)	OT sub	OT (2.0)	OT sub	ESTIMATED	ACTUAL
263 Airfares				0		0	0	0
264 Hotel				0		0	0	0
265 Per diem				0		0	0	0
266 Cabs and transportation				0		0	0	0
267 Extras casting director				0		0	0	0
268				0		0	0	0
269				0		0	0	0
270				0		0	0	0
271				0		0	0	0
272				0		0	0	0
273				0		0	0	0
274 Talent Agency fee (10%)				0		0	0	0
275 Pension & Health				0		0	0	0
276				0		0	0	0
TOTAL N							0	0

Producer To Producer Budget Template

O	EDITORIAL	Amount	Rate	X	ESTIMATED	ACTUAL
277	Post Production Supervisor				0	
278	Editor				0	
279	Assistant Editor				0	
280	Assistant Editor				0	
281	Transcription				0	
282	Edit equipment rental				0	
283	Hard drive purchase				0	
284	Visual SFX	1	1500	1	1500	1000
	TOTAL O				1500	1000.00

P	FILM TRANSFER	Amount	Rate	X	ESTIMATED	ACTUAL
285	Film to Tape Transfer				0	
286	Tape to Tape Color Correct				0	
287	Videotape Downconversion				0	
288	DVD/Videotape Stock				0	
289	Film to Tape Transfer				0	
290	Tape to Tape Color Correct				0	
291	Videotape Downconversion				0	
292	DVD/Videotape Stock				0	
293					0	
	TOTAL P				0	0

Q	AUDIO	Amount	Rate	X	ESTIMATED	ACTUAL
294	Audio Sweetening				0	
295	Audio Edit				0	
296	Audio Mix				0	
297	Audio Load In/Load Out				0	
298	Sound Effects Library				0	
299	Back-Up Audio files				0	
	TOTAL Q				0	0

R	MUSIC	Amount	Rate	X	ESTIMATED	ACTUAL
300	Music Composition				0	
301	Music Rights/Clearance				0	
302	Music Recording				0	
303	Music Supervisor				0	
304	Audiotape Stock/Files				0	
	TOTAL R				0	0

S	FILM FINISHING	Amount	Rate	X	ESTIMATED	ACTUAL
305	Negative Cutting				0	
306	1st Answer Print				0	
307	2nd Answer Print				0	
308	Additional Print(s)				0	
309	Blow up to 35mm				0	
310	Film Out				0	
311	Screening Room Rental				0	
312	Projectionist				0	125
	TOTAL S				0	125.00

T	MISCELLANEOUS	Amount	Rate	X	ESTIMATED	ACTUAL
313	Stock Footage Researcher				0	
314	Stock Footage Licensing				0	
315	Screener Copies				0	
316	Editor - transportation	1	265	1	265	218.5
317	Shipping				0	
318	Messengers				0	
319	Post Working Meals				0	
320	DVD/Videotape stock				0	
321	DVD Duplication				0	
322	DVD Authoring				0	
	TOTAL T				265	218.50
	TOTAL POST PRODUCTION			0	1765	1343.50

Budget Analysis

It's incredibly helpful and necessary to analyze the budget, line by line, after you have finalized it. There is a treasure trove of information that you have collected that can inform your future productions. With an actualized budget, you have the final answers to the questions you posed to yourself when you first created the estimated budget.

For *Red Flag* we came in under budget by $1,627, but there are still lessons to be learned. The cast worked deferred and crew all worked for free. We hadn't budgeted for working meals and we needed to pay for a few, so we were over budget in Section C. We were under budget on location fees by asking favors of locations that I frequented in NYC. We saved money for craft service for extras because we worked with them for less than six hours and kept their numbers to a minimum. We were a little under for props and on equipment rental with big favors from two vendors for the camera and lighting/grip. The red flag graphics person gave us a huge discount, so we were under budget in postproduction, as well. Overall, it was a realistic budget and we had a production without any mishaps. We also had a bunch of favors and discounts from key vendors, cast, and crew that allowed us to come in under budget.

For your production, you'll get a concrete idea of what those kinds of things will cost on future productions of the same size and scope. And if you have another production that is bigger or smaller you can scale up or down your calculations based on the per-day charges you had in this budget. You create your own budgetary database that allows you to estimate your future budgets with greater clarity and accuracy.

Petty Cash

Petty cash refers to the money that is paid out in cash for purchases and expenses. Each purchase is tracked by a written receipt and added up so you can track where all the cash outlay has gone. This gets entered in the Petty Cash log and is then transferred to the Actual column of the budget.

Wrap Paperwork

To wrap out the production there are many bits of paperwork that need to be taken care of. They include the following:

Cast Contracts — This includes any SAG, AFTRA, or non-union contracts for the cast. If you registered the production with a guild make sure to send all the guild paperwork back to the union and always keep a copy for your files.

Crew Deal Memos — All deal memos for each crew member.

Location Contracts and Release Forms — All contracts and signed location release forms for each location at which you filmed.

Actualized Budget — The final budget as discussed above including Purchase Orders, PO Log, Petty Cash Log, Payroll Log, Sales Log and Check Log.

Payment Paperwork — A copy of all payment documentation for cast, crew, and paid invoices.

Music Contracts — All negotiated and signed music licensing contracts including master license and synchronization documents (See *Music* chapter).

Daily Call Sheets — A copy of each call sheet for every day of principle photography.

Daily Production Reports — A copy of each production report for every day of principle photography.

Production Book — The production book that includes all contact info for cast and crew, vendor contact info, and any other production-related information.

Insurance Coverage Documents and Certificates — A copy of the insurance coverage and any insurance certificates that were used during the production.

Wrap Party

It's always nice to have a party for the cast and crew after you have wrapped production. Your budget will dictate what you can afford but it's a fun way for everyone to get closure (you've been through a lot together) and to thank all for their hard work and talent. On really low-budget projects, you can set it up at a bar or restaurant where the cast and crew can gather at a certain time. If you can pay for the first round of drinks it is always a generous and appreciated gesture. You also can invite people over to your home and serve some food and drink. It's mostly about everyone getting together to share in the sense of accomplishment of what you all have created.

For me, making a film is always an awe-inspiring feat no matter what the circumstances. I'm always uniquely aware of how impossible the odds are that you can pull it off and whenever you do, it is a small miracle. But it is a miracle that is manifested by every single person who put in his or her efforts and talent to realize the vision. Without the collective will of the cast and crew, a film can't be created.

RECAP

1. **Have all departments return rentals promptly after the wrap so the production is not charged for additional days.**

2. **Assess any lost, damaged, or stolen equipment and take care of the paperwork and payment promptly.**

3. **Retrieve deposit checks and credit card authorizations and destroy them properly.**

4. **Actualize the budget by entering and adding up all invoices and expenses through a PO log and a petty cash log.**

5. **Take some time to analyze the variance between the estimated budget and the actual one so you can accurately plan for future projects.**

6. **Create a binder and keep copies of all wrap paperwork on file. You'll need it for when you sell the film.**

7. **Based on the budget you have to work with, give a wrap party for all cast and crew to let them know how much you appreciate their hard work and talent.**

CHAPTER 13

POST-PRODUCTION

OR THIS CHAPTER, PRODUCER Paul Jarrett, founder of Rosetta Films (*www.rosettafilms.com*) lent his considerable expertise in the area of postproduction. Although editing begins only once you start shooting footage, postproduction actually begins during preproduction. Today, more than ever before, you need to plan for the finishing of the film when you are making your decisions on how to start the filmmaking process.

You need to consider the following:

1. What is the highest quality that you can afford to shoot on or master to?

2. What format (film, analog video or digital video) best suits the aesthetics of your film?

3. What will you need to do before, during, and after the shooting that will impact the finishing of the film?

4. What is the work flow for your film?

5. How will you "back up" the material that you have shot and the editing of your film to guard against loss, theft, or damage?

"In many ways, a director's job is how he uses all his second chances."

— *Twyla Tharp*

6. Whom do you need to consult and hire to make and implement these choices and decisions? When do they need to be brought into the process?

7. Where do you plan to show your film? Film festivals, television, theaters, Web, DVD, VOD, cell phones, media yet to be invented?

8. What are the technical requirements for each of these releases? What are the deliverables that will be required?

Picking a Format

As of the publication date of this book, the most common formats to shoot on for film and video are listed below:

FILM
IMAX
Super 35mm
35mm
Super 16mm
16mm
Super 8mm

DIGITAL VIDEO	*DEFINITION*
HDCam or HDCamSR (1080i, 1080p, 720p) RED Camera	High Definition — HD High Definition — HD (REDCODE RAW codec)
DVCPro (100) DVCPro (50, 25)	High Definition — HD Standard Definition — SD
HDV	High Definition — HD
24p mini DV	Standard Definition — SD
Mini DV	Standard Definition — SD
Digital Beta	Standard Definition — SD

ANALOGUE VIDEO	*DEFINITION*
Beta SP	Standard Definition — SD
Hi 8	Standard Definition — SD
S-VHS	Standard Definition — SD
VHS	Standard Definition — SD
Pixelvision	Standard Definition — SD

New formats and technology are created all the time. It's best to check in with the major manufacturers of these formats via technology conventions and trade publications to stay updated on the latest innovations. Manufacturer websites have a lot of information as they announce their new products and formats several times a year. Check out *www.ProducerToProducer.com* to find out about the links to manufacturers.

High Definition and Standard Definition Video

Video is either high definition (HDTV) or standard definition (SDTV). Aspects of differentiation between the two formats is: 1) resolution (measured by pixels); 2) the type of scanning; and 3) the aspect ratio. SDTV has a resolution of 480 x 640 pixels with interlaced scanning and a 4:3 aspect ratio. When shooting in HDTV video, there are several different resolutions — 720p, 1080i, and 1080p.

The number refers to horizontal lines of resolution and the letter refers to "i" for interlaced and "p" for progressive. The higher the number, the greater the number of horizontal lines of resolution. The term **interlaced** refers to the way alternate lines of resolution are put in alternate "fields." With **progressive**, each line of resolution is the same field. HDTV 1080i has a 1080 x 1920 pixel resolution, interlaced scanning, and 16:9 aspect ratio. HDTV 1080p is a 1080 x 1920 pixel resolution, progressive scanning, and 16:9 aspect ratio. This format is used for HD DVD and Blu-ray high definition DVDs. Although I just stated the tech specs on thosse two formats, it's very helpful to consult with the DP and DIT when sorting out different formats.

Camera Test

It is imperative that the DP does tests on the format(s) you are considering for your project. Unlike film cameras, each HD video camera has a different "look," based on the video metrics created by the manufacturer. And, of course, the lens, filter choices, and the innumerable menu settings on the camera will produce different looks and cinematic results.

When doing a camera test, try to create the lighting that you would plan for your film so the results will reflect the final look of your film as much as possible. Once you have found the look you like best, make sure to keep detailed notes and save the menu settings to a memory drive so they can be replicated when you shoot the project. One little menu setting change on a digital video camera and you can change the whole look.

A camera test is also a test of the postproduction work flow. It should involve bringing the media into an edit system and then delivering it to the house that will do the final mastering for the project. If the final deliverable for the project is film or film festivals, it would make sense to screen the camera test that has been color corrected and then projected (either digital projection or laser-to-film projection). This allows all the aspects of the post video process (camera, editorial, conform, color correct, and mastering) to take effect and give you the best insight into what final product will look like.

Once you have picked the format you will be shooting in, you need to figure out what format you will finish in and begin creating the workflow for the project. There are so many choices for acquisition formats and for delivery/release formats. A project can be shot in video and released on film, shot in film and released on video, etc. It's wonderful to be able to be flexible and tailor your decisions based on aesthetics, budget considerations, and final usage (theatrical 35mm print, HD master, TV broadcast, Web, etc.) Your plan for distribution and the deliverables you need to create will dictate some of your decisions on the acquisition format and how you finish the film. Figure out the work flow to the very end, at the beginning before you shoot one foot of film or one MB of digital memory. Do your research ahead of time to know what all the steps will be so you can maximize your project's final look, its technical specifications, and your postproduction dollars.

Telecine/Color Correct/Transfer

Before we discuss the sample workflows we need to go over the **telecine** process. It is often referred to as a **color correct** or **transfer**. These terms are relatively interchangeable. For the purposes of this section I'll use the term color correct. **Color correct** is the digital process whereby you can manipulate all photographic screen elements, including luminance (light and shadow) and chrominance (color and hue) levels to create the final video look you require.

If you have not seen a color correct session I suggest that you contact a postproduction facility and ask if you can sit in on a session, sometime. It helps to see the process in action to better understand the information discussed in this section. There is **film-to-tape** and **tape-to-tape** color correct processes. They refer to the material that you are transferring in the telecine machine — either film or video.

The basic purpose of a color correct is to make the visual material look its best — technically and aesthetically. In a telecine machine the film negative is put on a platter that gets fed into the digital machine that then converts it from a piece of film to a digital image that can be laid down onto tape or a digital hard drive. If your material originates as videotape or on a digital hard drive you'll load it into the machine digitally.

A color correct allows you to manipulate literally millions of bits of information to change the image in subtle and not-so-subtle ways. You can manipulate the chrominance and luminance of the images. You can change video frames to match to other film images and make them look similar. If a scene is too dark, it can be lightened and visa versa. The options are endless and it can be a very exhilarating experience.

For color-correct sessions, colorists run the telecine machines. They are highly skilled (and usually highly paid) and are fluent in the complex world of digital manipulation of film images. The director and the DP are also in the session (unless it is a "one-light" — see below). This is essential because the material was shot in a specific way with a plan on how it would be processed in the color-correct session. The shooting of the film or video is only the first step. The only way to get the full potency of the look of the material is to do a color correct with the DP present so it can be fully realized. The producer should be there as well. Supervised color-correct sessions are usually billed on an hourly basis, and you'll want to make sure they stay on track for the budget.

Types of Color Correct

There are several kinds of color correct. They relate to how much time and manipulation is done to the film in the process and are priced accordingly.

One-light/Unsupervised — The least expensive and least time-consuming color correct is a **one light or unsupervised** transfer. For this kind of transfer, the colorist sets up the general look for each lighting set up and then lets the film go through the telecine machine until the film shows a new lighting/location set up. Then the technician re-adjusts the machine and lets the film go on through the process. Often the colorist will have a brief discussion before the session with the DP and/or the director to get general notes. Otherwise there is no input into the process and it is done by the colorist alone in the work room. This process is often charged on a "per foot" basis (the same way the processing and development of the film is charged at the film lab.)

If you choose to do an unsupervised telecine you may decide later to re-transfer the **selects** (final sections of the film that end up in the final cut) at a supervised transfer at the end of the editing process. This will insure that they look as good as possible and properly reflect the aesthetics of the film.

Best Light — A **best light** transfer is the next step up from the one-light. This allows for more interaction and discussion with the colorist and more time for adjustment of the video.

Supervised — A **supervised** transfer is the most expensive telecine and it requires the DP, director, and/or producer to be in the session the entire time. The colorist works in tandem with the DP and/or director on every frame of the film to make it look exactly as it should, to complete the total aesthetic look of the film. This is a very dynamic process and the more experienced the colorist, the more expensive the session. This kind of session is billed on a "per hour" basis. I usually budget 3x the running time of the footage as a gauge of how much time and money it will take to do a supervised transfer.

Time Code/Edge Numbers/Keykode — **SMPTE** (Society of Motion Picture and Television Engineers) **time code** is a standard created by the Society to label individual video frames. **Edge numbers** and **keykode** are numbers that are placed on film frames in consecutive order to keep track of individual film frames. Make sure, during the telecine session, that you put the edge numbers/keykode and time code information on the videotape — either on screen (lower left, right or center of frame) or in another area of the videotape so it can be read by the editor but not seen on the television screen to a viewer. You will need the edge numbers/keykode info if you end up having to go back to your film negative and need to "match back," so you can find the exact film frame that corresponds to the exact frame of video. This process is necessary when you are cutting the film negative and it allows you to get the exact film frames to match the video frames that you edited for your film. The time code is needed so that your edit decision list (EDL) can properly record each edit and keep track of it in your editing system.

Film-to-Tape vs. Tape-to-Tape Color Correct vs. Digital Intermediate (DI) Session

Film-to-tape color correct occurs when you transfer film footage, color correct it, and then output to videotape. Film reels will be played on a platter and loaded into the telecine system.

Tape-to-tape color correct occurs when you transfer video footage, color correct it, and then output to videotape. It will be played from a videotape machine that is connected to the telecine. If the material originates on a digital hard drive, it will be connected directly to the telecine through a cable.

A **DI session** occurs when the film or video is transferred to a hard drive. For film, the EPX files can be lasered out back to film. For video, the DI files can be laid back to HD master videotape. A DI is usually done at a higher resolution and with greater color fidelity than is done at a telecine. The DI only uses digital tools and no analogue components.

Tape-to-tape color correct is usually only done after you have locked picture and are ready to finish the film. It is used to manipulate the footage to create the final visual look of the project and to match the shots in any given scene. It is either done at an outside postproduction facility as described above in the *Supervised* section or done on a system like Final Cut Pro (FCP) or Avid, with the color correct software that is a part of those systems.

CODEC Is King

As discussed earlier, in order to edit with your camera original videotapes/digital material, you'll have to digitize them into your editing system. You'll need to know the CODEC for the videotapes/digital material in order to load it in properly to your editing system. **CODEC** comes from the two words "coder-decoder" and refers to an encoding or decoding computer program that allows the digital material to be edited or played on electronic systems other than the camera. If you don't load your material into the editing computer with the correct CODEC it could compromise the technological quality of the video footage. It could cause inconsistencies with audio sync, shifts in time code and other problems that could affect the accuracy of your EDL.

You can find out what CODEC works for your digital material by asking the director of photography or video engineer from your shoot. Make sure the script supervisor takes notes on the menu settings from the assistant camera/video tech so you know the correct acquisition CODEC.

Postproduction Sample Workflows

Below I have created three sample workflows that will give you an idea of what needs to happen, step-by-step, to finish a film or video.

CASE STUDY #1
Acquisition format: Digital HD (high definition) camera
Release/Delivery format: 1080i HD Cam
Price: $

This process will have the same progression from acquisition of sound and image to editing, then audio mix, color correct final digital output to HD Cam.

Step-by-step workflow #1

1. Shoot in HD video. There are many cameras out there with many different price points that will shoot 1080i or 720p or 720 iHD. Each manufacturer's model will have a different intrinsic look and feel to the video it creates. As mentioned above, the DP will do tests to figure out what is the best camera based on the tech and budget requirements. With a limited budget there are more affordable cameras on the market now that deliver incredible results for less money.

2. Edit on a non-linear computer editing system. You'll first need to load your videotapes or digital material into the editing system. The two most popular systems are Final Cut Pro (FCP) and Avid. If you shoot digitally you'll have a digital hard drive that you will hook up with the editing system. If you shot onto videotape you'll need to digitize the tapes to get them loaded into the system. That will require a videotape deck to allow you to play and digitize the tapes. The editor usually works in tandem with the director. Each director and editor will decide how best to work together.

   The editor will cut the picture and the audio and create separate audio tracks for sync sound (usually actors' voices) and for music and sound effects. Remember throughout your editing period to *back up* your material, editing timelines, and whatever else is important in case the computer crashes. This is a usual occurrence during the course of editing a film so you need to plan for it. The editor should have at least one additional computer hard drive that has duplicates of the original material, the edited material, and timelines so you are protected from any computer problems during the postproduction period.

3. Decide on what kind of music you want to include in the film. You will either choose music that is already recorded or hire a composer to create an original score or a combination of both. Add the music into the film on separate tracks in preparation for the final audio work. (See *Audio and Music* chapter).

4. Lock picture. Once you have finished editing your film and there are no more changes, you will **lock picture**. No more picture editing will occur and the final stages of finishing the film will begin.

5. Do sound editing. Generally this work is done in a computer system that utilizes audio mixing software. ProTools is one of the most popular programs. The sound editor will take all soundtracks and make sure all the sound (including music and sound effects) that occur simultaneously at any given time in the film are on separate tracks. This means that you will have multiple separate tracks so the audio mixer can access them all and set them at different levels to make the best sounding soundtrack. The sound editor will also add in sound effects where necessary. (See *Audio* chapter).

6. Schedule Additional Digital Recording (ADR) if necessary. **ADR** refers to the process of recording actor's audio lines that were not audible originally or add lines where none existed before. ADR is usually done at an audio recording facility that has a recording booth for the actors and the ability to play the video so they can lip sync to the section they are replacing. If you are adding lines, it is sometimes a better audio match if you can re-record on a location similar to the place where the scene was originally recorded. It's best to use the same microphones, if at all possible, so it has a similar sound.

7. Schedule foley recording if necessary. **Foley** is the creation of additional customized sounds to match specific action in a film. For instance, someone will record footsteps and sync them up to the steps of the actor on the screen. Or if you need to have sounds of your clothing rustling to match something in a scene it might be recorded in a foley session. (See the *Audio* chapter for more information.)

8. Schedule the audio mix. Once all the tracks are properly laid out, the sound editor will hand off the project to the sound mixer who will mix the tracks so they are heard properly and in correct proportion to each other at any given time on the soundtrack. At one point in the film you may have a scene with a couple walking along the street at Times Square on a busy summer evening. You'll have one track for one actor's voice, one track for the other actor's voice, one track for the foley sounds of one actor's footsteps on the pavement, one track for the other actor's footsteps, one track for the street sounds of the noisy environment that the sound recordist recorded as wild sound on the shoot day, one track for the sound effect of a bus driving by, one track for the sound of a cab horn honking and two tracks for the stereo tracks of the music composition. All that is mixed so that the tracks are at different levels compared to the rest of the tracks so it sounds correct to the mixer and the director's ears.

Once that is completed all the way through the film, the levels are saved on the computer and it is usually "mixed down" to four final tracks. Tracks 1 & 2 for voice and Tracks 3 & 4 for music and effects (M & E). See the *Audio* chapter for more details.

9. Finalize and sign music licenses and/or Dolby/DTS licenses. You'll have been working on obtaining the proper music licenses for any soundtrack music and if you plan to utilize Dolby technology in the final audio track. Now is the time to make sure you have all the signed paperwork. See the *Audio and Music* chapter for more details.

10. Finalize and sign licenses for any visual archive material. If your film has any archive photos or video footage, you'll need to obtain signed agreements for the rights to use the material in your film. Make sure you sign the documents now so you don't have any loose ends to deal with after the film premieres. See the *Archive Materials* chapter for more information.

11. Schedule the final finishing work on the film or video. Please note that you can be doing this work while you are doing the audio work. Some people prefer to wait until after the mix to work on the film/video. That is fine if you have time in the postproduction schedule.

There are several options at this point for tape-to-tape color correct or a retransfer from the camera original footage. They are listed below from least expensive to most expensive:

a) In-system color correction

You can color correct your video in the FCP or Avid systems using the color correction tools that are a part of those systems. You can choose to do it yourself or hire a professional colorist who is proficient in using these systems. Afterwards, you will output from your digital master computer files to various videotape master formats.

b) Supervised tape-to-tape color correct at outside facility

Output your project from your edit system into a professional telecine system. This can happen via videotape or with a hard drive. In this scenario a professional colorist at a postproduction facility will color correct it with the director, DP, and producer in attendance.

c) Take your EDL and match back to your original film negative. As discussed above in the telecine section, if you need to match back to the negative you will use the keykode numbers to locate the particular film frames from the original film negative to retransfer the "selects." You'll go to the film negative reels and put up only the sections of the negative that are in the final master of the film. Once these are retransferred and color corrected, you'll need to re-edit or "auto conform" the new retransferred bits of film according to the EDL. This will enable it to be re-cut together exactly (frame by frame) to match the picture locked cut of the film. By finishing the film in this way, you are recreating the edited film with the highest-quality video possible of your original film in digital video.

12. Do the audio layback. Now you have the final version of your picture and the final version of your sound. It's time to marry them together to create your final master. The final step is an audio **layback** where the beginning of the mixed audio track is laid back to the beginning of the final edited video, so they are in sync. Now you have your final HD Cam video master!

13. Create protection master and dubs. Once you have created the HD Cam master, you'll need to immediately make a **clone** dub so you have an exact copy as a **protection master** in case anything ever happens to the original. It is also a good idea to use the protection master for making multiple dubs to have less wear and tear on the original. Make as many high-quality dubs as required on your deliverables list as you think you will need and can afford to do. **Deliverables** refers to the list of masters, protection masters, formats, screeners, dubs, etc., that will be needed for a sale to a distributor. It will be discussed more in depth later in this chapter.

CASE STUDY #2
Acquisition format: Digital HD (high definition) camera
Release/Delivery format: 35mm film via Digital Intermediate
(D/I)
Price: $$
This process will have the same progression from acquisition of sound and image to editing, then audio mix, color correct and technical processes to final delivery format. Toward the end of the postproduction process, we will be moving from video to eventual film output, so those steps will be different.

Step-by-step workflow #2

1. Shoot in 1080i HD video. There are many cameras out there with many different price points that will shoot 1080i HD. Each manufacturer's model will have a different intrinsic look and feel to the video it creates. As mentioned above, the DP will do tests to figure out what is the best camera based on the tech and budget requirements.

2. You'll first need to load your videotapes or digital material into the editing system. The two most popular systems are Final Cut Pro (FCP) and Avid. If you shoot digitally you'll have a digital hard drive that you will hook up with the editing system. If you shot onto videotape you'll need to digitize the tapes to get them loaded into the system. That will require a videotape deck to allow you to play and digitize the tapes. If you are on a tight budget, you can load in using the playback feature on the camera it was shot with. The preference is to load in from a separate video deck because it will save wear and tear on the camera.

3. Edit on a non-linear computer editing system. You'll first need to load your videotapes or digital material into the editing system. If you shoot digitally you'll have a digital hard drive that you will hook up with the editing system. If you shot onto videotape you'll need to digitize the tapes to get them loaded into the system. That will require a videotape deck to allow you to play and digitize the tapes. The editor usually works in tandem with the director. Each director and editor will decide how best to work together.

The editor will cut the picture and the audio and create separate audio tracks for sync sound (usually actors' voices) and for music and sound effects. Remember throughout your editing period to *back up* your material, editing timelines, and whatever else is important in case the computer crashes. This is a usual occurrence during the course of editing a film so you need to plan for it. The editor should have at least one additional computer hard drive that has duplicates of the original material, the edited material, and timelines so you are protected from any computer problems during the postproduction period.

4. Decide on what kind of music you want to include in the film. You will either choose music that is already recorded or hire a composer to create an original score, or a combination of both. Add the music into the film on separate tracks in preparation for the final audio work. (See *Audio and Music* chapter).

5. Lock picture. Once you have finished editing your film and there are no more changes, you will **lock picture**. No more picture editing will occur and the final stages of finishing the film will begin.

6. Do sound editing. Generally this work is done in a computer system that utilizes audio mixing software. ProTools is one of the most popular programs. The sound editor will take all soundtracks and make sure all the sound (including music and sound effects) that occur simultaneously at any given time in the film are on separate tracks. This means that you will have multiple separate tracks so the audio mixer can access them all and set them at different levels to make the best sounding soundtrack. The sound editor will also add in sound effects where necessary. (See *Audio* chapter).

7. Schedule Additional Digital Recording (ADR) if necessary. **ADR** refers to the process of recording actor's audio lines that were not audible originally or add lines where none existed before. ADR is usually done at an audio recording facility that has a recording booth for the actors and the ability to play the video so they can lip sync to the section they are replacing. If you are adding lines, it is sometimes a better audio match if you can re-record on a location similar to the place where the scene was originally recorded. It's best to use the same microphones, if at all possible, so it has a similar sound.

8. Schedule foley recording if necessary. **Foley** is the creation of additional customized sounds to match specific action in a film. For instance, someone will record footsteps and sync them up to the steps

of the actor on the screen. Or if you need to have sounds of your clothing rustling to match something in a scene it might be recorded in a foley session. (See the *Audio* chapter for more information.)

9. Schedule the audio mix. Once all the tracks are properly laid out, the sound editor will hand off the project to the sound mixer who will mix the tracks so they are heard properly and in correct proportion to each other at any given time on the soundtrack. At one point in the film you may have a scene with a couple walking along the street at Times Square on a busy summer evening. You'll have one track for one actor's voice, one track for the other actor's voice, one track for the foley sounds of one actor's footsteps on the pavement, one track for the other actor's footsteps, one track for the street sounds of the noisy environment that the sound recordist recorded as wild sound on the shoot day, one track for the sound effect of a bus driving by, one track for the sound of a cab horn honking and two tracks for the stereo tracks of the music composition. All that is mixed so that the tracks are at different levels compared to the rest of the tracks so it sounds correct to the mixer and the director's ears.

Once that is completed all the way through the film, the levels are saved on the computer and it is usually "mixed down" to four final tracks. Tracks 1 & 2 for voice and Tracks 3 & 4 for music and effects (M & E). See the *Audio* chapter for more details.

10. Finalize and sign music licenses and/or Dolby/DTS licenses. You'll have been working on obtaining the proper music licenses for any soundtrack music and if you plan to utilize Dolby technology in the final audio track. Now is the time to make sure you have all the signed paperwork. See the *Audio and Music* chapter for more details.

11. Finalize and sign licenses for any visual archive material. If your film has any archive photos or video footage, you'll need to obtain signed agreements for the rights to use the material in your film. Make sure you sign the documents now so you don't have any loose ends to deal with after the film premieres. See the *Archive Materials* chapter for more information.

12. Schedule the final finishing work on the film or video. Please note that you can be doing this work while you are doing the audio work.

Some people prefer to wait until after the mix to work on the film/video. That is fine if you have time in the postproduction schedule.

There are several options at this point for tape-to-tape color correct or a retransfer from the camera original footage. They are listed below from least expensive to most expensive:

a) In-system color correction

You can color correct your video in the FCP or Avid systems using the color correction tools that are a part of those systems. You can choose to do it yourself or hire a professional colorist who is proficient in using these systems. Afterwards, you will output from your digital master computer files to various videotape master formats.

b) Supervised digital intermediate (D/I) session at outside facility

Output your project from your edit system into a professional D/I system. This can happen via videotape or with a hard drive. In this scenario a professional colorist at a postproduction facility will color correct it with the director, DP, and producer in attendance.

c) Take your EDL and match back to your original film negative.

As discussed above in the telecine section If you want to go to film you are best suited by using color correction format of higher quality like 2K, HD SR, or 4K, if you need to match back to the negative you will use the keykode numbers to locate the particular film frames from the original film negative to retransfer the "selects." You'll go to the film negative reels and put up only the sections of the negative that are in the final master of the film. Once these are retransferred and color corrected, you'll need to re-edit or "auto conform" the new retransferred bits of film according to the EDL. This will enable it to be re-cut together exactly (frame by frame) to match the picture locked cut of the film. By finishing the film in this way, you are recreating the edited film with the highest-quality video possible of your original film in digital video. If shooting in HD then try to edit in HD at a lower resolution (720p). This also allows for easier storage than editing at full resolution, but makes sure that director and editor have a good image to work from. Editing with down-converted images runs the risk of the director and editor missing important details like continuity and performance. This also helps with making high-quality DVD screeners for festivals and further fund raising.

13. Create 1080i digital intermediate (D/I) — low contrast. This is the digital step in the process of creating a final film print.

14. Create 35mm film negative from the 1080i digital intermediate. From the D/I you will output to a 35mm film negative.

15. Answer Print #1 with optical soundtrack. This is the first print created from the 35mm film negative. It is created by the color grader manipulating timing lights to control the color and contrast of the print. It is the best guess of how the final film should look. The director and DP will give notes to the grader for the next pass. The soundtrack is converted to magnetic optical tape that is on the side of the film print.

16. Answer Print #2. This is the next print made by the grader based on the notes. It should look very close to the final look for the film.

17. Final Print. This is the final print that will play in cinemas. It will be duplicated to make as many prints as needed for a theatrical release and any other 35mm projector screenings.

18. Create protection master and dubs. You'll need to create a digital video master of you final film by doing a film-to-tape transfer. Once you have created the HD Cam master, you'll need to immediately make a **clone** dub so you have an exact copy as a **protection master** in case anything ever happens to the original. It is also a good idea to use the protection master for making multiple dubs to have less wear and tear on the original. Make as many high-quality dubs as required on your deliverables list as you think you will need and can afford to do. **Deliverables** refers to the list of masters, protection masters, formats, screeners, dubs, etc., that will be needed for a sale to a distributor. It will be discussed more in depth later in this chapter.

WORKFLOW #1
Acquisition format: Super 16mm Film
Release/Delivery format: HDCam (1080i)
Budget: $$$

This project plans to shoot in film and finish to High Definition (HD) video. The producer does not have enough money to shoot 35mm film, so has chosen to shoot in Super 16mm film.

Super 16mm is different from regular 16mm film. Instead of having perforations on both sides of the film negative, Super 16mm has single perforations on only one side of the stock. This allows the camera (when set up to shoot Super 16mm properly) to capture an image on a larger percentage of the area of the film negative. Instead of a 4:3 aspect ratio of 16mm film, the larger format gives a 1:85 aspect ratio which is analogous with the aspect ratio of 35mm film. Consequently you can "blow up" from Super 16mm to 35mm without any problems. Please note that Super 16mm cannot be projected on a 16mm film projector, so you can *only* blow up to 35mm if you wish to release the film as a film print. Of course you can also choose to finish your Super 16mm film to video and project it on a digital projector. For the purposes of this case study, we will plan to finish on **HD Cam 1080i (**see earlier in this chapter).

Step-by-step workflow #1

1. Shoot in Super 16mm film. This is generally shot at 24 frames per second (fps) in the U.S. and Japan and 25 fps in Europe. Depending on the film camera, you can shoot at a lower or higher frame rate to make it look faster or slower when played back at 24 fps.

2. Develop the film negative at a film lab. When instructing the lab, let them know you need it to be "prepped for telecine." They will make sure the film negative is ready for the next step of the process.

3. Do a telecine session. See the prior *Telecine* section to determine what kind of transfer session you require for your film-to-tape transfer. Make sure to budget enough time in your schedule to get all the material transferred. One light telecines take less time and money than a best light or supervised session. Plan accordingly.

4. Edit on a non-linear computer editing system. You'll first need to load your videotapes or digital material into the editing system. The two most popular systems are Final Cut Pro (FCP) and Avid. If you shoot digitally you'll load the editing system material from a digital hard drive or directly from the digital files. If you shot onto videotape you'll need to digitize the tapes to get them loaded into the system. That will require a videotape deck to allow you to play and digitize the tapes. The editor usually works in tandem with the director. Each director and editor will decide how best to work together.

   The editor will cut the picture and the audio and create separate audio tracks for sync sound (usually actors' voices) and for music and sound effects. Remember throughout your editing period to *back up* your material, editing timelines and whatever else is important in case the computer crashes. This is a usual occurrence during the course of editing a film, so you need to plan for it. The editor should have at least one additional computer hard drive that has duplicates of the original material, the edited material and timelines so you are protected from any computer problems during the postproduction period.

5. Decide on what kind of music you want to include in the film. You will either choose music that is already recorded or hire a composer to create an original score, or a combination of both. Add the music into the film on separate tracks in preparation for the final audio work. (See *Audio and Music* chapter).

6. Lock picture. Once you have finished editing your film and there are no more changes, you will **lock picture**. No more picture editing will occur and the final stages of finishing the film will begin.

7. Do sound editing. Generally this work is done in a computer system that utilizes audio mixing software. ProTools is one of the most popular programs. The sound editor will take all soundtracks and make sure all the sound (including music and sound effects) that occur simultaneously at any given time in the film are on separate tracks. This means that you will have multiple separate tracks so the audio mixer can access them all and set them at different levels to make the best sounding soundtrack. The sound editor will also add in sound effects where necessary. (See *Audio* chapter).

8. Schedule Additional Digital Recording (ADR) if necessary. **ADR** refers to the process of recording actor's audio lines that were not audible originally or add lines where none existed before. ADR is usually done at an audio recording facility that has a recording booth for the actors and the ability to play the video so they can lip sync to the sections they are replacing. If you are adding lines, it is sometimes a better audio match if you can re-record on a location similar to the place where the scene was originally recorded. It's best to use the same microphones, if at all possible, so it has a similar sound.

9. Schedule foley recording if necessary. **Foley** is the creation of additional customized sounds to match specific action in a film. For instance, someone will record footsteps and sync them up to the steps of the actor on the screen. Or if you need to have sounds of your clothing rustling to match something in a scene it might be recorded in a foley session. (See the *Audio* chapter for more information.)

10. Schedule the audio mix. Once all the tracks are properly laid out, the sound editor will hand off the project to the sound mixer who will mix the tracks so they are heard properly and in correct proportion to each other at any given time on the soundtrack. At one point in the film you may have a scene with a couple walking along the street at Times Square on a busy summer evening. You'll have one track for one actor's voice, one track for the other actor's voice, one track for the foley sounds of one actor's footsteps on the pavement, one track for the other actor's footsteps, one track for the street sounds of the noisy environment that the sound recordist recorded as wild sound on the shoot day, one track for the sound effect of a bus driving by, one track for the sound of a cab horn honking and two tracks for the stereo tracks of the music composition. All that is mixed so that the tracks are at different levels compared to the rest of the tracks so it sounds correct to the mixer and the director's ears.

Once that is completed all the way through the film, the levels are saved on the computer and it is usually "mixed down" to four final tracks. Tracks 1 & 2 for voice and Tracks 3 & 4 for music and effects (M & E). See the *Audio* chapter for more details.

11. Finalize and sign music licenses and/or Dolby/DTS licenses. You'll have been working on obtaining the proper music licenses for any soundtrack music and if you plan to utilize Dolby technology in the final audio track. Now is the time to make sure you have all the signed paperwork. See the *Audio and Music* chapter for more details.

12. Finalize and sign licenses for any visual archive material. If your film has any archive photos or video footage, you'll need to obtain signed agreements for the rights to use the material in your film. Make sure you sign the documents now so you don't have any loose ends to deal with after the film premieres. See the *Archive Materials* chapter for more information.

13. Schedule the final finishing work on the film or video. Please note that you can be doing this work while you are doing the audio work. Some people prefer to wait until after the mix to work on the film/video. That is fine if you have time in the postproduction schedule.

There are several options at this point for tape-to-tape color correct or a retransfer from the camera original footage. They are listed below from least expensive to most expensive:

a) In-system color correction

You can color correct your video in the FCP or Avid systems using the color correction tools that are a part of those systems. You can choose to do it yourself or hire a professional colorist who is proficient in using these systems. Afterwards, you will output from your digital master computer files to various videotape master formats.

b) Supervised tape-to-tape color correct at outside facility

Output your project from your edit system into a professional telecine system. This can happen via videotape or with a hard drive. In this scenario a professional colorist at a postproduction facility will color correct it with the director, DP, and producer in attendance.

c) Take your EDL and match back to your original film negative.

As discussed above in the telecine section, if you need to match back to the negative you will use the keykode numbers to locate the particular film frames from the original film negative to retransfer the "selects." You'll go to the film negative reels and put up only the sections of the negative that are in the final master of the film. Once these are retransferred and color corrected, you'll need to re-edit or "auto conform" the new retransferred bits of film according to the EDL. This will enable it to be re-cut together exactly (frame by frame) to match the picture locked cut of the film. By finishing the film in this way, you are recreating the edited film with the highest quality video possible of your original film in digital video.

14. Do the audio layback. Now you have the final version of your picture and the final version of your sound. It's time to marry them together to create your final master. The final step is an audio **layback** where the beginning of the mixed audio track is laid back to the beginning of the final edited video, so they are in sync. Now you have your final HD Cam video master!

15. Create protection master and dubs. Once you have created the HD Cam master, you'll need to immediately make a **clone** dub so you have an exact copy as a **protection master** in case anything ever happens to the original. It is also a good idea to use the protection master for making multiple dubs to have less wear and tear on the original. Make as many high-quality dubs as required on your deliverables list as you think you will need and can afford to do. **Deliverables** refers to the list of masters, protection masters, formats, screeners, dubs, etc., that will be needed for a sale to a distributor. It will be discussed more in depth later in this chapter.

How to Put Together a Postproduction Team

As the producer you'll need to put together a good postproduction team to help finish the film. In the production phase, the editor and assistant editor will come onto the project. If there is archive needed, you'll need to hire a researcher. For music, you'll either license music, hire a composer, or both. For the audio work, you'll need a sound editor and audio mixer. For the color correct, there will be a colorist. An online editor may be required, and a negative cutter, if you have to go back to a film negative to cut it for a print. Overseeing all of these people and the postproduction schedule will be the postproduction supervisor. Here's a breakdown:

Postproduction Supervisor — hires key postproduction personnel, creates and maintains the postproduction schedule, creates and delivers the deliverables.

Editor — edits the film beginning on the first day of principal photography.

Assistant Editor — assists the editor, loads in material, logs it, organizes the edit, keeps back up for all the material and EDLs.

Sound Editor — adds sound effects, edits the audio tracks, and organizes the tracks in preparation for the audio mix.

Sound Mixer — mixes the audio tracks down to the final two or four that are necessary for the finished master. Lays back the final mixed soundtrack to the final master for the film.

Foley Artist — creates sound effects in a foley studio that can't be effectively used from a sound effects library.

Colorist — manipulates the video using a telecine machine to digitally change the image to the desired look for the film.

Music Supervisor — interfaces with the director and the editor to find pieces of music for the film's soundtrack.

Music Composer — composes an original soundtrack for the film.

Archivist/Researcher — researches and finds archival material — photographs, film or video, newspaper articles — related to the film and its topic.

Online Editor — re-creates the film at the higher resolution material from the offline editor's Edit Decision List (EDL).

Negative Cutter — cuts the film negative to match the film's EDL.

Putting together this team for the postproduction phase is very important. As the producer you'll need to know what your deliverables and your deadlines are. Hiring the postproduction supervisor is a critical decision — this position is similar to the assistant director during the production phase of the filmmaking. **Postproduction supervisors** oversee the teams, create the schedules, coordinate bids from multiple vendors, and make deals during the post phase. They also are knowledgeable about the various post facilities and personnel and have experience with who/what would be best for your particular film. They have deep technological knowledge of the latest information and processes and are key to making those decisions along the way.

Preplanning Is Essential

Once you have a general plan for finishing your film you should set up a meeting with the postproduction supervisor at whatever postproduction facilities you are using. Often you will be using several places — one for audio work, one for your color correct and one for the online work. You'll need to set up meetings at each place and make sure you are coordinating between the three facilities. The earlier you have these meetings the better. The editor should know the master plan before he or she starts logging and cutting the film. There will be decisions and protocols that need to be followed from the very beginning or else it will cost time and money to your post schedule/budget.

In the meeting you'll go over what your plans are for the finishing timeline. You should know answers to the following questions:

1. Acquisition format

2. CODEC used

3. System and computer software used for editing

4. Delivery format

5. Delivery date

6. List of deliverables

7. Estimated $ budget to finish (Don't share this with the facilities, keep it to yourself)

The postproduction supervisor will ask you questions and give you suggestions on the best way to finish the film. You'll need to cross reference this with what the other facilities say and make sure everyone is "on the same page." The post supervisor will create a postproduction calendar and tentatively book time for your various sessions. Then take a step back and see if every step is covered.

When creating the calendar, don't schedule each step of the process, back to back. It may look like it all fits perfectly on the paper calendar but there are inevitable glitches, equipment failures, time overruns, etc., so it is always good to give a day or two extra for each process, i.e., audio mix, color correct, online edit, dubbing/standards conversions. For a narrative feature film, 14-16 weeks is a good rule of thumb. Feature documentaries often take longer to edit, depending on the amount of footage and what the film will require.

Deliverables

Deliverables refers to all the materials that are required when you deliver a film to a distributor or broadcaster. It is a slightly different list depending on what entity you are delivering to but there are certain requirements that are universal for most deliverables. It is time consuming and expensive to create and provide the deliverables and there are strict technical requirements that need to be met. There are legal and financial implications to a deliverables list. If you have a sale for your film, you will not receive the last payment until you provide all the deliverables to the company. Creating the deliverables can cost a lot of money so you'll need to work out your cash flow so that you have enough capital to pay for the delivery work before you receive your last payment.

Deliverables consist of videotapes and various versions of the material. It is also comprised of many documents that include deal memos, contracts, licenses, — most of the wrap paperwork you created in addition to any licenses for music and archive used in the film.

Here's a sample deliverable list:

SAMPLE DELIVERABLES LIST

HD master 16x9 Texted
Digital Beta NTSC 16x9 Texted
Digital Beta PAL 16x9 Texted
HD master 16x9 Textless
Digital Beta NTSC 16x9 Textless
Digital Beta PAL 16x9 Textless
100 – 300 dpi hi-resolution digital still publicity photographs
"Making of" video
HD video film trailer
Digital Beta 4x3 letterbox trailer
Website
Final shooting script in English
Closed caption files
Written press kit (including synopsis, bios and credit list)
EPK (Electronic Press Kit)
Advertising Key Artwork
Written credit list for all crew and cast
TV and Radio spots
Music cue sheet
Music contracts
Music licenses
Dolby music license
Paid Advertising statement
Union contracts
Non-union contracts
E&O insurance
Chain of Title documents
Original certificate of producer
Original certificate of authorship
WGA registration number
US Form PA Copyright Registration certificate
List of any residual payments

Editorial Notes

As producer, one of your key responsibilities is to give notes on the various cuts of the film as it goes through the editorial process. You will also schedule and coordinate screenings for small audiences during critical times in the edit process.

How you give notes is just as important as the content and quality of your notes. I always start with what is positive about the cut and what is "working." It may sound obvious but I have seen people launch into a litany of what needs to change and what isn't working first — without saying the positive — and it makes it difficult for even the most seasoned editors to "hear" the notes. Obviously the editor and director think what they have done is best so if you have a different opinion you'll need to advocate and explain your thoughts carefully. A blanket comment like "The first act isn't working, you'll need to fix that" isn't constructive. If you think the first act isn't working you should cite specific places where it is having problems and have suggestions as to how it could be fixed. But the notes are not edicts; they should be the beginning of a dialogue about what can be done with the editor and director. They may have felt the same way but didn't know what to do. That way you are working together to solve the same issue.

If you disagree on a key point in the film, then it will require a more in-depth discussion. You'll need to be able to speak freely and talk things through to try to get resolutions. It also may be helpful to have a work-in-progress screening to be able to bring in some viewers who have more objectivity to give feedback before moving forward in the edit room.

Work-in-Progress Screenings

A **work-in-progress screening** is a viewing of the film for anywhere from five or more people to give feedback on the cut to help gauge how it is working or not working as a film. The film should be in a good rough-cut form and in a good enough technical state (i.e., all the dialogue is audible and temporary music has been placed in the soundtrack) so the audience will not have trouble watching and hearing all dialogue. The screening can be helpful to answer certain questions that are hard to know the answers to after 10 weeks of editing. Is the film funny anymore? Is the plot easy to follow? How strong are the two lead actors' performances? Your objectivity becomes compromised the longer you are in the editing process.

The first thing you need to do is find a screening room that is big enough to screen for the amount of people who will attend. Twenty or more people are a good sampling if you can get that many people to attend. Ideally it is a small screening room with nice seats, clear sight lines, good audio, and a big screen. Arrange to borrow or rent it for a specific time and date, at least 10 days ahead of time. Do a tech test at that time so you are sure that your project will hook up to the system in place and there will be no technological problems. If you can't afford to rent a space, you might be able to use someone's living room if there are enough seats and a big enough screen with good sound.

Once you have a place reserved, contact at least 1.5x as many people as you want for the screening. Invite them by sending them the time, date, and place. Explain that it is a work-in-progress screening and give a log line and running time for the rough cut. Also give them the general rundown of the schedule — first the screening, a short break, and then a question and answer session. I prefer to have the audience fill out a questionnaire directly after the screening and then do a 30-40 minute Q&A to get consensus and discussion from the audience. Remember, they are giving you approximately three hours of their personal time to watch and comment on your project. You want to make sure you are considerate of their generosity and not wasting their time. Start on time, serve beverages and snacks, and keep to the schedule so people get out on time.

Again, Ira Deutchman, veteran film executive/producer and managing partner of Emerging Pictures (*www.EmergingPictures.com*) and his thoughts:

Maureen: What are the most important things to keep in mind when you are doing a work-in-progress screening.

Ira: Obviously, doing it on an independent level you don't have the budget to do it the way that the studios do it when you hire a market research firm, which has its own risks and rewards. The good part about doing it through an agency is you're doing it with complete strangers. The bad part about doing it with them is that it's very easy to skew the results by doing the wrong kind of a recruit, getting the wrong people into the room. So trying to reach a balance between those two things when you're doing it on your own is very difficult.

What I found very useful is to gather people whom I know and trust, but to make it absolutely crystal clear that what I'm looking for is the truth. No matter what you do when you're in a room full of people you like, you're going to end up getting lied to, not in a bad way but what they think is a helpful way because they're trying to boost you up.

So what you have to do is burst the dam. What I always do is start out by saying something that is an inherent criticism of the film that's coming from me so that I kind of bust the door down and allow them to understand that I'm really interested in hearing what they think about the movie.

So I'll start out by saying that, *Okay, so how many people in here think it's too long?* Or just something really right on the nose to kind of get them to open up and then you'd be amazed at how all of a sudden the people who would have said, *Oh, I love it. It's perfect* start giving you information.

There is an art to doing focus groups — when you get a small number of people and you try to have a discussion around the room. You try to, first of all, get everybody in the room to say something about the movie before you go into too much depth, so that everybody has been heard from. People have a tendency to start leaning in the direction of the opinion of the loudest people. So it's very common to begin a focus group with a show of hands about people who like it, would give it a five, give it a four, give it a three, so that you can get the lay of the land a little bit and get everybody to have expressed some kind of an opinion.

And it's also really valuable that once people start talking about the film, before you let them dominate the discussion, to let them reach a point where they've expressed their opinions about some aspect of it and then to turn and ask people, *Does anybody agree with that?* You can even do it as a show of hands. *Okay, who disagrees with that?* And then get the other opinion on the table and just see where the discussions goes because you just want to prevent one person from ending up skewing everybody in the room.

At a certain point you reach a moment where it becomes unhelpful because it all breaks down to gripping. It always turns extremely negative at a certain point where everybody begins to say, *Oh, and there's this. Oh, and there's that.* And then they start to heap on. Basically it's done at that point, because you've learned everything that you can really learn that's valuable. At that point it's just human nature that they're just going to keep going and begin to nitpick in ways that are really not going to be helpful. So you have to recognize that moment and say, *Okay, time for drinks* or whatever. It's just over.

Maureen: Do you suggest that people have a written questionnaire that is filled out? How do you like to do it?

Ira: It depends on whether I'm doing it with a group of people whom I'm close with and how big the group is. I would say that questionnaires are really not that helpful unless you have a big sample. Because if you only have five or 10 people in a room watching a movie, I think that questionnaires are things that would come out in a discussion and they'll come out with more value in a discussion.

I think if you get 50 people in a room, then the questionnaires are meaningful because then you're dealing with a sampling size that actually can give you results. You're still going to want to grab only a small number of them for a better discussion, afterwards.

Maureen: Do you usually have the director and writer and editor there?

Ira: It depends on the situation. With a big crowd, I would say they probably are there but they're just not identified, so that people don't know. Traditionally, even when the studios are doing it, the person doing the focus group at the end [of the screening] usually begins by saying something like, I have nothing to do with the film so you don't have to feel like you're going to bruise my ego. And I do that even when I'm running the discussion myself, if it's a group of strangers.

If it's like 5 to 10 people in my living room, then they know it's not true, so that's when I have to go for that opening line of trying to break people down and make sure that they understand that I really want to hear the truth and not a bunch of lies. In those circumstances sometimes the director and the editor might be there; sometimes not. I really don't have a preference because I think in those circumstances, it's all right for them to be there, as long as you handle the focus group well enough.

RECAP

1. **You need to consider myriad technical issues, deliverables, and distribution streams when deciding what format to shoot for your film. Research these factors and do tests before making the final decision.**

2. **Schedule a film-to-tape or tape-to-tape color correct to finish your film properly. Unsupervised, best light, and supervised are the three options.**

3. **Consult the three workflows to use as a guide for your postproduction process.**

4. **Put together a strong team starting with a knowledgeable postproduction supervisor.**

5. **Know your deliverables list before you plan or budget for postproduction.**

6. **Give specific editorial notes periodically throughout the post process. Consult the director and editor on how best to communicate the notes and set up a schedule for such screenings.**

7. **Arrange for work-in-progress screenings after the film is at the rough-cut stage to get objective feedback and notes.**

CHAPTER 14

AUDIO

I'VE BEEN EXPERTLY ASSISTED in this chapter by the talented sound designer Zach Seivers of Snap Sound in Los Angeles, CA (*www .SnapSound.tv*)

Sound Recording During Principal Photography

The audio work on your film begins with the recording of the sound on set during principal photography. The sound recordist/production mixer is a key member of the crew and your film will be greatly impacted by how well your sound is recorded "in the field." Low-budget projects are notorious for not having the best sound and the films suffer for it. If you don't invest wisely in professional audio recording, you'll be throwing good money after bad to try to fix things that weren't recorded properly the first time around. It's always more expensive to fix something in post-production than to do it properly at the time of recording.

Like all key crew department heads, interview your top candidates and check two references of your final choice for the position of sound recordist/production mixer. Then on the first day of shooting, if you haven't

Habitually creative people are prepared to be lucky.

— E.B. White

worked with the recordist before, take the time to listen on headphones to the first couple of takes after you have begun shooting. Make sure it sounds technically correct to you — no over modulation, no hissing, etc. — good, clean sound. If it doesn't sound good, you should discuss your concerns discreetly with the director and sound recordist, immediately, until you are satisfied that the problem has been corrected and that you have confidence in the recordist's abilities. If you do not, then replace him or her immediately.

I had a situation like this on a film I co-produced a few years ago. It was a very low-budget film so I couldn't hire the sound recordist I usually work with. We followed up on one recommendation but he was just starting out and didn't have any others. Unfortunately we realized after listening to the first few takes on set, that our recordist wasn't up to the professional standard we needed. We called our backup sound recordist (who was a bit more expensive) immediately and brought him in for the next day's shoot. It was a bit awkward, but it was imperative to get the best sound for the production.

How to Get the Best Sound on Set

As producer, your first job is to hire the best recordist/mixer you can. The next thing you need to do is *listen* to what the recordist/mixer tells you when you are shooting on set. In the hierarchy of production, the visual elements always seem to take precedence over the aural ones. But you should resist this urge to dismiss audio concerns raised by the recordist/mixer when on a tech scout or while shooting. You only have one shot at getting good, clean, well-recorded sound. If you don't get it in the field, whatever you do in post will never be as good as what was really happening on set that day. You might be able to get close but it won't be the same and it will cost more money.

AURAL ALERTS FOR TECH SCOUTS AND SHOOT DAYS:

Refrigerator (put your car keys in the fridge or put a big reminder note by the video monitor so you don't forget to turn it back on)
Telephones/cell phones
Electric generators/electric transformers
Airplanes/airports
Buses
Trains/subways
Construction
Landscaping work — lawn mowers and leaf blowers
Air conditioners
Muzak (in elevators and retail stores)
Barking dogs
Paper thin floors, ceilings and walls in apartments
Beach waves
Road traffic
Elevator shaft noise

Another area where the producer can make a big difference to over-all audio of the film, is to get the recordist/production mixer to discuss the strategy, tech specs, and workflow with the postproduction sound designer before principal photography begins. Establishing this line of communication has many rewards when your film enters the post phase. You can save lots of time and money and avoid costly mistakes.

Room Tone

Room tone is the recording of the sound of the room without anyone talking or making noise for at least 30 seconds. It is useful during sound editing so the editor can fill in "gaps" in the aural environment after the film is cut for picture. Room tone is usually recorded before you move onto another set up in another audio environment. You'll want to have the actors in their places on set in the way they were for the scene(s) you just recorded. Often they will be wearing **lavaliere** microphones (small mikes that can be clipped under a person's clothing) so sound will be recorded through those mikes, as well as the boom microphone. The assistant director or sound recordist/mixer will ask for "quiet on set" and then say "recording room tone." The recordist/mixer captures the sound of the room through all of the microphones for at least 30 seconds. If you are recording audio onto the video camera as well, the camera operator will often record a shot of a microphone so it is clear that this section is not sync sound from the film. Room tone is used in the editing room to mask a drop in audio when an edit cut occurs or to "fill in" for any audio post work.

There is a caveat to the issue of room tone. Some editors and sound designers do not use it. They use the recorded silence between dialogue from the film footage to fill the aural gap in postproduction. Consult the editor and sound designer before you begin principal photography to decide if you need to record room tone.

Wild Sound

Wild sound is any recorded audio that is not part of the sync sound recording while the camera is rolling. Examples of wild sound are the sounds of birds chirping in a park or the sound of a flag flapping in the wind.

The director, in consultation with the editor, should create a list of wild sounds they need the sound person to record during the shooting period. They should discuss the list with the recordist/mixer ahead of time and get suggestions, as well. The great thing about wild sound is that it is real and custom recorded for your production. It can help to fill out the sound design for your film and to reduce the need to purchase sound from an effects library.

Audio Postproduction

The audio recorded in the field will be used during the editing of the film. As discussed in the *Postproduction* chapter there are several different steps to the sound work that need to be done during the postproduction of a film. They are: 1) building the various audio tracks; 2) adding sound effects; 3) recording ADR; 4) creating and recording foley work; 5) laying in music tracks; 6) sound editing; 7) sound mixing; 8) audio layback.

Building Audio Tracks/Sound Design

When editing your project on a non-linear system, you have multiple audio tracks you can use for your project's soundtrack. By isolating each sound on its own track, you then can adjust each one separately when you are building your overall audio mix. The ambient background sounds will not be at the same level as the actor's voice. The music may be low in the soundtrack when it is under a dialogue scene but may be up full when it is played during a montage scene without dialogue. By putting each piece of audio on a separate track, the audio mixer can make the adjustments and set the levels individually to create the final mix. As a general rule — dialogue is put on certain tracks, sound effects on others, music on others, etc.

Usually, the picture editor will do a rough version of what a sound designer will do later in the postproduction process. As Zach Seivers said to me once, "the postproduction team works to support the canvas of the film."

Adding Sound Effects

A sound editor will fill in the soundscape of the film with the sounds needed to make the scene work. This is where wild sound from your sound recordist can be added to the soundtrack. There are also sound effects libraries that the sound editor uses to build the soundtrack. Often the sound editor owns the rights to use CDs or digital files from a sound library company. Also you may find it necessary to record additional sounds that need to be added. This is called foley.

Creating and Recording Foley Work

Foley is the craft of adding sound that specifically matches things that are happening on screen, i.e., the rustle of someone's coat as it is put on, or the sound of footsteps as they climb the stairs or the clink of a glass as an actor gives a celebratory toast in a restaurant. The craft is named after Jack Foley, the sound effects pioneer who virtually invented it when working on films in the early days at Universal Studios.

A foley artist works in a recording studio, watches the film and simultaneously creates the appropriate sound to match the action on screen. They often create sounds from things that have absolutely nothing to do with the unique action on screen, but it works. If you ever get a chance to watch a foley session — make sure you go — it's so entertaining.

In an ideal world, all added sound effects would be created by a foley artist. In the low-budget independent film world, it is often not affordable and sound effects have to be created from libraries and recorded sound exclusively.

Recording ADR

Additional Dialogue Recording (ADR) or "looping" is when you record or re-record dialogue with an actor to replace or add to the original audio that was recorded during principal photography. This can be needed for several reasons. If an actor didn't have the proper accent during the original recording, she can work with a dialogue coach and re-record the proper-sounding accent to make it work. Or if a scene took place at a very noisy place, like a beach or on a busy street — the original dialogue recording was inaudible and the whole scene would probably be looped so the lines can be heard. ADR also can be used to change or add to dialogue. If the shot is far enough away from the actor's face or we are seeing the back of the actor's head, you can add/change dialogue easily.

Laying in Music Tracks

Whether you acquire the rights to music that already has been recorded or hire a composer to create music specifically for your film/video, you'll need to lay down the music tracks in the places that you want it to be heard. Once again it is advisable to have the composer and sound designer discuss the project before the composer or designer begins work. They can "speak the same language" and sort out technical and creative issues together to maximize time and effort.

Sound Mixing

A sound mixer takes all the tracks that the sound editor has laid out on separate tracks and puts them in the right aural relationship to each other in the full soundtrack. They work with the director and editor to finalize the decisions on how each sound/piece of dialogue/music will be at what level in the mix. One section may be all dialogue with ambient sound in the deep background and no music. Another section may have an emphasis on the music, with no dialogue and minimal ambient tone to round out the soundscape. All of these decisions tie in with the director's overall vision for the film.

The sound mix takes place in a recording studio. The sound editor will have laid out all the tracks separately so the sound mixer can mix them all to create the proper balance and audio track. The director, editor, and producer are usually in attendance. The director and the mixer are constantly listening to the mix and discussing modifications with each other to get to the final mix. The mixer will mix the tracks and then play it back for all to hear. Then the director will give notes, the mixer will make adjustments, and they will listen again to the mix. The entire soundtrack is done this way until its completion.

Recording studios are fitted out with fantastic sounding stereo audio speakers. If you are doing a Dolby™ mix then you'll need to arrange for the license and technician to come into the process (see below). Otherwise you'll listen carefully in the best sounding audio environment you probably will ever experience for your film.

But don't be completely seduced by the awesome sonic technology. Your film will be watched in many different ways and places with differing levels of technological sophistication. It will be played in theaters with great audio equipment, in viewer's homes with fancy surround sound speakers, in other homes with old analogue television sets and on people's laptops and cell phones. Some will be a better audio experience than others. You need to keep this in mind as you mix your film. Always ask to listen to the mix on the **TV speakers,** at some point while you are in the mixing studio. It replicates the worst case audio scenario and lets you hear how the mix sounds to an average viewer watching/listening to it on not-so-great speakers. It can be a revelation — the fantastic music mix now drowns out the dialogue of your lead actor in the restaurant scene. Or the ambient track is too low in the mix and you can't hear the birds while your actors are walking through a park. Make sure you listen on the TV speakers before you finalize the mix. Once the entire soundtrack is mixed and locked, the next step will be the layback.

Dolby Digital™, DTS™, or THX™

As mentioned above, often a soundtrack will be mixed with trademarked technology (either Dolby or DTS) that is used to reduce audio noise. This is usually only done when the film will be playing in Dolby/DTX-enabled theaters on either 35mm prints or digital masters. It enables you to get the audio mix onto the final film master. If you wish to use Dolby or DTS you'll need to pay for a usage license and have a company consultant attend the audio layback to certify that it meets the technical standards of the proprietary technology. License prices depend on the usage. A film-festival-only license is a lower rate then a theatrical rate.

THX is a certification process for cinemas. Created by George Lucas, it requires movie theaters to follow strict technical specifications to receive the certification.

Layback

Layback is when the soundtrack is put in sync at the very beginning on the film and then "laid down" or "laid back" to match the picture of the master. By matching the time code at the head of the film, the audio should be completely in sync all throughout the piece. If you are creating a 16mm or 35mm film print, the final soundtrack will be converted to a magnetic optical track and married to the visual film track to create the final film print. If you have completed all the finishing work on the picture portion of the film, you will now have your final master!

RECAP

1. **Hiring a sound recordist/production mixer for principal photography is very important. Research references and choose the best person you can afford.**

2. **Facilitate communication between the recordist/mixer and the sound designer so they can plan ahead for audio postproduction while in preproduction.**

3. **Check with the sound designer to decide if room tone should be recorded at each location for use in the postproduction.**

4. **Sound editing includes the laying out of multiple audio tracks, ADR, sound effects, and foley work to create a full and proper audio landscape for your film.**

5. **Sound mixing is a collaboration between the director and the mixer to achieve the final mix that will maximize the aural experience of the film.**

6. **Depending on where your film will be screened, you may need to license proprietary audio technology (Dolby Digital™ or DTS™) for your mix.**

7. **An audio layback occurs when you match the audio track to the final visual master of your film.**

CHAPTER 15

MUSIC

Creating a Music Soundtrack

A MUSIC SOUNDTRACK IS USU-ALLY comprised of music that was previously produced and is commercially available and/or music composed specifically for the film by a composer. Either way, you'll need to obtain the music rights.

Music rights consist of two kinds of rights for each piece of music — the Master Recording License and the Synchronization (Sync) License. A **master recording license** refers to the rights for the performance of a piece of music — i.e., Bruce Springsteen's recording of *Santa Claus is Coming to Town*. These rights are usually obtained through the record label that made the recording — in this example — Columbia Records, a subsidiary of Sony Music. The **synchronization (sync) license** pertains to the rights for the song itself and is usually held by a publishing company that represents the person(s) who wrote the song. The writers of the song *Santa Claus is Coming to Town* are J. Fred Coots and Haven Gillespie. The publishing companies are EMI Feist Catalog, Inc. and Haven Gillespie Music.

> *Everything should be as simple as it is, but not simpler.*
>
> *— Albert Einstein*

To negotiate the master recording license, contact the record company and ask for the licensing department. Doing an Internet search is a good way to track down this information. If you have a CD of the song, you can get the information from the cover. To find out who is the publisher for the sync license you can search the websites of the two major publishing groups — *www.BMI.com* and *www.ASCAP.com*. As the producer, you need to contact each company — Columbia Records, EMI Feist, and Haven Gillespie and request the rights you require for your project. This process is often called **clearing the rights** to a song.

What Rights Do You Need?

Once you have the contact information for your music, you'll need to figure out what rights you require for your film and how long you need the license. Here are the rights generally available for any piece of music:

U.S. Theatrical
U.S. network television
U.S. cable television
U.S. DVD
U.S. VOD (Video on Demand)
International theatrical
International network television
International cable television
International DVD
International VOD (Video on Demand)
Internet/Web
Film festivals
Educational

For international rights, they can be sold per region or per country, i.e., UK/Ireland, Spain, France, etc. If you can afford it, the best rights level to ask for is *all* of the above. That is usually referred to as "all media worldwide." The other consideration is the length of time you own the rights. The longest time period is usually referred to as "in perpetuity." If you can afford "all media worldwide, in perpetuity" then you are covered for every scenario forever.

There is one other designation that you'll need to ask for and that is either an "exclusive" or "non-exclusive" license. Usually non-exclusive is enough for a film soundtrack and it allows the rights owners to license the same song to others for other purposes. Exclusive would mean the publisher and the recording artist couldn't license to other entities. Decide what you need before you contact publishers and record labels.

Depending on the artist, the song, the record label, and the publisher, you may not be able to afford all the rights you want or need. That's when negotiation comes into play. The publisher may be willing to give you the sync license for all media worldwide, in perpetuity for a reasonable sum but you can't afford the rights for the specific performance on the record. In regards to the Bruce Springsteen example, you might be able to obtain an affordable price for the sync license but Springsteen's record label will require a fee that is well beyond what you can afford to pay. You could decide to record your own version of the song with a singer that would be an affordable alternate. Then you would do a "buyout" with that vocalist so you had the rights for all media worldwide, in perpetuity. Or you may decide you *have* to have the Springsteen's version, but can only afford the film festival rights for two years. If you decide to license for film festivals only, you might be taking a big gamble.

If the film does well at film festivals and a company wants to distribute your film, you may not be able to afford all the rights you will need to accept the deal. The amount of money paid to you for the distribution rights for your film may not be enough to acquire the necessary rights for the song. Then you'll have to face a hard decision to either turn down the distribution deal, re-record the song by a different artist, or replace the song with a different one on the soundtrack. You would need to make sure that the distribution company would still want your film if you had a different song on the soundtrack.

My advice is to *not* take that gamble. Always plan for the success of your film and make sure to lock down all the rights you need for all markets, domestic and internationally. If you cannot afford to do that when you are finishing your film and want to take it out to film festivals only as the first step, then negotiate the future purchase price for all rights while you lock down the film-festival rights only. That way you will know how much the additional rights will cost in the future and it won't suddenly increase if your film becomes successful afterwards. You'll know what your music licensing costs will be and you will know what you need to get for a distribution fee if you go to sell the film, in order to cover the music licensing costs.

Putting in the License Request

Now that you know what rights to acquire, you need to decide when to ask for them in your pre/production/post timeline. If the song is sung or heard as diegetic sound in the film, then you need to obtain the rights before you shoot the scene during production.

For example, if you have a scene with a character singing a lullaby to her baby before the child falls asleep, you'll need to obtain the sync rights for the song from the publisher. You'll also need to ask the actor to sign a master recording rights license for her recording of the song. If a band is performing a song on a stage in a scene in which people are dancing to the tune, you'll need to obtain both the master recording rights to the performance and the sync rights for the song the band performs. This needs to happen *before* you film the scene. If you don't secure the rights for *all* the territories you need then you run the enormous risk of not being able to use any of the footage you shot for that scene in your final cut.

The only way to remedy this kind of problem in the edit room would be to get the rights to another song with the same beat to match the cadence of the actors who are dancing and the musicians who are performing. Then you would need to cut it into the soundtrack and then edit the footage in a way that would never show any of the musicians or singers in close up. It is incredibly difficult, perhaps impossible and a huge waste of time and energy in postproduction. It would be much smarter to get the rights before you plan to shoot the performance of the song on-camera.

The use of other music for your film's soundtrack that is seen being played in a scene should be acquired when you are fairly certain you will need it in the final cut. You want to contact the record labels and publishers early enough so there is enough time to get an answer before you have locked picture. If you find that you can't afford the rights, you have time to replace it with another piece of music. You also don't want to waste time on negotiating for rights to music that ends up on the cutting room floor, so you need to figure out what music has a good chance of ending up in the final soundtrack and begin contacting the appropriate entities for the rights. Lastly, if you have several recordings that are on the same record label, it may help you to negotiate a better deal by waiting until you have the list of everything on that one label before sending in your request.

The timing on getting rights is tricky because it can take many months to successfully negotiate a license. Start at least three to five months ahead of time for major record labels. They have more requests and bureaucracy so you need a longer lead time.

Music Rights Request Letter Format

Finding out who owns the master recording rights and the sync rights to any given piece of music can require a bit of detective work. If you have the CD that the recording is from, you should be able to get the name of the record label and the publisher from the printed material that comes with the CD packaging.

If you downloaded the music or don't know where the song came from you can use the Internet to do the research. The first place to start is the major performing rights society websites — *www.BMI.com* (Broadcast Music, Inc.), *www.ASCAP.com* (American Society of Composers, Authors and Publishers) and *www.SESAC.com* (Society of European Stage Authors & Composers) — they collect the fees and distribute the royalties to the songwriters and publishers. They each have fairly powerful search engines that allow you to type in the name of the song and give you the publishing information and often the name of the album that it was released on. From there you can find the contact information for the sync and the master recording rights. Remember to search each publishing website because they are separate organizations and usually a song is only registered under one of the groups.

If you still need more information, do an Internet search for the name of the song and/or the artist. You can look up the discography for the title of the album and the record label. From there you can search for the label's contact info on the Web. Once you have the contact info for the publisher and the record label, call them and ask for the music rights person. You will be given the name and number for that person or an email address. Often the phone number is connected to an answering machine that will give you a list of all the information they require before processing your rights request. Usually the request needs to be in writing and sent via fax or email. Expect to send the following information:

1. Title of recording/composition

2. Album title

3. Artist/band/orchestra name

4. Usage you require, i.e., background music under pictures, sung by the lead character. Also describe what is seen on the screen when the music is heard. i.e., someone being shot or a family driving in a car on a highway.

5. Short description of your film.

6. Time length of usage, specify minutes and seconds and if it is repeated later in the film, state the time length for the additional usage.

7. What territories you are requesting i.e., all media worldwide in perpetuity.

8. State if it is for exclusive or non-exclusive use.

9. What you can afford to pay for the rights (or gratis) and if you have already made deals for the same amount of money to other publishers/record labels.

Negotiating for the Music Rights

The record label or the publisher own the rights and they want to get as much money as possible for them and you want to pay as little as possible. Therein lies the negotiation process.

Use the sales skills that you perfected throughout the making of your film. Your film will give exposure to the songwriter or performer by being included on the film's soundtrack. There will be film festivals, DVDs, maybe a television or Internet sale, etc. Added exposure is not an incentive for a well-known musical artist but for an up-and-coming band or singer it should be of some value.

To increase your chances of a successful negotiation try to find a mutual friend or contact who can bring your request directly to the artist or songwriter. As we discussed in the *Casting* Chapter when you were attaching talent to your film, getting in direct contact can help make a much stronger case for your request. If you go through the label or the manager, you could get a "no" without the artist even knowing about it because the manager deemed the monetary offer too small. But if you can send the artist a copy of your film with a beautiful handwritten note from the director explaining why the song is brilliant and essential to the film, you might get a wholly different answer. This happened on a film I produced several years ago. We got a quick "no" from the manager but then sent a copy of the film and letter to the artist directly. He really liked the project and gave us the rights for an affordable sum.

Writer/director/producer Paul Cotter (*BOMBER, Estes Avenue*) has some advice regarding music soundtracks for low-budget films:

"If you've got a tight budget, it's great to be flexible about the music and who you get on the soundtrack. The basic rule I follow is 'like attracts like.' If you've got no money, find bands who have no money. You're then on a level playing field and they're usually cool, understand your predicament, and are willing to play along. Just be honest and upfront with them, which is something you should be with everybody (honesty goes a long, long way in low-budget filmmaking). Also, they need the publicity you can give them. Don't go for Lionel Ritchie. He's loaded and doesn't have time for riff raff like us."

Most Favored Nation

The term **most favored nation (MFN)** refers to the concept of paying everyone the same amount of money for the same thing. It comes from international trade agreements where each country signed to an agreement has the same terms as every other country. We discussed this in the *Preproduction* chapter regarding how to pay crew members and keep pay rates consistent across salary levels. Music rights negotiation uses the concept of *most favored nation*, as well. It is the industry practice to pay the same amount for the sync rights to the publisher as you do for the master recording rights to the record label. And usually you will pay the same amount for each of the rights per song. So if you are paying $500 for sync rights and $500 for master recording rights for one song, you will do that same deal for all of the other songs on the soundtrack. The only exception would be for a song by a very famous band, which would be a vastly higher number and would not be part of the MFN pricing system.

The best strategy for negotiating rights would be to go to the entity (publisher or label) you think will give you the best deal first. If the song is a well-known composition being sung by an unknown performer, go to the record label first to make a deal. Once you have an affordable negotiated rate in writing, then you go to the publisher for that song. Let them know that you already got the master recording license for X amount and ask if they would be willing to give you the sync rights for the same amount.

You'll use most favored nation when you are negotiating for the rights to several recordings. Let's say you have seven pieces of music you wish to clear — start with the five songs that will be the easiest and most affordable first. Then go to the last two and let them know that you have already negotiated the rights to most of your soundtrack and that the publishers and labels have agreed to X amount for the rights. Ask them to take the same deal for their song(s).

If they agree to it, be ready to send out the paperwork for signature. If not, you may have to agree to a higher amount for the last two songs to make the deal. If this happens, because it was all done on a MFN basis, you'll have to pay the higher amount to the first five publisher/labels, as well. It's like the tide in the ocean — it raises, or lowers all boats equally.

If the higher amount for each composition proves to be too expensive, you may decide to replace the expensive songs for those that will accept the lower amount you negotiated for the first five compositions and complete your soundtrack with different music.

Out of Copyright or Public Domain Music

Copyright law in the U.S. has specific rules that cover the length of the copyright for the creator of the material. After the copyright expires the work is considered in the **public domain (PD)** and you do not need to purchae a license. Here are the general guidelines below. Remember to consult an attorney to confirm a piece of music is in the public domain:

Works created after Jan. 1, 1978 — the life of the longest surviving author plus 70 years — earliest possible PD date is 1/1/2048

Works registered before Jan. 1, 1978 — 95 years from the date copyright was secured.

Works registered before Jan. 1, 1923 — Copyright protection for 75 years has expired and these works are in the public domain.

For a piece of music composed by Wolfgang Amadeus Mozart in 1777 there is no copyright on the material and you will not need to acquire the synch rights for the composition. But you will need to acquire the master recording license for the recording of the performance of that composition by a specific orchestra on a specific album. When you pick a recording of a classical piece of music it is wise to choose a smaller record label because you'll have a greater chance of negotiating an affordable price than if you go after the rights to the New York Philharmonic conducted by Leonard Bernstein at Carnegie Hall for a major record label.

The great thing about classical music is that there are often numerous recordings of the same piece of music and you have a choice in which one to use on your soundtrack.

HAPPY BIRTHDAY TO YOU VS. FOR HE'S A JOLLY GOOD FELLOW

Have you ever noticed in some films that instead of singing *Happy Birthday to You* in a party scene, everyone sings *For He's a Jolly Good Fellow*? It's because *Happy Birthday* is still under copyright until 2030 by Warner Chappell (ASCAP) and *For He's a Jolly Good Fellow* is out of copyright (the copyright has expired). If you put *HBTY* in your film you have to pay and if you use *FHAJGF* it is free!

Fair Use

Fair use is discussed fully in the *Legal* chapter. Please go there for a more in-depth explanation of the concept and its use. Two good websites for more information are at *www.fairuse.stanford.edu* and *www .centerforsocialmedia.org*. This is a definition from the Stanford website — "fair use is a copyright principle based on the belief that the public is entitled to freely use portions of copyrighted materials for purposes of commentary and criticism. For example, if you wish to criticize a novelist, you should have the freedom to quote a portion of the novelist's work without asking permission. Absent this freedom, copyright owners could stifle any negative comments about their work." At the American University's Center for Social Media there is a downloadable *Documentary Filmmakers' Statement of Best Practices in Fair Use* handbook that is very helpful.

E&O Insurance

As discussed in the *Insurance* chapter, if you need to purchase E&O insurance, you'll need to make sure you have all the music licenses completed. That paperwork will be used to prove you have the proper clearance in case there was ever a claim against the film.

Blanket TV Agreements

The term "blanket" music rights agreement refers to certain agreements that major broadcast television and radio networks obtain from the music performing rights societies (BMI, ASCAP, and SESAC). Networks like PBS, BBC, VH1, and MTV have these agreements because of the sheer volume of the music they use in their programming. The agreements grant them permission to use songs in catalogs represented by the society. The rates are based on the volume of music used and the type of usage.

Once a film is complete, you will need to fill out a **music cue sheet** (a list of each music composition used, length of usage, and publisher) and the broadcaster will pay the proper fee to each publisher. It saves time and money because the broadcaster has a pre-negotiated rate for any piece of music under its blanket agreement.

If you have sold your film to a network that has such an agreement, it is important to find out what it does and does not cover. It can save you from having to clear your music for certain markets (i.e., U.S. television only) or all markets, depending on the agreement they have in place.

Music Cue Sheet

A **music cue sheet** is a standard form that is filled out with information for each piece of music on your film's soundtrack. The cue sheet is then filed with the performing rights societies prior to a theatrical release or television broadcast so they can track payments due to the music publishers. There is an example at *www.ProducerToProducer.com*. It lists each piece of music, the publisher, the record label, usage length (minutes : seconds) and its use (is it in the background or sung by an actor, etc.) This is important because you will need to keep track of what music you used and you will need to provide it as a deliverable if you sell your film to a network or distributor, etc.

Cease and Desist

If you screen your film publicly without properly clearing the music you are in violation of copyright law and there are legal ramifications. If your film gets into a film festival, often you'll need to sign a document stating that you have all the rights to the material in the film, including music and visual archive. If you sign this form without the proper rights you are violating the agreement and are at risk for legal action, if you are caught.

If this occurs, you most likely will be sent a "cease and desist" letter from the record label or publisher's attorney. The letter will cite your alleged violation of their copyright and will insist that you immediately stop showing the film publicly (i.e., film festivals, DVD, Internet).

If their allegations are true, you then have two options after you stop showing the film. You can: 1) negotiate a deal for the rights at that time (and they will probably be more expensive than if you had asked nicely in the first place), or; 2) create a new soundtrack with different music that you can obtain all the rights to. Then you can go back to showing your film.

Don't take this risk. Make sure you have the proper rights to material before you screen it publicly.

What Happens if You Can't Find the Copyright Holder?

Sometimes, no matter how much research you do, you can't find the correct copyright holder for a given piece of music. In that case, make sure you document your attempts to find and contact the copyright holder. If the copyright owners come forward at a later date, you can prove that you made best efforts to find and contact them. Keep a phone call log and an email log of all your attempts to contact the rights holders. You'll still need to negotiate, at that time, for the rights but it will show that you did not willfully ignore the copyright law.

Music Rights Clearance Person/Company

By now you may have decided to NOT use any music because the prospect of clearing the rights yourself sounds a bit daunting. Have no fear, there are several companies and individuals that are in the business of clearing music rights for productions. After reading this chapter, you may decide that you will pay any amount of money not have to go through the steps I have outlined.

Clearance companies/individuals charge fees based on a per song, per project or hourly basis, in addition to the license fees. On the other hand, music clearance people have long standing relationships with all the record labels, so that can come in handy when dealing with a well-known artist or particularly difficult negotiation. On a film I produced a few years ago, several of the songs in the soundtrack were performed by a very well-known musician on a well-known record label. I tried to get the rights on my own for a low price and was turned down. Because we were on deadline and really needed to procure the rights, we hired an experienced music clearance company to contact the music label through their contacts. They did a great job with the negotiation and we were able to procure the rights in the end.

Original Music Composition for Your Project

Another option for your soundtrack is to hire a composer to create original music composition(s) for your project. Depending on the composer, the length of your film and how many pieces need to be composed, this may be the best option. It allows you to customize the music to fit your visual material, down to the second, and you will negotiate a composition fee for all the rights in perpetuity, worldwide, with the composer up front before you finish the film.

As described earlier, music licenses with composers are specific for each project, but generally fall under the category of "exclusive" or "non-exclusive" rights. Exclusive means that only your project has the rights to use the particular composition(s) for the territories and time period stated in the contract. "Non-exclusive" allows the composer to license the same music to other entities for the time period and territories stated in the contract. Non-exclusive is usually a cheaper rate than exclusive, so if you don't anticipate needing the exclusive rights to the music, you may decide it is acceptable to do a non-exclusive license so the composer can re-license to someone else at a future date.

If you do plan to create a CD of the film's soundtrack, you'll have to make sure to license all the music for that purpose. It is usually a different rate than a license for use in the film, only, and will often be more expensive.

Finding a composer is much like finding any other key department head. You should look up credits for the composers on films you really like and think will be appropriate for your film. Talk to other filmmakers to get recommendations. If you have a no/low-budget, go to the music programs at local universities and find out if there are music students who want to create a soundtrack for your film.

Music Libraries and Royalty Free Music

Using music libraries can be a cost-effective way to use licensed music in your film. There are some wonderful libraries that have a wide range of music genres to fulfill your particular need and use. Most of them have robust websites that allow you to search and listen to samples of music. Some also have CD sets with music to choose from. They have competitive rates and are very easy to use and license. Some libraries specialize in certain kinds of music, such as classical or pop. Others are exclusive to one composer's work and are an outgrowth of their original composition work. Check out *www.ProducerToProducer.com* for a list of stock music companies.

Royalty free or buyout music allows you to purchase the music for a particular usage in your film and you can use it as many times as you would like for the lifetime of the film. You still need to fill out a Music Cue Sheet, if the film is ever shown on television, so the broadcaster can make sure the proper money is disbursed to the writer of the music.

Music Supervisors

Music supervisors are hired to consult and create music soundtracks. They are experts at making recommendations about what song or composition would work well for your particular project. Their job is to know what bands and artists would be right for your film. They get pitched a lot of music from artists who want to be included on soundtracks. If you have a tight budget it may make sense to hire a music supervisor because he or she has relationships with musical artists who want to get onto soundtracks. Music supervisors also license music once it is confirmed for the soundtrack. Their relationships with music creators will help to negotiate licenses that are affordable and appropriate for your budget. Look at screen credits on films that you like for music supervisors who would be right for your project.

RECAP

1. **When licensing music for your film, you'll need to purchase the master recording license from the record label and the synchronization (sync) rights from the publisher.**

2. **The preference is to acquire "all media worldwide, in perpetuity."**

3. **Research the rights holders and submit a licensing request form via email or fax.**

4. **Negotiate the music rights with the entity that will be least expensive. Then use "most favored nation" to get the other entities to agree to the same licensing fee.**

5. **In the U.S., for music copyrighted after 1978, the copyright remains in effect for 70 years after the death of the author. Public domain music does not require a licensing fee.**

6. Some radio and television broadcast networks have blanket license agreements with performing rights societies. They pay performance royalties to the society for the song's writer(s).

7. Music cue sheets are used to track payments to the music publishers.

8. Make sure you clear all your music before your film is screened publicly.

9. If you can't find the copyright holder, keep written documentation of your attempts to find and contact the music's author and record label.

10. A music-rights clearance person is a professional who can assist you in acquiring and negotiating music licenses.

11. Look at screen credits and ask for recommendations for music composers if you wish to hire someone to create a music soundtrack for your film.

12. Music supervisors recommend music for inclusion in your soundtrack. They have relationships with music creators and can be invaluable in putting together a good soundtrack.

CHAPTER 16

ARCHIVE MATERIALS

Archive and Research

RESEARCH AND ACQUISITION OF archive material may be a part of your film. It is most common in documentaries but also plays a role in narrative films. There may be characters that watch television or listen to the radio or hold specific archive photos in their hands, at some point in the film. All of those bits of material will require research and acquisition for use in the project.

There are many online websites that allow you to view clips from their archives. Others require an in-person visit to view the material. If you find material that you wish to consider for your film, you'll need to request a screener. A screener usually costs a nominal fee and will contain the material with a time code number on it. When you are done editing you'll give the archive the time code numbers for the beginning and end of the bits you need. The archive will dub off that particular material at the highest technical quality without the time code and you will re-edit it into your film.

Most archives have charge rates for material on a per-second basis. Often they have a 10- or 30-second minimum. The per-second rate will

> *Do, or do not.*
>
> *There is no "try."*
>
> — *Yoda, from*
>
> The Empire Strikes Back

reflect the amount of rights you require. The most expensive rate will be for "worldwide, in perpetuity, in all media." They will allow you to use the material in your film forever, anywhere in the world and for all possible exhibition — theatrical, television, Internet, and any possible media yet to be invented. If you don't need or can't afford that rate, you can negotiate for specific rights like U.S. television, International theatrical, or Internet. The least expensive rights are usually for film festival only.

You may decide that you want to do a step deal — pay for film-festival-only now and then, if you get a sale (let's say for U.S. cable TV), pay for those rights at that time. The best way to do that would be to pre-negotiate those additional rights ahead of time, when you pay for the film-festival rights. That way you lock in a rate and don't have to worry that the rate could go up in the future when you might need it. Always remember to get it all in writing.

Often the price per second for material decreases with an increase in the amount of material you decide to purchase. So if you can get the same kind of material from the same archive and group them together you might be able to get a cheaper rate, overall.

Most archives also will require you to put the archive info in the screen credits. This will be stated in the license agreement you sign for the material. Make sure you abide by those instructions when creating the end screen credits.

Steps to Acquire and Use Archive in Your Film

There are several steps required to obtain and utilize archive materials for your film:

1. Research and find the needed material

2. Contact the rights holder and acquire a copy of the photo or a screener of the material

3. Edit the film utilizing the archive materials

4. Lock picture and create a list of all the archive materials needed for the final cut of the film

5. Contact the rights holder and negotiate a licensing fee for the rights you require

6. Obtain a copy of the highest-quality version of the material to re-edit into the final film

7. Sign paperwork and pay for the licensing fee

Archive Researcher

Depending on the project, you may need to hire an archive researcher to do the work — it can be a complex and time-consuming job. In some cases the archive materials may come from the people who are the subject of your film and you will not need to go to an archive library. That will reduce or eliminate the research phase of the process but you will still need to do all the other steps outlined above. Researchers know all the various libraries and archives and will log, track, and organize the material. They have relationships with many of the big archive libraries and can be helpful in brokering a deal to get the licenses for your film. Archive research requires a good understanding of where to go and how to sniff out the places that might have the right material for your film.

Archive Libraries

There are many archive libraries and most of them can be searched online. Check out *www.ProducerToProducer.com* to find out which ones may have the material you are searching for. Here's a list of the kind of places that will have material:

- Photo and film/video libraries
- National and International television news companies
- Local newscasts
- Historical museums and institutions — national, local, and university
- The National Archives
- Individual archives owned by a person or estate

Once you have found material at an institution you'll need to get a low-quality copy so you can work with it in the editing of your film. This is usually done by purchasing a screener copy. A **screener** is a video/DVD copy of the material, usually with burn in time code (BITC). For photos, you'd be sent a low-resolution copy of the photo. There will be a watermark on the photo or a running time code on the video that matches back to the original, higher-quality master for the video/film. You'll cut in the material you want for your film from the screener and decide if it belongs in the final cut of the film. Once you know all the elements that will be a part of the film, create a master list of the archive name, the time code numbers for the beginning and end of the clip, the length of the clip and a brief description of what is happening on screen. Once you have every photo or clip in a master list, you should collate it by archive name.

The next step will be to contact each archive and negotiate for the licensing of the clip/photo. Although you have locked picture on your film, you should not completely finish the film until you know you have successfully negotiated the rights for each archival element. If you can't afford a certain clip you may need to alter your film by removing the archival material and changing the final cut.

National Archives

The United States government maintains the National Archives and Records Administration (NARA) in College Park, MD. It was established in 1934 by President Franklin Roosevelt but has holdings that date back to 1775. It contains copies of the Declaration of Independence, the U.S. Constitution, and the Bill of Rights. More than 365,000 reels of film and 110,000 videotapes reside in the archives. Many of the films and videos are listed online, but usually you need to go to the archives or hire a researcher to see what holdings might be useful for your film. Go to *www.archives.gov* for more information about how to research and obtain reproduction copies of their materials. Usually you will need to pay for reproduction costs (which may include a digital intermediate copy for the archive itself, as well) at an approved vendor.

The archives were created by employees or agents of the U.S. government, so most of the records in the custody of the NARA are in the public domain. But some of the documentary materials may be protected by copyright. In that case, you'll need to contact the rights holder to get permission and perhaps pay a licensing fee.

Fair Use

Fair use is discussed fully in the *Legal* chapter. Please go there for a more in-depth explanation of the concept and its use. Two good websites for more information are at *www.fairuse.stanford.edu* and *www.centerforsocialmedia.org*. This is a definition from the Stanford website — "fair use is a copyright principle based on the belief that the public is entitled to freely use portions of copyrighted materials for purposes of commentary and criticism. For example, if you wish to criticize a novelist, you should have the freedom to quote a portion of the novelist's work without asking permission. Absent this freedom, copyright owners could stifle any negative comments about their work." At the American University's Center for Social Media there is a downloadable

Documentary Filmmakers' Statement of Best Practices in Fair Use handbook that is very helpful.

If you use material in your film and you think it falls under one of the guidelines for fair use, you should consult an attorney to make sure you are on solid legal ground. Once you feel certain you are in compliance, use it in your film with confidence and you will not pay a license fee.

Archive Usage and Negotiation

To negotiate the rights for the archive material you require you'll need to know a few things:

   1. The archive's identification number for the photo or clip.

   2. The name and contact details for the archive.

   3. If it's a piece of video, the length (measured by # of seconds) of the video required and the number of times it is used in the film.

   4. The type of rights you require (i.e., all media worldwide, in perpetuity or U.S. television and theatrical only, etc.).

   5. Are there any other photos or clips you need from the same archive?

Once you have all of this info you can contact the archive and begin the negotiation.

Each archive will have a price list based on the rights requested. The most expensive will be all rights worldwide, in perpetuity. The least expensive will be film festival only. And there will be a sliding scale between those two rights with different prices. For video, the rates will be based on a per-second charge and there is usually a minimum required — often 30 seconds. If you only need 15 seconds, you will still be charged for 30 seconds. That's why it is important to group your material by archive — you may have one 10-second clip, one 15-second clip and another 5-second clip — to maximize the money you are spending by not having to pay the minimum charge for clips under that amount. Sometimes multiple archives will have the same photo or clip and you can group your purchases to certain archives so you can get your total clip requests to total over the minimum and save money.

Everything is open to negotiation. The more you are using from one archive, the more leverage you have. Each archive will give you the standard charge as the first price but it is up to you to try to negotiate a better rate if you can't afford it. Go back to your contact person and ask for a better deal so you can afford to put the clip in your film.

License Paperwork

Once you have negotiated a price, ask each archive for the license agreement for the photos or footage. It is best to run it by your attorney to make sure that it covers all of the rights you are purchasing and gives you the usage you require. You also want to make sure that the document proves that the archive has the proper ownership of the material so they are legally allowed to give you the rights.

All of the archive licensing agreements will be needed when you apply for Errors & Omissions (E&O) insurance (see *Insurance* chapter). The insurance company may request copies when you submit the E&O application. This will prove to the insurance company that you have all the proper clearances for the all of the archive material in your film. The licensing agreements are an essential part of the legal paperwork for your project.

Cease and Desist

If you do not obtain the proper archive (and music) licenses for your film, you could receive a cease and desist letter from the copyright holder after a public screening or its distribution via the internet, theatrical or television. This letter would tell you to cease screening the film because you are in violation of the copyright laws governing the materials in question. If the accusation is valid, you'd have to stop showing the film until you had either obtained the proper licensing for the rights or removed the copyrighted material from your film before you could show the film again or distribute it publicly.

RECAP

1. **Use photo and video archives when you need to acquire historical material for your film.**

2. **Archive researchers are knowledgeable about archive resources and can find and procure material for your film.**

3. **Negotiate for the rights you require for the film — "all media worldwide, in perpetuity" is best.**

4. If your usage falls under the fair use criteria, consult an attorney to make sure you are correct and don't pay a license fee.

5. For video, archive material is usually charged by the second and there is often a 30-second minimum. Group archive clips together from the same archive to save money.

6. You may need to submit the archive license agreements when you apply for E&O insurance.

MARKETING/ PUBLICITY

O NCE YOU HAVE COMPLETED your independent film you'll need to come up with a marketing and publicity plan. If you already have received funding from a distribution company or a theatrical or television broadcast entity, then you will be working on marketing/publicity with those outlets and campaigns. There may be other territories that are unsold and you'll need to create a strategy for selling those territories so you can maximize your profits and/or pay off the costs of production, depending on how you have funded your film.

Marketing refers to how you brand, promote, and sell your film to sales agents, distributors, and the public. Publicity refers to the dissemination of promotional materials to make sales agents, distributors, and the public aware of your film and generate sales. Interviewing cast and crew is also a tool used for publicity purposes. The two areas go hand in hand and overlap. The following are the common ways to market and publicize a low-budget independent film.

Recognize and tell the truth. The truth is the most attractive thing of all, but it requires skills and awareness.

— Thomas Leonard

Press Kit

A press kit is an essential building block in the marketing of your film. Some of the material that was created in the investment plan (see *Development* chapter) will be re-used or amended for the press kit. The elements that make up a press kit are:

1. Log line

2. Synopsis

3. Director's Statement & Bio

4. Cast Bios

5. Key Personnel Bios (producer, cinematographer, editor)

6. Press clippings

7. Full Screen-Credit list

8. Photos (in a format that can be used easily for press articles)

9. Director's Filmography

As an example, here is the press kit for the case study short film *RED FLAG*:

RED FLAG

PRESS KIT

Contact information:
Name
Phone
Email address

RED FLAG

LOGLINE

A woman endures a series of blind dates, each one worse than the last. Tracy chooses to ignore her own personal warning system, making her unprepared for her unexpected meeting with Mr. Right.

SYNOPSIS

A comedic short film where Tracy, an "everywoman" in her early 30s, goes on four pretty bad blind dates. She emerges unscathed, even after ignoring red flag after red flag, and seems to have given up on dating. Free and alone, she stumbles upon a fabulous guy in the park. All is looking good until it's time to say goodbye.

FILM CREDITS

Tracy

James

Richard

Comb–Over Man

Matt

Written and Directed by
Sheila Curran Dennin

Produced by
Maureen A. Ryan

Executive Producer

Director of Photography

Editor

Casting Director

Unit Production Manager

Assistant Director

Production Coordinator

Assistant Camera

Gaffer

Key Grip

Grip/Electric

Sound/DIT

Production Designer

Art Director

Costume Designer

Assistant Costume Designer

Hair/Makeup/Wig creator

Script Supervisor

Animation Designers

Production Assistants

Background Actors

Music credits

Stock footage credits

Special Thanks

BIOS

Sheila Curran Dennin (Writer/Director)

Sheila Curran Dennin has been writing and directing for film video and multi-media over 20 years. Her work as been recognized by numerous awards, including two Freddies, considered the "Oscar" of health films for programs on HIV and AIDS testing for at-risk women and their partners, which is currently the Department of Health's official counseling and testing video in over 40 states, and the film *Advance Directives* aimed at gay couples living with HIV, encouraging them to generate living wills and health care proxies as legal protection for their partnership. Her programs for Big Brothers/Big Sisters motivating mentorship for the children of prisoners received numerous awards, including three 2006 Telly awards.

Her television work includes field production and interviews for several cable network programs, including *Villians, Vixens and Superheroes, The Road* and *"Biography."* Television writing credits include projects for the SciFi (now SyFy) Channel, Lifetime Television, Court TV and "COPS."

Sheila's work on public health related documentaries focuses on widespread dissemination of information with an emphasis on awareness, education, and motivation for "at risk" audiences. These include *Everything's Fine* starring Edward Asner, a film about the effects of alcoholism on the family, focusing on the principles of Adult Children of Alcoholics. She was honored with a Cine and several HeSCA and National Health Information awards.

Clearly, for Dennin, given this body of important work, this film marks a much-needed fore into dramatic comedy. Phew!!

Maureen A. Ryan (Producer)

Maureen Ryan, an award winning producer based in New York, recently enjoyed success as Co-producer of *MAN ON WIRE*, Grand Jury Prize winner at the 2008 Sundance Film Festival. She also Co-produced James Marsh and Milo Addica's *The King*, starring Gael Garcia Bernal and William Hurt, which premiered at the Cannes Film Festival. Other credits include Producer of the feature documentary *The Gates*, co-directed by Albert Maysles and Antonio Ferrera, which premiered at the Tribeca Film Festival and aired on HBO, *Grey Gardens: From East Hampton to Broadway*, which premiered at the Hamptons International Film Festival and *The Team*, a feature documentary following the U.S. homeless soccer team as they compete in the first Annual Homeless Soccer World Cup.

She also produced the BAFTA award-winning feature documentary *Wisconsin Death Trip* and the shorts *Torte Bluma* (Best Drama at the Palm Springs International Shorts Film Festival and Best Short at the Los Angeles Film Festival) and *Last Hand Standing* (finalist for the Chrysler Million Dollar Film Festival). Her television producing credits include *At the Ryman, The Road* and *Long Live the King: Country Salutes Elvis.*

Currently, Ryan teaches at Columbia University's Graduate Film Division and supervises student production at the school. She also teaches film producing at New York University.

Christo Tsiaras (Editor)

Christo Tsiaras has been editing in the Boston since 1982. Clients have included leading ad agencies like Arnold Worldwide and Hill, Holiday as well as Fortune 500 corporations, filmmakers, directors and independent producers. Christo has won many awards for his television commercials, music videos, documentaries and corporate videos.

Previous and current clients include Disney Channel, Tommy Hilfiger, CNN, Turner Classic Movies, USA Networks, Timberland, Boston Herald, Blue Cross/Blue Shield, Reebok, McDonalds and Animal Planet. His most recent project is editing the award winning independent film *Overserved* which is winning numerous awards around the country including Best Picture at the Boston Comedy Film Festival.

DIRECTOR'S STATEMENT

Red Flag is a film about looking for love. It came from my own experience in the dating world.... All of the blind dates in the film actually happened to me. Most were set up by well-meaning "friends" who thought these were great guys... me, not so much. The lesson? No matter how much we think we can, no one can predict chemistry!

One of the ways I got through it was to keep telling myself that it would be great fodder for a screenplay. Such was the genesis of this short film.

When you look at it, if we're in dating mode, we're much more willing to ignore obvious warning signs in the name of "giving it a try," "lightening up," "who knows, this could be it." Particularly when a friend thinks this is a great guy or gal. So, the film explores the questions, "should we pay attention to red flags? Ignore them? Or, after we've learned a lesson or two, *look* for them?" We are, after all, meeting strangers as potential partners. How best to approach this really strange and loaded process?

One of the things I wanted to stay away from in this film was "male bashing." It seemed too easy. The twist at the end grew out of my distance from the experience, but also my belief that we're all on the hot seat in these situations, whether we know it or not.

The other character in this film is the Red Flag itself. It needed to have, not just a presence, but also a "will"... a purpose as well as personality. We went through many discussions about how it needed to look and "act" and we came up with the post effect to make it work.

Red Flag is a film which makes us take a look at ourselves from an angle we perhaps hadn't thought of before. Careful the Red Flag...one never knows where it may fly!

PRESS CLIPPINGS/QUOTES

Add in articles and blurbs as reviews come in

Screeners

Once you create your protection master for your film, you'll want to make lots of screeners. **Screeners** refer to the DVD copies of your film that you send out to people who want to see your film — sales agents, distributors, acquisitions people at broadcast entities. You'll also need to send them out with film festival applications. Screeners need to have a watermark on them to prevent them from being stolen, duplicated, or used for any purpose other than that particular person viewing it. They should never be used for public screenings and that is why the watermark is important. **Watermarks** can be the name of your company on the lower part of the image, or a phrase like "Not for duplication." Watermarks can stay on the screen throughout the entire film or just dissolve on and off the screen every three to five minutes. You decide how you want to do it, but make sure it is on every screener you send out.

Writer/director/producer Paul Cotter (*BOMBER, Estes Avenue*) advises how best to deal with screeners. "Here's the deal. Everyone wants to check your film out on DVD. STOP!!! Wait! Think! First of all, can you still get that person to a festival screening to watch it in front of a live audience? If so, then don't send a DVD. Bust their arse [sic] and get them to come and watch it live.

If not, then send them a DVD but make sure it's watermarked. We all love piracy, until it happens to our own work. Maybe later down the line it's an honor to be pirated, but right at the outset of your film (and I'm talking features here — shorts filmmakers... be thankful if your film is pirated) you need to protect it. It's a commodity. Get it sold/distributed, then relax. But until then, don't let a 'piratable' copy get into the public domain. You'll be thankful in the long run."

Website

Creating a website for your film is also a necessary publicity tool. It doesn't have to be anything too fancy or expensive but it needs to include a few specific bits of information about your project. You also want it to be easy to update so you can add and delete information and keep it current. Before you set up the website, you'll need to acquire a URL address. Often people choose the title of the film followed by "the movie" or "the film." Two recent websites that were created for films I produced include *www.bomberthemovie.com* and *www.redflagthefilm.com*.

Here are the necessary elements for a website:

1. Home page — film title, graphic, and general info about the film.

2. Press Kit — available for download for publicity purposes.

3. Trailer — about a minute-long trailer of your film.

4. Publicity photos — in a high-resolution (300 dpi) format that press and others can use for articles and other publicity. It should include stills of the lead cast members in the film, the director working on set, and any other key features of the film you want to illustrate.

5. Schedule — an updated list of festival screenings, theatrical runs, broadcast dates, and DVD release dates in the coming months. Keep it current.

6. Awards list — an updated list of any awards the film has won.

7. Links — to press articles online, to social networking sites for the film, and any other material that is pertinent to the film.

Online Social Networking

The ability to create publicity for your film is enhanced by how many people know about it. Online social networking provides a cost effective way to get the word out and cultivate an audience for your film. Whatever site(s) you use, you can give people information about your film's screenings, film festival dates, direct them to your website, and inform them as to how to purchase the film. It's a vast landscape for getting the word out about your film and the direct costs are virtually nothing. It does cost time and you have to decide how much time you want to dedicate to doing it. The time commitment can expand and contract based on your own availability and where you are in the process of releasing your film, publicly. You'll probably spend more time when you start your film festival run and again when the film is released theatrically, on television, VOD, and DVD.

Blogs

Many directors or producers blog on their film websites as a way to generate interest and excitement about the film. You can create a blog or go on other website blogs to do interviews and guest blogs. Micro-blogging (i.e., Twitter) can also be used. Depending on your film's audience and the technology available at the time of its release you can decide what is the best platform to get the word out to your audience.

Media Outreach

For certain documentaries and for narrative films that are tied closely to a specific societal topic, media outreach programs are a great way to get the film out to larger audiences that will appreciate its message. **Media outreach** for films is usually done by creating a media packet about the film's topic as a way of connecting with people who are interested in the content. Scheduling screenings for interested groups, sending out press releases to organizations and their websites, and contacting local and national press to generate story ideas for articles about the film's subject are the best ways to launch a media outreach campaign.

Some nonprofit foundations provide grants to filmmakers to create and implement media outreach around their films' topics. If you have a film that is of interest to certain constituencies, you can build awareness about your film through those organizations.

How to Hire a Publicist

Hiring a publicist can be a good choice for your film. A publicist has long standing relationships with press, magazines, news outlets, and other places that are interested in the news about your film. They have email lists of all the people who write for print and online media and will send out press releases regarding your project to the various outlets that are interested. Publicists will determine what is newsworthy about your film and pitch story ideas for articles to try to get journalists to write about your film.

Depending on your funds and marketing strategy, hiring a publicist for your film can be a good investment. If your film appeals to mainstream media then you'll want a publicist with those connections. If your film's audience is more orientated to online outlets and blogs, you'll want a publicist who is orientated to that area of marketing.

Track which films were well publicized in the independent world over the last year. Find out who the publicist was and contact her to see if she would be interested in your film and what rates she charges. Local film organizations and online film communities can be a good place to get referrals for publicists, as well.

IMDb.com

www.IMDb.com stands for the Internet Movie Database. It is the go-to website to look up credits for any film, television show, actor, filmmaker, and crew personnel over the last several decades. When your film meets the IMDb criteria you can create an entry for it. As the producer it is best to be the person who adds the credits and makes sure they are accurate on the website. It's a public record of your film's screen credits and you want it to be correct.

The database also compiles profiles for anyone who has at least one screen credit so it also serves as a kind of online resume for anyone to see. It's very important to make sure your credits are correct and up to date whenever a film you have worked on is added to the database. If you find your credit missing or an incorrect attribution for your name, contact the producers of the film and ask them to correct it. Often people in the film industry look people up on the website if they want to get some sense of a person's background before a meeting or an introduction.

RECAP

1. **Marketing and publicity are vital to getting information out to the press and the public about your film when it is ready to premiere.**

2. **The tools for a marketing campaign are a press kit, screeners, website, online social networking sites, blogs, and media outreach programs.**

3. **Hiring a publicist may be an option if you have the budget and it will help publicize your film.**

4. **IMDb.com is used by the film industry as an online resume for everyone who has ever had a screen credit on a film.**

CHAPTER 18

FILM FESTIVALS

NOW THAT YOU HAVE completed your film you will probably want to send it out to film festivals. This is a great way to get your film out there — seen by audiences, distributors, talent agencies, sales agents, and scouts for other film festivals. If you haven't sold your film, screening it at film festivals can be very helpful toward making a sale — the film gets exposure, critical reviews, and press and has the potential to win awards.

If you already have sold your film to television, theatrical, DVD, or the Web, look at your contract(s) to make sure you are allowed to screen it at festivals prior to the transmission or release of the film. Some contracts have a "hold back" period that prevents you from having any public screenings (including film festivals.) If your contract has such a stipulation, it doesn't stop you from asking for permission to screen at a film festival(s). Often it can be helpful to a film's broadcast premiere and the network will be very supportive of any film festival participation.

If you decide you want to apply to film festivals, there are thousands of festivals all around the globe. It can

Art first. All else will follow.

— Jerry Saltz

be a bit overwhelming and expensive (each application usually requires an application fee), so it's important to do research on the various film festivals to figure out which ones are right for your project.

A great clearinghouse for information about film festivals is a website called *www.withoutabox.com*. The website has an in-depth database and customizable search engine so you can look for festivals that fit your criteria — narrative features, documentaries, experimental, short films, music videos, etc. The website also allows you to pay a fee to register your film online and then use its online system to send your application to film festivals electronically, thus saving you some time from the mind-numbing process of re-inputting the same info over and over again each time you apply to a different film festival. Not all film festivals use *withoutabox.com,* so for some festivals you'll need to apply directly through their own websites.

The application will require information about the key creative and cast members, including resumes, filmographies, press kit, and a director's statement. You'll need to designate the contact person and include information about a sales agent, if you have one. You'll also need to provide technical information about aspect ratio and how your sound is mixed, i.e., stereo, mono, or Dolby. Once you have filled out the application, you'll need to provide a credit card to pay for the application fee and then send off a DVD to the festival's application committee for consideration.

There are usually several deadlines for applying to a festival — Early, Regular, and Late. The earlier you send in the application, the less expensive the application fee. You can save a lot of money by sending in your film before the end of the Early deadline.

Fee Waivers and Screening Fees

Those film festival application fees can really add up. Requesting fee waivers and screening fees is a way to mitigate some of the expense. Depending on your film and your past relationship with the festival, you can sometimes request a fee waiver so you don't have to pay the application fee. You still will need to send in an application and a DVD screener, but there is usually a section on the application that allows you to put the fee waiver code in a certain box and you will not have to pay the fee. If you are a first-time filmmaker without a track record, chances are you won't be given a fee waiver. If you had previous films play at that festival, if the festival programmer saw your film at another festival and liked it a lot and asked you to apply, or if your film has won some top awards at other festivals — these are all valid reasons for a fee waiver request. If you are a student filmmaker, some film festivals will extend a fee waiver if you ask.

The screening fee is another little-known aspect of the film festival circuit. Some festivals have money budgeted to pay screening fees to certain films that they program. Each festival has different criteria and many don't have screening fee money available. Some will pay for your travel and hotel instead of a screening fee. But you might as well ask when you receive notification that your film was accepted into a festival. The screening fee could help pay for a few more application fees!

Film Festival Strategy

Getting your film into domestic and international film festivals can be a very competitive proposition. You'll want to have a cogent strategy so you can promote your film well and have a greater chance of your film getting accepted.

1. First think about what your film is about. Does it have well-known actors? Is it about a certain topic? What genre? What is the specific target audience? Is it similar, in type, to past films — what film festivals did they play?

2. Where do you want to have the world premiere for your film? What about a U.S., European and/or local (state or region) premiere?

3. Are you interested in trying to become eligible for Oscar consideration for your feature, documentary, or short?

4. Are you interested in becoming eligible for the Independent Spirit (West Coast) or Gotham (East Coast) awards for independent feature films?

5. Do you want to attend and/or compete at film festivals with or without "markets" attached to them?

Ira Deutchman, veteran film executive/producer and managing partner of Emerging Pictures (*www.EmergingPictures.com*), shares his advice on film festivals and sales:

Maureen: What are the essential steps to selling a low-budget indie film these days?

Ira: The most interesting thing about the whole myth about making a movie and then going to a festival with it is that you've got to first get into a festival, and it can't be just any festival. It has to be a festival where the buyers are actually paying attention. So there are certain kinds of films [that get into film festivals.]

There are a lot of people who would dispute me on this but "festival films" are a genre. There may be a lot of genres within that genre, but lots of movies get made with the hope that they're going to sell at a film festival and they're just not the right kind of movies. They're not the kind of films that the major film festival directors are really looking for.

Sometimes you can get surprised and they'll take something just because it hit them the right way or they think it's different enough from what's out there that they might take it — in spite of the fact that it doesn't fit into their normal sweet spot. But the truth is that certain kinds of movies get into film festivals.

Maureen: Give me the kind of principles of that genre.

Ira: There has got to be something distinctive about it. If it's kind of formulaic, it's not going to get into a film festival. Ironically, a lot of those kinds of movies get made because there is this feeling like, *Oh, I know how to make a studio movie. The problem is I don't have enough money to make it with stars. I'm going to make that movie without stars.* So what you end up with is a mainstream commercial movie, theoretically, with absolutely nothing that you can sell.

So those kinds of movies are really up shit's creek because they're not going to get well reviewed. They're not going to get into film festivals and nobody else is going to be interested in them because they don't have the star power to sell them. We refer to those movies as "tweeners." They're movies that are not this and they're not that, neither fish nor foul, whatever metaphor you want to come up with, but basically there is no market for them.

Going back to your original point, you can't even get into film festivals with those films except for, sometimes, C- and D-level festivals that are so desperate for premieres… or the hometown film festival where you shot the film… or something along those lines. So if you really want to be strategic about it, you try to create a film that you know is in the sweet spot of film festivals. It's a little quirky, a little outside the mainstream, perhaps a little outrageous, themes that have to do with issues that we know are of interest to the people who run film festivals. That would certainly be true of documentaries — hard-hitting, exposes of something.

Kiss Me, Guido [a film I produced] is a funny example of that because the filmmaker, right from the get-go, from the moment he pitched me, was really strategic about the fact that he thought the way to jumpstart his career was to make a gay-themed film, because he knew that there would be film festival interest in it. And even if there wasn't Sundance-level interest in it, which turned out to be case — we did get into Sundance — there would have been gay film festivals. There are certain things like that — there are Asian festivals, there are women's festivals. Those are the kinds of things you know have a place where these films can be played — Jewish film — and those festivals are all over the place.

Maureen: In that case, if you're making that kind of a film, you're targeting film festivals as your first step. You are looking to get into a film festival that you know is going to have buyers there.

Ira: That is assuming that you've got a movie that would be of interest to them and the only way you can find that is by trying. You've got to be very strategic about where your world premiere is going to be and then, beyond your world premiere, you have to think strategically — *Now what's my international premiere? What's my Canadian premiere?* You've got to try for the top-level festivals first. Truth be told, in terms of buyers, there is only a handful of them that really are meaningful. In the U.S., really, Sundance is just about the only festival that's truly meaningful.

There is an interesting B-list developing that includes Tribeca, the L.A. Festival, SXSW, and even Cine Vegas, to some extent. But those are definitely B-level festivals. The difference, really, between Sundance and all the rest is that all the buyers are there. There is a certain subset of buyers that will go to each of those other festivals I'm talking about, sometimes based on who they invite to be on the panels, sometimes based on the fact that there is a relationship that's developed between that particular buyer and that festival, but it's not the same thing [as Sundance].

And the other difference between that A-level festival and the B-level festivals is the level of press that it has. That really can push a film into the buyers' hands, in a sense, because you can develop a head of steam where people are buzzing about a movie and suddenly there is an article, even if it's just a paragraph in *Daily Variety* or *Hollywood Reporter* or *The New York Times*. That makes the difference between the film selling or not selling and that can't happen at these B-level festivals — and not to mention the C-level festivals that are even beyond that.

So aside from Sundance, which I think is the only A-level festival for buyers in the United States, there is Toronto and Cannes, of course. But the next level would be Venice and Berlin. You hear about buyers going to other markets or festivals but it just isn't the same thing. It's not the same numbers, it's not the same critical mass of press that can really push a movie over.

Maureen: Corollary to the film festival discussion, how important is winning an award?

Ira: It can make the difference to that movie but I don't think not winning an award is a strike against you. It could be. I mean, the major directors feel that way. Like if you're Francis Coppola and you've got a new movie you're going to premiere in Cannes — if you don't win an award, that's like a scar.

Film Festival Premieres

You can only have *one* world premiere for your film. It's a coveted event for a film festival to have your feature film's world premiere (for shorts it is not as much of an issue). It adds cachet to their festival and depending on the selectivity of each festival, they will weigh your application accordingly. The descending order of domestic premiere designations are world premiere, North American premiere, U.S. premiere, and U.S. regional premiere. For international film festivals, they usually want to know if it is a regional (i.e., European, Middle Eastern, Asian) or a country premiere. For features, some festivals will not screen your film if they can't have one of those classifications for their festival.

I suggest you send out a few applications at first and follow the rules that you used when you applied to college — there's the long-shot festival, the festival that you might have a chance at, and then there is the safety festival that you think you have a very good shot at. That way you cover all of your bases and have a good chance of getting into a festival with as few applications as possible.

The biggest and most competitive film festivals include Sundance, Berlin, Tribeca, Cannes, Telluride, Toronto, Venice, and New York. SXSW, Rotterdam, Edinburgh, Karlovy Vary, San Sebastian, Hamptons, and London are also well known and highly competitive and there are more film festivals added to the list each year. There are also festivals that concentrate on certain types of films or genres like documentaries, comedies, or horror. There is a festival for every film and it's just a matter of finding the right fit for your film and festival. Online research is important and there a several books about film festivals that can be helpful.

Oscar Eligibility

Many filmmakers dream of winning an Academy Award. The first step in that process is to have your film become eligible for one of the awards categories at The Academy of Motion Picture Arts and Sciences (AMPAS). The competition is fierce and odds of getting a nomination are akin to winning the lottery, but it can happen. There are categories for narrative features, live-action shorts, animated shorts, documentary shorts, and documentary features. Go to *www.oscars.org* to read about the specific rules and regulations for the eligibility requirements. For feature films there are theatrical distribution requirements. For short films there is a list of qualifying film festivals. If your film wins certain awards at one of the AMPAS-qualifying festivals then your film becomes eligible for a nomination in a live-action short or documentary-short category.

There are also Student Academy Awards. The awards are given in three categories — narrative, experimental, and documentary and the awards ceremony is in June in Los Angeles, CA. Check out *www.oscars. org* for more information.

Other Awards

There are almost as many awards shows as there are film festivals. The Independent Spirit Awards (given out by Film Independent) and the Gotham Awards (given out by Independent Feature Project) are two of the best known for independent films, but there are many others that are geared toward specific genres and indie categories. Research online for awards that your film may be eligible for.

Film Festivals vs. Film Markets

A film festival is usually a series of days and/or nights of film screenings, panel discussions, and parties. Some festivals have specific themes or categories, i.e., student, ethnic, genre, and gender. Festivals usually give out awards (with or without cash or gifts attached) at the end of the festival. Often there are jury prizes (voted on by a group of judges) and audience prizes (voted on by the audiences that go to the screenings.)

Film markets can be attached to a film festival or stand-alone events. Markets are where film buyers and film sellers (the filmmakers) meet to do the business of buying and selling and making deals.

In or Out of Competition

Film festivals often have several "programs" within the festival. Some of the programs are considered "in competition" and some are deemed to be "out of competition." If your film is in competition it usually means it is eligible for prizes. Out of competition means it will screen at the festival but will not be eligible for an award. The criteria for acceptance "in or out of competition" is determined by each festival. Sometimes a film is not in competition because it is not a certain premiere but the festival programmers still want to feature the film at the festival. Other times, the festival is so large that only a small number of the films can be viewed by the jury and so they create other programs to feature great work that they wish to include in the festival. Check each festival's individual website to find out the specific application rules for each program and the competition requirements for your film.

What to Expect from a Film Festival

Film festivals play an important role for independent films. They help to publicize and launch films that don't yet have distribution deals or publicity budgets. They help foster community within the film industry and introduce filmmakers to critics and tastemakers on the festival circuit. You meet and connect with film programmers who can help you get your next film into their film festivals later in the year. And programmers often move from one festival to another, over time. You may meet them at a small festival but by the time your next film is ready, they have moved on to a larger film festival. Your relationship will help get your film considered at the larger one. You can start to build a track record for you and your films.

Festivals are often filled with panel discussions where industry professionals speak about current topics and issues in the film business. It's a great way to get information and to meet people who can help you and your film. Some festivals have sections that highlight film-related businesses like film/video equipment, state film commissions, film-related computer software, etc. You can learn about cutting-edge technologies and other organizations that can be useful to you.

Often festival organizers will offer roundtrip airfare and hotel accommodations for filmmakers to be present for their screening(s). Festivals want the filmmakers to be present for Q&A sessions after the screenings so the audience can meet and discuss the film with the creators. It is a value-added for festival goers to get to see and meet the filmmakers. Usually the airfare/hotel is offered to the directors of the projects but, if they are not available, the producers or other key creatives on the film may be able to attend in their places. It really depends on the festival regulations. Once your film is accepted, the festival's hospitality department will coordinate these details.

Getting a festival pass is also an important perk for the filmmaker(s). Usually your film will be offered at least one pass that allows access to all screenings and panel discussions. If more than one person from the film is attending you can request more passes and tickets to your screenings. Each festival has its own policies about passes and tickets. Take advantage of all that the film festivals and markets offer so you can maximize your time and money while you are there.

Posters, Postcards, and Photos

When you get into a film festival, you will be asked to send the festival organizers several things — the film master (in the highest-quality format that the fest can project), a press kit (see *Marketing and Publicity* chapter), posters and/or postcards, digital publicity photos, and a photo for a festival ID badge.

Most festivals will request several posters and often they ask for a poster on poster card stock so they can put it on an easel or place it elsewhere around the festival. Postcards are needed to give to potential audience members, press, etc., and to put out on the tables around the festival lounges and venues. Both of these materials will cost money but they are a great way to publicize your film. There are many low-cost printers online that can print out posters and postcards from a digital image that you upload. A longer turnaround time will help keep costs down.

Email your publicity digital photos to the filmmaker press coordinator at the festival. They also will need a passport-type photo of you, ahead of time, so they can create your festival pass and/or badge.

Technical Issues at Festivals

Getting your film master or print to and from the film festival is usually coordinated by the traffic department. They will contact you several weeks before your film is due to screen and ask for the tech specifications (i.e., screening format, video standard, aspect ratio, audio format, running time) for your film. It's important to get that information back to them as soon as possible. You need to make sure that you have the correct video or film format for their projection system. Each festival is different and has different technical requirements. Some will screen HD Cam, some Digital Beta, others will screen in other video formats. Very few festivals require a film print any more. For international festivals make sure you confirm if they can screen NTSC. If not, find out what standard they require — usually PAL or SECAM. If you don't have that kind of master you will need to do a **standards conversion.** It's an expensive process and requires special equipment at a dub house. You should get an estimate and decide if you are able to pay for the cost to convert the master.

You've worked so hard to make the film the best it can be. You want to work hard to assure that it has the best technical presentation possible at every festival. To that end, request a tech test before it screens for the first time at the festival theater. A **tech test** is a quick screening of your master right before the festival personnel opens the doors of the theater to the public to see your film. The projectionist will play the first few minutes of your film and you should be there to check the following: aspect ratio (is the frame cropped in any way?); audio volume (is it too loud, too low or non-existent?); brightness (is it bright enough?); frame-rate speed (is it running too fast or in slow motion?). You know your film best and within a few seconds you'll be able to tell if all the technical aspects are correct for the best possible viewing experience in that theater.

Before the screening of a film I produced at a well-known international film festival, I asked to do a tech test. I was reassured that the projectionist had already done a tech test and everything was fine. I acquiesced and settled into my seat next to the director and DP. The audience arrived, then the lights went down and the film started. The aspect ratio was completely wrong and the audio volume was too low. It was devastating because although we could get the projectionist to raise the audio volume we couldn't change the aspect ratio unless we stopped the screening to correct it. Make the effort to get a tech test done in the few minutes before one film finishes and your film starts — it can make all the difference.

Jury and Audience Awards

Most film festivals give out awards at the end of the fest. They fall into two categories — 1) Jury prizes and 2) Audience awards. Jury prizes are usually decided by a panel of judges who watch all the films in competition at the festival. Often there are a few different panels that are devoted to a certain type of film — i.e., documentary, narrative features, short films. Audience awards are voted on by the audiences that attend all the screenings. Usually there is a ballot that is filled out and handed in by audience members after each screening. Then the festival organizers tally the votes and announce the winners.

If you win an award, congrats! If you don't, no worries. But if you do, use it to your advantage — send out a press release, announce it on your website, post it on your social networks and put it on your poster or postcard. It's a competitive world — celebrate and let everyone know.

RECAP

1. Film festivals are a vital part of any release plan for an independent film.

2. Create a film festival strategy for your film. Research which festivals are best for your film and will give it the audiences, press, and exposure you want.

3. Decide where you'd like to have the world premiere for your film. Be mindful of how best to exploit the various regional premieres at different film festivals.

4. Go to *www.oscars.org* to research the rules for Academy Award eligibility.

5. Film markets are focused on bringing sales agents and distributors together in pursuit of film acquisitions.

6. If your film is "in competition" it is usually eligible for various jury awards and special prizes.

7. Coordinate travel/accommodations with the festival hospitality department and send the film master to the festival traffic department.

8. Request a tech test with the projectionist before your first screening at the festival's theater to make sure that the film is projected properly.

CHAPTER 19

DISTRIBUTION/ SALES

P RODUCING AND COMPLETING
YOUR film is a tremendous
accomplishment. But that
is only the first half of the
process. Selling your film and getting it distributed is, in some ways,
THE most important part of making
the film. You need to pay back your
investors and make a profit so you
can go out and do it all again. If not,
no matter how impressive and brilliant your film, it is not a sustainable
business model. It's the film business
and people invest so they can make
a profit.

We are at a unique place in industry history right now with many
questions about what the new models
for distribution and monetization will
be. There are more questions than
there are answers and I don't know
what the new business models will be.
Lots of very bright people are trying
to figure it out right now. Whatever
happens it will need to enable independent filmmakers to make a living
producing films. For this chapter I
will outline the general principals and
steps necessary to sell and distribute
a film. Beyond that I will leave it up to
you to keep up with the latest industry information to figure out how best

Producers produce.

— Ira Deutschman

to sell your film in the changing winds of our times. Check out the latest information at *www.ProducerToProducer.com*.

Sales Agents

Sales agents are representatives of your film in the marketplace. They have contacts and relationships with distribution and DVD companies and work to sell your film for you. Sales agents usually delineate between North American and International sales markets. Some agents cover world rights but it is common to concentrate on either domestic or international because they are very different markets with different companies and countries in each one. Agents also leverage the other films that they represent so your film is considered when they make a pitch to a company for distribution consideration. If they have several films that distributors are interested in, it can help to get them to watch your film for possible acquisition, as well.

Sales agents charge a fee based on a percentage of the sales they get for your film. In addition, there are often expenses that get charged to cover the costs of travel to film festivals and meetings, as well as overhead costs for their offices and support staffs. Negotiating a cap on expenses is wise so you don't lose your revenue to lots of agent expenses. Make sure to read your contract carefully and consult your attorney before signing a sales agent agreement. The other point of negotiation is the time period that agents will represent your film and how long they can collect fees for deals that began during the time period, but concluded after the representation period.

Once you have a sales agent involved he or she will partner with you to build your film festival and marketing strategy, as discussed in the *Marketing/Publicity* and *Film Festivals* chapters. The sales agent will need marketing materials and DVD screeners to send out to various distribution companies to see if they are interested in your film. The sales agent will follow up and stay in contact with the companies to work toward selling the film. If you do not find a sales agent, this task will fall solely to you to do. It is a big job but essential to be able to find a buyer for your film.

Groundbreaking producer/executive producer and managing partner of Emerging Pictures Ira Deutchman (*www.EmergingPictures.com*) has good information about choosing a sales agent:

Maureen: How do you find a sales agent? How do you know if he or she is any good and good for your film? What do you need to be careful about when signing with a sales agent?

Ira: If you're talking about one of these low-budget indie movies that really doesn't have a whole lot of sales potential, then any sales agent who wants your movie — you DON'T want them because there is nothing to sell. All they're trying to do is get their hooks into a movie early, on the chance that it turns into something interesting. I think that's bad.

The time to look for a sales agent is when you just heard that you got into one of those major film festivals. I get asked all the time, *Well, yeah, but doesn't it matter who your sales agent is to get you into those festivals?* I really don't believe that. I think it can sometimes work against you. So don't even look for a sales agent until you have something to sell and you don't have something to sell until you're in a film festival, unless you have a star-driven movie.

Now, picking a sales agent once you are in that position — you want somebody who is not going to the film festival with too many movies. You want somebody who you've got some references from. Really call those people. Call the people they've worked with because you're going to be surprised at what kind of results you get. I mean I've had happy experiences with sales agents where the film didn't do real well but I was still happy with the effort that went into it. I felt like they didn't abandon the film the minute it didn't go well—that they stuck with it. And I've had bad experiences with sales agents even though they were selling. I felt like they had five minutes of attention that they gave to the movie, they sold whatever they could, and that the movie in essence sold itself.

You want a sales agent who is a marketer, who really sees the hooks in your film and who strategizes with you. I would definitely sit down with them and say, *Okay, so what do you think? Who is the audience for this movie? Who are the potential distributors that you think might be interested in it? What's going to get them interested? And what are you going to do that's going to help to foster that interest?* And it's not just about having a Rolodex. It's about really thinking strategically about where it fits in the festival and what they're actually going to do to earn their percentage.

Maureen: How do you check on them if you've never worked with them before?

Ira: Ask them for references.

Maureen: And then call the producer of that film.

Ira: That's right. Call up the producer and say, *Hey, what was your experience like? Do they pay you? Were they still interested in your movie six months after it premiered? Can you get them on the phone?*—that kind of stuff.

International Sales

International sales is usually done on a country-by-country or regional basis. An international sales agent would look to sell different countries like France, Japan, Mexico, or Australia separately, or sometimes the film will be sold by region such as the United Kingdom/Ireland or Asia. For international sales agreements determine if you have to pay for translation and subtitling – it will add to your deliverables costs.

Theatrical/Television Sales

Each country or region will allow you the opportunity to sell the film's theatrical (shown in theaters) and television rights. It doesn't mean that you will always sell both rights for a given country — it will depend on the marketplace and who is interested in buying which rights. Some films may not warrant a theatrical release and will only garner television sales.

Television has different markets and windows for licenses. In the U.S. there is network television (NBC, ABC, CBS and Fox), public television (PBS), subscriber cable (HBO, Showtime, Cinemax, etc.) and cable television (IFC, Sundance, Bravo, A&E, National Geographic, etc.). You can sell to one market for a certain period of time and then do another sale to another market after that license period expires.

Home Video/VOD Sales

Currently home video is about DVD sales. Additionally, there is Video On Demand (VOD) that will become a bigger share of the market as the business model and technology allow for more films to be directly downloaded to your television or computer monitor. Getting a deal for DVD and VOD can be in addition to a theatrical or television sale. More and more it may be the only way for audiences to see your film. Doing a theatrical release for a film is expensive and labor intensive and is not always possible for every film produced. VOD is growing and its role in delivering films to audiences will change in the coming years.

Deliverables

As discussed in the *Postproduction* chapter, deliverables are the materials that must be delivered to a buyer when you sell the film. The contract for each sale will dictate what your deliverables will be for your film for that buyer. This is a crucial part of the contract and before you sign, you must make sure you have all the deliverables necessary for the deal and can afford to supply them to the buyer. Depending on the list, it can be rather expensive to make all the masters, prints, dubs, copies of release forms, etc., and hire the personnel to put it all together. Make sure you are aware of the requirements and can meet the demands before you accept the sale and sign the deal. A deliverables list can be found in the Postproduction chapter. Remember to obtain E&O insurance if required (see *Insurance* chapter).

Self Distribution

If you do not get a theatrical distribution deal for you film, you can try to do your own theatrical run at selected U.S. cities. This is a lot of work and if you haven't ever done it before, there is usually a steep learning curve. You'll need to contact individual cinemas across the U.S. and work out a deal with the owners, one theater at a time. There are self-distribution consultants and books on the subject. I would recommend that you do your research to find out if it will be financially viable to self distribute your film.

Selling DVDs on the Internet is another way of recouping your money. You can expand your film's website to include a shopping cart and sell DVDs and ship them out yourself. There are also fulfillment companies that will charge you a fee to do this for you. Please keep in mind that if you get a DVD distribution deal later on, you will probably need to stop selling DVDs yourself online.

Future Distribution Models

Producer/executive producer and managing partner of Emerging Pictures Ira Deutchman (*www.EmergingPictures.com*) discusses the future of independent film distribution:

Maureen: What will be the way indie films are going to be distributed in the next five to 10 years and will it be enough to be able to make a living producing films?

Ira: I believe we're in the "post-major studio, pre-Internet age," which is to say we're nowhere. There is no real predictable business model right now with the exception of adapting comic books into hundred-million-dollar plus movies. That seems to be working and Pixar seems to have its finger on something.

But that business model, even the studios are acknowledging is only successful if they limit supply. That's the reason why the number of productions are going down at the moment because they know that there is only a certain number of times they can go to the well every year. The marketplace just isn't big enough for more movies than that. So that's one end of the spectrum.

There is a business model with examples of successes at the very lowest end of the spectrum. If you can make a movie for $50,000 or less, which people have done, then between selling it yourself via DVD on the Internet and doing DIY kinds of marketing, you can potentially make your money back and more. Develop your own following — there is a whole movement in the direction of that — specifically directors, but I think it can be just about anybody—can develop a fan base and monetize that fan base by solidifying them, by owning them.

There are a number of examples of people like that. Where that model seems to fall apart at the moment is how can you make a movie for a million dollars? How can you make a movie for two million dollars — and if you want any kind of production value, that's what you're talking about. The people who are really caught are the independent producer-directors, whatever you want to call it, who have been working for a long time — they're seeing the middle of the marketplace falling away and the DIY model just doesn't give them enough to live on.

So what will fill that gap? I don't think anybody knows the answer at this moment. The DIY thing can potentially grow into a real business. I have my doubts about that partially, because I believe that the people who are really idealistic about using the Internet to reach out to audiences are underestimating the power of big corporations to outspend them — if we're talking about whether it's available as a download on iTunes or whether it's available as a download on your own website or whether it's available on VOD in some form, or available from Netflix or Netflix Now. With all of those things, there is a tendency for the bigger movies to rise to the top, but bigger meaning — the ones with more marketing muscle behind them.

If you go and look at iTunes now, you can't find the independent films on iTunes. They're there but you can't find them. I actually think Netflix has a better model in terms of those films coming up because of their recommendation engine. There are a lot of danger signs, that once the major studios see a successful business model, whatever emerges from all of this, they'll either buy it or dominate it in some way. Just because it's available doesn't mean anybody is going to tune in. If everybody in the world is a filmmaker, which is where we're heading, [and if] everybody in the world can write a story, and if everybody in the world has the means of distribution — meaning that it costs $10 to create a website and suddenly your film is available whatever price you want to put on — if there are millions of those things out there, how are you going to get them to focus in on you?

I'm sounding like a real bummer now, but every mechanism that I'm aware of to try to get to an audience, whether it's through social networking or whatever — anytime somebody finds an angle and says, *Ooh, this is clever* and they do it and it works, you can't replicate it because then everybody is trying to do the same thing and then, suddenly, it's not so novel anymore — and now what do you do?

Every day I get invited to be in the fan group of some movie—I shouldn't say some movie—like several movies a day, and I just say *no* because what does it mean if I'm a member of all these groups? So the thing is that I sort of wonder whether there is anything that can become a replicable business model in that regard.

I do think that there will be breakthroughs and I do think that eventually there will be some model that will emerge, but it won't be a strictly DIY model. Maybe Netflix is pointing the way in the sense that what you've got to do is become a good enough marketer to get people to explore and try your movie and get the word out so that you can eventually build it into something else. That's the marketing part of it.

And the distribution mechanism: Is it pay per view? To some extent I think that it almost isn't as important because when the delivery systems are becoming mashed together they call it "convergence." It's really just that people don't even know the difference, at this stage of the game, whether they're getting Netflix Now or they're getting it over their cable box or whatever. The big corporations are the ones fighting over which boxes are going to be in your house and they're going to control, to some extent, the content.

But the more interesting aspect of it is that there really are only a certain number of ways that people can consume movies that are free, which is usually advertiser supported, otherwise there is no way of monetizing it. There is the subscription model where it's an all-you-can-eat [model]. You pay a certain amount per month and then you get whatever it is you get. Or, there is the pay-per-view model and basically going to a theater is a pay-per-view model. So you're paying for the specific showing of the movie, although the difference between in-the-home and out-of-the-home is that you can pay per view and have seven people watch it, whereas out-of-the-home, you pay per person.

So those are the business models. There is nothing else. Basically, there are a lot of people who believe that where we're heading is that all intellectual property will find its way to being free. If that happens then it's going to have to be advertiser supported, no matter what it is and that could be true in the movie theater, too. So there are all sorts of jumbly things going on right now and I don't know that anybody really knows the answer other than I think at some point we'll reach an equilibrium.

Maureen: So independent producers will still be able to stay in the business and support themselves in the future?

Ira: I hope so. I think the current wisdom on that front is that the only way they'll be able to do it is by also learning to become marketers. They can't just make the movie and then cross their fingers — that's like buying a lottery ticket. They're going to have to, right from the inception of the project, be thinking about who the market is and what's Plan B or maybe even making that Plan A, and if Plan B comes along it'll be a miracle that it always is.

RECAP

1. Look for a sales agent who really understands and believes in your film. Check out references and discuss strategy for your film before signing up with one.

2. Usually you'll have one sales agent for domestic and another for international sales.

3. Theatrical, television, VOD, and DVD are the key media outlets for distribution, these days.

4. Self distribution is a possibility for your film if you don't make a theatrical deal. Research your options to determine if you have the time and resources to undertake self distribution.

5. What will be the future distribution models that will allow producers to monetize their films effectively? Let me know when you know!

CHAPTER 20

WHAT'S NET?

WHAT COMES NEXT IN the world of independent film is anyone's guess. But what has happened and is happening now is that the "barriers" to producing films are lower than they have ever been. Many more people can get their hands on a camera, some lights and put together a cast and crew without much money. And that's great.

BUT just having access to the means of production doesn't make for a good film or one that it is well produced. And that is the reason I wrote this book. Film producing is a craft, passed down from producer to producer. You learn by doing it — day after day, year after year.

In the past, you had to work your way up through the ranks to get the opportunity to produce a film. But now access is not much of a problem. You can do it, but can you do it WELL? Film festivals are flooded with applications all year long. But how many of those films are actually any good? Finding a brilliant script, hiring a talented director, and producing well is still the only way to make a great film. Though the means of production have changed, achieving those goals hasn't

> *There is no libretto.*
>
> *We need wit and courage*
>
> *to make our way while our*
>
> *way is making us.*
>
> *— Tom Stoppard,*
>
> The Coast of Utopia

changed. It's still a tremendous challenge, especially when you don't have all the resources you require.

Please use this book and the website *www.ProducerToProducer.com* to help you produce all your films well. Enjoy the journey and have a great adventure on each and every film!

INDEX

ABOUT THE AUTHOR

MAUREEN A. RYAN is a producer based in New York concentrating on feature films and documentaries. She is co-producer of James Marsh's **MAN ON WIRE**, a documentary about Philippe Petit, the wirewalker who stunned the world when he walked between the World Trade Center towers in 1974. It won the 2009 Academy Award for Best Documentary and the 2009 BAFTA Award for Best British Film. Other awards include the Sundance Jury Prize and Audience Award for World Cinema documentary, the Critics Choice Award, the IDA Award, the National Board of Review, the NY Film Critics Award, the PGA Award and the L.A. Film Critics Award.

She also is a producer of the independent narrative film, **BOMBER**, which premiered at the 2009 SXSW Film Festival. Written, directed, and produced by Paul Cotter (*Estes Avenue, Last Hand Standing*), it was shot in Brighton, UK, and Bad Zwischenahn, Germany. She produced a short film, **Red Flag**, that was written and directed by Sheila Curran Dennin. The film was honored as part of the Best of the Fest for Comedy at the 2009 Palm Springs ShortFest. It also won the 2009 Best Short Comedy Award at the Woods Hole Film Festival.

Ryan is the producer of the feature documentary, **The Gates,** which chronicles the artists Christo and Jean-Claude as they create their latest installation piece — over 7,500 gates of saffron cloth that were placed in New York City's Central Park in February 2005. The film won the 2008 Peabody Award and was co-directed by Albert Maysles and Antonio Ferrera. It played on HBO.

In 2006, Ryan produced the documentary, **Grey Gardens: From East Hampton to Broadway**. It premiered at the 2007 Hamptons International Film Festival. Directed by Albert Maysles, it follows the story of transforming the classic American documentary into a successful

Broadway musical in the fall of 2006. Ryan also is the producer of **The Team**, a feature documentary that was shot in Graz, Austria and premiered on BBC Four and TV2-Denmark in 2006/7. The film follows the NYC-based U.S. homeless soccer team as they prepare and journey to compete against 18 other international teams for the 1st Annual Homeless Soccer World Cup.

On the narrative feature film, **The King**, Ryan served as co-producer. The film premiered at the Cannes Film Festival and was released in May 2006. It stars Gael Garcia Bernal, William Hurt, and Laura Haring and was co-written by director James Marsh (*Wisconsin Death Trip*) and Milo Addica (*Monster's Ball, Birth*). Marsh was nominated for the 2006 Gotham Award for Breakthrough Director.

In 2004, Ryan was co-producer on a short film titled **Torte Bluma**, which stars Stellan Skarsgård (*Good Will Hunting, Breaking the Waves, The Exorcist: The Beginning*) and Simon McBurney (*The Manchurian Candidate*). Directed by Benjamin Ross (*RKO 281, The Young Poisoner's Handbook*), the story takes place in the Treblinka death camp and was shot in and around New York City. The film won Best Short at the Palm Springs International Festival of Shorts and the Best Drama Award at the L.A. Shorts Film Festival in 2005.

In 2003, Ryan produced a short film titled **Last Hand Standing**. It was directed by Paul Cotter (*Jeff Farnsworth*) and was a finalist in the Chrysler Million Dollar Film Festival. The director and production team competed against nine other semi-finalists who each had 10 days in New York City to write, cast, shoot, and edit a short film before screening it on the last night in front of a live audience and the film jury.

Another feature documentary produced by Ryan includes the award-winning **Wisconsin Death Trip**. It premiered at the Telluride and Venice Film Festivals in 1999 and had a theatrical run that began at NYC's Film Forum. The film was produced under her production company, Hands On Productions, Inc., and ran on the BBC and Cinemax in 2000.

During its run at the National Film Theatre in London, David Thomson, the critic for the London *Independent* newspaper wrote "I doubt you will see a more important American film this year." **Wisconsin Death Trip** won the award for Best Cutting Edge Documentary at the First Annual BBC2 Awards ceremony in London, England. It also garnered the 2001 Royal Television Society Award for Best Arts Documentary and the 2001 BAFTA Award for Best Cinematography. It received a nomination for Best Arts Documentary for the 2001 BAFTA Television Awards and was nominated for an EMMY for Best Lighting Design. *Wisconsin Death Trip* also was short listed for the 2001 Academy Award for Best Documentary.

Ryan's first feature film, **Matchbox Circus Train**, premiered at the Boston Film Festival in September 1997. Jay Carr of *The Boston Globe* called it "an enticing low-key family drama". The 80-minute, independent feature film was shot entirely in Mackinac Island, Michigan. Because of the island's "no motorized vehicle" policy, the production was made with only horse-drawn dreys and bicycles for transportation of equipment and crew.

Ryan's past work has included producing commercials, television series, music television specials, music videos, and EPKs (Electronic Press Kits). This work has won three AICP awards, a Billboard award, a CMA award, an ACM award, and five Tellys.

While a thesis candidate for her Master of Fine Arts degree in Film at Columbia University, Ryan was awarded the Paramount Studio Fellowship in Producing. One of five nominees from the top American film schools, she was given a one-year contract as a producer with the Hollywood studio in its production division.

Since 1999, Ryan has taught Film Production and the Craft of Documentary Filmmaking at Columbia University's Graduate Film Division and supervises student production at the school. Ryan also teaches a course in Producing Essentials at New York University's Tisch School of the Arts.

To get in touch with Maureen Ryan, please click on
www.ProducerToProducer.com

Free downloadable production templates go to
www.mwp.com
Click on *Virtual Film School*
Click *Resources*

and also
www.ProducerToProducer.com

THE WRITER'S JOURNEY
3RD EDITION

MYTHIC STRUCTURE FOR WRITERS

CHRISTOPHER VOGLER

BEST SELLER
OVER 170,000 COPIES SOLD!

See why this book has become an international best seller and a true classic. *The Writer's Journey* explores the powerful relationship between mythology and storytelling in a clear, concise style that's made it required reading for movie executives, screenwriters, playwrights, scholars, and fans of pop culture all over the world.

Both fiction and nonfiction writers will discover a set of useful myth-inspired storytelling paradigms (i.e., "The Hero's Journey") and step-by-step guidelines to plot and character development. Based on the work of Joseph Campbell, *The Writer's Journey* is a must for all writers interested in further developing their craft.

The updated and revised third edition provides new insights and observations from Vogler's ongoing work on mythology's influence on stories, movies, and man himself.

"This book is like having the smartest person in the story meeting come home with you and whisper what to do in your ear as you write a screenplay. Insight for insight, step for step, Chris Vogler takes us through the process of connecting theme to story and making a script come alive."
> – Lynda Obst, Producer, *Sleepless in Seattle, How to Lose a Guy in 10 Days;*
> Author, *Hello, He Lied*

"This is a book about the stories we write, and perhaps more importantly, the stories we live. It is the most influential work I have yet encountered on the art, nature, and the very purpose of storytelling."
> – Bruce Joel Rubin, Screenwriter, *Stuart Little 2, Deep Impact,*
> *Ghost, Jacob's Ladder*

CHRISTOPHER VOGLER is a veteran story consultant for major Hollywood film companies and a respected teacher of filmmakers and writers around the globe. He has influenced the stories of movies from *The Lion King* to *Fight Club* to *The Thin Red Line* and most recently wrote the first installment of *Ravenskull*, a Japanese-style manga or graphic novel. He is the executive producer of the feature film *P.S. Your Cat is Dead* and writer of the animated feature *Jester Till*.

$26.95 · 300 PAGES · ORDER NUMBER 76RLS · ISBN: 193290736x

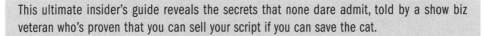

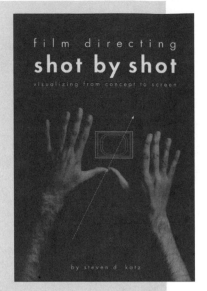

MASTER SHOTS
100 ADVANCED CAMERA TECHNIQUES TO GET AN EXPENSIVE LOOK ON YOUR LOW BUDGET MOVIE

CHRISTOPHER KENWORTHY

Master Shots gives filmmakers the techniques they need to execute complex, original shots on any budget. By using powerful master shots and well-executed moves, directors can develop a strong style and stand out from the crowd. Most low-budget movies look low-budget, because the director is forced to compromise at the last minute. *Master Shots* gives you so many powerful techniques that you'll be able to respond, even under pressure, and create knock-out shots. Even when the clock is ticking and the light is fading, the techniques in this book can rescue your film, and make every shot look like it cost a fortune.

Each technique is illustrated with samples from great feature films and computer-generated diagrams for absolute clarity.

Use the secrets of the master directors to give your film the look and feel of a multi-million-dollar movie. The set-ups, moves and methods of the greats are there for the taking, whatever your budget.

"Master Shots gives every filmmaker out there the blow-by-blow setup required to pull off even the most difficult of setups found from indies to the big Hollywood blockbusters. It's like getting all of the magician's tricks in one book."
> — Devin Watson, Producer, *The Cursed*

"Though one needs to choose any addition to a film book library carefully, what with the current plethora of volumes on cinema, Master Shots *is an essential addition to any worthwhile collection."*
> — Scott Essman, Publisher, *Directed By* Magazine

"Christopher Kenworthy's book gives you a basic, no holds barred, no shot forgotten look at how films are made from the camera point of view. For anyone with a desire to understand how film is constructed — this book is for you."
> — Matthew Terry, Screenwriter/Director, Columnist
> *www.hollywoodlitsales.com*

Since 2000, CHRISTOPHER KENWORTHY has written, produced, and directed drama and comedy programs, along with many hours of commercial video, tv pilots, music videos, experimental projects, and short films. He's also produced and directed over 300 visual FX shots. In 2006 he directed the web-based Australian UFO Wave, which attracted many millions of viewers. Upcoming films for Kenworthy include *The Sickness* (2009) and *Glimpse* (2011).

$24.95 · 240 PAGES · ORDER NUMBER 91RLS · ISBN: 9781932907513

THE COMPLETE INDEPENDENT MOVIE MARKETING HANDBOOK
PROMOTE, DISTRIBUTE & SELL YOUR FILM OR VIDEO

MARK STEVEN BOSKO

If you're an independent filmmaker looking for information on how to market, distribute, and find audiences for your movies and videos, you'll discover it here. This book is packed with street-smart savvy and real-world examples on how to promote and sell your productions. From landing a distribution deal and getting free media coverage to staging a low-cost premiere and selling your movie to video rental chains and over the Internet, this book is a must-have for any independent film or video maker looking to seriously launch and sustain a career in the entertainment industry.

"Get this book if you have a finished film you want to sell ! It's packed full with incredible ideas, gimmicks, and ploys to get little films out there and noticed. I wish we had this when we were doing Blair Witch.*"*

— Eduardo Sanchez
Co-Writer, Co-Director, Co-Editor,
The Blair Witch Project

"The best book that I have read about grass-roots film marketing. Troma Entertainment actually uses the marketing secrets described in this excellent book, and has for nearly 30 years! They work!"

— Lloyd Kaufman
President, Troma Entertainment
Creator, *The Toxic Avenger*

"NOTICE TO ALL INDIE FILMMAKERS: You've shot a great indie film. You're proud of it. Your mother loves it. Now what? You need this book. Buy this book. Read this book cover to cover."

— Elizabeth English
Founder & Executive Director
Moondance International Film Festival

MARK STEVEN BOSKO has been promoting and distributing independent feature films for more than 10 years. In addition to performing virtually every job on a film production, he has worked professionally in public relations, marketing, and magazine publishing.

$39.95 · 300 PAGES · ORDER NUMBER 108RLS · ISBN: 9780941188760

24 HOURS | **1.800.833.5738** | **WWW.MWP.COM**

THE MYTH OF MWP

In a dark time, a light bringer came along, leading the curious and the frustrated to clarity and empowerment. It took the well-guarded secrets out of the hands of the few and made them available to all. It spread a spirit of openness and creative freedom, and built a storehouse of knowledge dedicated to the betterment of the arts.

The essence of the Michael Wiese Productions (MWP) is empowering people who have the burning desire to express themselves creatively. We help them realize their dreams by putting the tools in their hands. We demystify the sometimes secretive worlds of screenwriting, directing, acting, producing, film financing, and other media crafts.

By doing so, we hope to bring forth a realization of 'conscious media' which we define as being positively charged, emphasizing hope and affirming positive values like trust, cooperation, self-empowerment, freedom, and love. Grounded in the deep roots of myth, it aims to be healing both for those who make the art and those who encounter it. It hopes to be transformative for people, opening doors to new possibilities and pulling back veils to reveal hidden worlds.

MWP has built a storehouse of knowledge unequaled in the world, for no other publisher has so many titles on the media arts. Please visit www.mwp.com where you will find many free resources and a 25% discount on our books. Sign up and become part of the wider creative community!

Onward and upward,

Michael Wiese
Publisher/Filmmaker

FILM & VIDEO BOOKS
TO RECEIVE A FREE MWP NEWSLETTER, CLICK ON WWW.MWP.COM TO REGISTER

SCREENWRITING | WRITING

And the Best Screenplay Goes to... | Dr. Linda Seger | $26.95
Archetypes for Writers | Jennifer Van Bergen | $22.95
Bali Brothers | Lacy Waltzman, Matthew Bishop, Michael Wiese | $12.95
Cinematic Storytelling | Jennifer Van Sijll | $24.95
Could It Be a Movie? | Christina Hamlett | $26.95
Creating Characters | Marisa D'Vari | $26.95
Crime Writer's Reference Guide, The | Martin Roth | $20.95
Deep Cinema | Mary Trainor-Brigham | $19.95
Elephant Bucks | Sheldon Bull | $24.95
Fast, Cheap & Written That Way | John Gaspard | $26.95
Hollywood Standard, The, 2nd Edition | Christopher Riley | $18.95
Horror Screenwriting | Devin Watson | $24.95
I Could've Written a Better Movie than That! | Derek Rydall | $26.95
Inner Drives | Pamela Jaye Smith | $26.95
Moral Premise, The | Stanley D. Williams, Ph.D. | $24.95
Myth and the Movies | Stuart Voytilla | $26.95
Power of the Dark Side, The | Pamela Jaye Smith | $22.95
Psychology for Screenwriters | William Indick, Ph.D. | $26.95
Reflections of the Shadow | Jeffrey Hirschberg | $26.95
Rewrite | Paul Chitlik | $16.95
Romancing the A-List | Christopher Keane | $18.95
Save the Cat! | Blake Snyder | $19.95
Save the Cat! Goes to the Movies | Blake Snyder | $24.95
Screenwriting 101 | Neill D. Hicks | $16.95
Screenwriting for Teens | Christina Hamlett | $18.95
Script-Selling Game, The | Kathie Fong Yoneda | $16.95
Stealing Fire From the Gods, 2nd Edition | James Bonnet | $26.95
Talk the Talk | Penny Penniston | $24.95
Way of Story, The | Catherine Ann Jones | $22.95
What Are You Laughing At? | Brad Schreiber | $19.95
Writer's Journey, – 3rd Edition, The | Christopher Vogler | $26.95
Writer's Partner, The | Martin Roth | $24.95
Writing the Action Adventure Film | Neill D. Hicks | $14.95
Writing the Comedy Film | Stuart Voytilla & Scott Petri | $14.95
Writing the Killer Treatment | Michael Halperin | $14.95
Writing the Second Act | Michael Halperin | $19.95
Writing the Thriller Film | Neill D. Hicks | $14.95
Writing the TV Drama Series – 2nd Edition | Pamela Douglas | $26.95
Your Screenplay Sucks! | William M. Akers | $19.95

FILMMAKING

Film School | Richard D. Pepperman | $24.95
Power of Film, The | Howard Suber | $27.95

PITCHING

Perfect Pitch – 2nd Edition, The | Ken Rotcop | $19.95
Selling Your Story in 60 Seconds | Michael Hauge | $12.95

SHORTS

Filmmaking for Teens, 2nd Edition | Troy Lanier & Clay Nichols | $24.95
Making It Big in Shorts | Kim Adelman | $22.95

BUDGET | PRODUCTION MANAGEMENT

Film & Video Budgets, 5th Updated Edition | Deke Simon | $26.95
Film Production Management 101 | Deborah S. Patz | $39.95

DIRECTING | VISUALIZATION

Animation Unleashed | Ellen Besen | $26.95

Cinematography for Directors | Jacqueline Frost | $29.95
Citizen Kane Crash Course in Cinematography | David Worth | $19.95
Directing Actors | Judith Weston | $26.95
Directing Feature Films | Mark Travis | $26.95
Fast, Cheap & Under Control | John Gaspard | $26.95
Film Directing: Cinematic Motion, 2nd Edition | Steven D. Katz | $27.95
Film Directing: Shot by Shot | Steven D. Katz | $27.95
Film Director's Intuition, The | Judith Weston | $26.95
First Time Director | Gil Bettman | $27.95
From Word to Image, 2nd Edition | Marcie Begleiter | $26.95
I'll Be in My Trailer! | John Badham & Craig Modderno | $26.95
Master Shots | Christopher Kenworthy | $24.95
Setting Up Your Scenes | Richard D. Pepperman | $24.95
Setting Up Your Shots, 2nd Edition | Jeremy Vineyard | $22.95
Working Director, The | Charles Wilkinson | $22.95

DIGITAL | DOCUMENTARY | SPECIAL

Digital Filmmaking 101, 2nd Edition | Dale Newton & John Gaspard | $26.95
Digital Moviemaking 3.0 | Scott Billups | $24.95
Digital Video Secrets | Tony Levelle | $26.95
Greenscreen Made Easy | Jeremy Hanke & Michele Yamazaki | $19.95
Producing with Passion | Dorothy Fadiman & Tony Levelle | $22.95
Special Effects | Michael Slone | $31.95

EDITING

Cut by Cut | Gael Chandler | $35.95
Cut to the Chase | Bobbie O'Steen | $24.95
Eye is Quicker, The | Richard D. Pepperman | $27.95
Film Editing | Gael Chandler | $34.95
Invisible Cut, The | Bobbie O'Steen | $28.95

SOUND | DVD | CAREER

Complete DVD Book, The | Chris Gore & Paul J. Salamoff | $26.95
Costume Design 101, 2nd Edition | Richard La Motte | $24.95
Hitting Your Mark, 2nd Edition | Steve Carlson | $22.95
Sound Design | David Sonnenschein | $19.95
Sound Effects Bible, The | Ric Viers | $26.95
Storyboarding 101 | James Fraioli | $19.95
There's No Business Like Soul Business | Derek Rydall | $22.95
You Can Act! | D. W. Brown | $24.95

FINANCE | MARKETING | FUNDING

Art of Film Funding, The | Carole Lee Dean | $26.95
Bankroll | Tom Malloy | $26.95
Complete Independent Movie Marketing Handbook, The | Mark Steven Bosko | $39.95
Getting the Money | Jeremy Jusso | $26.95
Independent Film and Videomakers Guide – 2nd Edition, The | Michael Wiese | $29.95
Independent Film Distribution | Phil Hall | $26.95
Shaking the Money Tree, 3rd Edition | Morrie Warshawski | $26.95

MEDITATION | ART

Mandalas of Bali | Dewa Nyoman Batuan | $39.95

OUR FILMS

Dolphin Adventures: DVD | Michael Wiese and Hardy Jones | $24.95
Hardware Wars: DVD | Written and Directed by Ernie Fosselius | $14.95
On the Edge of a Dream | Michael Wiese | $16.95
Sacred Sites of the Dalai Lamas– DVD, The | Documentary by Michael Wiese | $24.95